KU-572-947

Pelican Books
Local Government in Britain

Tony Byrne was born in 1937 and went to school in Liverpool. He took a degree in economics in the University of Bristol, and in government in the University of London. He has taught in schools in Liverpool and Somerset, was an adult education officer and an examiner for the Yorkshire and Humberside Council for Further and Higher Education, and is now lecturer in government and social administration at the Somerset College of Arts and Technology in Taunton and a student counsellor. He is chairman of the Taunton Marriage Guidance Council and has been secretary of the Taunton Workers' Education Association. His other books are *Social Services Made Simple* and *British Constitution Made Simple*, both written with the late Colin Padfield. He is a semi-professional musician and plays the saxophone with a local dance band.

Tony Byrne

Local Government in Britain

Everyone's Guide to How It All Works
Third Edition

Penguin Books

In memory of C.F.P.

Penguin Books Ltd, Harmondsworth, Middlesex, England
Viking Penguin Inc., 40 West 23rd Street, New York, New York 10010, U.S.A.
Penguin Books Australia Ltd, Ringwood, Victoria, Australia
Penguin Books Canada Ltd, 2801 John Street, Markham, Ontario, Canada L3R 1B4
Penguin Books (N.Z.) Ltd, 182–190 Wairau Road, Auckland 10, New Zealand

First published 1981
Second edition 1983
Third edition 1985

Copyright © Anthony Byrne, 1981, 1983, 1985
All rights reserved

Made and printed in Great Britain by
Richard Clay (The Chaucer Press) Ltd, Bungay, Suffolk
Set in Monotype Times

Contents

List of Text Figures

List of Tables

Glossary

See also Index

Abatement – the withholding of central grant to a local authority: see Holdback, below

Accountability – the condition of being held responsible and answerable for decisions and actions (or inactions) which affect others and are usually undertaken on their behalf: typically officers are accountable to councillors (members) and the latter are accountable to the local populace and electors (p. 96)

ACC – The Association of County Councils: one of several societies of particular types of local authority (p. 242)

AMA – The Association of Metropolitan Authorities: another local authority association, for those in metropolitan areas (p. 242)

APSAS – the Association of Public Service Administrative Staff

Audit – the checking of local councils' income and expenditure to detect errors, abuse, waste or illegality (p. 216)

Block grant – central government's financial aid to local authorities; it is not directly allocated to particular services; it forms part (the bulk) of the Rate Support Grant (p. 201)

Borough (or in Scotland, Burgh) – an old term still used to denote certain (mainly urban) local authorities entitled to have a mayor (or provost) instead of a chairman of the council, and other minor privileges. In England, such Borough (or district) councils may be metropolitan (of which London Boroughs are a particular case) or non-metropolitan (p. 42)

By-laws – legally enforceable regulations created by the council and which help to control social life in the local community (p. 226)

Capital expenditure – spending on 'real' and costly items (highways, land, house-building, machinery etc.), cf. current or revenue expenditure (on wages, heating etc.) (p. 209)

Cash limits – the maximum allowance made (usually by the government) for increases in the cost of expenditure due to inflation (prices and wages increases) (p. 214)

Chief Executive Officer (CEO) – a chief local official who often acts as head of his local authority's team of chief officers, often heads his own department and may sometimes be entitled Chief Administrative Officer or Director of Administration (p. 160)

CIPFA – the Chartered Institute of Public Finance and Accountancy, comprising accountants and financial managers from local government and the public services; publish data and journals and help in the development of SSAPs (p. 11)

Circular – a government document sent to local authorities for the purpose of explanation or guidance, on legislation etc. (p. 228). But note there are also 'circulars' sent out to local authorities by the local authorities' associations, and to local parties by party central offices

Clawback – the mechanism whereby excess spending of some councils is recouped from all. The government apportions money to councils according to a formula based on what they are deemed to need; if the total of councils' claims exceed the total grant available, money is 'clawed back' from every council (p. 283)

COG – Chief Officers' Group (p. 179)

Commissioner for Local Administration (CLA) – popularly known as the 'ombudsman', he or she is responsible for investigating complaints against local councils (p. 260)

Community council – a very local and small-scale form of local government, found in Wales and Scotland (p. 273)

Community politics – concern and action involving very local issues at street- or neighbourhood level (p. 278)

Corporate management – a system whereby senior administrators (especially chief officers) and/or councillors regularly meet to determine, and co-ordinate, the execution of policy (p. 158)

COSLA – the Convention of Scottish Local Authorities (p. 247)

Creative accounting – the practice of regularly adjusting allocations and nomenclatures of local expenditures to cope with changed circumstances or to remain within given strictures (e.g. government spending limits on capital or revenue accounts)

Derogation – a special relaxation of the government's rate limitation (p. 284)

DES – the central government's Department of Education and Science (p. 228)

Direct labour (DLO) – use of a council's own workforce, instead of an outside contractor (p. 282)

Director – a local authority chief officer such as Director of Social Services (p. 162)

DOE – the central government's Department of the Environment (p. 232)

GLC – the Greater London Council; the top tier of London's government (p. 91)

GREA – Grant Related Expenditure Assessment: a central estimate of what each local authority needs to spend; it helps determine (block) grants to councils (p. 201)

HIPS – Housing Investment Programmes: what the government agrees councils should spend on housing (building, repairs, renovation grants) (p. 211)

Holdback – the withholding of some of the (block) grant to those councils which exceed the spending targets set by the government (p. 283)

ICSA – the Institute of Chartered Secretaries and Administrators

ILEA – the Inner London Education Authority: a special committee which is responsible for education in part of the Greater London area (p. 92)

INLOGOV – the Institute of Local Government Studies, part of Birmingham University (p. 172)

LASS – local authority (personal) social services department(s) (p. 79)

LBA – the London Boroughs Association (p. 247)

Local authority associations – groupings of councils of the same type (p. 246)

Local income tax (LIT) – a proposed council tax on income-receivers (p. 208)

Metropolitan – a conurbation area containing a metropolitan county and metropolitan districts (or boroughs) (p. 53)

NALGO – a trade union: the National and Local Government Officers' Association (p. 172)

Neighbourhood councils – very local, non-executive, semi-official bodies (p. 276)

Ombudsman – see Commissioner above

Penalties – loss of grant where a council exceeds GREA and/or target (p. 283)

Policy and Resources Committee (P and R) – the main committee of the council; here councillors are responsible for overall policy, management and finance e . 158)

Precept – the (rate) tax collected by rating authorities for county councils and parish/ community councils (p. 202)

Prescribed expenditure allocation (PEA) – the blocks of capital expenditure allocated to local authorities by the government (p. 211)

Privatization – contracting out councils' work to private firms (p. 282)

PSS – social services department of the local authority (p. 79)

PWLB – the Public Works Loan Board: a government body which lends to local authorities (p. 210)

Qualgo – quasi-local government organization; a form of 'quango' or semi-independent board in the field of local (as opposed to central) administration (p. 84)

Rates – a tax on property levied by councils for their own or (as a precept) others' revenue; based on property's (rateable) value (p. 202)

RIPA – the Royal Institute of Public Administration

SAUS – the School of Advanced Urban Studies, part of Bristol University

Shire – the non-metropolitan county (p. 52)

SOLACE – the Society of Local Authority Chief Executives (p. 177)

Special responsibility allowances – payments to councillors with additional duties (p. 136)

SSAP – Statement of Standard Accountancy Practice – describe methods of accounting (approved by the accountancy bodies), a number of which are being developed for particular application to local authority accounting practice

SSD – local authority social services department (p. 79)

Surcharge – a financial penalty on those responsible for illegal spending (p. 336)

Supplementary rate (or precept) – an extra levy, in addition to the regular, annual local tax (p. 214)

SWD – local authority social work department (Scotland) (p. 79)

Taper – the diminishing proportion of grant attracted by a council's spending when it exceeds a threshold level (p. 283)

Target – a level of council expenditure set by the government (p. 283)

Ultra vires – beyond the powers; illegal (p. 65)

Preface to the First Edition

There is much public ignorance of and misunderstanding about local government: according to one survey, some 20 per cent of the British public cannot accurately name a single local government service. But local government is not unique in this respect, judging by the similar results produced by surveys of public understanding of the national government, the EEC and the legal system.

Such widespread ignorance, sometimes referred to as 'political illiteracy', may be understandable if not excusable. It takes energy, persistence and patience to master the intricacies of any large organization, be it the Ford motor company, the National Health Service or a government department such as the Ministry of Agriculture.

This book seeks to provide a reasonably clear and up-to-date account of what local government is, what it does and how it does it. I have aimed to achieve a balance between description and analysis, between law and practice and between institutions and issues. Being based essentially on secondary sources, the book makes no claim to originality, nor does it attempt to contribute to theory.

In writing this book, I have had in mind a number of overlapping groups of reader:

(a) the *consumer* who needs to know how local political decisions affect him;

(b) the *activist* who, as a citizen, wants a part in the decision-making process;

(c) the *student* who seeks an understanding of local government as part of his academic studies;

(d) the potential or *new entrant* to local government who wishes to know something about the world of the local authority.

It is ambitious to try to satisfy all these groups, and in a book of this size one can hope to do little more than provide an outline and an introduction to certain themes. I have treated the subject in a fairly conventional way, and I make no apology for this, since the book is intended as an introductory text. Detailed references, and a bibliography of more specialized works, are provided for the benefit of those who wish to pursue the various themes and issues in greater depth. Some of the works mentioned, such as Stanyer's *Understanding Local Government*, are highly original and commendable.

Comments or questions from readers will be welcome so that the text can be suitably amended at a later date.

Local government is a branch of public administration, and its study helps to form one of the 'social sciences': that is, studies which seek to apply to social affairs the scientific methods of observation, comparison and conjecture. But social science is not an exact science and there are many areas where ideas about relationships and the causes and consequences of events remain inconclusive. There are many 'ifs and buts' because we are dealing with a world (human society) which lacks certainty or uniformity; it is dangerous therefore to generalize. This is perhaps especially true of local government in Britain, which includes 500 principal local authorities and covers such different territories as England, Scotland and Wales, highlands, lowlands, conurbations, market towns and seaports. Each area and local authority is unique: it has its own traditions, history, problems and social structure . . . in short its own political culture.

However, as the late Professor J. Mackintosh said, the study of political institutions and theories connected with it depends on the patient accumulation of instances. Furthermore, local authorities do have many common features and are subject to a number of common influences and constraints, not the least important of which is the law. Consequently we can say that a local government 'system' does exist and we are able (with caution) to suggest some general tendencies which operate within it.

One thing which can be said with certainty is that local authorities live in exciting times! Nationally, our economic performance has faltered and we have sought salvation (at least in part) by joining the Common Market. At the same time, a diminished faith in our political system has been manifested both in a review and reform of a number of our institutions (the civil service, the House of Commons, the National Health Service) and in our adoption or contemplation of certain exotic devices (ombudsmen, referendums, proportional representation, a written constitution).

Local government has not escaped scrutiny: indeed it can claim to have had more than its fair share of searching inquiry over the past twenty years; and since the 1960s local authorities have undergone substantial changes in their structure, in the allocation of responsibilities and in their internal organization. Confidence and optimism, sustained and reflected in their expanding budgets, have given way to retrenchment of spending plans and reductions in services. Local authorities have (perhaps only for the moment) been spared the challenge posed by devolution, but they are experiencing a longer-term and less conspicuous threat. This has been described as 'de-localization' and it is caused by the loss of certain services, the greater quest for equal (national) standards and the insinuation into local politics of national parties and pressure groups. In these ways local authorities are being homogenized – just as our town centres are losing their local character by the spread of national chain stores and building societies. However, there may be some gains from these developments, and in any case they are still far from complete.

Students, councillors and officers have had to cope with these developments, and it has not always been easy. This book deals with a number of them. Its preparation has been stimulating for the author, but it would have been an impossible task without the generous assistance of a number of friends, colleagues, specialist practitioners and students (past and present). My debt to published work will be obvious to the reader. I have also received helpful information and documents from central and local officials in England, Wales and Scotland. In particular, however, I wish to acknowledge the help I have received from the Rt Hon. Edward du Cann, MP; from Brian Bailey, John Blackmore, John Chant, Mike Dearden, Mr S. E. Harwood, John Pentney, David Perrin, Brian Tanner, Barry Taylor, Phil Trevelyan and Colin Vile (all of Somerset County Council); from Don Alder, Michael Clark, John Davis, Mr I. Locke, Mr S. Price, Mike Porter and Derek Rumsey (all of Taunton Deane Borough Council); and from Rosemary Morris (Kent County Council). I am confident of the accuracy of their answers: I only hope I have asked the right questions. Any errors of omission or commission are entirely mine and while I have tried to make it entirely up to date, the book has come to fruition at a time of considerable change in local government.

I am also grateful to David Hencke of the *Guardian* and David Peschek of Local Government Information Services for advising me on certain sources, and to David Smith of the Conservative Central Office for allowing me access to local government records.

I should also like to thank my teaching colleagues Barrie Foster and Russell Pearce; the library staffs of the Somerset College of Arts and Technology, Bristol and Exeter Universities and Taunton library (in particular Bryan McEnroe); the NJC for allowing me to quote extracts from their scheme; and the Controller of HM Stationery Office for his permission to reproduce material from official sources.

Neil Middleton of Penguin Books has been most considerate in regard to unavoidable delays over deadlines. And his encouragement and help have been most welcome.

Finally, I must thank my wife Sari and my children Celie and Dan for their support and for enduring my more than usual preoccupation and periods of silence.

Taunton, February 1981   Tony Byrne

Preface to the Second Edition

An American wit, parodying Lord Acton, has opined that 'Government is boring; Local Government bores absolutely'. Many people in local government would it were true! They seek more settled times – a return to normalcy, where they can get on with administration and the delivery of services, instead of adapting to the latest change and awaiting the next one. Professor Stewart's description of local government as 'the government of difference' is perhaps more apt, though for unfortunate reasons.

The exciting times referred to in the First Edition of this book have continued and this new edition takes account of the related causal and consequential changes (up to January 1983). The book was originally scheduled as a reprint with corrections. Fortunately I was able to take advantage of the opportunity to thoroughly revise the text and bring it up to date; I am grateful to the publishers for agreeing to this.

I must also express my gratitude to a number of people who have contacted me or otherwise communicated their generous and encouraging remarks about the first edition, or have provided me with additional information or perspectives. In particular I wish to thank Professor George Jones of the London School of Economics, William Thornhill of Sheffield University, Professor Ken Newton of Dundee University, Professor D. E. Regan of Nottingham University, John Gyford of University College, London, Alan Parker of Teesside Polytechnic, Mr K. J. Bridge, Chief Executive, Humberside County Council and Arthur Godfrey of the *Local Government Review*. I am also grateful to Peter Stuart of Somerset County Council Law Library, Bryan McEnroe of Taunton Library, Stuart Macwilliam of Exeter University Library and Phil Lawton of Somerset Health Authority.

For local government watchers there has been a lot to see in the past two years – legislation, legal battles, resource restrictions and service reductions. Unfortunately our sights are being narrowed here by government economy measures. Thus as part of the 'Rayner exercise' in cutting 'waste' in public expenditure, the OPCS has now ceased to collect and collate the local government election returns; consequently, after forty years, it is now impossible to follow trends and patterns in local government voting turnout. This, in itself, is not a vitally important matter; but it is another indication of the unfortunate recent tendency to downgrade Local Government in Britain.

Taunton, January 1983   Tony Byrne

Preface to the Third Edition

It is tempting to suggest that for local government in Britain George Orwell's choice of the year 1984 was remarkably prescient, for 1984 saw the passage into law of the Rates Act. This permits, for the first time, the limitation of local councils' rates by (Big Brother) central government; and eighteen local authorities have been selected to have their rates thus capped in the year 1985-6.

As this legislation proceeded through Parliament there was massive protest and lobbying, and considerable opposition among MPs including many prominent members and former leaders of the Government's own party; indeed, one former (Conservative) Secretary of State for the Environment described the legislation as 'a deplorable Bill which raises major constitutional issues. It is a classic example of elective dictatorship' (Geoffrey Rippon, House of Commons, 22 December 1983).

With the Government's overwhelming majority (of 144 seats) in the House of Commons, parliamentary opposition is weak and frustrated, and as a result many detect that the task of opposition has, at least to some extent, shifted out to local government. In so far as this is (or is perceived to be) true, it helps to explain the acrimony which has characterized local-central relations in recent years – and is likely to continue, with arguments over rate-capping and derogation, and over targets and grants: already a number of councils are threatening to 'do a Liverpool' and deliberately to refuse or delay the declaration of a rate/budget. And 1985-6 will witness the débâcle over the abolition of the metropolitan authorities and the redistribution of their responsibilities; members (especially Labour members) in metropolitan counties are resigning or threatening to resign their seats in order to force by-elections and thus test public opinion on the issue in the hope of embarrassing the Government and discrediting its plans.

Such is the continuing pace of change in the world of local government that I have found it necessary to undertake a further revision of the text, for which opportunity I am grateful to Penguin Books. However, I have left some of the figures unaltered either because the recent changes are not significant, or (as with the election turnout figures) because the data is unfortunately not available.

Taunton, September 1984

Tony Byrne

1. What Local Government Is

The governance of a modern society is an enormous task. In Great Britain, for example, half of the nation's annual income flows through the hands of the government, and some 30 per cent of the labour force are employed in the state sector. Government is, therefore, 'big business'.

For this reason most countries find it necessary to decentralize their administration, in other words to arrange for services to be provided and decisions to be made away from the centre or capital and 'in the field' or locally. Such decentralization can take a number of forms. The simplest is known as *deconcentration*, whereby the officers of the central government (the civil servants) are dispersed into local and regional offices such as the local tax or National Insurance office. Another simple form is *functional decentralization*, in which a particular service or function is hived off from the central government to a semi-independent organization commonly referred to as a 'quango' (quasi-autonomous non-governmental organization). Among their estimated 3,000, examples include the Post Office, the Manpower Services Commission, the Gaming Board, the Housing Corporation, the Council for Small Industries in Rural Areas and the Scottish Development Agency. *Regional devolution* (or regionalism) is more complex and involves the limited transfer by the central government of political and administrative authority to a regional body, such as a Scottish or Welsh Assembly. Local government is an example of such devolution, but on a more local basis. Local government is self-government involving the administration of public affairs in each locality by a body of representatives of the local community. Although subject to the central government in many ways, it possesses a considerable amount of responsibility and discretionary power.

Local government, then, is one of a number of forms of decentralization. This fact helps to explain why it can be so confusing: it resembles so many other administrative structures to be found in the modern state – ministries, departments, authorities, boards, corporations, bureaux, councils and so on. Consequently it is not surprising that many people mistakenly believe, for example, that local authorities run the hospitals (which are actually the responsibility of appointed Health Authorities) or think that teachers are paid by the Minister responsible for education (in fact they are employed by the local authorities, who pay their salaries out of the rates).

There are, however, a number of characteristics which mark out local government as a distinctive form of public administration. Thus local government is *elected*. Although some areas (parishes and communities) are small enough to need only a simple meeting of the local people, most local authorities consist of representatives chosen by the members of the community at properly constituted elections. These elected members form the local 'council', which then recruits the full-time paid staff of the authority, including engineers, accountants, teachers, clerks and bin-men. These employees are not civil servants, though they are organized at the town hall or county hall into departments such as the Education Department, the Housing Department or the Social Services Department.

It follows that local government is *multi-purpose*: every local authority has many jobs to do and a variety of services to provide. An individual local authority may be responsible for the provision of schools, homes for the elderly and training centres for the handicapped; fire services; road building and maintenance, and traffic management; and the control of the environment through the regulation of building and land development. By contrast, the 'quangos' and public corporations tend to be concerned with just one particular service or field of activity, such as health (the Health Authorities), water (the Water Boards) or transport (the National Bus Company).

The third feature of local government is the *local scale* of its operations: each authority has responsibility in its own area only. As we have seen, some of these areas (the parishes and communities) are very local in scale. But most of the more important authorities operate over the area of a county or region, or over a district (part of a county or region).

Fourthly, local government has a quite clearly *defined structure*, essentially of two tiers made up of sixty-six large county or regional councils and 455 smaller district councils. (In some parts of Britain, the parish or community make a third tier.) Thus, wherever we may live in Britain, we shall find ourselves under the jurisdiction of two local authorities. This is illustrated in Figure 1 (the diagram is not intended to suggest a hierarchical or power relationship between the two tiers).

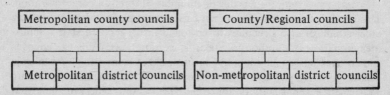

Figure 1 *The structure of British local government (up to 1968)*

The next feature of local government is that it is *subordinated* to the national authority, which is Parliament. Local authorities come into existence as a result of legislation passed by Parliament, and all such authorities are subject to the law. If a local authority steps outside the law (for example by failing to do something which the law requires it to do, such as not providing schools) it will be liable to the rigours and sanctions of the law in the same way as private people are. Parliament alone has sovereignty: local authorities exercise power to the extent that Acts of Parliament allow.

Although local authorities carry out those responsibilities handed on to them by Parliament, it is misleading to see them simply as agents acting for the central government in the administration of certain services. While subject to certain controls operated by the central government, the local authorities work in partnership with it, and they possess a freedom and initiative which justifies their being described as bodies exercising local *self*-government.

Enabling them to do this, and the last important feature of local government, is the *rating system*. Rates are a form of taxation and have been exercised by local authorities for centuries. Although rate revenue is no longer the most important source of local government income, it is very substantial (see Chapter 11) and provides local authorities with a significant degree of independence and flexibility.

Local government forms part of the administrative structure of the country, and it may be useful, before going further, to summarize the work of the two other main components, central government and the quangos.

Central government and the quangos

Central government is composed of about a hundred Ministers of the Crown, responsible to Parliament. Most of them are elected MPs (from the majority party in the House of Commons), though some will be peers (members of the non-elected House of Lords). The central government forms the executive branch of the nation's political system, and it is headed by a Cabinet of senior Ministers, under the leadership of the Prime Minister. Central government is national, not local, and has to take the whole country into its consideration, administering services uniformly across the nation. Thus the services carried on are national, not local, in scale. The necessary finance is derived by the Treasury from national taxation.

Civil servants are recruited to carry out the policies and administer the statutes passed by Parliament. They are both advisers to the government and administrators of government policy. Although the main government departments (or Ministries) are in London (for the most part in Whitehall) there are regional and local offices in the main towns and cities of Britain. So we have Ministers, each heading a government department, and civil servants who are directly responsible to the Ministers through a hierarchical structure ranging from the permanent secretaries (civil servants) at the top advising Ministers personally, down to the assistant clerical officers at the bottom, who put the laws and regulations into effect at the community level (for example, by assessing and collecting income taxes).

Quasi-governmental organizations are independent agencies set up to perform some service or to administer an industry free from direct government control (though subject to some restraints exercised by Ministers, who are responsible to Parliament). There are an estimated[1] 3,000 such bodies, and in addition to those previously mentioned (p. 17) examples include British Aerospace, the British National Oil Corporation, the British Steel Corporation, the National Coal Board, the Atomic Energy Authority, the Independent Broadcasting Authority, the National Enterprise Board, the Location of Offices Bureau, the University Grants Committee, the Arts Council, the Countryside Commission and Remploy.

The role of these organizations varies. They may be *advisory* (for example the Schools Council or the British Safety Council); *executive* (the Manpower Services Commission or the Public Works Loan Board); *industrial–commercial* (British Airways or the Central Electricity Generating Board); *promotional* (the Industrial Training Boards, the Research Councils or the General Practice Finance Corporation); *regulatory* (the Monopolies Commission or the Council for National Academic Awards); *semi-judicial* (the Commission for Racial Equality or the Health and Safety Commission); or they may be *conciliatory* in function (the Advisory Conciliation and Arbitration Service or the Central Arbitration Council). Many in fact combine several roles and are therefore difficult to classify.

The number and variety of these organizations and bodies reflect the range of activities which fall within the sphere of 'government' in its widest sense. At the beginning of the last century, the main task of government was internal peace and defence against external enemies. Gradually government has widened its view and extended the scope of its activities, particularly with the development of the Welfare State and the 'managed' economy.

The degree of control over these bodies exercised by government Ministries varies. Most of the boards or managing committees, however, are appointed either by the Prime Minister or a Minister, and they are given a general responsibility defined in either a charter (like the BBC and the Arts Council) or a statute (like the Countryside Commission, the Commission for New Towns and most of the others). The staff of these bodies are not civil servants; they are employees of the particular corporation, commission, council or board. Nevertheless, the political responsibility rests with the government Minister.

Quangos are given considerable freedom from direct government control so as to keep politics, which may be irrelevant or prejudicial to their various ostensible functions, out of their day-to-day operations, whether commercial (as with the nationalized industries such as the British Gas Corporation or British Rail) or cultural (such as the BBC) or semi-judicial (such as the Charity Commission).

The administrative structure in Britain is summarized in Figure 2.

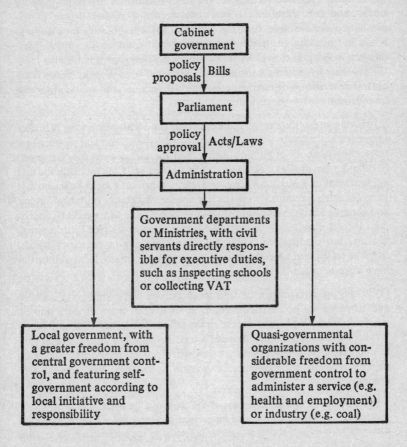

Figure 2 *British administrative structure*

The justification for local government

Local government exists and it is difficult to imagine its disappearance. However, it is worth considering some of the reasons which are advanced to justify its existence.

(1) Local government is seen as an *efficient* method of administering certain services. This efficiency is explained on one or more of the following grounds: (a) local authorities consist of members who are drawn from the local populace and who therefore have local knowledge and a commitment to the local area and its people; (b) local authorities are multi-purpose bodies and can therefore, theoretically, secure a greater degree of co-ordination: for example, since the same council is responsible for planning, roads and housing, the liaison between these different services and departments is easier and closer; (c) public administration generally benefits from the existence of local authorities because they off-load responsibilities from central government departments and the civil service, who would otherwise be overburdened with work.

(2) Having a fair degree of independence, the local authorities can take initiatives and *experiment*. In this way they may innovate and pioneer new services or methods of administration, and successful ideas may be spread to other authorities. For example, in 1847 Liverpool Council made the first appointment of a Medical Officer of Health; other authorities followed suit later. Similarly, certain cities in the late nineteenth century (notably London and Birmingham) developed the first council housing. More recently individual local authorities have originated such schemes as free birth control, comprehensive education, advice centres for housing or consumer affairs, free bus travel and special housing for pensioners; many local authorities have since adopted these ideas.

(3) Local government can be said to encourage citizenship or *democracy* and to promote 'political education' in its widest sense. It does this by involving large numbers of people in the political decision-making process. While people may find the affairs of a modern state too large and complex to understand, it is suggested that they will more easily and naturally participate with their neighbours in helping to manage local community affairs:

Nowhere has democracy ever worked well without a great measure of local self-government . . . Where the scope of the political measures become so large that the necessary knowledge is almost exclusively possessed by the bureaucracy, the creative impulses of the private person must flag.[2]

In Britain, there are currently some 26,000 local government councillors, that is members of the public who are elected to the principal local authorities. A significant proportion of these are members of social groups which are distinctly under-represented in national politics, for example women and manual workers. Furthermore, experience in local government has frequently proved to be a stepping stone to national politics: as many as one third of MPs are or have been local councillors.

Councillors of course are elected, and the frequent elections which occur in local government give the general public an opportunity to exercise and practise the right to vote. In some ways this relationship between elector and elected is closer at the local than at the national level, and helps to create an awareness among local voters of their ability to influence decisions.

(4) Local government is seen by some as a barrier or *defence* against an all-powerful central government and the abuse of power. Certainly in the nineteenth century it was held that the existence of a strong local government system helped to disperse political power and diminish the danger of an over-centralized state.[3] Today we tend to see local government more as a means to influence central government; for example, through the various local authority associations (see p. 246), which may seek to influence government policy in such matters as transport subsidies, conservation, rural postal services or electrification.

(5) Local government may be justified simply on the grounds of *tradition* – that it has from time immemorial been a part of the British way of life, part of our heritage and of our culture. A more sophisticated view is that of Edmund Burke (1729–97): 'That which *is* must be good because it has stood the test of time.'

(6) Finally there is support for local government from those who, like the American Founding Fathers of the eighteenth century, believe that there should be no taxation without *representation* – that since local authorities have the power to impose taxes (rates), the ratepayers should be represented on the body which determines how that money should be spent. This is a fundamental precept of parliamentary government (and has been since the signing of Magna Carta in 1215). Many feel it is equally applicable at the local level of government.

The critics of local government

However, the case for local government is not overwhelming or unanimous: there exists a contrary view, that of the 'centralists', who are critical of its existence on a number of grounds:

(1) Local government allows a variation in the standard of provision of local services which may be regarded as inequitable or unfair in an age of equality, or at least equality of opportunity. For example, in operating the '11-plus' examination and selective secondary education, some authorities allowed half of their secondary pupils to go to grammar schools, while in other areas the figure was only 20 per cent. Similar variation may be found in other areas of education (such as in nursery or adult education) and in other services, such as the provision of special housing for the elderly, hostel accommodation for the mentally disordered, or the levels of provision of home helps, occupational therapists and social workers.

(2) Doubt is cast on the efficiency of local government administration. Many authorities are felt to be too small to be effective in the provision of some or all of their services (see p. 57). In addition, there is scepticism about the amount of co-ordination and integration of services which is achieved in practice among local authorities. Moreover, the speed of modern communications means that central government can be as effective in dealing with local problems even though local government is nearer.

(3) Though local authorities may be progressive and pioneer new services, equally they may drag their feet and be closed to new ideas and change. Thus local government is criticized as encouraging narrow or 'parish pump' attitudes and policies.

(4) Finally there is the danger of exaggeration and over-idealization. The notion that local government acts as a bastion against excessive state power and as a catalyst to the release of simmering community participation may be far too ambitious a claim. In practice, as we shall see later (Chapter 12), the central government exercises considerable control over the policies of local government, and the general public shows a considerable lack of enthusiasm for local government matters.

Arguments or views such as these may convince some people that local government should be abolished altogether. The main consequence, in practice, has been a tendency to closer control and supervision of local authorities from the central government.

2. An Evolving System

The British are renowned for their respect for tradition. The British system of government is equally famous for its reliance on conventions and unwritten codes of behaviour, in preference to formal written codes which often purport to be immutable. Change, however, is inherent in laws and constitutions, as it is inherent in life. The way in which local government has adapted to changing circumstances is the subject of this chapter.

History has imprinted itself with particular clarity on our system of local government. Understand our history and you go a long way towards an understanding of the local government system, for we still have the same essential forms (for example, committees), the same basic geographical divisions (such as counties and parishes), the same sort of local leaders (the councillors) and the same sort of offices (such as mayors and provosts) as we have had for centuries. All the main elements have evolved to meet the new challenges of a complex society and to ensure sensible democratic government.

Before 1800: the early system

The feudal system in England lasted until the sixteenth century. It was based on land tenure or holding, with the king, as lord paramount, granting tracts of land to barons, nobles or bishops, who in turn granted portions to freemen. It was a social order or hierarchy, each person having duties towards or rights over those above and below. Central government was carried out by the king with his *curia regis* (or council). Justice was administered by judges, holding the king's commission, who visited the localities to supervise local administration and ensure justice, order and peace.

Local government grew out of the local communities of parishes, townships (some of which were boroughs) and counties, the boundaries of which were found even in Anglo-Saxon times. The local communities formed naturally, and leaders (such as the hundredman, the shire reeve or sheriff, and the Justice or Conservator of the Peace) emerged or were appointed by the king to help to carry out the basic tasks of the local communities – the prevention of crime and punishment of offenders, poor relief and welfare, the control of nuisance, the management of common lands and property, etc.

These essential local government activities were in fact dealt with by various bodies: self-help groups, voluntary associations and sometimes commercial undertakings. Formal legal authorities, what today we would call 'local authorities', provided a fourth agency, but they were not necessarily the most important, and in many areas the units of civil government merely filled in the gaps left by the other bodies.

In the course of time, many of the non-statutory bodies (charities, guilds, the Church and the manor) declined, and many of their functions were taken over by the nascent local authorities. From the late Middle Ages, around the fifteenth century, three types of civil authority became firmly established: the parish (based on the church parish), the shire (county) and the corporate town (borough or burgh).

The parish became responsible for local law and order (appointing a local constable), for providing common amenities (through a surveyor of highways) and for dealing with social distress (through overseers of the poor). These officers were elected or served on a rota basis. Some general supervision was exercised by the 'vestry', a local committee which in some places was elected and in others was appointed or self-selected. Further oversight was provided by Justices of the Peace, who were appointed by the Crown and who exercised authority on a county-wide basis. They were responsible for checking local affairs and administration, inspecting accounts and making appointments, but they had direct responsibility for such matters as highways and bridges, weights and measures, as well as the traditional duties of maintaining the peace and punishing petty crimes.

The corporate towns (called 'boroughs' in England and Wales, 'burghs' in Scotland) were those urban areas which had at some time obtained a charter from the Crown entitling them to certain privileges. These included the right to establish their own administration (in the form of a 'corporation'), to own corporate property (guild halls and town halls) and to have a separate 'bench' of magistrates or JPs.

This was the picture, much simplified, of local government at the end of the eighteenth century. The real picture was very complex, however, and there were many variations among the regions and areas. In some areas charities were strong and active; in others responsibilities had been taken over by special statutory bodies, such as Turnpike Trusts (to build and maintain roads) or Improvement Commissioners (to provide water, lighting or sanitation). And there was considerable variation in the method of election or selection of officers, vestries and corporations. A generalization that can safely be made, however, is that the 'system' was rudimentary, and by today's standards many local authorities were inefficient and corrupt.

Over the course of the next two centuries (the nineteenth and twentieth centuries) local government appears to have undergone three distinct phases of development, which we now consider.

1800–1880: stress and improvization

By the beginning of the nineteenth century the impact of industrialization and urbanization was becoming clear. Problems of poverty, disease, crime and squalor were demanding attention.

The response was substantial, though piecemeal and sometimes reluctant,[1] so that by the mid nineteenth century there was more active concern about the problems of society than there had been at any time before. However, it was a community response rather than an official response: private enterprise developed estates and provided water and gas; voluntary groups and charities provided schools, housing and hospitals; self-help and pressure groups urged the provision of parks and other cultural and social amenities.

From the official side it was soon apparent that the existing authorities could not cope with the problems they were now facing. The parishes were too small or inept, and they began to lose some of their traditional functions to higher authorities. For example, in England and Wales the inadequacy of the parish constables led to the setting-up of police forces in the boroughs in 1835 and in the counties in 1839 and 1856 (all modelled on the Metropolitan Police, created in 1829). Similarly, being unable to cope with the mounting social distress, the parishes lost their individual responsibilities for poor relief in 1834, when the Poor Law Act placed this responsibility on to groups (or 'unions') of parishes, which then operated under *ad hoc* elected Boards of Guardians.

Such *ad hoc* (or special-purpose) authorities were not new: a number of Turnpike Trusts and Improvement Commissioners had been created by Local (or Private – see p. 67) Acts of Parliament in the eighteenth century. These bodies proliferated in the nineteenth century (often by-passing the existing public authorities), so that we find local commissions or 'boards' for cleaning, paving or lighting the streets, for road building, for slum clearance, sewers, burial and for water supply.

Furthermore, general Acts of Parliament led to the creation of more *ad hoc* bodies, just as the Poor Law Amendment Act 1834 had created Boards of Guardians. Local health boards were set up under the Public Health Act 1848, highways boards under the Highways Acts 1835 and 1862 and elementary school boards under the Education Act 1870. Each of these local boards had its own elected body (the board itself), its own officials and its own rates.

Some existing local authorities showed initiative and foresight: they promoted local Acts and obtained the powers to take action themselves.[2] There was thus some administrative tidying-up, as corporations, and especially Boards of Health, took over some of the functions of the Improvement Commissions.

In addition, there were some attempts to reform local government in the towns, since it was the towns which were most affected by economic and social changes (including an astonishing growth in population[3]). In 1835 the Municipal Corporations Act, affecting 178 corporate boroughs in England and Wales, was passed. In an attempt to remove corruption and inefficiency, the Act required the corporations to be elected by ratepayers, to hold council meetings open to the public and to have their accounts regularly audited. In this way, a uniform constitution for most (about two thirds) of the boroughs was established.

The Municipal Corporations Act 1882 added another twenty-five old boroughs to this scheme, and in the meantime all new boroughs (some sixty-two were created between 1835 and 1876) adopted this form of local government. Uniformity was enhanced by the Public Health Act 1872, which *required* the establishment of health authorities throughout England and Wales – whether they took the form of borough councils (for the towns and cities), Boards of Health (for urban areas) or Boards of Guardians (for rural areas) – and the obligatory performance of health functions and responsibilities.

But a number of the old corporations had gone unreformed and had dwindled into insignificance as the *ad hoc* bodies assumed real power. In other towns and villages there was no common pattern either: the vestry, manorial officers, guardians, Improvement Commissioners, charity trustees, Justices of the Peace, all jostled each other for authority. Consequently local government was fittingly described in the 1870s as 'a chaos of areas, a chaos of authorities and a chaos of rates'. The structure was the product of a continuous patching-up exercise: it was not purpose-built.

1888–1930: the period of ascendancy

Such chaos as existed in England and Wales before 1888 was described and condemned by the Royal Sanitary Commission (1868–71), and there was some attempt at improving and tidying up the situation by the Public Health Act 1872, which divided the country into *rural* and *urban* areas for the purpose of public health services such as sanitation. But the demand for a more thorough-going reform had been growing since the 1830s. In particular there was a call to set up in the counties a form of representative government similar to that established for the boroughs. The call was resisted by the country gentry, largely because of fear of an increased rate burden which they thought would result from a more open and more active county government.

The Reform Act 1832 had revised the allocation of parliamentary representatives to reflect the changed distribution of the population. In removing the parliamentary franchise from many ancient boroughs ('rotten' or 'pocket' boroughs), the effect was to leave the disfranchised boroughs somewhat powerless and exposed. Hence the reforms of the Municipal Corporation Act 1835 (see p. 28). In a similar way, the Reform Act 1884, by extending the parliamentary vote to agricultural workers, threw into sharp relief the anomaly of the non-elected character of the county authorities composed of Justices of the Peace. Consequently the Local Government Act 1888 created elected *county councils*, based largely on the existing counties.[4] Initially their responsibilities were limited to highways, asylums, weights and measures, and police, but these were increased substantially over the next forty years.

The Local Government Act 1888 also created *county borough councils*. These were to be all-purpose authorities, independent of the county councils and based on existing boroughs. The criterion for their creation was population: a town with a population of 50,000 or more could claim county borough status. Some eighty-two towns[5] did so, much to the dismay of the county MPs, who had originally sought a qualifying figure of 150,000 population. Those boroughs which failed to gain county borough status remained as non-county boroughs and became *district councils*, for local government purposes, within the counties.

The rationalization of the local government structure was largely completed by the Local Government Act 1894. This created elected *urban district councils* (UDCs) and *rural district councils* (RDCs), which were based on consolidated sanitary districts. Like those of the *non-county borough councils*, the main functions of the district councils were public health and highways.[6] Under the same Act, *parishes* were revived by the creation of parish councils, which, except in parishes of under 300 electors (where they might simply have meetings of all parishioners), were elected.

The system of local government was completed in 1899 when twenty-eight *metropolitan borough councils* were established for the London area, which had at that time the largest city population in the world. In 1888 a separate London county area had been created by removing parts of Middlesex, Kent and Surrey, and the *London County Council* was established on a similar basis to other county councils. In 1899 the 'district' authorities were being added, with the City of London (the square mile in the heart of London) being left as a separate authority in deference to its unique character and tradition.

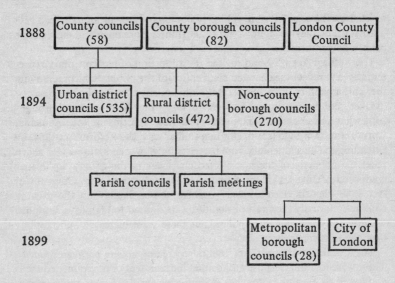

Figure 3
Local government in England and Wales at the end of the nineteenth century

Local government now had an established structure which was based on rational principles and provided a large measure of uniformity. In addition, all local authorities (councils) had a constitutional basis and operated on openly democratic lines. The stage was set for the local government system to enjoy some fifty years of ascendancy. It enjoyed increased status in the eyes of the general public, it became a pathway to a desirable career, and, above all, the central government was increasingly willing to entrust it with important responsibilities.

Some of these responsibilities were simply transferred from existing local government bodies when the new authorities were set up: in 1888 the county councils and county borough councils acquired the administrative functions of the Justices of the Peace, which covered rating, licensing, asylums, highways, weights and measures and police. Similarly some of the J P's functions were passed on to the new district councils in 1894, though the districts' most important functions came in the same year from the transfer of the functions of the public health and highways boards. Further important transfers were soon to follow. In 1902 the School Boards (see p. 27) were abolished and in their place local authorities set up committees (known as 'local education authorities') to provide schools and other educational services such as meals (introduced in 1906) and medical inspection (introduced in 1907). Under the Local Government Act 1929 the Boards of

Guardians (see p. 27) were abolished and their functions transferred to local authorities, who created Public Assistance Committees to continue the Guardians' former financial and welfare services.

Meanwhile new responsibilities were being assumed by the state, and many of these were placed in the hands of local government. In 1890 local authorities were permitted to build low-cost houses, and in 1919 they were given central government subsidies to encourage them to do so (as a result of which 1 million council houses were built in the years 1919–39). Under the Town Planning Act 1909, local authorities acquired the power to control the use and development of land, and while the legislation was modest in its provisions, it was greatly strengthened in 1919 and was extended to rural areas under the Town and Country Planning Act 1932.

Following the Unemployed Workmen's Act 1905, local authorities were permitted to anticipate the creation of a national network of Labour Exchanges by setting up local labour bureaux to help the unemployed to find work. (They could also finance the voluntary emigration of those out of work.) The same legislation strengthened their powers to spend money on public works for the purpose of creating jobs, a scheme originated in 1886 by Joseph Chamberlain. For school-leavers, the Education (Choice of Employment) Act 1910 allowed local education authorities to make special provision for advising and placing young people in employment (later to become known as the Youth Employment Scheme or the Careers Service).

During this period, local authorities were also providing employment opportunities directly, as a result of their expanded trading activities. There was considerable development by local government, by means of the Private Bill procedure (see p. 67), of what are usually called 'public utilities' – public transport, water, electricity and gas supply – although some of this apparent expansion was due to 'municipalization', that is, the takeover of private enterprise provision by local authorities. Apart from these activities there was considerable variety in the nature of municipal enterprises, which included the provision of a racecourse (Doncaster), a municipal bank (Birmingham), river ferries (Birkenhead), a telephone system (Hull), a civic theatre (Manchester) and numerous crematoria, slaughter-houses and dock undertakings.

In the meantime, local authorities' powers in respect of health – already well established in the environmental field (see p. 28) – were being extended to personal services. These included the provision of sanatoria for tuberculosis (1921) and community care services for the mentally subnormal (1913) and the mentally ill (1930). Concern at the welfare of children and young people found expression in the Midwives' Act (1902), the Children's Act (1908) and the Maternity and Child Welfare Act (1919), all of which had an immediate effect on the role and scope of local authorities.

Thus, over a period of some fifty years local government enjoyed something of a 'golden age', the symbol of which was the Local Government Act 1933. This was a consolidating measure, designed to clarify, confirm and in effect set the seal on the constitution, structure, powers and functions of local government in England and Wales.

1930–74: the period of 'decline'

For the next forty years, local government was in retreat: it no longer assumed such pride of place in the career orientation of bright school-leavers; it was losing status in the eyes of the public and became the subject of a number of unlikely sounding television serials; its management processes came in for criticism when the aldermanic system, the proliferation of committees and the ethos of 'Buggins' turn next' were contrasted with foreign systems and in particular with modern business management.[7] But the more tangible evidence of a decline lay in four other directions:

(1) *Loss of functions.* As the result of a policy of nationalization, local authorities lost their responsibilities for electricity and gas supply when these were taken over by electricity and gas boards in 1947/8. Local government had never been the sole provider of these services, but its role was a substantial one, supplying about one third and two thirds respectively of the nation's gas and electricity consumption in 1945. Similarly, under post-war legislation (notably the Water Act 1945) many local authorities lost their responsibilities for water supply, as smaller water authorities were absorbed by the larger local authorities or joint water boards. Between 1945 and 1970 the number of water undertakings shrank from 1,250 to about 300. More recently, under the Water Act 1973, local authorities lost responsibility for water altogether to the new regional water authorities.

These developments have been described as a return to the *ad hoc* system of the nineteenth century. But this resurgence is not confined to the field of public utilities. Under the National Health Service Act 1946, all local authority hospitals (about 1,700) together with voluntary hospitals (about 1,300) were transferred to Regional Hospital Boards. Under the National Health Service Act 1973 local government lost the remainder of their personal health services (including vaccination, health visiting, district nursing, ambulances and health centres) when these were transferred to the newly created *ad hoc* Regional and Area Health Authorities in order to create a more unified (and uniform) health service.

Similar developments occurred in the field of social security, for while local government inherited the function of public assistance (or poor relief) from the Boards of Guardians (see p. 27) when they were abolished in 1929, the local authority Public Assistance Committees which administered the system within the local government soon found themselves deprived of clients (whom they could barely afford to support) when, in 1934, the central government set up its own *ad hoc* Unemployment Assistance Board. In 1948 this became the National Assistance Board (and subsequently, in 1966, the Supplementary Benefits Commission) and it removed from local government completely the function of public assistance.

Further instances of the transference of local government functions to *ad hoc* bodies may be cited: under the River Boards Act 1948 (extended by the Water Resources Act 1963) the control of river pollution became the responsibility of River Boards. Under the Road Traffic Act 1930, the responsibility for licensing passenger road services passed from local authorities to regional traffic commissioners. The Transport Act 1947 transferred many canals and harbours to the British Transport Commission, and under the Transport Act 1968 special Passenger Transport Authorities have been established to manage the provision of local buses and trains in the larger urban areas (see p. 321).

However, the re-emergence of semi-independent public boards was not the only way in which local authorities lost functions. The central government itself has taken over direct responsibility for a number of services, for example the building and maintenance of trunk roads (under the Trunk Roads Acts 1936 and 1946) and rating valuation (under the Local Government Act 1948). For a short time, 1972–4, local authorities in effect found that central government had become responsible for the determination of council housing rents (under the Housing Finance Act 1972).

It is felt by some that another element in this aspect of local government 'decline' is the upward transfer of functions from the lower-tier authorities to the upper-tier ones. This has occurred most clearly in the case of the district councils. Although there were some exceptions, in 1944 district councils lost to the county councils their responsibility for providing elementary schools; in 1946 they lost their health and police functions, and in 1947 their fire services and planning functions.

This transfer between tiers has occurred in another sense. Under the direction of the Home Secretary, the number of police forces in Britain has been reduced from over two hundred in 1946 to fifty today. This is partly a consequence of the transfer from district to county councils under the 1946 Police Act. But it is also due to the fact that many police forces are now administered by joint committees of neighbouring county councils (for example the Avon and Somerset Constabulary).

(2) *Failure to attract new functions.* It has been suggested that local authorities have failed to acquire certain new responsibilities to which they would

seem to have a claim. Under the New Towns Act 1946, the development of New Towns (such as Cumbernauld, Milton Keynes and Cwmbran) was placed in the hands of appointed boards instead of the proximate local authorities, and for nearly twenty years (1959–77) it was intended that the New Towns when completed should be transferred from the Development Corporations to the New Towns Commission rather than to local authorities. (This was changed in the 1977 Act and local authorities will now acquire the New Towns' assets and management, though some authorities are apprehensive about the costs involved.)

In 1949, under the Special Roads Act, the government announced plans to build motorways. It was not, however, the major local authorities who were to be responsible but the Ministry of Transport (operating through Road Construction Units). In 1967, in pursuance of a policy to preserve and enhance the environment, the Countryside Commissions were set up. Yet their functions (of encouraging the provision and development of facilities for open-air recreation) could perhaps have been undertaken by local authorities, if necessary through joint committees.[8] In 1965, under the government's National Plan, regional economic development machinery was established, in the form of Regional Planning Boards and Councils.[9] Although local authorities had representatives on these Planning Councils, at the time of their creation it was felt that local government was again being overlooked and by-passed. Indeed, in a leading article entitled 'Exit the Town Hall', *The Times* said, 'It is beginning to look as if confidence in it [local government] and practice of it may prove to be a passing phase in British political evolution.'

(3) *Loss of financial independence.* One of the characteristics of local authorities is that they have the power of taxation (see p. 19) and are thus able to finance their activities. Rates have never been the sole source of income, however, as local authorities have also received income by way of rents, sales, service charges, fines and legacies. Since the nineteenth century, beginning with police grants, local authorities have also received grants from the central government. Over the past forty years the proportion of this grant revenue in local authority budgets has grown substantially, as the figures in Table 1 indicate. As a result, it is argued, local authorities have lost much of their independence – 'he who pays the piper calls the tune'. (See Chapters 11 and 12.)

(4) *Increased central control.* In the course of the twentieth century, the central government has sought to control the activities of local authorities in a number of other ways. Legislation in the 1940s, setting up the post-war health, education and welfare services, required local authorities to submit their proposed schemes (for the administration and development of these

services) to the Minister, or else gave him wide discretionary powers over local authorities undertaking those services. The central government has also developed substantial powers to intervene in local authorities' appointment of senior officers, to inspect certain local government services and to determine the charges which local authorities make for certain services. In addition, the volume of informational and advisory documents from the central government (called 'circulars') has grown in such a way as to give the central government considerable additional powers of persuasion and influence over the affairs of local government. The situation is well illustrated by the career of Aneurin Bevan. He is said to have been elected to Tredegar Urban District Council (in 1922) only to find that power resided in the county council. Having got himself elected to Monmouth County Council (1928), he found that power had gone to the central government. Subsequently he went there (1929) becoming Minister of Health (1945) and thus responsible for local government!

Table 1. *Local government income* (*revenue account*)

Year	Grants		Rates		Other	
	£m	%	£m	%	£m	%
1933	122	27	149	33	176	40
1953	469	36	443	33	413	31
1963	1,158	37	1,031	33	901	29
1973	4,422	45	2,682	28	2,660	27

Source: *Local Government Finance* (the Layfield Report), HMSO, 1976, Table 25; W. A. Robson, *Local Government in Crisis*, Allen & Unwin, 1966, Table 1.

A number of explanations have been put forward to account for the apparent decline of local government. Firstly, it is suggested that rates as a source of income are inadequate: they lack 'buoyancy', that is to say that they do not automatically produce a higher yield in revenue as incomes rise generally (see p. 205). As a consequence local authorities have of necessity come to rely more and more on central government grants.

Secondly, local authorities lost another source of income when gas and electricity were nationalized. The notion of nationalization and centralization are normally associated with the rise of socialism. The Labour Party was swept to power in 1945 (remaining in office until 1951) and while Labour is usually seen as an ally of local government (having historically developed many of its roots there) this time its commitment to central state ownership outweighed its predisposition to municipal enterprise.

Thirdly, the notion of equality had been gaining general approval throughout the century. The privations and camaraderie of the Second

World War gave it a substantial boost. Thus, following the Beveridge Report (1942),[10] the Welfare State was established. Social security and health services were unified and centralized to secure more uniform and equal treatment throughout the nation. And to the same end the activities of local government in the fields of education, welfare and housing became subject to greater central government oversight.

Fourthly, the radical doctrine of state intervention in the economy, usually associated with the economist J. M. Keynes (1883–1946) and often referred to as 'Keynesian economics', became official government policy during and after the war. In 1944 the government pledged itself to a policy of full employment (in contrast to the heavy unemployment of the 1930s) and this required 'budget management' by the government, that is to say that in times of threatened depression the government would spend money to boost the economy, even if it meant that its budget was in deficit and not balanced with income from taxation. Conversely, where demand in the economy was excessive and inflation threatened, the government would seek to reduce state expenditure and perhaps private spending too, for example through higher taxes, tighter credit facilities and higher interest charges. This is generally known as fiscal and monetary policy. Local authorities have inevitably been caught up in this new 'demand management' role of government as they are big spenders, and in this way they have lost some of their freedom and autonomy.

Fifthly, local government may be said to have 'declined' because of its outmoded structure, which was mainly established in the nineteenth century, when the population was much smaller and population settlement quite different. At that time there were few if any suburbs, nor was there a 'drift' of population such as we have experienced in this century towards the South and East. Increased mobility, especially with the spread of motoring, and modern transport and communications, have made the nineteenth-century local government boundaries meaningless. In many ways, therefore, the structure was out of date from its inception: boundaries were wrongly drawn (for instance, county boroughs were made too small) and with the possible exception of London (see p. 89) insufficient account was taken of the nascent conurbations (the large urban areas, which stretch around the cities of Birmingham, Manchester and Glasgow, for example).

Coupled with this was the notion that local government units were too small to be efficient. Business enterprise had shown that 'bigger is better' in the sense that economies could be achieved in large-scale units – increasing the size of production unit can lower the unit costs (just as a double-decker bus can carry twice as many people as a single-decker but still only needs one driver and four wheels). Thus 'the process of technical change, by making such economies possible, encourages a shifting of responsibility for particular functions from lower to higher levels of government'.[11]

Assessing the fortunes of a private company or the business sector in general can be a fairly objective and precise exercise: one can refer to profits records, balance sheets etc. It is much more difficult to make a similar evaluation of local government, which is very subjective and open to varying interpretations.

In the previous pages we have indicated some ways in which local government generally has declined since the 1930s, in contrast with its expansionary and optimistic phase from the later nineteenth century. However, we must beware of the danger of exaggeration. It could be argued that a number of the functions lost by local government were not very significant. For example the central government, in building motorways and taking over trunk roads, became responsible for less than 5 per cent of the nation's public highways; local authorities have retained responsibility for the remainder. Overall, it is not unreasonable to suggest that local authorities have retained their most important functions, and indeed they have markedly expanded their provision of these, as for example in the fields of education, leisure and the welfare services.

In addition, local government has acquired some new or enlarged responsibilities: for instance in the environmental field (including planning, town development, National Parks, pollution control and civic amenities) and in the field of welfare (such as children's services, consumer protection and community care for the mentally disordered). As a result of these developments, local government expenditure in the 1950s and 1960s increased not only in real terms but also as a proportion of total national expenditure (see Chapter 11).

Moreover, we must distinguish the substance from the shadow. Extensive central government control exists in law, but how much is exercised in actual practice? For example, although he has the legal power to do so, only rarely does a Minister issue general directions to local authorities (and not always successfully even then – see p. 230 and 237).

In so far as local government has experienced a decline in the ways described in this chapter, this *in itself* is not to be decried, for society changes and the machinery of public administration must change accordingly. What appears as a loss to local government may represent a net gain to society: thus the removal from local government of public assistance or gas supply may provide the greater benefits of lower costs and less uneven standards of service.

Finally, it may be added that local government has to some extent suffered at its own hands – by failing to take advantage of existing permissive powers and by failing to adapt itself and its structures to changing circumstances.

Scotland

The development of local government in Scotland quite closely parallels that of England and Wales. However, the relatively large number of burghs and their tradition of local self-rule provided Scotland with a more pervasive framework on which to build the structure of modern local government.

Burghs, like the English boroughs, were established in the Middle Ages as trading communities. Their primary function was to make profits and so supplement the king's revenues, but they were also set up to extend royal influence within the kingdom. In the course of time many of these burghs flourished and grew into towns, and councils of burgesses were entrusted to collect the revenues and regulate trading practices. Subsequently they began to assume responsibility for the management of local affairs generally. Alongside these 'royal' burghs there developed a considerable number of 'barony' and 'regality' burghs, established by landowning Scottish nobles and bishops and having similar trading privileges. By the end of the sixteenth century, there were some 350 burghs of one kind or another in Scotland.

The Church, in the form of the 'kirk session' (similar to the English parish vestry – see p. 26), had long taken upon itself the responsibility for caring for the helpless poor and for providing some school education. In practice the cost of these services was met largely from church collections. But they were also partly financed from rates levied on the property owners (or 'heritors') of the parish. Assessment for rating was undertaken by committees of local landowners in each county, known as 'commissioners of supply'. Gradually the functions of these magnates widened to include such matters as the establishment of police forces, registration of electors and the management of roads, though in some cases the responsibility was shared with the Justices of the Peace.

So in the eighteenth century there was a rudimentary form of local government in both the urban and rural (or landward) parts of Scotland. But, as in England and Wales, Scottish local affairs in the late eighteenth and early nineteenth centuries suffered from the twin defects of corruption, due to the closed, self-appointing system of selecting councillors, and of impotence in the face of the problems arising from rapid industrialization, population growth and urbanization.[12] One consequence was that the larger, mainly royal, burghs were reformed: under the Burgh Reform Acts 1833 these councils were made subject to open election.[13] Many burghs, however, remained unreformed until 1900 (see below).

A second consequence was the creation of numerous *ad hoc* bodies. In the smaller burghs, alongside the old councils, popularly elected commissions were set up to provide police and basic improvement services, such as sanitation, lighting and water. Following the Police Acts of 1850 and 1862 new (non-burghal) towns were allowed to establish similar multi-purpose police commissioners, and by the end of the nineteenth century there were about one hundred such 'police' burghs.

In 1845, following a Royal Commission report, elected parochial boards were established to take over responsibility for the relief of the non-able-bodied poor. Subsequently, these boards became responsible for certain aspects of public health. In 1857 local boards were set up to take care of the mentally disordered. And under the Education Act 1872, locally elected school boards were formed to administer the new system of popular education.

In 1889 elected county councils were established in Scotland which took over most of the functions of the commissioners of supply and the JPs (both of which remained in being, partly to administer the police through joint committees), together with some of those of the *ad hoc* bodies. Similarly, under the Burgh Police Act 1892 the functions and relationships between the police commissioners and the burgh councils were clarified and rationalized. The reform momentum continued under the Town Councils (Scotland) Act 1900, when *all* burghs were required to have regularly elected councils, each headed by a 'provost' (or mayor) and 'bailies' (aldermen). At a lower level, elected parish councils were created in 1894 and given responsibility for poor relief.

For administrative purposes county councils were obliged to delegate a part of their responsibilities to county road boards (appointed by the county council) and to district committees, comprising representatives from the county council, town councils and parish councils and responsible for roads and public health. Consequently, despite some measure of rationalization, Scotland's local government in the early twentieth century was a complex network consisting of 200 town councils (the burghs), 33 county councils, 869 parish councils, nearly 1,000 school boards and a host of police commissions, county road boards, district committees and joint standing committees.

However this complex structure was somewhat simplified by the Education (Scotland) Act 1918, which replaced the school boards with thirty-eight education authorities based on the counties and large burghs. And finally, the whole local government structure was re-cast by the Local Government (Scotland) Act 1929, under which:

(1) The various types of burghs were reduced to two, 'large' or 'small',

depending on whether their population exceeded or fell below 20,000. (Towns with under 700 inhabitants lost their burghal status. In 1947 this figure was raised to 2,000.)

(2) The four largest burghs (Glasgow, Edinburgh, Dundee and Aberdeen) became 'counties of cities' (all-purpose authorities like county boroughs in England) and they, together with the county councils, became responsible for the provision of school education.

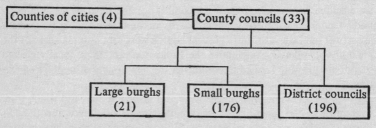

Figure 4 *Local government in Scotland 1929–74*

(3) Parishes, district committees and standing joint committees (with their commissioners of supply) were abolished and their functions transferred to the county councils.

(4) District councils were set up in the landward (rural) areas.

(5) The rates of the various authorities were combined into a consolidated county and burgh rate.

(6) Functions were divided between the county councils and the more local authorities: (a) the large burghs were responsible for all *except* education and valuation; (b) small burghs were responsible for housing, public health and amenities; (c) district councils had statutory responsibilities for amenities (parks, allotments, entertainments, footpaths) but might also receive delegated authority from the county council for such services as lighting, sewerage and refuse.

(7) As a consequence of the division of functions, the councils of the counties were to contain representatives from the town councils of the burghs.

Like local government in England and Wales, the Scottish system had its critics. The need for structural revision was officially recognized in 1963, when the government published a White Paper, *The Modernisation of Local Government in Scotland* (Cmd 2067). This was not acted upon because, following a change of government, a Royal Commission was appointed in 1966 (under the chairmanship of Lord Wheatley) to undertake a thoroughgoing review of local government in Scotland. This Commission thus ran parallel to the Royal Commission, under Lord Redcliffe-Maud, which was considering local government in England (see pp. 49–52).

3. The Structure of Local Government

Local government today has a two-tier structure. This is a relatively new arrangement, being the result of the Local Government Act 1972 (England and Wales), the Local Government (Scotland) Act 1973 and the London Government Act 1963. (Each Act came into operation after two years.) The new structure is also the product of a great deal of criticism, inquiry, debate and argument.

As we saw in the previous chapter, the old structure, established mainly at the end of the nineteenth century, had become out of date and inappropriate to twentieth-century circumstances. It was increasingly seen as an incubus and has been blamed for local government's loss of functions and general decline.[1] The words of the Royal Commission on Local Government in Scotland could have referred to the whole country: 'Something is seriously wrong with local government . . . the system is not working properly . . . At the root of the trouble is the present structure of local government.'[2]

The old structure: 1888–1975

Until the reforms of the 1960s and 1970s, local government in Britain comprised three different structures:

(1) The single-tier all-purpose authorities called 'county boroughs' in England and Wales, and 'counties of cities' in Scotland. About 15 million people, or about 25 per cent of the population, lived under this system in 1965.

(2) The two-tier system which existed in the administrative county of London, the London County Council (LCC) having responsibility over the whole area for such functions as education, planning, health and welfare, and the twenty-eight boroughs having responsibility for public health and housing. About 3 million people, or about 5 per cent of the population, lived in the LCC area in 1965. (About 8 million, or 15 per cent, lived in the area of Greater London. See Chapter 5.)

(3) The three-tier system of the counties, districts (including urban district councils, rural district councils and non-county borough councils – see

p. 30), and parishes which operated in the remainder of Britain[3] and thus covered about 40 million, or about 70 per cent of the population. Under this system, the county councils had responsibility for the broader functions of education, planning, welfare and police, and the district councils for public health, housing and amenities. Within the RDCs, parishes held meetings of all parishioners or, where the population was large enough (200 or over), formed councils with responsibility for such things as allotments, footpaths and recreation grounds, some of these being exercised concurrently by the RDC.

The faults which have been detected in this structure over the course of the century are numerous. They may be summarized as follows:

(a) Many local authorities had become too small, with the consequence that they were unable to provide some of the services expected of them,[4] or they provided inferior services.

(b) There were great disparities in the sizes of local authorities of the same type. In 1966, out of a total of 140 top-tier local authorities in England and Wales (outside London), twenty-two had populations of over 500,000 and forty-one had populations of less than 100,000. Similarly, at district level, out of a total of 1,298 local authorities ninety-five had populations of over 50,000 while 184 had populations of less than 5,000. As a result, many top-tier local authorities were actually smaller than some second-tier authorities, so that population size was no longer an accurate guide to the status or functions of a local authority. (In Scotland, this was less of a problem because in 1929 the Scottish burghs were revised to take some account of population variations. See p. 40.)

(c) The structure no longer reflected the social geography of the nation: what may have been appropriate for the later nineteenth century no longer suited Britain in the second half of the twentieth. Movements in the population and developments in transport and communications, electricity, housing and medicine made many local government boundaries seem irrelevant and redundant. For example the distinction between town and country (as exemplified in the county council–county borough and the rural district–urban district bifurcations) no longer seemed appropriate, as people were regularly moving between the two environments for employment, leisure or education: they were no longer distinctive communities. A similar situation existed in the conurbations, where there were collections of separate local authorities and no authority with an overall responsibility or perspective.

(d) The division of functions among local authorities inhibited their effective performance. This occurred in two ways. Firstly some services were complementary to one another, but their close liaison and co-ordination was obstructed because responsibility for them lay in the hands of different local authorities. For example, housing was the responsibility of the district councils while welfare functions – accommodation for the homeless, care of the elderly, community services for the mentally and physically handicapped – were carried out by the county councils. Secondly, the *same* function could be divided among different local authorities, and this fragmentation could reduce its effective performance, as, for example in the area of the comprehensive planning and control of land development and transport.

Generally, therefore, it was felt that there were too many local authorities (about 1,500, excluding parishes) and that larger units would be more effective and more economic. Furthermore the existing system was regarded as confusing for the public, especially since it was compounded by complexities such as delegation, joint schemes and *ad hoc* provision.[5]

Some of these anomalies were inherent in the sense that they were allowed into the original structure. For example in 1888 four county boroughs came into existence with populations well below the statutory requirement of 50,000 (see p. 29). But most of them have arisen as a result of social and economic developments. It is perhaps surprising that the system did not respond to these changes and adapt itself to them. We consider this in the following section.

Attempts at reform 1900–1966: England and Wales

The local government structure created at the end of the nineteenth century did not remain completely unaltered until the reorganization of the 1970s. The founding legislation did allow for boundaries to be changed and for councils to be merged or altered in status. The process was quite cumbersome, involving the relevant local authorities, the central government and, for major changes, Parliament. But the system was used, and it led, for example, to the creation of twenty-one new county boroughs and over a hundred county borough boundary changes in the years 1889–1925. These changes cost the county councils an estimated 3 million loss of population and some £14½ million loss of rateable value (revenue). It thus caused them considerable anxiety and heightened the enmity which existed between town and country authorities.

The consequence was a full-scale inquiry in the form of the Royal Commission on Local Government 1923–9. Essentially, this had two consequences: (i) it stemmed the growth of county boroughs by recommending that the minimum population be raised from 50,000 to 75,000 (enacted in 1926); (ii) it led to a massive reduction in the number of district authorities (UDCs and RDCs) from 1,606 to 1,048 during the years 1931–7.[6] This followed from the Royal Commission's recommendation (enacted 1930) that county councils should be *required* to conduct a review of the district authority areas. Nevertheless, the central government was moved to comment that 'the changes have not in every case been as comprehensive as would have been wished'.

The 1939–45 war prevented the issue of reform being taken any further, but in 1945 the government appointed a five-man Local Government Boundary Commission to 'consider the boundaries of local government areas in England and Wales (except London) and related questions such as the establishment of new county boroughs'; their objective was to secure 'individually and collectively effective and convenient units of local government administration'. They were also advised to take account of such factors as community of interest in the localities, their physical, economic and social characteristics, financial resources and local opinion.

The Commissioners felt that they had been given plenty of instructions but not enough powers. In their report for 1947 they made some very trenchant criticisms of the local government structure, and on the ground that a major disorder demanded drastic treatment they went beyond their terms of reference and recommended a substantial reorganization. Their proposals included: (1) two-tier county systems (like that of London – see p. 29) for the conurbations; (2) most-purpose authorities for the medium-sized towns (like the Scottish large burghs – see p. 40); (3) a uniform system of district councils formed from the UDCs, RDCs and boroughs. But the government, in the form of the Minister of Health, Aneurin Bevan, in effect rejected the report and the Commission was later dissolved.

In taking this action, the government declared that it was not the right time to introduce far-reaching changes in local government structure. It also acknowledged the fact that the various types and tiers of local government were at odds with one another over the direction which reform should take, since inevitably one authority's gain was another's loss. This divergence of opinion was revealed most clearly in 1953, when the local government associations (the organizations representing the different types of local authority – see p. 246) held a number of joint conferences and issued reports. These reports were largely concerned with defending and espousing the virtues of their own particular types of local authority, and generally supporting the existing system with some modifications. However the Association of Municipal Corporations, representing the county boroughs and non-county boroughs, was alarmed at the others' suggestion that county boroughs with populations of under 75,000 (nineteen of them) should be demoted, while no new county boroughs should be created without a population of at least 100,000. In reply, the AMC advanced the figure of 50,000 as the population minimum for county borough status.

The government sought to cool tempers among the local authorities by announcing that it had faith in the existing system and did not propose to embark on any extensive reform. 'The present system has, over many years, stood up to the severest tests. It responded well . . . There is no convincing case for radically reshaping the existing form of local government in England and Wales.'[7]

The Local Government Commissions 1958–65

Nevertheless some changes were needed and to this end the government set up two Local Government Commissions (for England and for Wales) under the Local Government Act 1958. They were to be advisory, not executive; that is they could propose changes but the government and Parliament would make the decisions. They were also given some general guidelines, based substantially on an amalgam of the local authority associations' earlier proposals. Thus, in what were called 'General Review Areas', the Commissioners could propose changes in the area and status of county councils (which would then review district council areas) and county boroughs (taking 100,000 as a loose population criterion for the latter). In the five 'Special Review Areas', based on the conurbations apart from London, the English Commission could be more assertive and (a) deal with *all* the local authorities, (b) re-distribute functions, and, in particular, (c) propose 'continuous counties' (counties in which there would be no 'islands' of independent county boroughs) where they thought it appropriate.

For a number of reasons, the work and achievements of these Commissions were limited. In the first place, their terms of reference were inadequate: in one sense they were too vague and in another too restricted (for example, by excluding the consideration of functions in the General Review Areas). Secondly the procedure was cumbrous, providing as it did for innumerable consultations and opportunities to raise objections, so that delay was inevitable and inordinate (some reports took up to four years to produce[8]). Furthermore, a number of the recommendations were rejected outright (those of the Welsh Commission for example – see p. 48). Finally, the English Commission was prematurely dissolved in 1965 when the government announced its intention to set up a Royal Commission, under Lord Redcliffe-Maud, to undertake a more fundamental review of local government. (The Welsh Commission had already completed its work – see below.)

Nevertheless, a number of reports were issued[9] and some changes took place. For the General Review Areas, proposals were made to revise a number of county boundaries and to amalgamate some of the smaller counties. Similarly, boundary changes were proposed for county boroughs, with some demotions and new creations. For the Special Review Areas, apart from some adjustments to the boundaries and status of counties and county boroughs, the 'continuous county' system (an urban two-tier system like that in London) was recommended for Tyneside and South East Lancashire, while a joint board of neighbouring county councils was recommended for Merseyside.

Some of these recommendations were accepted by the government and became operative. For example, the Isle of Ely was merged with Cambridgeshire and a number of county boroughs were created, including Torbay, Luton, Solihull and Teesside. Other proposals were rejected, either outright (such as those for Wales) or after sustained protest and inquiry (such as the proposed abolition of Rutland County). The remainder languished and lapsed when, in February 1966, the setting-up of the Royal Commission was formally announced.

It has been suggested that 'the significance of the period from the Second World War to the passage of the Local Government Act 1958 is that it was a period of great changes in local government, *except* in the structure of local government'.[10] As we have seen, the structure has not changed fundamentally throughout the century (until the 1970s). We now consider why this is so.

Why reform was delayed

Despite the fundamental changes in society and the mounting pressure for structural reform, local government remained substantially unchanged until the 1970s (except for London – see p. 89). This may be partly explained by exigencies, such as the costs involved in reorganization, the pressures on governments' legislative timetables and the problems caused by war and reconstruction. Nor was there any real fervour from the general public.

Secondly, there was no agreed alternative: a number of schemes were proposed of more or less equal appeal (or repugnance). Differences of opinion were bound to arise as some groups sought to promote *efficiency* (which frequently meant larger or single-tier units), while others sought to emphasize and enhance the cause of *democracy* (which often amounted to the retention of small local authorities, usually in a two-tier structure) and yet others pursued the goal of *simplicity* (which implied a uniform pattern of authorities). In other words, the whole basis of reform was in dispute and implied deadlock or compromise (as exemplified in the numerous boundary changes outlined above).

Finally, there were political reasons for delay. Any reform was bound to threaten some interests, and every local authority or group of authorities sought to justify its own continued existence. The government at Westminster could not afford to ignore or alienate large blocks of local government opinion. (A more cynical view was that the central government preferred to keep local authorities small, numerous and divided in order to sustain a dominant position.) Moreover, party politics were involved, since changing local government authorities and boundaries could affect the composition of constituencies and so large numbers of local government votes and party majorities.[11] In fact, it appears that when reform did appear it was to a large extent the result of pure chance.[12] Before examining this reform, it is appropriate to consider developments in Wales's local government structure.

Wales

The Local Government Commission for Wales (see p. 46) produced a draft report in 1961. It recommended the reduction of counties from thirteen to five. Following considerable protest, it deliberated further and revised its recommendations to seven new counties. Again there was strong reaction from the local authorities, and indeed the Commission itself was not entirely happy with its own conclusions, as it felt that its terms of reference were somewhat inadequate: '. . . we cannot help wondering whether, had we been allowed to consider at least the redistribution of functions, we might not have done a better job.'[13]

In response, the government thanked the Commission for its report, but rejected its proposals. It then acknowledged the limitations of the terms of reference by setting up a departmental inquiry (under the Welsh Office) in 1965 to consider the functions and finance, as well as the boundaries, of local authorities in Wales. Despite the inauguration of a Royal Commission in England in 1966, it was decided to persist with the Welsh inquiry, and in 1967 a White Paper was published.[14] This proposed that the county boroughs should be reduced from four to three, the counties from thirteen to five, and the districts from 164 to thirty-six. The scheme also proposed the introduction of an appointed Welsh Council with advisory functions.[15]

Inevitably, with various ideas for reform going before the English Royal Commission, it was felt that the proposals for Wales were premature. Subsequently, the proposals were changed, partly as a result of the Royal Commission's report (see p. 51) and partly as a result of a change of government in 1970.

The Redcliffe-Maud Report

Local government is the only representative political institution in the country outside Parliament; and being, by its nature, in closer touch . . . with local conditions, local needs, local opinions, it is an essential part of the fabric of democratic government. Central government tends, by its nature, to be bureaucratic. It is only by the combination of local representative institutions with the central institutions of Parliament, that a genuine national democracy can be sustained.[16]

Thus did the Royal Commission on Local Government in England 1966–9 (led by Lord Redcliffe-Maud) defend the concept of local government. It went on to say that a local government system should possess four qualities: the ability to perform efficiently a wide range of important tasks concerned with the well-being of people in different localities; the ability to attract and hold the interest of its citizens; the ability to develop enough inherent strength to deal with national authorities in a valid partnership; and the ability to adapt itself to the process of change in the way people work and live. These qualities were missing from English local government, which was found to be suffering from four structural defects, namely:

(1) The local government areas did not fit the pattern of life and work of modern England, and the gap was likely to widen with social, economic and technological changes.

(2) The fragmentation of England into seventy-nine county boroughs and forty-five counties, exercising independent jurisdictions and dividing town from country, had made the proper planning of development and transportation impossible. The result had often been an atmosphere of hostility between county boroughs and counties and this had made it harder to decide difficult questions on their merits.

(3) The division of responsibility within each county between county council and a number of county districts, together with the position of county boroughs as islands in the counties, meant that services which should have been in the hands of one authority were fragmented among several, making it more difficult to meet needs comprehensively.

(4) Many local authorities were too small in size and revenue and consequently lacked qualified manpower and technical equipment to be able to do their work well.

Furthermore, and partly as a consequence of these failings, there were deficiencies in local government's relationships with the general public, who saw local government as too complex and irrelevant to their daily lives, and with the national government, who doubted the ability of local governors to run local affairs and consequently restricted their activities.

As a result of this analysis, the Royal Commission members were unanimous in their view that the structure needed changing, and there was near unanimity on the principles which should underlie the reformed structure. These stated that:

(1) Local authority areas must be so defined that they enable citizens and their elected representatives to have a sense of common purpose. Consequently,

(2) The areas must be based upon the interdependence of town and country.

(3) In each area, all environmental services (planning, transportation and major development) must be in the hands of one authority. These areas must be large enough to enable these authorities to meet pressing land needs, and their inhabitants must share a common interest in their environment.

(4) All personal services (education, personal social services, health and housing) must also be in the hands of one authority.

(5) If possible both the environmental and the personal groups of services should be in the hands of the same authority: through the allocation of priorities and co-ordinated use of resources, this single authority can relate its programmes for all services to objectives for its area considered as a whole.

(6) Authorities must be made large enough to be able to command the resources needed for the efficient provision of services.

(7) The size of authorities must vary if areas are to match the pattern of population, but a minimum of around 250,000 is essential.

(8) On the other hand, authorities must not be so large that serious managerial problems arise or elected representatives cannot keep in touch with constituents. Consequently a maximum of around 1 million is appropriate as a general rule.

(9) Where the area required for environmental services contains a very large population, a single authority for all services would not be appropriate; here, responsibilities must be divided between environmental and personal services and allocated to two operational tiers of authority.

(10) The new local government pattern should as far as practicable stem from the existing one.

In trying to determine the appropriate units for the new local government structure, the Royal Commission was thus laying down four criteria: efficiency, democracy, the pattern of living and the existing structure of local government. These were not all necessarily compatible. For example, research for the Royal Commission had shown that there existed some 130–140 areas which could be described as coherent socio-geographic units (that is, having patterns of living which combined town and country). But these areas were of varying sizes and were generally too small for the effective performance of the main services. The Royal Commission therefore had to strike a balance between the claims of efficiency, democracy, community and continuity.

In striking this balance, the Royal Commission concluded that most of England should be divided into fifty-eight areas, each having a population in the range of 250,000 to 1 million with a *single-tier* or 'unitary' authority to carry out all the local government responsibilities (that is, it would resemble the county borough system). In three other areas of England, all densely populated conurbations, the environmental group of services would have to deal with such large populations that a single authority would be too unwieldy, too difficult to control democratically and, for the purposes of the personal services, too remote. In these 'metropolitan' areas therefore, a *two-tier* structure was recommended (somewhat like the London system of local government – see p. 91). The top-tier metropolitan authority would be responsible for the mainly environmental services, while the smaller metropolitan district authorities were to provide the more personal services.

In addition, the Royal Commission recommended two partial or non-operational tiers of local government. At very local level, 'local councils' were to be elected with the duty of representing local opinion and perhaps with some powers to provide some local services. At the regional level, eight 'provincial councils' were to be set up to represent the main local authorities in those regions and be responsible for drawing up the provincial strategy and planning framework within which the main authorities would operate.

Reactions to these radical proposals were mixed. The Association of Municipal Corporations (representing the boroughs and county boroughs) accepted the report to some extent. The Labour Party endorsed most of the proposals, although the Labour government's projected legislation[17] included plans to increase the number of metropolitan areas to five and to defer its decision on provincial councils until the Royal Commission on the Constitution had reported.[18]

Hostile comment came from those, notably the Rural District Councils Association and the County Councils Association, who argued that the large unitary authorities would be remote, bureaucratic and unresponsive to local needs, and that the proposed local councils were inadequate, a mere sop to satisfy the demands for local democracy. In effect, these critics were saying that unitary authorities were government but not local, that local councils were local but not government, while the provincial councils were neither local nor government. Instead they favoured a two-tier system of local government throughout England.

They were not alone in this. Many other critics thought that the Royal

Commission had sacrificed democracy in the pursuit of consistency and of efficiency (even though, as others pointed out and the Royal Commission acknowledged, there was no conclusive evidence that larger units of administration were more efficient). Indeed the Royal Commission did not produce a unanimous report, for one member wrote a powerful memorandum of dissent[19] because he believed that the main report had given too much weight to the principle of concentrating responsibilities into single-tier authorities, but that in making these areas the appropriate size for effectiveness (between 250,000 and 1 million) it had undervalued the important principle of population settlement. He felt that his colleagues on the Commission had compromised in the wrong direction and had gained the worst of both worlds, as many of the proposed areas would be too small for environmental services and too remote for personal services. His own proposals for a two-tier structure (plus local and provincial councils) sought to give greater recognition to the 'facts of social geography' (rather like the Royal Commission on Scotland's local government – see p. 59) by creating small regional authorities, to exercise mainly strategic functions, and district authorities, for the more personal services.

In June 1970 the Conservative Party won the general election and local government reform was back in the melting pot. The Conservatives were anxious to avoid unitary authorities for a number of reasons. In the first place there was no great enthusiasm from any quarter – for many of the public the whole exercise was somewhat remote, and most people were at least used to the two-tier system (only 25 per cent lived in county boroughs). For members and officers, the unitary system threatened possible redundancy. For a number of Conservative M Ps, the parliamentary constituency changes which may have resulted from the proposed local government reforms appeared unwelcome (especially where a rural constituency might be merged into an adjacent city). Fear of amalgamation and perhaps loss of political control also caused a number of county councillors to press the new government to retain the two-tier structure.[20]

Then in 1971 the government published its own proposals,[21] which accepted the two-tier system for the metropolitan areas, but rejected completely the unitary authorities which had been proposed for the rest of England. Instead, the whole of England (and Wales[22]) was to have a two-tier system. The first tier was to be based largely on existing counties; the main change was to occur at district level, in the second tier.

The Local Government Act 1972

Under this Act (operative from April 1974) the eighty-two county boroughs were abolished outright. The fifty-eight *county councils* in England and

Wales were reduced to forty-seven (thirty-nine in England and eight in Wales), with populations ranging from 100,000 (Powys) to almost 1½ million (Hants), and responsible for most of the planning, protective and personal services. Within these counties, 1,249 borough, urban and rural district councils were replaced by 333 *district councils* or *boroughs* [23] (of which thirty-seven are in Wales). Their populations ranged from 422,000 (Bristol) to 18,670 (Radnor), and these councils are responsible for such services as housing, environmental health and amenities. However, a number of responsibilities such as planning and amenities (parks and museums etc.), are shared between the two sets of authorities.

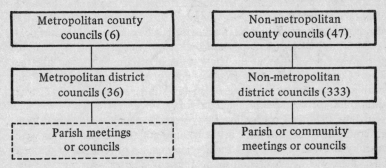

Figure 5 *Local government in England and Wales* (*outside London*) *since 1974* (Note: from 1986 Metropolitan Counties will cease to exist)

The Act also created six *metropolitan counties* (Greater Manchester, Merseyside, West Midlands, Tyne and Wear, South Yorkshire and West Yorkshire), ranging in population from just over 1 million (Tyne and Wear) to 2·7 million (West Midlands) and having responsibility for the broad environmental services (planning, transport, highways). Within these metropolitan counties are thirty-six *metropolitan districts* or *metropolitan boroughs*, ranging from 173,000 (South Tyneside) to over 1 million (Birmingham) and having responsibility for such services as housing, education, welfare and environmental health. A number of other services, such as planning and the provision of amenities, are shared.

In England, the parish was retained as a third tier of local government. In those districts where they existed before 1974, parish councils have been re-established. Elsewhere they have been created either automatically (if the population is large enough) or at the discretion of the district council (see p. 273). There are currently some 7,200 parish councils in England. In the other parts of the non-metropolitan counties local government electors may hold parish meetings to discuss parish affairs and perhaps to take some

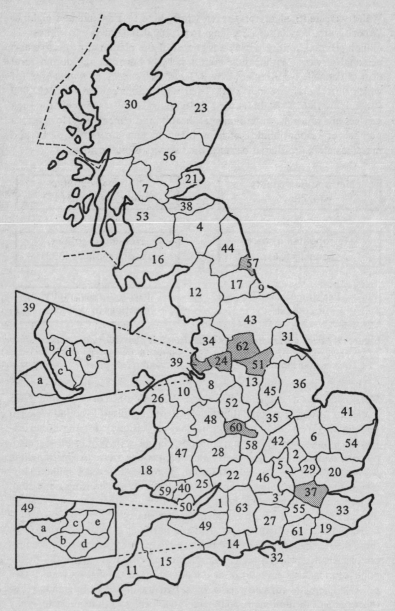

Figure 6 *The local government areas of Britain: counties and regions*

Key to Figure 6 (opposite page)

	Population			Population
1. Avon	921,900	38. Lothian		750,308
2. Bedford	494,700	39. Merseyside		1,545,500
3. Berkshire	672,600	a. Wirral		344,500
4. Borders	100,407	b. Sefton		301,300
5. Buckinghamshire	525,100	c. Liverpool		528,000
6. Cambridge	570,200	d. Knowsley		187,700
7. Central	271,816	e. St Helens		189,500
8. Cheshire	919,800	40. Mid Glamorgan		537,900
9. Cleveland	568,200	41. Norfolk		679,800
10. Clwyd	382,100	42. Northampton		516,400
11. Cornwall	414,700	43. North Yorkshire		661,300
12. Cumbria	472,400	44. Northumberland		289,200
13. Derbyshire	896,200	45. Nottinghamshire		973,700
14. Dorset	586,500	46. Oxford		450,600
15. Devon	948,000	47. Powys		106,000
16. Dumfries and Galloway	143,469	48. Shropshire (Salop)		365,900
17. Durham	603,800	49. Somerset		411,100
18. Dyfed	325,000	a. West Somerset		29,200
19. East Sussex	652,500	b. Taunton Deane		82,200
20. Essex	1,435,600	c. Sedgemoor		86,300
21. Fife	343,077	d. Yeovil		127,100
22. Gloucester	495,300	e. Mendip		86,300
23. Grampian	464,194	50. South Glamorgan		385,600
24. Greater Manchester	2,663,500	51. South Yorkshire		1,304,100
25. Gwent	438,000	52. Staffordshire		997,000
26. Gwynedd	226,400	53. Strathclyde		2,445,283
27. Hampshire	1,453,400	54. Suffolk		592,700
28. Hereford and Worcester	610,100	55. Surrey		995,400
29. Hertford	947,100	56. Tayside		402,930
30. Highland	188,524	57. Tyne and Wear		1,165,100
31. Humberside	844,900	58. Warwick		469,500
32. Isle of Wight	114,300	59. West Glamorgan		366,900
33. Kent	1,449,000	60. West Midlands		2,711,600
34. Lancashire	1,369,600	61. West Sussex		633,600
35. Leicester	833,300	62. West Yorkshire		2,067,900
36. Lincoln	530,100	63. Wiltshire		516,200
37. London	6,918,000			

Under 39 and 49 districts are included to illustrate the pattern of second-tier authorities.

Shaded areas opposite show the six Metropolitan counties and the Greater London Council: in 1986 these will be abolished.

decisions (see p. 273). In Wales the situation is similar except that parishes have been replaced by 'communities', which are entitled to have community meetings and/or community councils with a role similar to that of parishes in England, acting as a forum and a voice for the locality. In particular they can claim to be consulted on planning applications, and they may opt to exercise control over the provision of allotments, burial grounds, footpaths, bus shelters, recreation grounds and street lighting. Altogether, throughout England and Wales (though not in every district – see p. 276) there are about 11,000 parishes and communities, of which about 8,000 have elected councils. Collectively, they are known as 'local councils'. (See p. 273.)

The Local Government Boundary Commissions

The Local Government Boundary Commissions (not to be confused with the Local Government Boundary Commission 1945–9) are permanent bodies set up under the Local Government Acts of 1972 (England and Wales) and 1973 (Scotland). There are three such Commissions, one each for England, Wales and Scotland, and each comprises about half a dozen people (usually from an academic or public service background – Sir Edmund Compton, an ex-civil servant and the first 'ombudsman' in Britain, was the chairman of the English Commission until 1978).

It is the Commissions' function to keep under review the local government areas (including their names) and their electoral arrangements (including the number of councillors and the patterns of wards and county divisions – see p. 95). They would normally be expected to undertake reviews of principal areas at intervals of ten to fifteen years, unless otherwise directed by the Minister.

Following their reviews, they are required to make proposals to the appropriate Secretary of State for changes which they consider desirable 'in the interests of effective and convenient local government'. Such proposals may include the alteration of boundaries, the abolition or creation of local government areas, the conversion of a metropolitan area into a non-metropolitan and vice-versa. As regards areas, most of their work so far has been to consider the districts' reports on parishes and communities in England and Wales, and certain anomalous boundaries in other local authorities generally. Alterations are effected, with or without alteration, by the Secretary of State by means of an order (or statutory instrument) which is passed through Parliament, some of the objections, if any, having been already heard at a local inquiry if necessary. Meanwhile, the Commissions have been busily engaged in reviewing electoral arrangements in most local government areas (see Chapter 6).

Reorganized but not reformed?

The Local Government Act 1972 has substantially altered the face of local government in England and Wales. Apart from the creation of the six metropolitan areas (with their county and district councils) and the reduction of county districts by 75 per cent, the county borough 'islands' have been abolished; some of the smaller counties have disappeared through amalgamation (especially in Wales); some new counties have been created; and there have been innumerable boundary changes (only five counties retained their territories completely intact). It was widely anticipated that these changes would promote efficiency and improve services while at the same time retaining an ample measure of democratic control and involvement:

There is considerable advantage in having units of population sufficiently large to provide a base for ... effective organization and a high quality of service ... The Government obviously must seek efficiency, but where the arguments are evenly balanced their judgement will be given in favour of responsibility being exercised at the more local level.[24]

However, the critics of the reorganized system have been legion. The substitution of the two-tier system for the proposed unitary authorities has not assuaged the feelings of those who declare the new system to be remote and insensitive. In some ways the prescribed antidote has become poisonous, as the parish and town councils have acted as a focus and rallying point for old loyalties so that the hoped-for melding of new communities is slow to develop.

A different kind of criticism has come from those on the left of British politics. They see the reorganization as a stratagem for the greater centralization of power. This has occurred in two directions: firstly from local to central government, and secondly from significant levels of working-class participation and influence to the more exclusive, elitist influence of the business and professional sectors of society.[25] In effect, the capitalist state is seen as mopping up pockets of resistance which local councils represent (see p. 340, note 45).

Most of the criticisms, however, tend to point in the other direction – that, broadly speaking, the scale of reorganization was inadequate and far too many small authorities remain and exercise vital responsibilities (such as education and social services). Even the metropolitan counties are felt to be too small in that their boundaries have been drawn rather tightly around the urban areas, thus incorporating too little of the rural hinterland.[26] This arrangement to some extent re-instates the town–country dichotomy (see Chapter 10) and hinders successful planning and housing programmes, which often require inter-authority co-operation. Relations between local authorities have been soured in other ways, in particular by the division of responsibilities under the 1972 Act. The most contentious area here is that of 'concurrent' powers, where both tiers were given responsibilities for the same service (notably planning, but generally too in the provision of amenities). In many parts of the country this has not been working smoothly and there have been some notable cases of outright hostility (see p. 244). Recent legislation should improve matters here (see p. 321). A further criticism concerns the effectiveness of the county or regional tiers. They are supposed to exercise a broadly strategic role, but this is made difficult by the fact that they do not control the administration of so many services – those which lie in the hands of the districts and of *ad hoc* bodies. This is particularly the case in the metropolitan areas.

Apart from any other consideration, this system of sharing responsibilities (compounded by 'agency' arrangements – see p. 69) adds to the public confusion about local government. The reorganization was intended to 'demystify' the system for the man in the street by making the structure simpler and clearer, but the creation of a double two-tier system, the complicated division of services (not just as between the metropolitan and the non-metropolitan areas, but between England and Wales) and the proliferation of names (including boroughs, cities and town councils) makes the system apparently as complex and perhaps irrelevant as ever. This criticism would appear to be reflected in the fact that election turnout has not improved since the reorganization (see p. 102).

Finally, the government's removal from local government of personal health services and responsibilities for water provision [27] has not only added to public confusion, but also suggests a continued lack of confidence in local government by the central government – in contrast to the aspirations of the Royal Commission, which declared:

The whole Commission is unanimous in its conviction that if the present local government system is drastically reformed, its scope extended to include functions now in the hands of nominated bodies and the grip of central government relaxed, England can become a more efficient, democratic and humane society.[28]

The reorganized system of local government is essentially an evolution from the system established in the late nineteenth century, and in this respect it carries with it the virtues of that system. But it also has many of its defects. The reorganized system does work, but there are many who believe that it does not meet the major problems that local government has to face as effectively as a more radically reformed system would have done.

At the 1983 General Election all three major party manifestoes contained commitments to reorganization (see p. 279). The Labour Party had already put forward two sets of proposals: one, known as 'organic change',[29] involved a limited redistribution of responsibilities in favour of the larger, urban, non-metropolitan county districts (such as Bristol, Hull or Nottingham). The other had a longer-term perspective and envisaged a regional structure throughout England. It was based on the criticism that reorganization was a 'botched job' and that for planning purposes in particular the 'two-tier county–district structure ... [was] irrelevant'.[30] Consequently, in 1978 the Labour Party came out with the proposal for twelve regional councils, with 200 most-purpose authorities forming the second tier (like Scotland's Island Councils). (See p. 279 below.)

Clearly the issue of local government is not settled and major changes affecting the metropolitan authorities are now taking place (see pp. 64 and 94). Local government structure is becoming a party political football, albeit one of third division impact as a result of its limited public appeal: a public attitudes survey in 1970 showed that 77 per cent favoured no change in local government or didn't know or care about it.[31]

Scotland: The Wheatley Report

The Royal Commission on Local Government in Scotland 1966–9 (under Lord Wheatley) praised the work of the local authorities in Scotland, but found the structure of local government to be gravely defective:

Something is seriously wrong with local government in Scotland ... the local government system is not working properly – it is not doing the job that it ought to be doing. At the root of the trouble is the present structure of local government. It has remained basically the same for forty years, when everything around it has changed. (paras. 1 and 2)

More specifically it pointed to the following defects:

... local authorities on the whole are too small. The boundaries pay little heed to present social and economic realities. Services are often being provided by the wrong sorts of authorities and over the wrong areas. The financial resources of authorities do not match their responsibilities. (para. 3)

And as a result:

... the services that local government provide do not operate as well as they should. Staff are not always deployed to the best advantage. Plans ... are often not fully realized. Friction tends to build up between neighbouring authorities because of an artificial conflict of interest, created by the structure of local government and nothing else. The ratepayer's – and the taxpayer's – money is frequently wasted on maintaining two or more separate organizations where one would do perfectly well. Some important services have outgrown the structure, and have had to be taken away from local authorities altogether. (para. 4)

Thus the faults are similar to those diagnosed for England's local government (see p. 49). Not unexpectedly, the overall consequences are also similar:

Looked at as part of the machinery for running the country, local government is less significant than it ought to be. It lacks the ability to speak with a strong and united voice. Local authorities have come to accept, and even rely on, a large measure of direction and control from the central Government. The electorate is aware of this ... The question is being asked ... whether ... local government is worthwhile maintaining at all. (para. 5)

The Royal Commission answers this last question with a firm 'yes' – 'local government of some kind is absolutely indispensable' – but only if it is fundamentally reformed.

The Royal Commission believed that the structural defects 'were so deep seated that surface patching would not do'. Consequently, the reforms were to be thorough-going and were to rest on a foundation of solid principle which would allow the new structure to (a) function as a whole and (b) be capable of coping with future social changes and demands on local government.

In order to provide the groundwork for such a system, the Royal Commission then set down four basic objectives of reform:

(i) Power: Local government should be enabled to play a more important, responsible and positive part in the running of the country – to bring the reality of government nearer to the people [and in particular away from central government].

(ii) Effectiveness: Local government should be equipped to provide services in the most satisfactory manner, particularly from the point of view of the people receiving the services. [This implies a reallocation of functions for discharge at appropriate levels.]

(iii) Local democracy: Local government should constitute a system in which power is exercised through the elected representatives of the people, and in which those representatives are locally accountable for its exercise. That is, local councils should be genuinely in charge of the local situation and elected local councillors really answerable for its actions.

(iv) Local involvement: Local government should bring the people into the process of reaching decisions as much as possible, and enable those decisions to be made intelligible to the people. (paras. 126–160)

These were to be the ideals of the new structure as a whole. But in the quest for appropriate *units* of local government, the Royal Commission emphasized three criteria:

(1) Functional viability. The Royal Commission examined the main functions (actual or potential) of local government and, after considering the scale on which they should be discharged and the extent to which they could be combined in the same hands, drew conclusions about the size of area, population and resources requisite for each. On this basis it said there was a *prima facie* case for three levels of local government (regional, intermediate and local).

(2) Correspondence with communities. It was felt important to match authorities with communities as closely as possible. After examining the social geography of Scotland, the Royal Commission concluded that a pattern existed, made up of four types of community – the region, the shire, the locality and the parish.

(3) Democratic viability. Local authorities must have a sufficient range of functions to create local interest and provide opportunities for councillors to exercise real choice while at the same time keeping the councillors' duties within the compass of ordinary members of the public serving in a part-time capacity.

Clearly these criteria were not entirely compatible. Some sort of compromise was inevitable. In order to avoid fragmentation and to ensure that all local authorities had a sufficient range of functions, the Royal Commission rejected the idea of a four-fold structure to match the four-level community. Instead it sought to concentrate responsibility on just two sets of local authorities. This would have the added virtue of consistency – of as uniform a structure of authorities as could be achieved without undue violence to the pattern of communities.

The final result of the analysis [32] was the recommendation of a two-tier structure consisting of:

(1) Seven regional authorities, based on an amalgamation of existing counties and ranging in population from $2\frac{1}{2}$ million in the West Region to 145,000 in the South West Region;

(2) Thirty-seven district authorities, based on counties and counties of cities which had been enlarged and/or partitioned;

(3) At a very local level community councils could be set up throughout the new districts where there was sufficient local/popular support. They would have no statutory powers and would not be local authorities as such. Essentially their role would be a representative one: to give expression to the views of the community. They would also be entitled to do anything to improve the amenity of the area, and indeed might act as agents for the local authorities in the day-to-day running of certain services.

(4) Responsibilities would be divided between the two sets of authorities. The regional authorities would be responsible for transportation, water, sewerage, drainage, education, social work, housing and police; the districts for environmental health, libraries, building control and licensing. Functions such as planning, parks and recreation would be shared between them.

The Conservative government at Westminster made no radical changes to these recommendations – as it has to the Royal Commission report on English local government – partly because the proposed scheme fitted in with that party's preference for a two-tier system of local government, and partly because they had less at risk politically in Scotland than in England.

Nevertheless the government did respond to the criticism that the district authorities would be too few, too remote and too restricted in function. Consequently the number of districts was increased and they were given more responsibilities (notably housing). In addition, the island authorities were given a separate, virtually all-purpose (region *and* district) status, and another two regions were added to the seven proposed. (Some of these changes were forced on the government during the Bill's passage through Parliament.)

The Local Government (Scotland) Act 1973

The resulting Act created, with effect from May 1975:

(1) Nine regions, each with a Regional Council, and ranging in population from under 100,000 in the Borders to nearly $2\frac{1}{2}$ million in the Strathclyde region, and in area from 500 square miles in Fife to 10,000 square miles in the Highlands.

(2) Three island councils, two with populations of about 20,000, one with 30,000.

(3) Fifty-three districts, each with a district council and ranging in population from 856,000 in Glasgow to just over 9,000 in Badenoch and Strathspey in the Highland region.

Functions were divided between the two sets of authorities largely as recommended by the Royal Commission, except that housing became a function of the district authorities and the island authorities were each given responsibility for most functions (except fire and police services, for which purposes they combine with the Highland Regional Council).

Provision was made for the creation of community councils along the lines recommended by the Commission. (By 1979 some 1,343 such councils had been approved by the government.)

Predictably, the regional tier has been criticized as too big and remote; as over-bureaucratized, cumbersome and inefficient; as varying too greatly in area, population and resources.[33] In particular, the huge Strathclyde region (containing half of Scotland's population) has come in for criticism.

The Royal Commission had anticipated some of the criticisms, saying for example that while the Strathclyde region was big, it nevertheless did comprise a meaningful and identifiable community.[34] Furthermore, it stressed that democracy could be enhanced rather than diminished by increasing the size of the local government unit:

> It is when local government operates at the scale which its services demand that true local democracy emerges; because that is the point where power and responsibility can be properly entrusted and where the administration of services can be responsive in the right way, that is through pressures from within [the local authority] rather than from without [from central government]. (para. 162)

However, the expectation that the bigger and more powerful local authorities would stimulate a greater public participation has been disappointed: voting turnout and the contesting of seats has not noticeably increased since the reform, apart from an initial improvement in the first elections in 1974[35] (see p. 108).

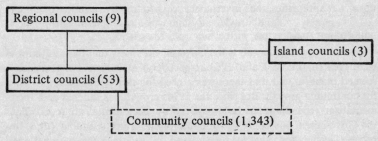

Figure 7 *Local government in Scotland since 1975*

The other main criticisms have been directed at the distribution of functions, and in particular at the transference of housing and refuse disposal from the regions to the district councils[36] and the souring of relations between the two tiers of authorities over the vexed question of shared responsibilities for certain services (as has happened in England and Wales).

On the other hand, one potential problem – devolution – has disappeared (at least for the present). At one time, there was speculation that Scottish local authorities (whatever form they were to take) might have had their functions gradually usurped by the prospective Scottish Assembly.[37] Following the referendum in March 1979 (where only 34 per cent voted in favour of the devolution proposals) the scheduled devolution of power to Scotland (and Wales) was formally dropped by the government.

In 1979, the Secretary of State for Scotland set up a committee of inquiry into local government in Scotland (under the chairmanship of Anthony – now Lord – Stodart). Its terms of reference limited its scope to a tidying-up exercise, though many of the district councils were hoping for something more radical. The Report (February 1981) formed the basis of the Local Government and Planning Act 1982 which (among other things) rationalized the division of concurrent responsibilities among the two tiers of local authorities by some modest adjustments (mainly in favour of the districts) in the fields of tourism, planning and leisure provision, and (in favour of the regions) in the field of industrial promotion and development. In April 1984 another committee (Montgomery) reported on its inquiries into the workings of the Island Councils. The Report applauded the operation of these most-purpose authorities and recommended that their powers be consolidated and perhaps extended (e.g. into airport management).

Streamlining the Cities (Cmnd 9063, October 1983)

This White Paper outlines Government plans for the abolition of the six Metropolitan County Councils and the GLC in 1986. In eliminating these upper tier authorities, the Government seeks to 'remove a source of conflict . . . save money . . . [and] provide a system which is simpler for the public to understand' (Para 1. 19).

Underlying the proposals is the Government's view that these authorities were created (in 1972 and 1963 respectively) at a time when resources seemed plentiful and that there was a need for strategic planning to cater for continuing growth. But since the 1970s growth has faltered and 'incrementalism' (spending) has been replaced by 'decrementalism' (cuts). Thus the Government is seeking (i) to reduce public sector spending, (ii) to improve efficiency (or value for money) and (iii) to attack the 'national overhead' through cuts in the civil service, the removal of one tier of the NHS (see p. 80) and higher revenue targets for nationalized industries. Abolition of the upper tier of metropolitan local government is to be local government's contribution to this and to the Government's prime objective to 'tackle inflation and to improve efficiency in all sectors of national life'.

The Government sees metropolitan counties as secondary and superficial; they have 'too few functions' which has resulted in their finding it 'difficult to establish a role for themselves' – indeed they have sought to encroach on that of the district councils, thus producing 'conflict and uncertainty'. Worse has been their inclination to 'promote policies which conflict with national policies which are the responsibility of central government'. Thus the capital offence of the metropolitan counties has been to 'consistently exceed [the] targets' of expenditure set by the Government. However, *The Times* (1.8.84) has commented, 'A convincing case for abolition has yet to be made with intellectual vigour and sufficient fact . . . ministers will seem to believe that in this matter assertion can substitute for argument.' Private management consultants suggest that the Government's assertions about the metropolitan authorities' excessive spending was overstated and misleading, and that abolition will produce no significant savings.[38] (See pp. 84 and 94 below.)

4. The Functions of Local Government

Local government has a number of functions – providing a voice for the local community, acting as a buffer to the central government, supplying local services, recruiting people into the political process and off-loading the central administration. More briefly we can say that local government has a *political* (or representative) role and an *administrative* (or executive) role. In this chapter we are concerned with the latter.

The principle of 'ultra vires'

An essential element of any democratic system of government is the rule of law: that government is not arbitrary but operates according to the law of the land, and members of the government are subject to the law in just the same way as ordinary members of the public.

As public authorities, local authorities in Britain are subject to the rule of law. Before they can act (collect rates, build schools, acquire property etc.) they must be able to point to the statutory authority (normally an Act of Parliament) which authorizes such actions. If a local council were to take action which was not sanctioned by the law (say by opening a chain of fish shops) or if they exceeded their lawful powers (providing a laundry service where they were only permitted to provide public wash-houses [1]), they would be acting illegally, or *ultra vires*. When a court finds a local authority thus acting beyond its powers, it will declare these actions illegal and may punish members of the authority (see p. 222). In contrast, private organizations or individuals such as you or I can act in any way whatsoever as long as it is not forbidden by law. We can do what is not prohibited; local authorities can do only what the law explicitly allows them to do: what is permitted.

However, local authorities do have some freedom to act. In the first place, besides those powers explicitly conferred on them, there are those which are derived by reasonable implication or inference – powers which facilitate the discharge of their explicit powers, such as acquiring special equipment or appointing and training staff. Secondly, while Acts of Parliament mostly require local authorities to undertake certain 'mandatory' duties (such as building schools or providing gipsy caravan sites), some statutes merely allow local authorities to exercise optional or permissive powers as they see fit (such as rating unoccupied properties or providing general caravan sites). Thus local authorities have a certain discretion as to which services to provide and indeed in what form they will be provided.[2]

Thirdly, local authorities have the freedom to spend a certain sum of money for any purpose which in its opinion would be to the benefit of the area (except where this runs counter to other statutory provisions). Such spending is limited to the product of a 2p. rate in any one year (when the scheme started in 1963 it was 1d: see p. 235). In fact, councils spend under 10% of what is permitted here.[2a]

The justification of the *ultra vires* principle is that it protects the community against possible tyranny, extravagance and hare-brained or politically motivated adventures by its local council. However, it could be argued that the ballot box is a sufficient safeguard and that the operation of the *ultra vires* rule is too restrictive. Professor Keith-Lucas has written, '. . . our local councils are narrowly limited in their powers and duties. There is a lack of enterprise among them, and a feeling in many people's minds that they are unimportant and rather dull'.[3] Apart from thus inhibiting enterprise, voting turnout and council membership, it was argued strongly by the Maud Committee[4] that the principle of *ultra vires* 'robs the community of services which the local authority might render . . . encourages too rigorous oversight by the central government . . . contributes to the excessive concern over legalities'. (And it was pointed out that foreign systems of local government do not have such restrictions.)

Consequently, Maud recommended that local authorities should be given a 'general competence' to do whatever in their opinion is in the interests of their areas, in addition to what is already specified in legislation and subject to their not encroaching on the duties of other governmental bodies and to appropriate safeguards for the protection of public and private interests.

Official response to this suggestion has taken the form of a marginal increase in the power of local authorities to spend money for the benefit of their inhabitants (see above). However, the Local Government Acts of 1972 (England and Wales) and 1973 (Scotland) do make provision for local authorities to acquire statutory powers somewhat more easily (through the rationalization and consolidation of many private Acts and making them of general application to local authorities, as happened through the Local Government Miscellaneous Provisions Acts of 1976 and 1982). We now therefore consider the acquisition of powers by local authorities.

The source of powers

As we have seen above, local authorities are required to operate according to the law. Parliament is the source of law, but there are different kinds of law which can apply to local government. The most important derives from

Public Acts (the most usual kind of legislation). Some of these Acts, such as the Local Government Acts of 1972 and 1973 or the Local Government Social Services Act 1970, apply specifically to local government. Others deal with a general service or function and confer powers on local authorities along with other official bodies, as did for example the Education Act 1944, the National Health Service Act 1947 and the Housing Finance Act 1972.

There are some Acts which permit local authorities to exercise certain powers if the authorities themselves formally 'adopt' them and thus choose to exercise them. These are usually called 'adoptive' or 'enabling' Acts. A recent example is to be found in connection with the licensing of private hire vehicles in the Local Government (Miscellaneous Provisions) Act 1976. They are of relatively little importance these days.

An individual local authority (except a parish or community council) wishing to extend the range of its powers beyond those conferred by public legislation can promote a *Private Bill* in Parliament. The procedure involves special meetings of the council, compulsory advertisement and public announcement, and the engagement of legal counsel for part of the parliamentary proceedings; it is thus complex, lengthy and costly,[5] and only about ten local authorities a year promote such Private (or 'Local') Acts. Recent examples include the Southampton Corporation Act 1960 (which empowered that local authority to construct a bridge across the River Itchen), the Abingdon Market Place Act 1978 (which allows that authority to ban vehicles from the market place in order to help conserve the historic town centre), and the Kensington and Chelsea Corporation Act 1977 (which enables that borough to ban the leaving of refuse outside commercial premises, and also empowers it to carry out the work necessary for the maintenance of the external decoration of any listed building or any building in a conservation area).

Finally, local authorities can seek to extend their powers by applying to the Secretary of State (the Minister), who has the authority, delegated to him by Parliament, to confer certain powers or duties. In some cases he alone has discretion (for example, if a local authority is seeking power to acquire property by compulsion, the 'compulsory purchase order' needs to be confirmed only by the Minister). In most cases however the Minister will have to submit his 'orders' for parliamentary approval. Parliament seldom rejects such Ministerial orders, though they are often challenged (for example by other local authorities) and may be amended.[6]

Who does what

In examining the reorganization of local government in Chapter 3 we had an indication of the division of responsibilities among the various tiers and types of local authority. It may be useful at this point to draw the threads together before analysing the various functions in further detail. Table 2 attempts to do this.

There is some logic underlying this distribution in that the 'bigger' services are administered by the 'bigger' authorities. Broadly, the functions are allocated between the two main tiers on the basis of operational efficiency and cost-effectiveness. Thus it is both cheaper and more effective to have responsibilities such as major planning, police and fire services operated over fairly large areas. Similarly it was strongly argued by the Redcliffe-Maud Report[7] and the Wheatley Report[8] that the education service should be

Table 2. *The responsibilities of local authorities*

	Responsible for:
ENGLAND	
Metropolitan areas	
6 counties	Overall planning, transport, police, fire services
36 districts	Education, personal social services, housing, local planning, environmental health, leisure services
Non-metropolitan areas	
39 counties	As metropolitan counties, *plus* education and personal social services
296 districts	As metropolitan districts, *minus* education and personal social services
Over 7,000 local (parish and town) councils	Local amenities
LONDON	
Greater London Council	Transport, overall planning, some housing
Inner London Education Authority	Education in inner London
32 London boroughs	Housing, social services, leisure, public health, education (outside inner London)
WALES	
8 county councils } 37 district councils }	Much the same as non-metropolitan authorities in England
About 800 community or town councils	Local amenities
SCOTLAND	
9 regions	Overall planning, education, social work, transport, water, police, fire services
53 districts	Housing, local planning
Over 1,200 community councils	Local amenities
3 island areas	All regional and district powers

For a more detailed analysis, see Appendix 2, pp. 292–8, and Appendix 8, p. 309.

administered over an area containing at least 200,000–250,000 in order that such authorities should have at their disposal 'the range and calibre of staff, and the technical and financial resources necessary for effective provision' of the service. On the other hand services such as allotments, public health and amenities can be effectively administered over smaller areas, and are thus the responsibility of district (and even parish/community) authorities.

There is, however, no universal agreement about this general distribution of functions. There is even less agreement about such services as housing and social services (social work): on operational grounds a good case could be made out for their being administered by either tier; their administration varies among the different parts of Britain (see Table 2).

However, the scale of operations is only one criterion. In the allocation of responsibilities, regard has rightly been given to the need for democratic control and responsiveness to local needs. Furthermore, in practice, the rationality of the system has been undermined by the respect which has been paid to history and tradition: the district authorities in England and Wales for example not only have long experience (and expertise) in housing, but they have substantial political influence which they could use to defend themselves against any threatened loss of the housing (or other) function.

Another complication is that the allocation of responsibilities among the local government tiers is not clear-cut: many responsibilities are *shared*. Shared responsibilities can take a number of forms, including (a) *concurrent provision*: whereby several types of local authority all provide the same service, such as car parking, amenities or caravan sites; (b) *joint provision*: whereby several local authorities join together by forming a joint committee or board for the provision of a common service such as crematoria or communications (for instance, the Forth Road Bridge Joint Board, a combined provision by the Lothian and Fife Regional Councils); (c) *shared but divided provision*: whereby several tiers are responsible for a service, but each is responsible for a separate part or aspect of that service, as with refuse collection and disposal (in England) and planning development and control;[9] (d) *reserve powers*, as in the case of housing (and, until recently, planning control), whereby the English county councils may assume responsibility under certain circumstances (for such undertakings as providing houses for certain employees, such as police or teachers); (e) *claimed powers*: whereby certain responsibilities are initially allocated to one set of authorities, but may be claimed by individual local authorities from another tier, such as the district councils in England and Wales, who can claim to maintain unclassified roads in urban areas;[10] (f) *agency powers*: whereby a local authority can arrange (by mutual agreement) for another local authority to carry out functions on its behalf and be suitably re-imbursed. This power to delegate or transfer responsibility is widely available, except that it is specifically prohibited in the case of education, police, social services, national parks, finance (other than rate collection and valuation) and diseased animal control. It is quite widely used, but it varies considerably among both local authorities and services. Services may also be transferred when an authority defaults (see p. 226).

Further complications arise from the fact that in some cases non-providing local authorities must be advised and consulted about matters relating to certain services. For example parishes and community councils must be consulted about planning matters by the appropriate planning authority. Similarly, district authorities are normally given representation on bodies which are the responsibility of the counties (as in the case of school governing bodies in the English and Welsh non-metropolitan areas).

Enough has been said to illustrate the main point: that while it may be possible to indicate in a broad way the allocation of responsibilities among local authorities, for any particular local authority its range of responsibilities will depend on its status, the use it makes of agency and claiming powers, and the use it makes of its permissive powers – all of which will depend in turn on its size, local needs, finance, party politics and the vitality of local voluntary organizations and pressure groups.

The range of services

The range of local government responsibilities is extensive: it is no exaggeration to say that it provides services 'from the cradle to the grave'. Table 2 gives a stark indication of this, and Table 16 (p. 192) shows the relative importance of each function in terms of expenditure. Here we shall try to put some flesh on the bare bones by describing some of these responsibilities in more detail. We can conveniently group them into five categories (Table 3); though it is not always easy to decide the allocation of some services.

Table 3. *Categories of local government services*

Protective	Environmental	Personal	Recreational	Commercial
Fire	Highways	Education	Sports facilities	Markets
Police	Environmental	Careers	Museums, galleries	Transport
Consumer	health	Housing	Theatres	Smallholdings
protection	Transport	Social work	Camp sites	
Disease of	Planning	Homes		
animals		Aids		
Licensing		Meals		

(1) Protective services

Protective services seek to protect the citizen from various dangers.

Police. The organized provision of local police services has been a local government responsibility since the mid nineteenth century, but since the Police Act 1946 small local forces have disappeared and some of the county-based forces have been amalgamated (or 'combined'). It might well be that in the not too distant future Britain's police forces will be organized on a regional basis, and indeed some people argue strongly in favour of a national system.[11]

Police forces are superintended by the police committee of the local authority. This committee is special in that it comprises two thirds councillors and one third magistrates. In London the GLC has no police committee, as the Metropolitan Police Force is under the direct control of the Home Office. In fact the Home Secretary has considerable powers of inspection and regulation of all local police forces and he must approve the appointment of chief constables. However, of greater public concern is the effectiveness of the control exercised by local police committees. It is widely felt to be inadequate, partly as a result of the amalgamations producing bigger and remoter forces. (Since 1946 the number of forces has fallen from 200 to 50.) But this unease is also due to the fact that under the Police Act 1964 the duties of the police committee are limited to maintaining the police force and appointing the chief constable. The latter is responsible for the general operational management of the force and consequently many committee members' questions and probings are allegedly blocked and deflected by the chief constable on the grounds that members are trespassing into his operational territory or that revealing certain information would be contrary to the public interest.

Fire. The provision by local authorities of fire-fighting services was not generally obligatory until 1938. Under the Local Government Acts of 1972 and 1973, fire authorities are required to co-operate and assist one another and, like police services, fire brigades may be amalgamated under a single chief fire officer. Apart from fire-fighting, fire authorities are also concerned with fire prevention, and under a number of statutes (notably the Fire Precautions Act 1971 and the Health and Safety at Work Act 1974) a wide variety of premises (residential, educational, leisure and employment) are required to obtain fire certificates. These are issued by the fire authority (county councils, the GLC, regional and island councils) if they are satisfied that adequate fire precautions and safety facilities (such as fire escapes, alarms, fire doors) exist. Local authorities may provide loans to enable such adaptations as are necessary. In the first instance, it is normally the district authorities who (in the pursuance of building regulations) inspect and require the occupier of premises to obtain fire certificates.

Consumer protection. Local authorities appoint inspectors (often known as trading standards officers) whose task it is to test the weights and measures of local trading concerns and to take legal proceedings against fraudulent traders and similar offenders – those giving short measure, for example. In recent years their work has extended into other areas of trading practice such as charges and credit facilities and false or misleading descriptions of goods and services. Consequently, local authorities are empowered to make purchases locally for test purposes, and inspectors have the right of entry to premises.

Local authorities have similar powers in relation to their food and drug responsibilities, which include the enforcement of regulations regarding the production and sale of food and drugs – their purity, safe storage, labelling and fitness for consumption. For this purpose local authorities appoint inspectors and many will also appoint a qualified public analyst. Inspectors have the right of entry of premises and the right to take food samples for testing.

Local authorities are empowered to set up consumer advice centres. These provide general pre-shopping and post-shopping advice to consumers, assessing product claims and facilitating the investigation of complaints. There is considerable variation across the country in what is provided here, and some local authorities rely on local voluntary provision (by Citizen's Advice Bureaux, for instance). This variation is due partly to financial stringency but also to differences of principles and politics: councillors have varying opinions about how far local authorities should go in advising consumers on appropriate purchases and how far it is the proper role of local authorities to take a pro-consumer stance and campaign against questionable trading practices.

Diseases of animals, such as tuberculosis, swine fever, foot and mouth or rabies, can be directly or indirectly injurious to humans. Consequently, legislation seeks, through local authorities, to control such disease by regulating the movement of livestock and by promoting certain preventive measures (such as sheep dipping). Local authorities issue licences for the movement of animals, and farmers must keep records of such movements.

Licensing has already been mentioned. Broadly it takes two forms: (a) Licensing which seeks merely to regulate certain trades or activities such as pawnbroking, money-lending, taxis, massage treatment, gun-ownership, street-collecting, cinemas, theatres, employment agencies, child-minding or private nursing homes. Such licensing or registration normally involves inspection or compliance with particular regulations (such as safety facilities or refraining from exhibiting certain films). (b) Licensing which involves regulation, but also provides a source of revenue or local taxation, such as dog licences or licences required for killing or dealing in game. The amounts of money raised here are very small.

(2) Environmental services

Environmental services control and improve the physical environment.

Environmental health is perhaps the best known and most firmly established local government function (see Chapter 2). Although in 1974 local authorities in England and Wales lost their responsibilities for the supply of water and main sewerage to *ad hoc* water authorities, they have for instance in recent years become responsible for smoke and noise abatement, the regulation of caravan sites, the control of poisonous waste disposal and the enforcement of health and safety at work regulations. Their more traditional responsibilities, undertaken by environmental health officers, include: the control of nuisances (such as waste tips, insanitary or overcrowded premises, unfenced mines and quarries) and offensive trades (such as glue-making, fat-extraction and tanning); the enforcement of building regulations (which lay down criteria for the construction and design of buildings, including such matters as the adequacy of drains, insulation and accessibility); refuse collection, street cleaning and the instituting of proceedings against litter offenders; the provision of public toilets; the provision of cemeteries and crematoria (and the disposal of dead bodies where no one else can be found to be responsible); and the control of vermin (by requiring or perhaps undertaking the destruction of vermin – most commonly rats, mice and lice – affecting persons or premises).

Many of these activities aim at preventing the outbreak of disease. When an outbreak of a 'notifiable' infectious disease (smallpox, diphtheria, typhoid, cholera, dysentery or anthrax) does occur, local authorities have the duty to inform the local health authority. Local authorities also have powers to prevent the spread of diseases through disinfection of premises and people and the compulsory removal to hospital of infected persons.

Highways, traffic and transport. Roads take a number of forms and local authorities are involved in all of them. Motorways are the responsibility of the central government,[12] which organized their construction through Regional Construction Units (which then broke down into sub-units run by local authorities and acting as agents for the central government). However, these have been recently disbanded (with much of their remaining work being contracted out to private contractors). Trunk roads are also the responsibility of the central government, but it is normal practice for local authorities to act as agents and undertake their building, maintenance, lighting and speed restriction. When such roads become 'de-trunked' (as when a parallel motorway is built) they become the full responsibility of the local authorities. The county councils have recently been pressing for the outright responsibility for trunk roads to be transferred to local authorities.

All other public roads and bridges are the responsibility of local authorities, mainly the county and regional and island councils. District councils have the right to claim responsibility for the maintenance of urban non-classified (i.e. less busy) roads; in practice they often undertake maintenance of these and other roads as agents of the (county) highways authorities. Responsibility for lighting may be similarly delegated, as may the provision of pedestrian crossings, footpaths, seats, shelters, speed limits etc. Such agency agreements are often preferable to the claiming arrangement, as the latter can give rise to discontinuous or patchy coverage of responsibility.

Traffic management involves responsibility for such devices as signals and roundabouts and for regulations such as those covering one-way streets, speed limits and the prohibition of certain vehicles. They are the responsibility of the highway authorities, but may be delegated along with highway maintenance. Decisions concerning street parking restrictions rest with the highway authority, but district authorities may provide off-street parking in their own right. Local authorities have a statutory duty to promote road safety and the prevention of accidents. For this purpose they usually appoint a road safety officer who organizes publicity to encourage road consciousness and the formation of local voluntary groups (for cycling, motor-cycling proficiency etc.), often in conjunction with the police and the schools.

Local authorities may provide passenger transport services. In practice such direct provision is confined to the metropolitan counties, the GLC, the Strathclyde Regional Council and about forty district councils.[13] Otherwise, county and regional councils are responsible for co-ordinating and rationalizing such provision, for which purpose they must draw up and submit to the central government five-year transport programmes which are revised annually. Local authorities may assist in the provision of public transport through grants (including subsidies for the running of mini-buses in rural areas).

Planning. Britain is a small and densely populated country. Land space is limited and its use needs to be carefully monitored, guided and if necessary controlled in the interests of the community as a whole. This is the realm of town and country planning, an essentially twentieth century function of local government.

Planning is important therefore because it affects the way individuals dispose of their property (land) and because it affects their living environment. Broadly, local authorities are charged with responsibility for the preparation of plans, the control of development and the conservation of the environment.

'Structure plans' set out for a ten-year period the broad policy or strategy of the local authority for the use of land in the area of the county or region/island. They cover such concerns as the lines of proposed roads, the sites of public buildings and open spaces, and the allocation of areas for such uses as housing, schools, agriculture and commercial premises, and they thus imply an element of economic planning. These plans are based on a survey of various factors, including population, economic activity, communications and traffic, each of which is likely to affect the scale and nature of land use and development. In drawing up its structure plan, the local authority must consult other appropriate bodies (including district councils) and must submit the plan to the Secretary of State for approval. 'Local plans' cover smaller areas, filling in the details, and are also submitted to the Secretary of State, but do not necessarily require his confirmation.

All of these plans must be well publicized and there must be ample opportunity for objections from the public.[14] The consequence of objections is a public inquiry or a local hearing, and the final decision rests with the Secretary of State in the case of structure plans and with the local planning authority in the case of the local plan.

Having settled their plans, local authorities are then responsible for the implementation of those plans through the process of the control of development. All development – from the big housing estate or shopping centre to the individual house extension or conversion, and the location and size of advertisements – must obtain prior planning permission[15] from the local authority (the district council). Where such permission is refused or involves unacceptable conditions, appeal may be made to the Secretary of State, who may hold an inquiry before making a decision. In practice, the Minister's decision rarely overturns the decision of the local authority. (In some cases, involving matters of national, regional or technical importance, the Secretary of State may appoint a Planning Inquiry Commission.)

Planning often appears to be a rather negative exercise, and planners are sometimes characterized as 'inverted Micawbers', waiting for something to turn down. However, town and country planning has many overtly positive aspects. Local authorities may acquire land (perhaps through compulsory purchase orders) with a view to its development either directly or by attracting industry (through the provision of loans or factory space). They also have powers to reclaim and improve derelict land. In both these respects the powers of councils in the inner urban areas are especially great.

Councils also have certain powers related to conservation. They can require special planning applications for the demolition or alteration of 'listed buildings' (those listed as of special architectural or historic interest or importance). Trees and woodlands may be protected by local authority 'preservation orders'. Local planning authorities may make grants or loans available for the maintenance of listed buildings. Finally, councils are empowered to preserve and enhance the natural beauty of the countryside by creating country parks and setting up nature reserves. They are also responsible for the recording and protection of rights of way. A number of their conservation functions are exercised in conjunction with the Countryside Commission.

Emergencies. Local authorities have made some sort of provision for the possibility of Britain being involved in a war, such provision normally including the formulation of an emergency plan (though 150 councils, have virtually opted out by declaring themselves 'nuclear free zones'). They also have contingency plans for natural disasters or hazardous conditions, such as abnormally heavy snowfalls, floods or extensive oil pollution. Under such circumstances, the emergency planning officer would be responsible for the co-ordination and execution of the appropriate services (perhaps in conjunction with outside bodies, such as the armed forces or health services).

Environmental services often seem dull in the sense of their being devoid of conflict and controversy. There are good reasons for this – we can normally expect the bins to be emptied, the dead to be buried or the public lavatory to function without a fuss. On the other hand there are many areas of dispute in this field. In the area of planning, apart from issues such as compulsory purchase or refused planning applications, there are the larger-scale issues of planning blight, the damage caused to communities by large-scale redevelopment and the running down of town centres etc. which give rise to neighbourhood action groups and civic societies. In the field of transport, there are the problems of routing, parking and pedestrianization, and the broader questions of social need and loss of amenity.

(3) Personal services

Personal services seek to enhance personal welfare.

Education, taken as a whole, is the local authorities' most costly service (see p. 192). Their basic responsibility laid down in the Education Acts of 1944 (England and Wales) and 1945 (Scotland) is to provide, without charge, adequate primary (including nursery) and secondary education for the 10 million schoolchildren in Britain. This implies the provision and staffing of schools, the enforcement of regular school attendance and the provision of transport and maintenance grants for the children. Other welfare services include the supply of milk, meals and child guidance services, as well as special arrangements for the education of handicapped children at home, in hospital or in schools.

State schools are 'maintained' by local education authorities (LEAs). Many of these in England and Wales – about one third – are known as 'voluntary aided' or 'voluntary controlled', implying their foundation by a voluntary organization (usually the Church) which continues to exercise a management role in spite of dependence on LEA financial support. The management committees or boards of governors of schools and colleges are currently being reformed (following the Taylor Committee Report 1977 and the Education Act 1980) to include a stronger (perhaps a majority) representation of members of the public and especially parents (see p. 78).

Beyond the secondary school stage, LEAs are responsible for the provision of full- and part-time courses in a vast range of vocational and academic studies in tertiary or technical colleges, sometimes known as colleges of further education. (An alternative is the sixth-form college, which provides full-time GCE courses for school pupils aged sixteen to nineteen.) Local authorities (on a joint or 'pooled' basis) are also responsible for part of the higher education system in the form of polytechnics and monotechnics. They also provide grants for students entering higher education courses.

Despite the trauma of public expenditure cuts in recent years, there is still much talk of 'continuing education' – the opportunity for those who wish to go on learning after leaving school, or who fared badly in school and need a second chance, or who need to keep up with and adapt to economic and technological change in society. Apart from further education, what is known as 'adult education' plays an important role here, especially for those whose schooling finished early (and about one third of Britain's population left school before the age of fifteen). Except for some formal and examination-orientated studies, adult education is largely associated with so-called leisure-time classes – needlecraft, cookery, woodwork and art, for example. In recent years a fusion has occurred between adult education and youth services (but often including also schools, voluntary groups and volunteer tutors and parents), giving rise to 'community education'.

The main educational issue of the 1960s, however, was the comprehensive school. The post-war system of segregating secondary school children according to the results of tests given between the ages of ten and eleven (the '11-plus') was increasingly condemned as unfair and elitist. By the mid-1970s most LEAs had 'gone comprehensive' and the Education Act 1976 sought to compel the remaining LEAs to do likewise. However, the Conservative government's Education Act 1979 restores to local authorities their freedom to determine their own system of secondary education. In doing so the government is also attempting to enhance parental choice (of their children's schools) and parental participation (in the management of those schools, as governors). However, over the past twenty years it is in the field of nursery and primary education especially that parents have been encouraged to participate, as helpers and quasi-'teachers'. At the same time, the policy of designating certain parts of towns as 'educational priority areas' (EPAs) was an attempt to equalize educational opportunities by diverting extra resources to areas of deprivation.

Freedom is a strong feature of the British education system, for although the Secretary of State is required 'to promote the education of the people . . . and secure the effective execution by local authorities, under his control and direction, of the national policy' of education, in practice LEAs are given a substantial degree of autonomy. The British system of education is perhaps the most decentralized in Europe. However, this can have its disadvantages in that it may create too great a variety (of teaching methods, of subjects, of exam standards). The periodic discoveries of low levels of literacy and numeracy have given rise to the 'great debate' on education and the greater monitoring of standards, with demands for closer links with the world of industry. These developments are moving government policy in the direction of greater curriculum uniformity: the freedom to choose has its limitations.

Careers. Most local authorities have had long experience in providing employment services for young people. Since the Employment and Training Act 1973 all local (education) authorities are required to provide a vocational advice and guidance service for pupils and students attending educational institutions (except universities) and an employment service for those leaving or having recently left such schools and colleges. If the local authority so decides, this service may be extended to young people in employment, thus providing a parallel and alternative service to that provided by the employment division of the Manpower Services Commission.

The 2,000 or so careers officers may be visited at their local careers office or they may hold interviews with individual school and college students on school and college premises. Some may specialize in work with the disabled or the long-term unemployed. More generally they visit educational establishments regularly to talk to groups of students about local and perhaps national employment opportunities and prospects, explaining the requirements and facilities for training and further education.

In the 1970s the careers service tried to cast off the rather unfavourable image of the old youth employment service. It has also had to face the problems of serious juvenile unemployment. However, together with the

Manpower Services Commission it is playing a large part in a wide range of schemes to try to deal with the situation, such as work experience, job creation, community work and the youth training scheme (YTS).

Personal social services are concerned with the social welfare of people of all ages and conditions, but their main attention is focused on the more vulnerable groups in society – the elderly, children and the handicapped. Broadly speaking, local authorities are required to promote social welfare by making available advice, guidance and assistance, and by providing a range of facilities. These facilities include residential homes or hostels and foster care; day-time care, training and occupation centres; help in the home, including laundry, meals and practical aids; and the support and advisory work provided by social workers, be it on an individual (casework) or group basis, or in a community setting (working with voluntary and tenants' groups).

Traditionally the emphasis has been placed on residential care and even today over 50 per cent of welfare expenditure takes this form. However, since the 1950s, increasing emphasis has been given to the concept of 'community care'. Thus, in order to avoid or postpone the need for residential care of the elderly, community support has been broadened by way of home helps, aids and adaptations, special equipment, recreational facilities and help with travelling. Special 'sheltered' housing schemes have also been developed (in conjunction with housing authorities and voluntary associations). Consequently, only about 3 per cent of persons of retirement age are in residential or hospital care.

Similar forms of provision, including facilities for occupational therapy and sheltered employment, have been developed for the physically and mentally handicapped, often in co-operation with local voluntary groups. The intention here is to provide rehabilitation and reduce the numbers in long-stay hospitals and homes, partly to avoid the danger of institutional neurosis (or over-dependence) and partly to lower costs.

There has been a significant increase in expenditure on these community services over the past ten years, following the Social Work (Scotland) Act 1968, the Local Authority Social Services Act 1970 and the Chronically Sick and Disabled Persons Act 1970. But recent restraints on public expenditure have halted this expansion. Furthermore, there are many wide variations between the different local authorities' provision, due in part to differences in resources, but also to differences in councillors' values, priorities and political wills. The mixed result is sometimes described as 'territorial injustice'.

Similar difficulties exist in the provision of services for children. Recent legislation is placing extra demands on the local authority social services departments. Apart from their traditional role as provider of care for children deprived of normal family life (through fostering and residential care in community homes) they have now to devise comprehensive adoption facilities, provide a thoroughgoing monitoring system to prevent child-battering, and supervise young offenders in the community on a caring rather than a punitive basis. Some of these services will only be adequately developed as more resources become available to the personal social services.

The National Health Service. The NHS, until its reorganization in 1974, was a tri-partite organization: one arm (the hospitals) was administered by appointed hospital boards; another arm (the family practitioner services) was administered by appointed local executive councils; and the third arm was administered by local authorities, who were responsible for a number of health services including health centres, home nursing, health visiting, maternity and child clinics, school medical services, family planning, vaccination and ambulances. Local government lost responsibility for these services when they transferred (in 1974) to Scottish Health Boards (15) and English and Welsh Regional (14) and Area (98) Health Authorities. The 98 Areas became 201 District Health Authorities in 1982.

These health authorities are appointed bodies and are responsible for nearly all health services.[16] Their geographical boundaries largely coincide with those of the main local authorities. This co-terminosity of boundaries was deliberate, in order to facilitate liaison between local government and the health services. Furthermore, in order to promote the co-ordination of health and welfare services (especially for groups such as the elderly, the mentally disordered and discharged hospital patients) joint consultative committees and jointly financed projects have been established. Another aspect of the NHS is of particular interest to local government: the community health council or, in Scotland, local health council. There is such a local health council for every health district. Their purpose is to monitor the health services and represent to the health authorities the views of the consumer. By law at least half of the members of health councils must be drawn from neighbouring local authorities.

Thus local government has a continuing interest in the nation's health services. This is perhaps inevitable, since the boundary between health and welfare service is not clear-cut, and many people felt that a reorganized and strengthened local government system could be strong enough to take over responsibility for the NHS.[17] While this now seems out of the question in the immediate future, the idea is by no means dead and buried.[18]

Housing covers a wide range of services, some of which could be said to fall within the environmental and protective fields. Thus, as an adjunct to public health, local authorities have long been empowered and (through subsidies) encouraged to clear slums and re-develop or rehabilitate whole areas (now known as 'general improvement areas' and 'housing action areas'). Similarly they have developed powers to control overcrowding. In general, their principal statutory duty is to undertake periodic reviews of housing conditions in their areas.

It was in response to the need to rehouse persons displaced by slum clearance that council housing was introduced in the nineteenth century. However, it was not until general subsidies began after 1919 that the building of council houses began on a large scale. Local authorities currently provide about a quarter of housing accommodation in Britain (i.e. they supply about 6 million dwellings).

Central government grants have been paid to encourage local authorities to provide housing. They are also intended to reduce rent charges to tenants. However, when it was felt that such subsidized rents were too indiscriminate and wasteful, the Conservative government passed the Housing (Finance) Act 1972 which required local authorities to charge 'fair' (generally higher) rents, but with reductions for those on low incomes. This policy was welcomed in many quarters as fair, rational and long overdue, as well as contributing to a reduction in state expenditure. Elsewhere (generally on the Left) it was condemned as inflationary, exploitative and profiteering, and also autocratic, since local authorities were no longer free to decide their own rents. Councillors at Clay Cross (Derbyshire) actually refused to implement the law and were displaced by housing commissioners, appointed by the Secretary of State. These councillors were saved from threatened imprisonment by the Labour government, who restored local authorities' housing powers in 1975. However, the other main part of the 1972 Act was left intact. This is the scheme whereby tenants in *privately* rented accommodation receive rent allowances according to their income. Rents are settled (if necessary with the assistance of rent officers and rent panels) and the role of local housing authorities is to process tenants' claims and disburse the appropriate allowances (for which they are re-imbursed by the government). Since 1982/3, rent rebates and allowances are called 'housing benefits'.

In recent years governments have tended to give added emphasis to the policy of housing conservation and improvement. Local authorities are responsible for the distribution of housing renovation grants and for ensuring that any conditions attaching to them are complied with. Generally speaking the grants are payable for housing conversions (into flats, for instance) and for improvements (like the installation of amenities such as running water or a w.c. or thermal insulation). Local authorities have the power to compel owners to improve their properties. The most important grant condition concerns future occupation: in order to prevent abuse, restrictions are placed on the immediate future use or occupation of the improved properties. In addition certain grants are not payable if the property exceeds a certain rateable value. Overall the number of such grants increased substantially in recent years, from 128,000 in 1968 to 200,000 in 1980, but have since declined.

The most controversial aspect of housing is the sale of council houses (see Norwich case p. 337). Since 1980 it has become incumbent on local housing authorities to sell some of their housing stock. The broad objective is to extend the property-owning element of our democracy. However, critics point out that there should always be a sizable proportion of rented accommodation (which the private sector is failing to provide) and that the private sector can be left to supply adequately for owner-occupation. In addition, local authorities already promote owner-occupation through the provision of mortgage advances (up to 100 per cent in some cases) and also by guaranteeing the repayment of loans from building societies.

Local authorities have other important housing responsibilities. These include the provision and control of caravan sites in general, and of gipsy sites in particular. Local government retains its ancient responsibility of providing accommodation for the homeless, but since the Housing (Homeless Persons) Act 1977 the responsibility (currently affecting some 30,000 households) has been transferred to local housing authorities from social service departments. Another more recently developed 'welfare' service is the local authority provision (either direct or indirect) of housing advice and aid centres.

(4) Amenity services

Amenity services provide for citizens' leisure time and, more than any other, tend to be taken for granted, mainly because they have long been provided by local government and have become very closely identified with it – museums, art galleries, parks and gardens (now including country parks), libraries and playgrounds are typical examples. Many were established in the nineteenth century, the formative years of local government, and their foundation stones and commemorative plaques bear the names of many civic leaders of earlier generations.

The past thirty years has witnessed a significant growth in leisure time, and local authorities have made an equally significant contribution to the provision of facilities for active forms of recreation, either indirectly through grants and assistance to sports clubs, or through the direct provision of facilities such as sports centres, swimming baths, squash courts, ski slopes and skating rinks as well as the longer-established bowls, golf, tennis and other recreational grounds.

On the cultural and entertainments side, local authorities have continued to subsidize art galleries, museums and exhibitions in addition to making their own direct provision, and their library services have diversified into such areas as information provision, audio-visual materials, sound archives and special services for the disadvantaged groups.

There has been a noticeable expansion too in the number of municipal theatres, and in local authorities' promotion of groups and festivals of drama, music, crafts and dancing as well as such events as regattas, flower and agricultural shows, particularly in areas where local authorities are promoting tourism and holiday-making. For this purpose they may also provide long-distance footpaths, camp sites and perhaps hotels and restaurants. Since the Local Government Acts of 1972 (England and Wales) and 1973 (Scotland) the financial limits on local government expenditure on such entertainments have been removed. But public expenditure cuts are jeopardizing existing provision.

(5) Trading services

Trading services are services for which local authorities make commercial charges. They charge fees for a large number of services, including further education, day nurseries, school meals, residential care, home helps, car parks and sports facilities. These charges are generally below the full economic cost and are often scaled to take account of users' ability to pay. Apart from housing, such charges bring in only about 15 per cent of the costs. Consequently they are substantially financed by local government rates and central government grants (see Chapter 11) and are not classified as *trading* services. What distinguishes the trading services is, firstly, that their charges aim substantially to cover costs (in aggregate they cover about 90 per cent of costs) and, secondly, these charges do not normally allow for differences in the incomes of users. (In addition it may be added that it is only the profits and losses of the trading services – and unlike other services, not their gross income and expenditure – which are brought into account in the general rate fund.)

This distinction is not always clear, as certain services traditionally classified as trading (such as markets) may regularly make losses and have to be subsidized from the rates. Some are perhaps run at a loss because they bring wider benefits – such as making the area more lively and attractive, which enhances local property values and job opportunities (and so rate revenues). The best illustration of this is local authorities' attempts to attract commercial enterprises to their areas through offering low-rented land and premises (using their 2p. rate power under Sec. 137 of the Local Government Act 1972). For example, the G L C is setting up a technology centre where newly-formed companies can develop their ideas for new products.

As we have seen, there are some rather unusual municipal trading services, including Birmingham's bank, Hull's telephone system and Doncaster's racecourse, but more generally they include allotments and smallholdings, markets, civic airports, conference and exhibition centres, estate development and beach undertakings.

The importance of trading services has declined, especially since the nationalization of gas, electricity and water. And there is a general reluctance to involve local government further in competition with private enterprise, partly for political reasons (to avoid 'creeping socialism') and partly for economic reasons (to avoid the waste of inefficient management). Such arguments are not conclusive and are examined further in Chapter 11.

Reorganization 1986

The proposed abolition of the metropolitan counties (see p. 64) and the GLC (see p. 94) in 1986 will involve a significant redistribution of functions among local authorities in those areas. Briefly, it is intended that most of the functions of the metropolitan counties will transfer to the metropolitan district councils (which thus become the sole principal tier local authorities in these areas). A number of these functions (e.g. planning, highways and traffic management, waste disposal) will require that there is considerable coordination, cooperation and sharing of specialist resources. However certain functions – those of a 'county-wide' nature (such as police, fire, public transport) – are to be transferred to statutory joint authorities or boards (or what are becoming known as 'qualgos': quasi-autonomous local government organizations).

These *ad hoc* arrangements have been widely criticized as confusing, diminishing accountability and further manifesting the 'corporate state' (or corporatism). It is also widely believed that bodies such as boards tend to be wasteful of expenditure (though for the first three years, the Minister is to have control over the boards' finances (precepts: see p. 202) and manpower levels).

The proposals are also criticized as (a) piecemeal tinkering, (b) motivated by party political considerations rather than administrative rationality, (c) unnecessary, since local authorities' expenditure is soon to be controlled through 'rate-capping' (see p. 284) and (d) too hastily devised and lacking research. (Indeed the Government produced no figures or estimated savings, though the Conservative Central Office has suggested some £200m. p.a.)

5. London's Local Government

London, like the rest of Britain, has a two-tier system of local government. But it has a number of distinctive features – a consequence of its importance as the nation's capital and of its preponderant size. With a population of nearly $7\frac{1}{2}$ millions, London contains one in seven of the nation's population.

Local government in London has always posed difficulties owing to the rapid and continuous growth of its urban population. An immediate problem is to determine what and where exactly London is. Up to the nineteenth century, for local government purposes, it consisted essentially of the ancient City of London: the square mile of heartland which was governed by a Corporation consisting of aldermen, sheriffs, liverymen, freemen and justices – all functionaries of medieval origin. Around this nucleus lay the ancient counties of Middlesex, Kent, Surrey and Essex, which were governed by JPs and parish vestries. The increasing urban development of London led to the creation of numerous *ad hoc* authorities – turnpikes trusts, Commissioners of Police, Boards of Guardians, and Boards of Commissioners with powers of sewerage, paving and water supply – all operating over limited areas. Thus by the mid nineteenth century there were some 300 such bodies (with about 10,000 members) all functioning in the area which became known as the 'metropolis' owing to its substantial population growth and urbanization. (In the period 1801–61 the population increased from 865,000 to 2·8 million in the area subsequently covered by the LCC.)

The Municipal Corporations Act 1835 (see p. 28) had not applied to London. Instead, because of its special problems, London was the subject of a separate report by the Royal Commission on Municipal Corporations in 1837. This considered the feasibility of placing London directly under the jurisdiction of the central government. On balance the report recommended a system of local self-government for London by extending outwards the authority of the City Corporation. This was not acted upon, but in 1854 another Royal Commission reported and emphasized the problems created by a multiplicity of unco-ordinated authorities and communities within the vast urban sprawl of the metropolis and its surroundings, promoted by the railway development of the mid nineteenth century. However, this Commission rejected the notion of a single elected council for the whole of the

London area on the grounds of size: that local government should be based on local knowledge and a community of interest, neither of which, it felt, would be possible with a single authority. London was more a collection of communities. The result was a compromise. Under the Metropolis Local Management Act 1855 a two-tier system was to replace the haphazard arrangements then existing. An area of 75,000 acres (containing 2·8 million people) was clearly defined. It contained ninety-nine parishes, but most of these were grouped into districts, each under a district board. These vestries (fifteen) and district boards (twenty-three), together with the City, which remained unchanged, were to continue as the primary units of local government in London, with responsibility for local sewerage and drainage, paving, lighting and street cleaning. Superimposed on this pattern of authorities was a new central body, the Metropolitan Board of Works. It had forty-five members, indirectly elected from the constituent parish vestries and district boards, with a term of office of three years, and it was given responsibility for main sewers throughout the metropolis. However, it was to become more than just a sanitary authority, for subsequently it acquired responsibility for (and achieved some notable successes in) flood prevention, fire services, housing provision, building controls and street improvements. It also had a supervisory role in relation to the public health activities of the primary authorities.

However, such control was weak and did not prevent some dereliction of responsibility by the vestries and boards. The Board of Works lacked authority (being indirectly elected) and failed to inspire civic pride. Furthermore its position was undermined by the continued existence of a number of *ad hoc* authorities within its territory. These included the Metropolitan Asylums Board (established 1867), which arranged for the grouping of Boards of Guardians and their provision of accommodation and hospitals; the London School Board (established 1870), with responsibility for the provision of state elementary schools in London; and the Port of London Sanitary Authority (established 1872), providing for public health in the dockland areas. Meanwhile, water supply was in the hands of nine private companies and gas in the hands of three more.

Subsequently there developed a movement for the reform of local government in London. Various pressure groups were involved – the Municipal Reform Association (founded 1866), the London Municipal Reform League (1881) and perhaps above all the Fabian socialists, who saw London as pioneering a 'brave new England' of municipal enterprise (otherwise known as 'gas and water socialism'). Such notions aroused the hostility of the City and the fears of those who foresaw the ignorant masses holding sway over the richest and most prestigious city in the world. Consequently, the argument became not whether to rationalize the government of London, but how to do so, and in particular which tier or level of authority was to predominate – the county or the district authorities.

The reform of local government in London took place as a result of the insistent pressure of those who argued that, like every other town, London should have a directly elected body to represent ratepayers. But the more immediate reasons were (i) the alleged corruption and investigation of the Metropolitan Board of Works (in 1888) and (ii) the fact that the rest of English local government was being reorganized (see p. 29). However, the reform was controversial and modest in scope, partly because of the widespread fears and opposition of those who foresaw a socialist London recreating something approaching the Commune, the left-wing revolutionary government which ran Paris in 1871, after the Franco-Prussian war. Thus under the Local Government Act 1888 an elected London County Council (of 124 councillors and twenty aldermen) replaced the Metropolitan Board of Works and became responsible for its functions. But the new LCC was given few additional powers and its area of administration, to be known as the Administrative County of London, covered only the Metropolitan Board of Works' former territory, despite the growth of population. Furthermore, the forty-one vestries and district boards plus the City remained untouched, thus detracting from the authority of the LCC to speak for London – a situation which was exacerbated by the continued existence of numerous *ad hoc* bodies including the Metropolitan Asylums Board, the Boards of Guardians, the Metropolitan Police, Burial Boards, School Boards and the Thames Conservancy Board.

Despite its inauspicious beginnings, the LCC soon grew in stature, partly because of its endeavours and achievements, and partly because of the eminence of its members, such as Lord Rosebery, who became Liberal Prime Minister in 1894–5, and Sidney Webb, a leading member of the Fabian Society. Socialist members[1] and non-members called for greater powers for the LCC. They wanted a municipal takeover of water, gas, transport and the docks. They also envisaged a programme of action to deal with housing, unemployment and land speculation. In the process, they sought the abolition of the numerous vestries and boards in their midst.

These proposals were offensive to Conservative opinion and, following the recommendations of a Royal Commission Report of 1894, but partly also under pressure from the larger vestries themselves, the government passed the Local Government Act 1899. This Act reorganized the lower tier of London's local government by replacing the mass of vestries and boards with twenty-eight municipal boroughs, each with an elected council. (The City remained unaffected.) They were given significant responsibilities for public health, housing, libraries, recreation and rating, and the whole arrangement seemed clearly aimed at reducing the power of the LCC by enhancing that of the boroughs: a counterweight to the actual or threatened excessive power of the top tier. Consequently, the Act was criticized as having, in effect, broken up London into a collection of twenty-eight power centres (or 'Birminghams'), and further that, being artificial creations, these centres lacked any civic identity of the sort that Birmingham and other county boroughs could reasonably claim.

However, it would be inaccurate to see the London boroughs as county boroughs. They were really a new genre of local authority: something more than town councils but less than county borough councils. Equally the LCC was unique as a county council, for it lacked some of the powers and authority which other counties possessed. Nevertheless, in the course of time, its prestige mounted and in parallel with other local authorities in Britain the LCC became responsible for a whole range of functions, some of which were new, such as planning (1909) and education welfare (1907), and some of which were transferred from *ad hoc* bodies, such as school education (1902) and health and welfare services (1930).

Meanwhile, the population pattern was changing (see Table 4). The population of inner London (the 117 square miles of the LCC area) stopped growing in the twentieth century and indeed began to fall. The surrounding area of nearly 600 square miles (outer London – the area which covered that originally designated to the Metropolitan Police in 1829) continued to grow rapidly.

Table 4. *The population of London*

	City of London	Inner London*	Outer London†	Greater London conurbation
1801	128,269	959,310	157,980	1,117,290
1851	127,869	2,363,341	321,707	2,685,048
1901	26,923	4,546,267	2,050,002	6,596,269
1951	5,324	3,347,956	5,000,041	8,347,997
1961	4,767	3,492,879	4,499,564	7,992,443
1971	4,245	3,031,935	4,420,411	7,452,346
1981	5,893	2,496,756	4,199,252	6,696,008

*Comprising the County of London after 1888 and the inner boroughs after 1965.

†After 1965 the outer London boroughs.

Note: this Table is based on the official (Census) definition of Inner London, comprising 14 boroughs; it thus differs slightly from the area of ILEA (see p. 91).

Developments in electricity, slum clearance, transport and communications were increasing the mobility of the population and thus reducing the validity of the administrative boundaries and the division of responsibilities.

Under the impetus of the LCC, the concept of 'metropolitanism' began to emerge: the idea of a government for Greater London as a whole (both the inner and the outer areas) and having responsibility for services such as public health, planning, housing and transport, on the grounds that these could be effectively handled only by a single authority operating over the wider area.[2] As if to demonstrate the point, in 1933 the LCC's transport functions were transferred to the London Passenger Transport Board, a new *ad hoc* body with responsibility for services in and beyond the Greater London area.

In 1940, the Royal Commission on the Distribution of the Industrial Population (Barlow) drew attention to the growth of London, which was being accelerated by the 'drift' of the population to the South and East. Also, the problems of re-construction after the war, coupled with the increase in commuting[3] between inner and outer London, were threatening the integrity of the Green Belt (the zone of protected countryside surrounding London) and led to the urgent consideration of a strategy for planning in the London region.

The immediate result was the Abercrombie Plan of 1944 which recommended the creation of a ring of small new towns around London and the setting-up of a regional planning board. But planning was not the only problem and clearly something more comprehensive was needed.

In 1945, while the Boundary Commission looked at the rest of England and Wales (see p. 45), a special committee under Lord Reading was appointed to inquire into and advise on the local government problem within the County of London. But this committee was soon disbanded when it was realized that the scope of the inquiry was too narrow and the problem of London government needed to be considered within a regional context. This wider inquiry took the form of a Royal Commission.

The Herbert Commission

London had outgrown its nineteenth-century local government structure. In recognition of this fact, the Royal Commission on Local Government in Greater London (1957–60) was to examine the Greater London area, within and beyond the LCC area, and it therefore included those built-up areas which identified with London but technically formed part of the separate counties surrounding London (the 'Home Counties'[4]). Thus the social unit of Greater London was not reflected in its local government structure: services were administered by seven county councils, three county boroughs, twenty-eight London boroughs, the City Corporation and seventy-one UDCs, RDCs, and non-county boroughs, apart from half a dozen *ad hoc* authorities. As the Royal Commission commented,

The machinery is untidy and full of anomalies. There is overlapping, duplication, and in some cases gaps . . . The fact that local government in London does manage to hang together and avoid breakdown says much for the British knack of making the most cumbrous machinery work . . . judged by the twin tests of administrative efficiency and the health of representative government the present structure . . . is inadequate and needs overhaul. (paras. 286, 696) . . . none of these major functions [except environmental health] can be discharged best by the local authorities which exist under the present structure of local government, and . . . some of them cannot be adequately discharged at all. (para. 672)

The report of the Royal Commission, published in 1960 (Cmnd 1164), was unanimous in its recommendations for change. Its detailed proposals for a two-tier structure were based on the principle of having as many services as possible concentrated in the hands of the borough councils, except where these could be better performed over the wider area and thus by an 'umbrella' or supra-borough authority. This body was to be the Greater London Council. The Commission recommended that:

(1) The London County Council and the Middlesex County Council be abolished and replaced by a Greater London Council (GLC) whose jurisdiction would also include the metropolitan areas of Essex, Kent, Surrey and Hertfordshire together with the county boroughs of Croydon, East Ham and West Ham. The area thus created would cover about 600 to 800 square miles and contain some 8 million people.

(2) Within that area covered by the GLC, the existing local authorities were to be reduced from ninety-five to fifty-two, to be called Greater London boroughs (except the City, which was to retain its ancient identity).

(3) Greater London boroughs were to have responsibility for the local services of housing, health, welfare, libraries and non-major roads. The GLC would exercise the wider, strategic, functions of fire, ambulances, main roads and refuse disposal. In education and planning the GLC would be the main authority, but the boroughs would have executive powers, that is the GLC would draw up the development plan for Greater London, but the boroughs would deal with local planning applications; in education, the GLC would be the local education authority, owning the schools and appointing teachers, but the day-to-day running and maintenance of the schools would rest with the boroughs. The GLC would also have some concurrent and supplementary (shared) powers in the fields of housing, open spaces, sewerage and drainage where these functions cut across or involved several boroughs, such as large housing and re-development schemes or the very large London parks.

The government responded favourably to the report, though it did propose some amendments. Reactions elsewhere were more hostile: some, such as Middlesex, sought to preserve their own existence; others, such as the LCC, were afraid of the upheaval to services which the reorganization would cause; and inevitably there were fears, especially in the Labour Party, about the threat to party fortunes. An independent panel considered the local authorities' comments and there was further acrimony and review as the Bill went through Parliament. The result was the London Government Act 1963 (which came into operation in 1965). Under the Act:

(1) An area of local government, somewhat smaller than that suggested by the Royal Commission, was designated as Greater London. It was to have an elected council of a hundred councillors (reduced to ninety-nine in 1973) and sixteen aldermen. (Aldermen were abolished in the GLC in 1977 and in the London boroughs in 1978.)

(2) The area was divided into thirty-two London boroughs (plus the City), each with an elected council comprising councillors and aldermen.

(3) Functions were allocated largely as recommended in the Royal Commission report,[5] with the notable exception of education. Since the boroughs were now to be fewer and larger than originally envisaged, it was felt

Figure 8 *Greater London and the London boroughs (reproduced by permission of the Greater London Council)*

appropriate to give them responsibility for education. However, in order to preserve the unity of the education services built up by the LCC, it was decided that the inner London boroughs would not individually control education. Instead, in that area (the original LCC area) education would be administered by a special committee of the GLC, called the Inner London Education Authority (ILEA), consisting of members of the GLC from inner London, together with a representative from each of the twelve inner London borough councils (who were responsible for rate-funding the service).

Various criticisms have been levelled at the reform outlined above. There were those who thought that the reorganization did not go far enough, and that the boundaries of the GLC area had been too tightly drawn, and others who argued for a regional structure for the local government of London and the South-East. At the other extreme were those who genuinely believed that no major reorganization was necessary.[6] In between were those who felt that the allocation of functions was unsatisfactory and that inadequate attention had been paid to the functions of the *ad hoc* bodies.

Nevertheless the new London system was, to some extent, used as a model for the reorganization of local government in the other conurbations of England (see p. 53). And a subsequent study of the London system of local government concluded that 'neither the best hopes nor the worst fears of the protagonists in the discussion which preceded the reforms appear to have been justified . . .' and on balance 'the new system represents a distinct advance in the evolution of London's government'.[7] Clearly, the study envisaged further change and drew particular attention to the problems caused by the sharing of responsibilities between the two co-ordinate tiers of authority (the GLC and the boroughs). This problem was reiterated in the Marshall Report in 1978.

The Marshall Report (1978)

The original aim of the 1963 Act was to create a mainly strategic authority (the GLC) for the Greater London area, while leaving the delivery of services in the hands of others (the boroughs). In practice it has been felt, especially by the Conservative members of the GLC, that the GLC's strategic role has gone by the board and it is involving itself in too many other activities. Consequently, when the Conservatives gained power in the GLC elections of 1977, they appointed Sir Frank Marshall, a lawyer, ex-chairman of the Association of Municipal Corporations and a former Conservative leader of Leeds City Council, to undertake an inquiry.

The Marshall report rejected the idea either of the abolition of the GLC or of expanding it to a wider-ranging regional authority (as some have suggested). Instead its recommendations sought to clarify and enhance the GLC's strategic role while leaving the boroughs with local executive functions. For example, to deal with the areas of greatest dispute, the GLC would drop out of the ILEA and from housing provision. It would thus concentrate on the setting of broad objectives for all London; it would oversee local policies; and it would assume overall control of resources (authorizing capital expenditures and distributing the central government grant among the boroughs). The scheme envisaged other transfers, including the transfer of some functions from the central government to the GLC (such as London's trunk roads and public transport – especially British Rail – pricing and investment). The plan thus involved some devolution of power: from the central government to the GLC and from the GLC to the London boroughs. As *The Times* concluded, the report was 'a constructive attempt to find a useful and clearly defined role for the GLC in the middle of the sandwich of power'.[8]

In 1979 the Conservatives won the General Election and replaced the Labour Government; conversely (but being in mid-term, quite typically) in 1981 Labour won control of the GLC from the Conservatives. Whilst there has been no legislative action on the Marshall recommendations, there have been a number of other significant developments. Firstly in 1980 the Government set up an inquiry into the future of the ILEA – much to the chagrin of most of the (Labour) inner London boroughs. The inquiry followed an earlier report by a group of London Conservatives which referred to ILEA's poor educational standards and lack of democratic and financial responsibility, and urged its dismantlement. In 1981 the Government announced that the ILEA was to be retained, but this did not stop the argument or the uncertainty. The 20-year-old ILEA system is now to be replaced: see p. 94.

Secondly, in December 1981, the House of Lords declared the GLC's transport subsidy – known as 'Fares Fair' – to be excessive and illegal thus confirming Lord Denning's earlier judgement in the Court of Appeal. Apart from the immediate financial turmoil, this decision brought allegations that the Lords and the judiciary were being political and helping the Government to implement its public expenditure (local government cuts) policy. The case had been brought by Bromley Borough Council and also illustrated an element of the conflict which can arise between the boroughs and the GLC when their party complexions differ – and when ratepayers baulk at the GLC's precept (see p. 202). But the issue also increased calls for the removal of GLC responsibility for transport.[9] This took place in 1984 when London Transport was replaced by London Regional Transport (a 'quango' appointed by the Transport Secretary)[10] because under the GLC 'transport services were not integrated, not economic and . . . not efficient'

(Secretary of State for Transport in the debate on the London Regional Transport Bill 1983).

Finally, there has been mounting pressure for the total abolition of the GLC – partly from those who wish to see its functions transferred to the boroughs (as housing virtually has been); partly from those who see it as merely duplicating the functions of other authorities; and from those who argue that it is redundant since it has so few responsibilities, having lost planning responsibility for the docklands area to a development corporation in 1980 and now losing transport. Such abolition is now also declared government policy (declared in its election manifesto 1983).

The abolition of the GLC and *Streamlining the Cities* (White Paper)

The Government sees the GLC (and the metropolitan counties) as 'a wasteful and unnecessary tier of government'; as lacking in functions and *raison d'être* especially since policing ('the Met') is the direct responsibility of the Home Secretary and the responsibility for London Transport (with the GLC since 1969) is to be transferred to the Government. But, in addition, the GLC is the country's principal 'overspender' (i.e. above the Government's target guideline) to the extent that it has lost entitlement to any government block grant (see p. 200–202). Within this context, the villain of the piece is the radical and outspoken leader of the (Labour) GLC Mr ('Red Ken') Livingstone. So the rationale behind the abolition of the GLC is an unfortunate mixture of politics, personality, economics and administration.

While the boroughs (plus the City of London Council) will take over responsibility from the GLC for most of its functions, special arrangements are laid down for most areas. Firstly, in the case of planning, although the boroughs will ultimately become responsible for the structure plan (see p. 75), the Minister is to be involved to the extent that he is to establish a London Planning Commission to advise him on the strategic issues involved in that task. Secondly, for most of the transferred functions, the Minister will require adequate cooperative arrangements among the boroughs and will exercise reserve powers where such cooperation is lacking. Thirdly, for certain services (e.g. fire and civil defence) statutory joint boards (comprising borough councillors) will be established. The ILEA is to be abolished but, as a result of much protest, replaced by a similar but directly elected body. Apart from these functions, London Transport is to be transferred to the Government, and the GLC's land drainage and flood protection responsibility will go to the Thames Water Authority.

Thus will London become unusual among capital cities in lacking a metropolitan governing body.

6. Local Government Elections

We have seen that one of the main features of local government is that it is elected. The members of local authorities – the councillors – are chosen by popular ballot, in keeping with the democratic nature of Britain's system of government. Both in theory and in practice, the electoral system in Britain's local government displays a number of democratic features – the right to vote is widespread, as is the right to stand as a candidate; the administration of elections is impartial and uncorrupt; there is plenty of advance notice about elections; the ballot is secret, and it is simple. Finally, the result of the election is direct and immediate: the composition of the council is changed to reflect the voters' preferences, the candidates who gain the majority of votes being deemed elected and becoming councillors for a fixed period of 'office'.

On the other hand, there are a number of aspects of local government elections which diminish its democratic impact. They include the low turnout at the polls; the numerous uncontested seats; the ignorance and confusion about such things as 'warding' or 'election by thirds'; and the possible injustice of the simple majority system of choosing winners. We examine these aspects in more detail below.

The administration of elections is the responsibility of the Returning Officer, usually a senior officer who often doubles as Registration Officer (see below). He is responsible for advising voters of the pending election and the location of the polling stations or (in Scotland) polling places. He also appoints polling officers, who distribute the ballot papers and supervise the polling stations (schools, village halls, public buildings, etc.). The Returning Officer oversees the counting of the votes and declares the winners. He must also receive the nominations of the candidates and check their qualifications (see p. 98) and their election expenditures (see p. 98).

The boundaries of local authorities are not determined by those authorities: this is the responsibility of the Local Government Boundary Commissions (see above, p. 56), who are also responsible for reviewing the electoral districts within local authorities (called 'divisions' and 'wards').

The right to vote

There is a widespread franchise in local elections; indeed the right to vote is almost universal. Anyone who is at least eighteen years of age and a British subject (or a citizen of the Irish Republic) is entitled to vote. But certain people may be disqualified: those detained in psychiatric institutions; prisoners convicted of felony or treason; and persons convicted of corrupt and illegal practices in elections.[1] In order to vote, however, an elector's name must appear on the local authority's Register of Electors. This Register (which is used for national as well as local elections) is compiled each year by the Electoral Registration Officer (usually a senior official of the council). He lists the names of residents in the electoral area who are of voting age on the qualifying date (10 October), together with 'attainers' – those who will reach voting age during the following twelve months. (In the City of London, non-residents may register to vote on condition that they occupy property there with a rateable value of at least £10 p.a. This additional qualification had applied to all local authorities prior to the 1969 Representation of the People Act.) The Register is published in draft form (in about December) and, following appeals over omissions and exclusions or other errors, the final Register is published and is ready for use on the following 16 February.

Voting

Voting is simple enough – a matter of marking an 'X' against the name of one of the candidates listed on the ballot paper (unless there are several seats to be filled, in which case a number of Xs will be required – see p. 100). The Representation of the People Act 1969 allowed candidates to add to their names a short description (in no more than six words) of themselves and what they stand for. In practice that often means simply stating his party or putting the word 'Independent'. This has helped to remove some confusion and erroneous voting, especially in those constituencies, such as Wales, where several candidates might have the same surname (such as Jones or Thomas).

Voters who cannot attend the poll are allowed to vote by post if they are ill and housebound or if they are engaged in religious observance for the day of the election. (You cannot claim a postal vote if you have moved from one local electoral area to another since registration, as you can in parliamentary elections.) Electors who are working outside Britain, such as fishermen or military service personnel, are allowed to vote by proxy, that is they can nominate a person to vote on their behalf. On average only about 2 per cent vote by post or proxy, and about 1 per cent of adults are legally debarred from voting.

The winner

The winner of an election is determined on the basis of 'the first past the post' – a simple majority is all that is required. Thus if there are three candidates and they receive votes as follows – Ellington 4,000, Basie 3,000, Herman 2,000 – Ellington is declared the winner. The same system is used in the General Election for Members of Parliament and it has come in for severe criticism in recent years on the grounds that:

(a) It exaggerates victories and distorts the true results. Thus in our example, while Ellington had 4,000 votes and was declared the winner, he actually had more electors against him (the 5,000 who voted for the other two candidates). The distortion is magnified if we introduce political parties: for example suppose that Taunton is divided into five electoral divisions for the purpose of electing five councillors to Somerset County Council. Suppose also that Ellington is a nominee of the Conservative Party, and that in the other four divisions his party colleagues were equally successful (that is, they each had simple but not overall majorities). That would result in a 'clean sweep' for the Conservative Party in representing the Taunton area, and the other parties would be completely unrepresented even though they attracted sizable voting support. Islington L B provides a recent case.[2] In practice, parties gaining the most votes may even fail to gain power (a majority) in the council.

(b) It creates upheavals whenever power changes hands. Thus, when a council changes hands from say Conservative to Labour, there is a lurch in policy in such matters as secondary school organization, council house rents or concessionary bus fares.

(c) Somewhat contradicting the previous point, it is argued that the simple majority system creates permanent majorities on local authorities – areas come to contain 'safe' Labour or Conservative councils. Consequently it may be that complacency or even corruption develops because there is no effective opposition.

The remedy for such defects in the voting system is often held to be some kind of *proportional representation*, in which parties would be allocated seats in proportion to the volume of votes they attracted. This would be fairer and it might well produce coalition councils which could avoid lurches in policy. On the other hand, it might add to public confusion and obscure accountability and a clear choice for voters, since there may be no clear party majority (see Chapter 7). Problems would also arise under the proportional system at by-elections.[3]

The right to stand

A candidate must be at least twenty-one years old and be a British (or Irish) citizen. In addition, he or she must possess one of the following qualifications:

(1) be registered as an elector for the area;

(2) have occupied land or property in the area for at least twelve months prior to nomination;

(3) have his main or only place of work in that area for at least twelve months prior to nomination;

(4) have been resident in the area for the previous twelve months, or within three miles in the case of the parish/community council in England or Wales (requirements for Scottish communities vary).

On the other hand, a candidate (or elected councillor) may be *disqualified* if:

(1) he is (or has within five years of the election been) a declared bankrupt;

(2) as a member of the council he has been found to have incurred or authorized expenditure which is unlawful and exceeds £2,000[4];

(3) he has been found guilty of an offence which leads to a prison sentence (without option of a fine) of at least three months;

(4) he has been found guilty (in his local authority area) of the criminal offence of corrupt and illegal practice at an election (this would include such actions as bribing or using undue influence on an elector, impersonation, hiring vehicles to convey electors to the polls, indiscriminate sticking of posters or exceeding permissible election expenses – see p. 99);

(5) he is a paid employee of the local authority (though there are certain exceptions here; for example, state school teachers can be co-opted on to committees – see p. 137 – and as an employee of the county he can be a member of a district council even though that authority appoints members to the County Education Committee).

All these disqualifications except (5) last for varying lengths of time, but most typically for five years. It is perhaps surprising that members found guilty of corruption (receiving bribes, non-disclosure of a financial interest etc. – see p. 142) are not subsequently disqualified unless they come into category (3).

Perhaps the most controversial of these disqualifications is the last, and many people (especially trade unionists) have argued for a relaxation of this part of the law. It is said, for example, that it is unreasonable to exclude council employees while allowing local businessmen such as estate agents, architects, building contractors etc. to qualify, since the latter may have just as much to gain from influencing council policy. The issue was considered by the Committee on Conduct in Local Government (see p. 144), which concluded that on balance it should remain unchanged. The rule reflects a more general principle, the 'separation of powers',[5] in that it attempts to avoid the situation in which a councillor who is in the employment of his own local authority might be tempted to manipulate policy to his own advantage (for example in the grading of posts). To make doubly sure, a councillor may not become an employee of his authority within twelve months of his ceasing to be a member.

Election expenditure

Candidates in parliamentary elections are required to put down a 'deposit' of £150 (£600 for the European Assembly election) as an indication that they are contesting the election seriously; the money is returned if they achieve not less than one eighth of the total poll. This requirement does not apply to local government elections, but candidates are required to produce the written support of a proposer and seconder and (except in parishes and communities) eight other electors for that area. Each candidate is also required to nominate an election agent (he can if he wishes act as his own agent) whose function is to assist in the election campaign, but who is specifically charged with keeping an accurate record of the candidate's election expenditure. These accounts must be submitted to the returning officer, who will check to see that the statutory limits have not been exceeded. The object of these restrictions is to equalize election chances between rich and poor candidates. Currently, the limits are £120 per ward or electoral division plus 2·4p. per elector[6] (£500 + 3p. for the GLC).

The electoral sequence

Normally we do not know more than a few weeks in advance the date of a forthcoming General Election for members of Parliament: the decision rests with the Prime Minister (the only limitation being that a Parliament must not go beyond five years before it is dissolved and faces re-election). Local councils, however, have a fixed term of office, so that their election arrangements follow a regular sequence (apart from by-elections – see p. 323 – and exceptions which occur as a result of boundary changes), and local government elections normally occur on the first Thursday in May.

All councillors are elected for a fixed term of office of four years. In most local authorities (counties, parishes and communities in England and Wales; all London authorities; all Scottish authorities) councillors are elected *all together* every fourth year: this is known as the 'whole council' system (or the 'county system'). For the purpose of these elections, the local authorities are divided into electoral 'divisions' or 'wards' [7] each usually returning one member. In the metropolitan districts, *one third* of the councillors are elected in each of the three years when there is no county election. This is known as 'election by thirds' (or the system of 'partial renewal' or of 'rolling elections') and the local authority is divided into wards with each ward returning (usually) three councillors (or a multiple of three according to the size of the council). Non-metropolitan councils may themselves choose which of the two systems to adopt. If they opt for the whole council system (and most – 65 per cent – have) they normally hold these elections in the mid-term year of the counties. Thus the election sequence runs as follows:

Table 5. *The local elections cycle in Britain*

	1978	79	80	81	82	83	84	85	86
All counties and Greater London Council**	.	.	.	√	.	.	.	√	.
Metropolitan and some non-metropolitan districts	⅓	⅓	⅓	.	⅓	⅓	⅓	.	⅓
Most non-metropolitan districts,* all parishes and communities (England and Wales)†	.	√	.	.	.	√	.	.	.
Scottish regions and islands, and London boroughs	√	.	.	.	√	.	.	.	√
Scottish districts	.	.	√	.	.	.	√	.	.

*The election year of any particular non-metropolitan district council will depend on the year it opted for the 'whole council' system. A local authority can apply to change its electoral system at any time, but not more than once every ten years, and it must have a 60 per cent majority vote at the council meeting in support of the proposal.

†In Scottish communities, the election arrangements vary considerably.

**1985 elections will occur only in non-metropolitan counties.

It is argued by its supporters that the system of elections 'by thirds' has the merit of keeping in closer touch with public opinion, as there are elections in three years out of four. Also there is greater continuity in council policy and administration as new members of the council will form only a minority and can be 'shown the ropes' by existing councillors who form the majority. Some would claim that this system of gradually changing the composition of councils prevents the full-time officials from 'getting on top' by browbeating new and inexperienced councillors. But it has been argued more cynically that the system of election by thirds is favoured only because the frequency of elections is a device to keep local party machines in motion. In practice it is the large town district councils (apart from metropolitan districts) which have opted for the 'thirds' system: these areas have a longer tradition of local party politics.

Against this system, and in favour of 'whole council' elections, is the argument that elections can be frustrating where they provide only for partial change: that it takes three or four years for a complete change to occur. Apart from frustration and disillusionment, it may be that the public get confused by these partial elections, and perhaps their frequency reduces public interest. Certainly elections cost the councils time and money, not just in terms of the formal electoral arrangements, but also time spent electioneering, and, perhaps above all, the need to recast the membership and chairmanship of committees and representation on outside bodies.

Voting behaviour

Since elections in Britain are conducted on the basis of secret ballot, we cannot know who votes, how they vote or why they vote as they do (or do not). We must rely substantially on social survey evidence, which is inevitably somewhat limited and patchy.

It is also often inconsistent. A survey for the Maud Report[8] suggested that those with the most favourable attitudes to voting are 'likely to be men, to come from the middle age group (35–64), to come from socio-economic groups 1 and 2 and to have had more than a primary type education'. Those with less favourable attitudes are 'likely to be women; to be under 35 and over 64; to be semi- or unskilled manual workers; and to have had only an elementary or secondary education'. When the same survey investigated those who said they had voted at the last local elections, it found a close relationship to the attitude findings, except that there was no difference in (claimed) voting between men and women.

Other surveys[9] confirm some of these findings, but contradict others. Thus, in general:

Age seems to make a difference in preparedness to vote: people under thirty-five appear to be less likely to vote than their elders. (It may be, of course, that older people exaggerate their declared readiness to vote in response to survey questioning.)

Sex seems to make no difference (there is no 'gender gap'), as men and women appear equally likely (or unlikely) to vote, though young married women appear to be the group least likely to vote.

Class appears to make little difference in influencing the propensity to vote (somewhat in contrast to America, where studies suggest that the middle class are more ready to vote than the working class).

Activists, that is party members and those who are strongly committed to a party, show a greater than average inclination to vote.

Owner-occupiers are more likely to vote than are tenants who rent their accommodation.

Mobile people, especially recent newcomers to an area, are less disposed to vote in local elections.

It is important to bear in mind that these are no more than tendencies drawn from a few local surveys. Any individual local election can reveal considerable variations in behaviour patterns. One particularly interesting development in recent years is the apparent emergence (or restoration) of local factors in voting for councillors. Much has been said and criticized about the overbearing influence of national attitudes and trends on local elections (e.g. how people feel about Margaret Thatcher's Conservative Government will be manifested in how they vote for local authority councillors). And there is much evidence of such local impact by national politics. But there is evidence too that *local* issues are often influential and these are perhaps becoming increasingly significant (see p. 122), hence the (not unwelcome) difficulty of discerning national or general swings and trends in local election results.

Voting turnout

One well-documented area of electoral behaviour is that of turnout. An examination of the electoral statistics shows considerable variations in the pattern of voting between different parts of Britain (for example Wales compared with England); different types of local authority (for example metropolitan county councils compared with non-metropolitan county councils in England); different (individual) local authorities of the same type; and the same local authority at different times.

One of the factors which affects turnout is the existence of political parties. Generally, it is believed that parties boost popular participation in elections (through canvassing, greater publicity etc. – see Chapter 7). However, this can be offset where parties dominate or virtually monopolize particular authorities (typically the Tory shires or certain Labour boroughs).

Here elections are seen as foregone conclusions and of relatively little importance, though in recent years voters have become more volatile in their voting allegiances, so that even 'safe' seats are changing (party) hands. In contrast, it is evident that polling tends to be higher where seats are marginal and the result is uncertain.[10]

It was suggested earlier (p. 101) that too frequent elections may cause a decline in local political interest. If this were so, we would expect to see a lower turnout of electors in those local authorities, notably metropolitan districts, which hold annual elections (using the thirds system) as compared to those authorities, such as counties, which hold elections every fourth year. The figures in Table 6 (p. 108) give some support to this view, since the metropolitan districts consistently poll below 40 per cent while the counties mainly poll over 40 per cent. On the other hand, those non-metropolitan districts which elect their council by thirds experience turnouts which exceed those of the metropolitan districts: in 1978 the average was 42·3 per cent (compared to 36 per cent for the metropolitan districts) and in 1979 the figure was 77 per cent (compared to 74·4).

Clearly, there are other factors influencing events. One such factor is almost certainly the incidence of non-contested seats. In general, turnout tends to be higher in those authorities where a larger proportion of wards/divisions are left uncontested: in other words, where there is a fight it will tend to be a good one.[11] Two other important influences seem to be population size and stability of population. The larger the local authority's population, the lower the turnout tends to be. And a mobile and changing population will also lower the turnout.[12]

The most striking and apparently consistent feature of the statistics in Table 6 is the low level of turnout by voters.[13] At around 40 per cent, the poll is low in comparison to that in Parliamentary elections (which have ranged from 72 per cent to 84 per cent since 1945). The exception was 1979, when the local and parliamentary elections were held simultaneously: electors simply put their 'X' on two ballot papers instead of the usual one. The uniqueness of this event was shown in 1980 and subsequent years, when the average poll in elections for nearly 200 local authorities was back to 40 per cent. Clearly, the reorganized (post-1974) local government system has not succeeded in attracting voters as had been hoped by some advocates of reorganization in the early 1970s[14] (see Appendix 3, p. 295). In 1983 the average poll for England was 42 per cent.*

The low polls in local government elections are widely held to reflect a lack of interest, and local electorates are derided as apathetic. There may be some truth in this: an inquiry for the Maud Committee (1967) showed that

* Figures supplied by the Conservative Central Office; official figures ceased to be published in 1979.

among those who did not vote in local elections were substantial proportions of electors – over 20 per cent in some places – who said they were not interested in local elections or they did not know, or did not know enough, about the election taking place.[15]

However, instead of blaming the public for their ignorance or apathy, perhaps we should look elsewhere for an explanation. It may well be, for example, that people see local authorities as essentially administrative rather than decision-making bodies, so that it little matters to electors who sits on the council: even if the election totally changes the composition of the council, the administrative end-product will be the same. Rightly or wrongly, council decisions may be seen as not very important, since it is felt that the central government and Parliament make the strategic decisions (hence the impact of national politics on local elections – see p. 122). At local level, much policy-making is often no more than an adjustment here and there – whether to raise the fees for adult education classes by 50p. rather than £1; which particular schools to close down; what kind of comprehensive school system or sheltered housing design to adopt. These are administrative details which may be of interest to councillors and officers, but are hardly issues of principle to excite the general public. In the nineteenth century the 'improvers' battled with the 'economizers' to persuade the public of the need for municipal provision of water, public health or building controls, but perhaps all the battles of principle have been won, so that now local authorities can be run on a simple care and maintenance basis.

Yet there *are* issues in local government, and policy decisions *can* give rise to considerable argument – the sale of council houses, concessionary bus fares, direct labour *v.* contracting out ('privatization') are current and widespread examples. As Professor George Jones has said,

Political parties are not artificially imposed on local government. They grow out of a local environment, and competition between them reflects clashes of local interests and views on public policies. They differ in their attitudes as to what is prudent spending, over priorities, the pace of development of services, and over who should receive what benefits. Such differences involve differing concepts of equality and liberty, different attitudes about who is deserving or the under-dog and about the scope of public collective activity and enterprise.[16]

To a considerable extent, the current centrally-imposed expenditure cuts have re-introduced the nineteenth-century argument, only these days it is more a matter of the 'cutters' versus the 'preservers' of services.

Why, then, does the low turnout persist? Some people blame the councillors – 'they're all the same, so what's the point?' Others blame the complexity of the local government system. There is the confusion caused by the voting system(s), which is compounded where elections occur out of sequence (as when boundaries are changed) or where the districts' partial elections coincide with the whole council elections of the parish/community (often involving many of the same candidates).

Another possibility is that the low poll is a deliberate and adverse comment on local government – that people are voting with their feet. Yet the converse may just as well be true: that people are basically satisfied with the services provided and do not therefore wish to promote any significant changes. The low poll is thus seen as an accolade for local government.

Rather than take too rosy or pessimistic a view of election turnout, maybe we need to adjust our perspective. It may be argued, for example, that the 70 per cent turnout in the General Election is an unreasonable paradigm – after all, General Elections occur infrequently and are accompanied by a lot more publicity and 'bally-hoo'; there is far more personalizing in national politics, with the media concentrating on the party leaders in particular (there are often no such obvious leaders in local authorities). Many people may thus be turning out to vote for rather superficial or synthetic reasons. Besides, voting in a General Election may be held to be a civic duty (like filling in one's tax return) and this attitude has not yet penetrated to local elections. Is it fair, then, to compare local with national elections? Perhaps the 40 per cent figure is a good indication of a genuine interest in politics in Britain – after all, in both the 1979 and 1984 EEC Assembly elections the poll was only 32 per cent. It might even be argued that the local government figure is a *desirable* level of participation, since too avid and active an interest in politics can be politically de-stabilizing and dangerous.[17]

Furthermore, it may be argued that elections should not be seen as the sole or even the principal criterion of political interest. The vigour of the local press and other media, the growth of 'consumerism' in the form of welfare rights groups or direct action events (rent strikes, marches, sit-ins), the formation of local pressure groups such as civic societies or education campaigners – all of these indicate a vitality of local political awareness and commitment, but using methods which supplement or substitute for the electoral system: after all, polling is only one means of gathering opinions.

Lack of candidates

Less defensible is the large number of uncontested seats in local government elections. The figures in Table 6 show that the proportion of uncontested seats in recent years has amounted to over 20 per cent in many areas, (especially in the Welsh and Scottish districts though the emergence of the SDP in 1981 has probably led to more electoral contests);[18] though in 1982 the overall figure was only 1 per cent.* However, before the reorganization of 1974/5 the figures were often much worse: in 1967 the Maud Report

* *Local Government Studies*, Annual Report 1983.

commented that 'Recruitment of candidates . . . was a problem in almost all the authorities we visited. In some areas it was difficult if not impossible to find sufficient people of even the minimum calibre considered adequate willing to accept nomination.'[19] The Committee found that over 40 per cent of members of principal authorities had been returned without having to contest elections. 'It seems likely that about one in three of county councillors and about one in two of rural district councillors have never had to fight an election.'[20] (See p. 299 below.)

By contrast in General Elections, despite higher costs and more demanding campaigns, there is no shortage of contestants: no constituency has fewer than three candidates. In the elections of 1974 (Oct.) and 1979 there were 2,252 and 2,576 candidates respectively for the 635 seats and in 1983 there were 2,579 candidates for the 650 seats.[21]

Why is there a shortage of public-spirited citizens willing to run for election locally? Many explanations have been put forward, and these are dealt with in some detail in the next chapter. Here it will be sufficient to say that there are two main reasons:

(1) Many of those who have *been* members give up for reasons of time; loss of income; frustration with the methods and controls or with party politics; mobility, especially in pursuit of a career.

(2) Many members of the public do not seek to *become* councillors because they think it might interfere with their business interests or their voluntary activities elsewhere; they are insufficiently informed about local government; or they are just not interested.[22]

In response to such attitudes a number of proposals have been made to try to improve the situation. These were elaborated in the Maud Report (Vol. 1) and include:

(a) the internal reorganization of local authorities by streamlining committees and departments, concentrating responsibility and making greater use of management services – all with a view to making council membership less time-consuming and less frustrating (see Chapter 10);

(b) reducing the degree of Whitehall interference in local government, and giving local authorities a greater general competence (see Chapter 12);

(c) providing more publicity about the activities of local government through open meetings, improved facilities for the press and publication of discussion papers, and a greater encouragement to schools to include local government studies in their curricula (see Chapter 13);

(d) improving the image of local government, partly through (c) above, and partly through such changes as the abolition of the aldermanic system and compulsory retirement from membership at the age of seventy;

(e) increasing the opportunities for membership by increasing the scope for release from employment to undertake council duties; reducing election costs by allowing a free postal delivery of election material; and by allowing candidates to stand in the local authority area of their principal place of employment;

(f) the payment of part-time salaries to the leading councillors who give most time to their council duties;

(g) the building of closer relations between local authorities and voluntary organizations;

(h) more training courses for members.

Some of these suggestions – the abolition of aldermen, payments to councillors, the expansion of public relations and the reform of internal structures – have been acted on over the past ten years. Most occurred at the time of reorganization in 1974/5. It is difficult to compare the incidence of non-contested elections in the pre- and post-reorganization periods, but there appears to be some evidence of improvement: for example, in the non-metropolitan county councils, the proportion of non-contested seats fell from a figure of about 50 per cent in the 1950s and 1960s (see Appendix 3, p. 295) to a figure of 12 per cent in the 1970s. However, bearing in mind that the number of local authorities has been reduced (from 1,500 to 500) and the number of members similarly reduced (from 42,000 to 26,000) it would be surprising if the recruitment picture had not improved.

However, the proportion of seats which remain uncontested is still significant. It may be that service on the newer, larger authorities is more demanding of councillors. But it may also be that the local government changes were too much for some of the older or longer-standing members, as they were for many London councillors in the early 1960s: in 1973 there were murmurs from some of them about the authorities becoming too big, too remote, too managerial or too bureaucratic. In terms of the 'brave new world' of efficient local government and in terms of attracting members of the 'right calibre', this shedding effect may have been no bad thing. But many felt that, in the process of change, local government was losing its 'soul': it was being seen purely as a mechanism for effective administration and the delivery of services (the 'instrumental' view). What was being overlooked or devalued was its 'organic' aspect: that local government should be seen as an extension or a natural expression of the community. The Maud Report showed an awareness of this problem:

Table 6. Local government elections: principal authorities in Britain (selected years)

Area/Type of authority	Year	Total of electors	Total of councillors	Councillors returned unopposed	% returned unopposed	Councillors elected	Electors in contested areas	Total poll	% poll
COUNTIES – ENGLISH									
Metropolitan	1973	8,327,570	601	22	4	579	8,146,605	3,023,891	37·1
	1977	8,470,954	601	6	1	595	8,278,108	3,328,933	40·2
Greater London Council	1973	5,302,893	92	0	0	92	5,313,470	1,966,270	37·0
	1977	5,229,160	92	0	0	92	5,183,668	2,250,332	43·0
Non-metropolitan	1973	19,354,642	3,129	396	12	2,731	17,386,510	7,399,655	42·6
	1977	20,195,908	3,129	376	12	2,753	18,397,510	7,795,341	42·3
	1984	—	—	—	—	—	—	—	(39·2)
COUNTIES – WELSH	1973	1,982,126	578	109	19	468	1,647,836	906,830	55·0
	1977	2,055,199	578	122	21	456	1,714,085	874,323	51·0
REGIONS – SCOTTISH AND ISLANDS	1974	3,704,758	507	77	15	430	3,445,472	1,708,792	50·1
	1978	3,809,212	508	134	26	374	3,356,403	1,509,476	45·0
	1984	—	—	—	—	—	—	—	(46·0)
DISTRICTS – ENGLISH									
Metropolitan	1973	8,327,570	2,514	66	3	2,445	8,204,197	2,744,195	33·4
	1976	8,466,953	2,517	13	2	838	8,116,271	3,151,964	38·8
	1978	8,482,364	2,517	7	1	930	8,327,862	3,099,025	36·1
	1979	8,652,318	2,508	9	1	978	8,291,576	6,174,319	74·4
	1984	—	—	—	—	—	—	—	(40·2)

7. The Political Parties

It is very difficult to assess the real extent of party politics in local government, partly because it is changing (especially as a result of reorganization), but mainly because of the problem of definition – when does a group of like-minded councillors become a 'party'? Is a group of active campaigners who seek but lack representation on the council a political party? Do labels always mean what they say – for example how many 'Independent' members are really disguised party men, and how many of those councillors bearing party labels really participate on a party basis?[1]

The vast majority of local government decisions involve no party politics.[2] Yet in some authorities they obtrude into virtually every issue, no matter how minor or routine,[3] and will vary so considerably among the different types of local authority and the different areas of the country that generalization is difficult. Much will depend on:

(1) whether the local parties are branches of national parties (Labour, Conservative, Liberal, Scottish Nationalist etc.) or

(2) are purely local organizations, not connected with a national party (ratepayers' associations, tenants' groups etc.);

(3) the personalities, experience and motives of the councillors, especially the local party leaders;[4]

(4) the political culture,[5] traditions and conventions of the local area. Consequently, the local party system may be:

(i) *one-party monopolistic:* where it holds an overall majority of seats (80 per cent or more) and maintains that position over a long period;

(ii) *one-party dominant:* where one party persistently has a majority of seats of about 60 per cent and over;

(iii) *two-party:* where the leading party has no more than 60 per cent of seats and there is genuine competition from another party, with the reasonable possibility of power changing hands between the two rival parties (as is basically the situation in British central government);

(iv) *multi-party:* where third and other parties have at least 10 per cent of seats and power is shifting among the parties following elections or is held jointly in coalitions (several parties combining to form an alliance and thus together enjoying a majority position). Where there is mutual hostility and a failure to co-operate, the parties exercise only a negative form of 'power'; these may be known as 'hung' councils;

(v) *non-existent:* where the majority of the council, say 60 per cent or more, are non-partisan (that is independents); party members of the council are in a minority and perhaps divided into several small parties.

Within these categories may be found a host of others – for example where parties fight elections under their own labels but drop their separate identity within the council chamber. Parties will vary enormously in the extent to which they exercise discipline over their members, appoint party 'whips' (who resemble school 'prefects') or hold party meetings to predigest council business. Some parties are no more than loose groupings, perhaps bound together by a vague philosophy or by a dominant personality. Like national parties, local parties are outwardly monolithic but inwardly fragmented and often fall out among themselves over policy issues in order to protect a sectional interest, a locality or a particular service. This is often the case where there is a dominant party: in practice that party may divide into several rival semi-parties or factions.

The variety of party systems is rich in local government. The pattern is illustrated, though not completely, in Table 7 (which accepts at face value the labels supplied by the local authorities).

Table 7. *Party systems in local government*

	Number of LAs	%	Definition
Non-party	81	16	60 per cent or more seats held by Independents
One-party monopolistic	52	10	80 per cent or more seats held by one party
One-party dominant	187	36	60–80 per cent seats held by one party
Two-party	109	20	Two parties, with the leading party having not more than 60 per cent of seats
Multi-party	92	18	Third party or parties having 10 per cent or more of seats
	521	100	

Based on information from *Municipal Year Book 1980* and press reports.

Local party politics in the past

It is often suggested, usually by critics of party politics, that parties are something new to local government: a twentieth-century phenomenon. This is not an unreasonable belief, for to some extent it was the Labour Party, seeking to create a power base, which penetrated local (urban) politics and established at large the devices of party organization, discipline and local policy programmes. These devices were new to local government[6] and the other parties were slow to copy them, but the concept and experience of political parties were not new. Acknowledged historians of local government have stated, 'By 1890, it would indeed be difficult to find any great English town ... with a municipal council elected on other than party lines.'[7] Numerous studies attest to the vitality of party politics in nineteenth-century local government – in Leeds, Sheffield, Exeter, Liverpool, Manchester and Oldham for example, where the parties were in conflict over such issues as public health expenditure,[8] municipal transport, education and its relationship to religion. The broadest division was between the 'improvers', who wanted to spend along the lines of the 'gas and water socialists', and the 'economizers', who did not. Such a division was well illustrated by the London County Council virtually from its inception in 1889, when the 'Radicals' (or 'Progressives') clashed with the Conservatives (or 'Moderates') over just this issue.[9] What is mainly new to twentieth-century local government is the form rather than the fact of party politics.

However, it is apparent that in the course of the last eighty years party politics have become much more widespread in local government. On the evidence of the last few years, this trend is continuing, especially as a result of reorganization in the mid-1970s. This is illustrated in Table 9.

Table 8. *Political control of local authorities in Britain, 1983 (and 1979)*

Overall majority of seats on each council held by:	ENGLAND AND WALES				SCOTLAND			GT BRITAIN
	County Councils	District councils	London councils	Total	Regions and islands	District councils	Total	Total
Labour Party	20 (5)	95 (79)	12 (14)	127 (98)	3 (4)	21 (6)	24 (10)	151 (108)
Conservative Party	19 (40)	161 (179)	16 (18)	196 (237)	1 (2)	5 (8)	6 (10)	202 (247)
Other parties	1 (0)	14 (3)	0 (0)	15 (3)	0 (1)	3 (8)	3 (9)	18 (12)
Independents	3 (4)	28 (54)	1 (1)	32 (59)	6 (4)	16 (18)	22 (22)	54 (81)
Mixed: no majority	10 (4)	71 (54)	5 (1)	86 (59)	2 (1)	8 (13)	10 (14)	96 (73)
	53	369	34	456	12	53	65	521

Based on information from *Municipal Year Books 1984, 1980* and press reports.
NOTE: The discrepancy between the mixed system of Table 8 and the multi-party of Table 7 arises from different definitions – a multi-party system can have a majority party.

Table 9. *Local authorities run on party lines (as a percentage of all local authorities of that type)*

	1983 %	1979 %	1972	%
County councils	92	92	County councils (England and Wales)	59
London councils	98	97	London councils	97
District councils (England and Wales)	92	88	County borough councils	99
District councils (Scotland)	72	66	Scottish counties	68
Regions/islands	50	67	Scottish burghs	43
			Non-county boroughs/ rural boroughs	63
			Urban district councils	70
			Rural district councils	27

Source: *Municipal Year Books 1984, 1980, 1973* and press election reports.

Prior to reorganization, the smaller and more rural authorities were the ones least likely to operate on party lines. It was anticipated that this situation would change as the rural authorities were merged with the urban and as the smaller authorities were thus enlarged. The figures indicate the extent to which this has occurred, though they cannot tell us how active these parties are or whether they are no more than old wine in newly labelled bottles – perhaps no more than electoral ploys. (It may also be that erstwhile Independent members have taken off their masks of neutrality and openly adopted the party label to reveal their true affiliation.) We must therefore examine the consequences of party politics in local government.

The operation and effects of local party politics

As so often elsewhere in local government, it is difficult to make safe general statements about the role of party politics – so much will depend on the local party system, the local political culture and the influence of personalities. All that can be done here is to indicate some of the effects. The existence and the form of political parties is likely to affect local authorities in the following areas:

(1) Elections;
(2) Public interest;
(3) The authority's operation and policy decisions.

(1) *Elections.* There are a number of likely effects here. In the first place, the existence of party competition is likely to reduce the number of un-

contested seats.[10] Even where the seat is 'safe' and the likely result is well known (a fact which will probably deter the independent), a rival party is likely to field a candidate if only to 'wave the flag' or give new candidates their first experience of elections.

Secondly, the existence of parties will influence the number and composition of the candidates who stand for election. As we shall see (p. 128), a large proportion of councillors have said that they entered local government at the suggestion of a party. And it is far easier to fight an election on a party 'ticket' than organize and finance your own campaign. Thus parties are responsible for the entry of many members to local government office: they are important agencies for recruitment.[11] In many, especially urban, areas, party competition is keen and so too is competition to stand for election. For this purpose, the candidate has to be selected and nominated by his party (usually by a relatively small committee of the local party). Who we as electors can vote for is therefore often determined for us by the party machines. And while there may be some guidance from the national party on policy, on campaign procedure or in respect of choice of candidates, local parties are usually free to follow their own judgement (or prejudices). Some will choose intellectuals or those from a professional background; some will choose the party loyalist regardless of background; and others may prefer the ideological 'hardliner'.

Thirdly, election turnout is likely to be higher where there is a party contest. This is partly because voters can easily recognize or identify (national) party labels, whereas it requires considerably more effort to discern individual non-party candidates and their election 'platforms'. The better turnout[12] is also a consequence of the better election organization and greater publicity which the parties are likely to foster – for example in informing the public about the issues, the candidates and even simple things such as the location of the polling stations. (Not that this increased turnout is necessarily a good thing, for example if people have simply turned out to vote like zombies, without considering the issues or seeking to exercise any real sanction over the elected representatives.)

(2) *Public interest.* We have already seen how parties are likely to encourage members of the public to participate as candidates or as electors. In addition it is likely that the parties will help to stimulate interest in local government affairs by spreading knowledge about issues and personalities, and indeed even by performing an 'educative' role by providing information about such basic aspects as the structure and functions of the local authority. (Such a consequence would be mainly as a by-product of the campaign.) Much of this information will get little further than its own party members,

though even this is not insignificant as a step to public participation. But in the process of campaigning, canvassing, sloganizing and conducting arguments through the local press and other media, the parties will have some impact on the stimulation of public awareness and interest.

(3) *The authority's operation and policy decisions.* This is the most difficult area in which to make general statements, since so much will depend on the number of parties; their 'style' (structure, discipline, outside links etc.); the local traditions and experiences; the size of the council and the size of the authority's area; whether there is a majority party etc. Here we must deal in general tendencies, and many of these are based on the operation of local parties in the more 'political' urban areas. This narrowing of focus is partly due to the fact most academic research has tended to concentrate on the bigger urban authorities,[12] so that we know rather more about their party systems. They also tend to have developed a broadly 'Westminster' pattern of party politics which can provide a useful model for the study of local party politics generally. One general finding is that Labour councils are most likely to provide services to members (Thomas Report: see note 30, p. 332 below)

It is common practice for Labour, Conservative and Liberal councillors to form themselves into party groups within their local authorities. Such groups, depending on their size, will often appoint officers – chairman, whip, secretary, leader (if not the chairman) – from among their own members, and perhaps a policy committee. Inevitably, there is a more or less close relationship between the group and the local constituency party (especially in the Labour Party) and members of the latter may actually attend and speak (though not vote) at group meetings. (These 'outsiders', together with the group's officers, form what is called the 'caucus'.[13]) However, this relationship varies among local authorities. It also varies among parties in that Labour, compared to the Conservatives, has a much more systematic and structured relationship set down in the model standing orders originally drafted by the national party organization in 1930. These purport to give the local party some potentially significant influence over the local groups' policy-making powers. In practice, that influence appears to be limited or variable, and is complicated by the cross-membership of councillors who are also active members and office-holders in their local party.

What is the *role* of the party group? It is here that we observe the significant impact of parties on the operation of local authorities. The functions of the party group are numerous[14] and may include:

(a) Choosing members to serve on various committees, to act as chairmen of those committees, to choose the leader of the party group and to nominate the mayor/chairman or provost/convenor of the council (where this is separate from leader);

(b) formulating policies for the various council services;

(c) determining the group's attitude to policy proposals which emerge from other sources – especially from chief officers of the authority and from committee reports and recommendations. In this task, individual differences can be thrashed out in the privacy of the group meeting, so that in council or committee meetings all members of the group will speak and vote according to the party 'line';

(d) determining tactics regarding debates, votes and other procedures at council and committee meetings;

(e) enforcing discipline and helping to present a united front in the public activities of the council;

(f) keeping members informed and primed, especially on the work of committees (since most members will sit on only a few such committees);

(g) scrutinizing existing policy and administration, and perhaps dealing with constituents' complaints;

(h) as a consequence of several of the above points, helping to promote the co-ordination of the authority's policy and administration.

Many of these activities resemble those of Parliament, and in some respects the local party groups go further than the parliamentary parties, for example in the holding of 'epitome' or dress-rehearsal meetings (prior to council and perhaps committee meetings) at which they vet committee minutes and reports, determine their party 'line' on policy and devise their tactics – who is to speak, in what order, whether they will move for a referral back etc. The result is that the subsequent council or committee meeting will have been pre-empted: the proceedings will be cut and dried and the result a foregone conclusion.

However, not all party groups will attempt to pursue all those objectives. This is obviously the case where no party has a clear majority (e.g. as was the situation in Liverpool 1974–83) and there has to be compromise and co-operation. But even where a majority does exist, there may be strong differences within the party which disciplinary threats or patronage blandishments cannot overcome. Thus, where party cohesion is weak, there can be frequent conflict between members from different districts of the authority or among different age groups (the young Turks *v.* the old guard) and perhaps, above all, between members of different committees – especially over such issues as economies and where cuts should fall.[15] Further, while it may be frequent practice for the majority party, by virtue of its superior numbers, to assume a majority on the key committees and to monopolize the key posts (the chairmanship of committees and perhaps of the council),[16] not all such parties take full advantage of their opportunity.[17]

Generally the Conservatives claim to have little truck with many of what they see as inflexible and restrictive party devices[18] such as 'whipping'; and while there may be more need for a formal structure and discipline in the Labour Party (for ideological and other reasons),[19] even here there are considerable variations among local Labour groups. By analogy, just as the Labour Party at national level is constantly trying to settle the issue of the proper relationship between the Parliamentary Labour Party and the mass party outside (especially as manifested in the party conference), so there are numerous local disputes over the same theme – how autonomous is the local group, and how independent-minded can individual councillors be allowed to be?

Similarly there are variations in the extent to which local party groups initiate policies. Some groups have policy or advisory committees which act as a source of policy ideas, and it has been claimed that 'in many authorities operating on party lines the party group makes a more significant contribution than any single "constitutional" committee towards general policy initiation'.[20]

That was written in 1967 and even then it was probably unusual for such policy initiation to occur. More often party groups appear to be so overwhelmed with the size and complexity of their existing programmes that they are unable to disentangle themselves and think in broad and longer terms. Consequently, policy emerges instead from individual committees or the senior officers of the authority. (The introduction of policy committees throughout local government since reorganization is intended to change this situation – see p. 158.)

To sum up, we may conclude with Gyford[21] that

party Groups provide a useful means of exchanging information between members, of pleading cases before a sympathetic audience, and, if effectively organized, of securing the passage through committee and full council of approved recommendations, whatever their source. They also serve to encourage debate and criticism and to ensure, through the existence of Minority Groups, that local Government enjoys the equivalent of a Parliamentary Opposition ... They find it more difficult to operate as co-ordinating devices and as policy initiators.

These limitations are even more apparent in those local authorities where the party system is little developed. And in local government generally it is worth repeating that a great deal of business is not transacted on party lines. 'In committees and sub-committees free discussion and even "cross-voting" is quite common and on many issues there is little evidence of party discipline.'[22]

Political parties: curse or blessing?

There is some evidence to suggest that Labour control of a local authority will tend to increase the levels of that authority's expenditure on education, housing and welfare services, in contrast to expenditure when the Conservatives are in control.[23] Thus in terms of the size and the composition of a local authority's provision, which party is in control is clearly important. However, as we have seen, the mere existence of parties can have very significant effects on the working of local government. The question is whether these effects are desirable or not. The arguments are extensive and quite evenly balanced. Here we must content ourselves with a résumé of the main points.

The arguments *in favour* of parties in local government can be grouped as follows:

(1) *Participation*. As we saw earlier (p. 115), parties help to mobilize voters. Turnout tends to be higher where parties contest local elections. This is partly because of the better organization and publicity which they bring. But it is largely due to the fact that parties simplify and crystallize the main issues for the general public. Parties present a publicly known set of principles and policies and at the very least party labels will provide instant indicators of the candidates' policy orientations – what they stand for (or against). In contrast, for electors to sift through a collection of independents' election addresses is to expect too much from the real world.

We also saw (p. 115; see also p. 128) how parties help to recruit council members and reduce the number of non-contested seats. It is also worth pointing out that membership of local government tends to be more representative of the community than the House of Commons[24] (or the British component of the European Assembly). It is unlikely that local authorities would draw on such a cross-section of the community if it were not for the recruiting activities of the parties.[25]

(2) *Public interest*. We have pointed out that parties can help to stimulate and sustain a general interest in local government (p. 115), though it is difficult to gauge the extent of this. Again, at the very least, the party 'dingdong' at council and committee meetings provides plenty of copy for the local press, and to a lesser extent local radio and television.

(3) *The working of the council*. The main advantage claimed for political parties here is the coherence they can bring to the work of the authority. Parties are 'organized opinion' and where they hold a majority position within the council they can provide a programme of internally and mutually consistent policies. This is much more difficult to achieve in an authority

comprising independent members. And there is the added gain of responsibility: with a single party holding a majority and in office, the electors can pin responsibility for the authority's achievements and failures fairly and squarely on the shoulders of that party: it alone may be held accountable in debates, public meetings and above all at election time when people can vote for or against the incumbent 'team' of party councillors.

It is also claimed that having parties in the council chamber helps to diminish the possibility of domination by officials: parties will have their own views on policy and perhaps some research facilities with which to challenge official reports.[26] Issues like council house sales, education priorities, transport policy etc. can receive deeper and more structured analysis than would be the case in the non-party authority (an argument which resembles the one that favours the entry of 'political advisers' or 'departmental cabinets' into central government). Party groups keep members better informed and may also enhance regularity of attendance at council meetings (members' absences often have to be explained to the party whips). In a number of councils, the leader (i.e. head of the majority party) and committee chairman form a policy group (or 'cabinet').

(4) *Central government relations*. It is frequently asserted that central government is stifling local government (see p. 230). Supporters of party politics point out, however, that in terms of local government's relations with the central government the existence of local parties can facilitate some influence in an upward direction. Members of local party groups – many of them respected and influential figures within the national parties – can have the case for local government raised in Parliament either directly (where the councillor has become an MP) or through sympathetic MPs of their own party, and this may be particularly effective for the party whose national leaders constitute the central government (see p. 342).

The advocates of parties claim too much. To a large extent this is because they take the 'ideal-type' two-party system as their model. In practice it cannot be assumed that parties will produce majorities, and thus the pursuance of consistent policies and constructive opposition cannot be assured. The benefits of local party government will depend on the nature of the local party system. Besides, as we have seen (p. 117), parties often take little initiative in the development of policy, and some of the claimed advantages of parties have been obviated by internal reforms of local authorities (see p. 158). Furthermore, in terms of elections, it is not necessarily the case that parties increase the poll, and even where they do so, it is not necessarily a good thing since many can be induced to cast their vote through blind loyalty or prejudice and in complete ignorance of the points at issue.

The arguments *against* parties can be considered under the following headings:

(1) *Participation.* Parties distort the composition of councils by squeezing out the independents: the bearing of a party label has become the necessary if not sufficient condition for election success. Apart from voters' actions, there is a certain amount of self-selection (or denial) here as independent-minded people will be deterred from local politics by the party regimentation and the 'rail-roading' of decisions in the council chamber. Others are discouraged from standing, not because they are non-partisan but because they do not wish to reveal (e.g. in election campaigns) their affiliation for social or business reasons. This latter group may be small (the Maud Committee believed it to be only 1 per cent), but they are significant because they represent sections of the community (such as business or professional people) who arguably should be adequately represented.[27]

Another aspect of this issue arises from the fact that, in the process of selecting candidates, parties may use the wrong criteria – rewarding loyalties and services to the party and perhaps thereby overlooking those with the desirable qualities of a councillor (see p. 115). The whole process may also create cynicism if it appears to degenerate into a self-perpetuating clique arrangement – especially likely where one party dominates the council.

(2) *Elections.* Where one party does so dominate, electors may be discouraged from voting because they see the result as a foregone conclusion. However, perhaps the greatest indictment of parties in this field is the impact of national issues. Rightly or wrongly electors identify local party groups with the national parties and either vote for their party election after election through blind loyalty and without regard to local issues, or they switch their voting support among the local parties in response to the actions (or inactions) of the central government party: in effect it is national rather than local politicians who are being held accountable on local election day. Thus a general dissatisfaction with the Thatcher government, or say its regional aid policy, will be reflected in a uniform swing against Conservative councillors throughout the country regardless of their individual worth and irrespective of local issues. Local elections thus become miniature general elections, and the good councillor is penalized along with the bad if his party is out of favour nationally: the councillor becomes 'protest fodder' and the quality of local government is jeopardized.

This is well displayed in Figure 9. It shows a remarkably close relationship between voters' attitudes to the national parties and the local parties in one local authority.[28] Further illustration occurs in Table 10 which shows a congruence between the local voting in 20 large cities and in proximate General Elections.[29]

Table 10. *Local (city) elections and General Elections, 1965–79*

Date	Labour	Conservative	Other or no overall control
1965	17	2	1
1966 General Election – Labour wins			
1970	1	16	3
1970 General Election – Conservatives win			
1973	16	3	1
1974 (Feb) General Election – Labour wins			
1974	14	3	3
1974 (Oct) General Election – Labour wins			
1978	6	11	3
1979 General Election – Conservatives win			

The close relationship between national trends and local voting patterns appears to be further confirmed by more recent events. In 1981 a series of spectacular Parliamentary by-election successes by the Social Democrat/ Liberal Alliance was accompanied (though somewhat less spectacularly) by Alliance gains in local elections. Then in May 1982 we witnessed the 'Falklands factor' – when the widespread national support for the Government's policy of armed retrieval of the Falklands carried unusually large numbers of Conservative candidates to victory in the local elections. (It should be noted, however, that even in these elections there were many aberrations and unexplained local variations, when Conservative candidates lost heavily. Such variations can occur as a result of candidate personality or local performance, and so on. Indeed, it is suggested that local issues are actually becoming a more significant factor in local elections: that with the limitations on resources since the mid 1970s, difficult *local choices* are having to be made about priorities, what services to cut, which staff to shed, which client groups to disappoint.[30] Intense involvement with parochial issues – known as 'community' or 'pavement politics' – has long characterized the Liberal approach to politics. See p. 274).

(3) *The working of the council.* The main criticisms in this area are five-fold. Firstly, party-based councils are prone to treat too many items of business as party issues (see p. 117).[31] This may not only prevent the issues being dealt with on their own merits, as national policies are adopted in doctrinaire fashion by local party groups, but it may slow down the whole process of decision-making and implementation, as parties seek to obstruct and score points off one another. There is the danger of too much party bickering and not enough civil engineering! This is especially likely in a

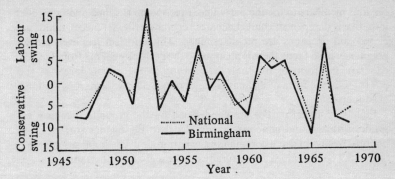

Figure 9 *Birmingham and the national swing*
(Note: *Swing* = (% *gain by major party* + % *loss by other*) ÷ 2)

multi-party system where no party has a majority. Some such criticisms were directed at Liverpool City Council following the Toxteth riots in July 1981 and the school disturbances in May 1982. There is the added danger that deadlock in the council chamber can result in power slipping into the hands of the officials.

Secondly, and conversely, wise decision-making can be jeopardized because chief officers (to preserve their impartiality) are normally absent from the meetings of party groups and cannot therefore provide the sort of guidance and advice which they would be called on to give at council and committee meetings in non-partisan authorities. Where there is a party system, the party group decisions are often final, the council/committee meeting becomes a formality and officials are too late to make a contribution (for example it is suggested that the GLC's legal conflict over its fare subsidies could have been avoided if it had been more fully advised by its officers[32]). Furthermore, where the official does make a contribution to the council/committee discussion he will often feel frustrated by seeing his advice ignored and decisions being made 'on the nod'.

Thirdly, where control of the council is subject to frequent, see-sawing change of party control (every four years at 'whole-council' elections) policy lurches can be time-consuming and wasteful, and again may be very frustrating to the officers and staff, as well as the local population (as in Tameside's switchback on comprehensive schools – see p. 230).

Fourthly, the party system is condemned as undemocratic. As in Parliament, the elected members are expected to 'leave their minds outside the chamber' and slavishly obey the dictates of the party caucus. They cannot exercise their independent powers of judgement: once the party decision is made – even where only one vote had decided the issue – party solidarity requires members to toe the party line. Free speech is stifled and individual initiative is dampened; council debates become sterile, set pieces; minds are closed and decisions are pre-determined. This criticism has even greater poignancy in so far as there is an input to the decision-making from outside, either in the form of the 'outsiders' sitting in the caucus meetings (see p. 116) or in the form of the manufacture of policies by the parties' national headquarters.

Finally, political parties are condemned on the grounds that they engender artificial and unnecessary conflict, that 'the regular stirring up of political feeling in small communities is harmful'.[33] The implication here is that small communities are naturally consensual and in harmony.

Clearly a number of these points are based on exaggerations. For example, party discipline and 'rubber-stamping' is by no means universal even in those authorities with a developed party system (see p. 116), for not only are there different party systems but local parties operate in more or less their own unique way.

As regards the absence of chief officers from crucial group meetings, there is evidence of ways having been found round this problem[34] and besides, as we have seen (p. 118), most business is transacted without regard to party considerations. And the assumption that the small community is more in harmony without political parties is even more questionable. Even if there were no parties, there would be conflicts of personality (among councillors or between officials and councillors); or clashes over sectional interests (such as tenant groups or shopkeepers); or rivalry among territorial blocks (councillors from a formerly autonomous area forming a separate identifiable group within the council and protesting their area's relative neglect within the larger amalgamated unit of local government); or there may be functional competition between different committees and services. When 'independent' councillors thus form cliques or unspoken agreements we have an emergent or concealed party system. The 'open' political parties cannot create conflict from nothing: their aim in this respect (if indeed they are aware of having an aim) is to heighten people's awareness of issues and their relationship to those issues. Indeed local parties can help to overlay some of the local divisions and reduce petty squabbles and parish-pump attitudes. Further, it may be argued that parties make a positive contribution to the well-being of the community in that many councillors are initially recruited by the parties and subsequently move on to give service to voluntary organizations.[35]

The assertion that there ought to be 'no politics in local government' and that the council should 'pull together in the best interests of the community' leaves two vital questions unanswered. First, what *is* the community? Is it the adult population? people who live in families? sport fanatics or culture vultures? motorists or pedestrians? And, second, what is *best*, and who decides what this is? Politics is about choice – 'who gets what' – and it is not at all obvious whether the town would benefit, say, more from the provision of a new sports centre or from the installation of central heating on a council housing estate. Parties may distort some of the issues, but they do not create them, and to a large extent they help to articulate and clarify them for the public at large. Above all, parties do not exist by command of the law: they exist because they attract popular support. If they were as dreadful as their critics suggest, independent candidates would do far better in elections than is currently the case. In England and Wales in 1975 there were thirty-one councils wholly non-party or entirely composed of independents; in total there were some 4,000 independent or non-party members (17 per cent of all councillors). In 1983 there were no such councils, and the number of independents or non-party members had fallen to 2,350 (under 10 per cent).[36]

Some critics of political parties in local government find solace in the thought that, as the standards of services become more uniform throughout the nation and as control by the central government is extended, so the scope for local party politics diminishes. Whether this optimism is justified is doubtful, but they also like to comfort themselves with the thought that the extensive nature of party politics in Britain reduces the scope for what many people see as a far more sinister phenomenon – the pressure group (see p. 248).

8. The Councillors

There is something of a shortage of people willing to stand for election as councillors. As we have seen (p. 105), in some areas there are as many as 27 per cent uncontested seats for major local authorities, and overall the figure is something like 20 per cent. In addition, there are a small number of vacancies on the local authorities of Britain – council seats which remain unfilled because no one is willing to serve (although some of these vacancies are temporary – the result of death or resignation – and awaiting a local by-election).

Who'd be a councillor?

Such deficiencies are not altogether surprising considering the disadvantages of being a councillor. Chief among these is the time it consumes – the average councillor spends 79 hours per month on his public duties (see p. 133). This is a large amount, and it can cut severely into his social life. It can also interfere with business and earnings. Others find it a physical and mental strain, and many councillors find their duties frustrating. This may be the result of experience with the administrative machinery – the limited powers of local authorities, restrictions by the central government, delays in reaching or implementing decisions or difficulties in obtaining finance (see p. 288).

Alternatively, the reluctance to serve may be the result of bad relationships with other councillors, either on a personal level or via party politics. Others may be put off by what they see as hostility or ignorant attitudes of the public. We get some idea of the scale of these difficulties from Table 11, which is based on a survey of councillors.[1]

There are other reasons why people are unwilling to enter or remain in local government service. For some, the times of meeting[2] are inconvenient – for example, evening meetings may not suit those who dislike night driving, while afternoon meetings may be awkward for housewives and mothers. Meetings at any time may be difficult for those in full-time employment and attendance may involve some loss of income. Although the Employment Protection Act 1975 requires employers to allow their employees to take reasonable time off to attend public duties, it may be done grudgingly, jeopardize promotion prospects and create friction with colleagues. Other potential councillors may be put off by what they see as the image of local government (parochial, bureaucratic, corrupt etc.). Further, some local seats are so safe, either in personal or in party terms, that it is regarded as a hopeless task to fight an election there.

Table 11. *Councillors' probable reasons for eventually giving up council work, and ex-councillors' reasons for leaving*

	Councillors'* probable reasons for giving up %	All ex-councillors' reasons for leaving %	Ex-councillors' (under 65) reasons for leaving %
Personal reasons:			
Ill-health/tired/found it a strain	22	23	} 21
Old age	21	7	
Interference with business or family life	17	14	15
Amount of time given	5	18	25
Moving from area	5	13	16
If became MP	1	—	—
Council reasons:			
Frustrations of party system	5	8	} 22
Frustrated by other aspects of local government organization	12	13	
Other answers/not answered	12	4	1
Total	100	100	100
(Numbers)	(1,044)	(401)	(289)

*Excluding those who said: 'Can't think of anything.'
Source: *The Management of Local Government* (Maud Report), HMSO, 1967, Vol. 2.

Although professional and business/managerial occupations appear to be well represented in local government (see also *Local Government Studies*, Sept/Oct 1982), there is a feeling in some quarters that many potential councillors from such a background are lost to local government on account of their mobility, especially in the pursuit of their careers. However, while there is clearly something in this, a study in Bristol[3] suggested that many such people are lost to local government because they prefer to give their services to voluntary organizations (partly because it affords greater status).

In spite of these obstacles why are so many people willing to become councillors? For example, in 1978 for the 3,466 seats in England and Wales which were contested (about 200 were not) there were some 9,000 candidates. According to one survey[4] only a minority of councillors themselves had the idea of standing: these were often driven to seek election in order to promote or campaign against a specific issue. Over three quarters said they were asked to stand, and most of these said they had thought little or not at all about becoming councillors beforehand. About one third had been asked to stand by political parties and another third by personal friends or acquaintances. Others were asked by organizations such as trade unions (which may 'sponsor' them, as they do M Ps),[5] or religious, welfare, business or civic groups.

Once on the council, there are a number of satisfactions to be gained from being a councillor:

(1) One of the most important seems to be that of giving service to the community. (Some may treat it as a form of apprenticeship before standing for Parliament. See p. 232.)

(2) There is a certain prestige attached to being a councillor (although the Maud Report doubts the importance of this these days[6]).

(3) Many find satisfaction in council work (decision-making, leadership, involvement) as a contrast and compensation for their paid employment (which may be more routine and undemanding or lacking authority). Retired members may find it a substitute for their former employment. And the hen-pecked husbands or intimidated wives may find it a compensation for their lack of status at home.

(4) The town hall has been described as 'the best club in town' and many councillors do find that membership of the council can enhance their private and social life.

Portrait of the councillor

There are about 26,000 councillors in Britain's principal local authorities (plus some 70,000 parish and community councillors). Like M Ps they are elected as local representatives. But just how *representative* of their community are they? How typical are they of the man in the street?

The pattern varies somewhat among communities and types of local authority – for example, London borough councillors tend to be younger than the national average councillor; there are fewer women councillors in Welsh and Scottish councils. Overall the picture[7] reveals that councillors are not a cross-section of the community: they are *un*typical. Compared to Britain's population as a whole, councillors tend to be:

(a) older – 50 per cent of councillors are over the age of fifty-four, and less than 10 per cent are under thirty-five years of age; this contrasts with the national population figures of 38 per cent aged fifty-five and over, and nearly 30 per cent aged between twenty-one and thirty-four;

(b) male – less than one councillor in five (17 per cent) is female;

(c) owner-occupiers – 76 per cent of councillors own their home, compared to 53 per cent (in 1972) for the population as a whole;

(d) white-collar in occupation – only one in four has a background in manual employment although nationally 60 per cent of occupations are manual in nature: on the other hand, 65 per cent of economically active male councillors are from just four occupational groups (sales, administration/management, professional/technical and clerical work).

Table 12. *Councillors by age, 1976*

Age-range	% of whole population		% of councillors	
21–24	8·5	28·5	—	8·5
25–34	20		8·5	
35–44	17	35	16·5	42
45–54	18		25	
55–64	16	29·5	29·5	47·5
65–74	13·5		18	
75 and over	8	8	2	2
	100	100	100	100

Source: *The Remuneration of Councillors,* HMSO, 1977, Vol. 2, Table 1 adapted and rounded.

Table 13. *Councillors by sex, 1976*

	% of whole population	% of councillors
Male	48	83
Female	52	17

Source: *The Remuneration of Councillors*, Vol. 2, Table 2.

(e) better educated – while only 8 per cent of the population experienced higher education (1972 figures), the proportion of councillors is 50 per cent.

(f) better paid – earnings of occupied councillors were approximately one third higher than the national average: no doubt a reflection of their educational and occupational background, and age.

These are national average figures: the social composition of any particular council will vary with local circumstances. For example, in rural areas farmers will tend to be well represented; in Labour-dominated areas there will tend to be more members from a working-class background; there are more women councillors in London Boroughs.[7a] Much too will depend on the turnover of councillors in the area, and on the method of recruitment (whether members are recruited through political parties, for instance, see p. 288).

It may be argued that our local councils should be more of a cross-section of the community: that only in this way can councillors really understand the issues and problems which are felt by the ordinary man in the street. For example, does the lack of women councillors explain the apparent inadequacy of nursery provision, while there is an arguably ample supply of municipal golfing facilities? In other words, better balanced councils would make for a better balance of services, of priorities and of justice.

On the other hand, it may be felt that the atypical (some would say elitist) composition of our local authorities has certain advantages – that age brings experience and wisdom; that certain occupations (especially business and managerial) bring useful contacts; and that, above all, managerial and administrative ability is necessary for the work councillors have to do.

The Maud Committee[8] concluded that

It is neither possible, nor in our opinion is it desirable, that councils should in some way be representative of all the varying interests, economic groups, income or education levels in the community ... The qualities of the member should be related to what he is expected to do ... The qualities required ... are:
(a) The capacity to understand sympathetically the problems and points of view of constituents and to convey them to the authority and, at the same time, to interpret and explain the authority's policies and actions to those whom they represent.
(b) The capacity to understand technical, economic and sociological problems which are likely to increase in complexity.
(c) The ability to innovate, to manage and direct; the personality to lead and guide public opinion and other members; and a capacity to accept responsibility for the policies of the authority.

The councillor's role

The duties of a councillor are little stated in law and to a large extent therefore he must turn for guidance to the conventions and practice of his local authority. (Many of these will have been set out in the authority's standing orders – see p. 149.) Legislation – the Local Government Acts 1972 (England and Wales) and 1973 (Scotland) – does require his attendance at council meetings (see p. 327) and his disclosure of financial interest (see p. 141). He has the right of access to the local authority's official documents in so far as this will enable him to carry out his responsibilities as a councillor (but see p. 186) and he can by law claim an attendance allowance (see p. 133). Normally it is understood that individual councillors have no lawful authority: that executive power is exercisable only by the council as a whole, as a corporate body (and operating within the powers given to them by law – see p. 221). Consequently all questions are decided by the vote of the members of the council, each voice and each vote counting equally.

However, local authorities have the power to delegate responsibility, and they frequently use it, especially in relation to committees (see p. 150). As a consequence of this and of other practices and conventions[9] in individual local authorities, the theoretical parity (of authority) among members is very different in practice.

A councillor will find that he has a variety of overlapping and perhaps conflicting roles and responsibilities, and he must try to achieve a satisfactory balance among them. Thus, he is:

– a *representative*: he is elected to represent his ward or division, but he is also expected to have regard for the interests of the whole of the local authority area. This dual role can be difficult, especially justifying it to his local constituents[10] – a problem compounded in the case of the councillor who also sits on a lower-tier council (see p. 245).

– an '*ombudsman*' or citizens' referee. As such he has to deal with, or 'trouble-shoot', problems and issues raised by individual constituents' grievances (such as school closures or allocations, adult education fees, road or council house maintenance, and planning permission).

– a *manager*. Here he must oversee the administrative machinery of officers and staff, to see that it is fair (as above) and efficient.

– a *policy-maker*, helping to shape policies and plans in the council and committees. In this and the previous role, he is expected to identify needs, set objectives and establish plans to meet those needs, and subsequently to review achievements (sometimes known as monitoring or 'progress chasing').

– above all, the councillor is a *politician*, seeking to resolve conflicts. In pursuit of this aim, he will exercise some of his other roles, but he must also be a motivator and a persuader, trying to influence, sway, convince – be it his committee members, his constituents or his party fellows. Inevitably, many councillors will also adopt a narrower political role in having a commitment to a political party.

In Parliament, some MPs become Ministers and shape government policy. Other MPs play a supporting role or, in the case of the Opposition, a critical and probing role (asking questions, making critical speeches, attempting to influence policy, especially through committee investigations etc.). Finally, there are those MPs who are content to play a more passive back-bench part (going along with the party directives, raising constituency matters from time to time etc.).

Similarly, councillors vary in the roles they play. Some, variously known as 'delegates' or 'tribunes',[11] are mainly interested in playing the representative role – dealing with complaints and speaking for particular areas or groups. This seems to be especially the case with the newer, less experienced, 'lighter' members. Others, known as 'statesmen' or 'trustees', will seek to play a more active part in policy-making, whether in broad terms (setting general objectives, determining priorities etc.) or in the area of particular services, such as housing or education. Thus, in local government, we have something equivalent to the parliamentary front- and back-benchers.

The demands of council work

Being a councillor is a heavy commitment: the Robinson Committee[12] (1977) found that on average a councillor spent seventy-nine hours a month on his duties. This is a significant increase since the Maud survey (1967) which found the average to be fifty-two hours. But it has since apparently risen to 100 hours (or even more)[13] – a reflection among other things of the fact that since 1974/5 the number of principal local authorities (that is excluding parishes and communities) had been reduced from 1,857 to 521 and the number of councillors from 46,000 to 26,000.

This average figure conceals substantial variations, however. There are variations among individual councillors, since obviously they are not all equally devoted to their duties. For example, councillors who are retired from employment appear to give more time than do councillors who have a self-employed occupation. There are also variations among local authorities, for example, according to the number of committees in the council (see p. 149). Furthermore, being a leading councillor, such as mayor,[14] Lord Provost, committee chairman or party leader, usually involves a far greater commitment – up to and even well over a hundred hours per month.

Table 14 gives a breakdown of the time spent by the average councillor on public duties. In more detail, they include:

(1) Council and committee meetings, including sub-committees. These involve attendance, preparatory work (reading relevant papers such as reports, etc.), attending party meetings, personal contacts, meeting council officers and travel.

Table 14. *Time spent by councillors on their public duties*

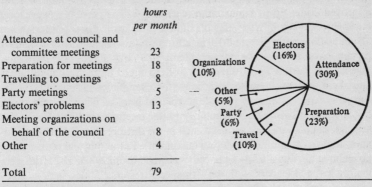

	hours per month
Attendance at council and committee meetings	23
Preparation for meetings	18
Travelling to meetings	8
Party meetings	5
Electors' problems	13
Meeting organizations on behalf of the council	8
Other	4
	——
Total	79

Source: *The Remuneration of Councillors*, HMSO, 1977, Vol. 2.

(2) Dealing with electors' problems (especially housing matters) and holding 'surgeries' at which the councillor makes himself available for consultations by constituents, including pressure groups. Sometimes councillors will visit constituents and they may organize open forums on local issues of the day.

(3) Serving as a nominee of the council on other organizations, such as health authorities, school governors and water authorities.

(4) Miscellaneous duties, including conferences, training courses, meetings of local organizations (such as Age Concern, Round Table and Shelter), site visits, ceremonies, speech days, fetes and various other semi-social functions.

But the average councillor is hard to find. The number of hours any one councillor will spend on his public duties will depend on whether he is a member of the controlling group, his seniority and the amount of time he is prepared to give.

Payment

In view of the considerable time which is involved in being a councillor it may seem reasonable to suggest that councillors should be paid for their endeavours. Up until the reorganization of local government in 1974/5, councillors received no payment as such, just expenses and loss of earnings allowance, which had been introduced on a systematic basis in 1948. This arrangement was superseded as a result of the Local Government Acts of 1972 and 1973, when attendance allowances were introduced, and councillors in principal local authorities (that is, excepting parish and community councils) are now entitled to claim an *attendance allowance* for approved duties up to a maximum (currently £15.52 per day). Most local authorities do actually pay this maximum to their members (although not all councillors bother to claim). The allowances are taxable, after deducting certain expenses. Absence through illness also now qualifies for payment.

What constitutes 'approved duties' is determined by each local authority and there are considerable variations (for example, some may recognize 'surgery' expenses or may provide secretarial help, while others may not), but all must recognize council and committee meetings for this purpose. On average, councillors claimed £320 each in the session 1976–7 (when attendance allowances were £10 per day maximum). But about one in five made no claim at all, and a few – 1 per cent – claimed over £2,000. The latter were mainly 'council leaders' – those with special responsibilities such as committee chairmen – and on average these councillors claim about double that of the 'backbench' councillors. Nearly all local authorities pay special non-taxable allowances to the chairman of the council (the mayor, convenor or Lord Provost) of between £500 and £3,000 per annum, to cover the extra expenses of that high office. In addition, all councillors can claim for travel and subsistence expenses necessarily incurred in the pursuit of council business. An estimated 100 councillors (mainly Labour) live on these allowances (which may amount to £6–7,000), i.e. they are professional local politicians.

The issue of payment is controversial. Members of the public are often quick to accuse councillors of self-seeking and not deserving of trust. Yet being a councillor can be costly: according to 1976 figures, about 40 per cent of working councillors lost pay if they stayed away from work, and about one in five of these lost as much as £50 or more a month, even taking attendance allowances into account.

The Wheatley Report (p. 59 above) and the Robinson Committee (1977) recommended a more substantial and uniform payment to councillors. In the words of the former, 'There is a job to be done, and the labourer is worthy of his hire.' It argued that a better system of payment would attract more people to stand for election: that in the light of 'the demanding and responsible nature of local government service . . . service given [ought no longer] to be its own reward' and that a standard system of payments would be far simpler and less invidious than the current arrangements.

The payment of councillors may have other merits. It might help to bring in a broader cross-section of the community (assuming this is desirable) and possibly a more committed, professional approach to the task. It might also help to stimulate public interest in the work and workings of local government. Finally, it might be argued that the adequate payment of councillors would help to eliminate corruption by reducing the disparity between the financial position of so many councillors and that of their officials and of the businessmen they must regularly meet.[15]

However, the Robinson Committee rejected the notion of a full-time salary on the grounds that it

would irretrievably damage the voluntary principle ... would endanger the relationship between elector and elected ... would endanger the relationship between members and officers by tending to blur the well-established distinction between their respective roles ... Further, we do not believe that public opinion is ready to accept the idea of full-time salaried councillors.[16]

It was also concerned about the likely cost.

While many of these points are by no means self-evident, it may be added that on the one hand such payments might attract the wrong sort of person on to local authorities, while on the other hand there is little if any evidence that payment would attract candidates: according to the Maud Report some two thirds of the elected members questioned thought that councillors should not be paid, and it did not appear that finance was a dominant influence on ex-councillors in giving up council work (see p. 127 above). In the survey of electors, only just over 10 per cent mentioned finance as a means of attracting more people into local government.[17]

Consequently the Robinson Committee recommended the abolition of the current attendance allowance (both because it was unfair and because it was surrounded by public misunderstanding and suspicion) and its replacement by a multi-component system of payment. This would comprise:

(a) a basic nominal payment for all councillors,

(b) an element to take account of expenses incurred (travel and subsistence to be dealt with separately);

(A figure of £1,000 for members of main authorities was suggested for (a) and (b) together.)

(c) a financial loss allowance, to compensate for lost earnings as a result of engaging in approved council duties (as existed up to 1974/5, when the Local Government Acts were implemented);

(d) special responsibility payments for those councillors, such as committee chairmen, who have to spend extra time on council affairs. The burden of office on such 'leaders' would vary with the size of the local authority and so a sliding scale was suggested for these extra payments (from £3,000 per annum in an authority with 400,000 population to £750 per annum in authorities below 50,000 – 1977 figures).

The overall cost of this scheme was estimated at some £30 million per annum, assuming full take-up of payments. Under the Local Government, Planning and Land Act 1980, local authorities are now able to pay *special responsibility allowances* (current maximum £445) to certain (leading) councillors, such as committee chairmen. In addition, councillors are given the option of claiming attendance allowances (as above) or alternatively of claiming a *financial loss allowance* (to compensate for loss of earnings caused by attendance at council meetings; current maximum £22.50 per day).

Non-elected council members

In addition to elected members (councillors) local authorities have often drawn in other members of the public by the appointments of (a) *aldermen* (though this office has now been abolished) and (b) *co-opted* members, neither of them directly or publicly elected.

Aldermen, or in Scotland 'bailies', were elected to individual councils by existing councillors.[18] They had no special role as aldermen/bailies. They tended to be older and somewhat more prestigious than the average member. In some respects they were more 'powerful' in that they often chaired committees, and in England and Wales their term of office was twice that of ordinary councillors (six years instead of three years, before 1974). In Scotland, their term of office was the same as that of (burgh) councillors.

For the most part aldermen were actual or former councillors, though legally anyone who was qualified to stand for election as a councillor (see p. 98) could be appointed. However, their numbers were limited to a maximum of the equivalent of one third of the council (one sixth in the London boroughs): thus a council of twenty-one councillors could add seven aldermen to their number.

The aldermanic system was introduced mainly to secure a measure of stability and continuity, especially where the whole council could be replaced in a 'clean-sweep' election. In addition, it was justified on the grounds that it could bring on to the council persons of ability and experience who might have been unable or unwilling to gain a place through open election. However, the system was clearly undemocratic and there were some notable instances of abuse – a marginally superior party might shore itself up by taking all the seats on the aldermanic bench. Consequently, under the Local Government Acts of 1972 and 1973 the office of alderman/bailie was abolished.[19]

Co-opted members are similar to aldermen in that they are chosen by the council itself (on the recommendation of its committees). The system of co-opting members is often used in parishes to fill council vacancies, or the appropriate district council may have to resort to co-option if the parish council is too low in membership through lack of candidates. The procedure is used in other local authorities to augment the membership of committees, but these co-opted persons do not become members of the local authority (the council) as such but they can claim expenses and allowances.

Legally, any local authority committee (except the finance committee) or sub-committee may co-opt persons from outside the council, and normally the council will set down in its standing orders (see p. 149) its arrangements for co-option, such as the numbers and composition (for example a certain percentage of women on the social service committee). Some committees may be obliged to co-opt because the law may require the representation of specific groups or interests, and without co-option the committees may be deficient in this respect. The 1944 Education Act requires education committees to include people who are experienced in education or acquainted with educational conditions in the area. Existing councillors (such as teachers in private schools) may themselves fulfil this requirement but otherwise they will need to be co-opted in order to comply with the law.[20] In Scotland, the law is more precise in this respect: Scottish education committees must appoint outsiders, including at least three persons interested in the promotion of religious education and two teachers from maintained schools (Local Government (Scotland) Act 1973).

In practice, apart from Scotland, education committees do tend to co-opt fairly regularly, while other committees are far less consistent (especially in district councils). But rarely do co-opted members form a substantial proportion of committee membership. Legally they can comprise up to one third of the membership of most committees, but they can constitute up to 49 per cent of education committees, and even 100 per cent of sub-committees, though they rarely ever do so.

Co-opted members usually become full committee members, with powers to speak and vote, and it is not unknown (though rare) for a committee chairman to be a co-opted member. However, co-opted members do not become members of the local authority (the council) as such; they will usually be confined to the field of their committee.

There are two broad types of co-opted member: (i) a person chosen on an individual or personal basis as having expertise or local notability (perhaps as a long-serving ex-councillor) and (ii) a person chosen as a representative of some outside interest – the Church, a teachers' union, a welfare society or the local chamber of commerce. In the case of 'representative co-option', the local authority will often leave it to the outside body itself to select the representative.

The sort of people who get co-opted to local authority committees are of a very similar mould to councillors themselves – which is not altogether surprising, since they must have the qualifications of a councillor[21] (see p. 98), and they are likely to be interested in council work and to know council members (perhaps as relatives). Some are chosen to provide them with a trial run at local authority committee work; others are chosen for party political reasons (and may as a consequence be subject to the party whip system). Allegations of party manipulation or of nepotism call in question the whole principle of co-option.

Briefly stated, the *advantages* claimed for co-option are as follows:

(1) It can provide expertise (cheaply) which may be lacking among the members and the officials or which may be sought as an alternative or counter-weight to that of the local government officers. (In a rather similar way, some Ministers bring in 'outsiders' to their departments in Whitehall.)

(2) Outsiders can give a wider, perhaps fresher perspective and reduce the danger of parochialism; and, in so far as they are independent, they can help to diminish a preoccupation with party politics.

(3) A larger number and a wider range of people can be brought into the political process, especially those who can give only a limited amount of time, or who would be otherwise deterred by having to go through the election process.

(4) In the 'representative' form, co-option can promote the exchange of ideas with outside organizations and so enhance mutual understanding and co-operation between them.

The *disadvantages* may include the following:

(1) The involvement of co-opted members may be regarded as undemocratic, not simply because they are not elected and are therefore not accountable to anyone, but because they may be appointed for purely party motives and may even include candidates who stood unsuccessfully in the election.

(2) They may upset committee relations with the local authorities' own 'experts' – the officers – and indeed, in so far as co-opted members are unfamiliar with local government procedures, they may upset councillors with their biased or 'starry-eyed and impracticable' ideas.

(3) They may provide dangerous openings for pressure groups, with the consequent unreasonable distortion of priorities in individual local authorities' provision.

(4) They can become the 'tail that wags the dog' in those councils where they hold the balance among the confronting parties.

It is difficult to generalize about the balance of advantage here, but the author believes that there is a place for co-option in local government and that, if anything, its possibilities should be more fully explored by local authorities.

Standards of conduct

Self-denigration is said to be a national pastime in Britain, especially in recent years, and local government is as likely to run the gauntlet as are trade unions, management, Parliament, moral standards, British Leyland or education. So, from time to time it is alleged that the quality of local government is not what it used to be.

Such denunciations have become especially intense in the years since the Second World War. In 1948, a respected historian commented on 'candidates of illiterate speech and low social standing . . . tongue-tied [in council debates]'.[22] In 1960, a senior civil servant[23] averred that '. . . despite the first-class people there are on every sort . . . of local authority . . . by and large local government is not drawing as good a quality of councillor or as many outstanding leaders by way of councillors as it used to do'. In 1961, a professor of government wrote that '. . . our councils are filled with retired people, with women whose children have grown up, and with a few others who can afford the time, or see some particular advantage in being on the council'.[24] In July 1963 *The Times* headed an article 'Petticoat and Pensioner Rule in Council Chambers'.

Partly as a consequence of this onslaught, the government appointed the Maud Committee on the Management of Local Government (1964–7). Its terms of reference were 'to consider in the light of modern conditions how local government might best continue to attract and retain people of the calibre necessary to ensure its maximum effectiveness'. This implied that the government had confidence in the quality of current councillors (and officers), but that there were doubts about the immediate future.

These doubts were reinforced in the research work which was undertaken for the Maud Committee:

Many chief officers . . . thought that members were unable to grasp issues of any complexity . . . only a small minority . . . made any real contribution in committee . . . Instances were found of dismal standards of discussion . . . Evidence on a decline in calibre is insubstantial. It does seem clear, however, that the increasing complexity of proposals for innovations are tending to increase the gap in understanding between member and officer, and ... frequently ... members take decisions without an adequate understanding of the issues involved.[25]

To be fair, the blame clearly did not always lie with councillors themselves; it was at least partly due to the fact that 'in many spheres, local government had become so highly technical that its intricacies were in large measure incomprehensible to the layman'[26] – be it environmental planning, engineering and building techniques or finance and budgetary procedures. As the Salmon Commission put it, '... members [of local authorities] may enter public life with little preparation and may find themselves handling matters on a financial scale quite beyond their experience in private life'.[27] An ex-leader of the GLC has recently condemned the shortage of young, enthusiastic and discerning councillors (see p. 186).

The Maud Committee itself declared that it is difficult both to measure the quality of councillors and discover hard evidence for its alleged decline. Instead, it looked to the future, and suggested that councillors should possess the following qualities:

(a) The capacity to understand sympathetically the problems and points of view of constituents and to convey them to the authority and, at the same time, to interpret and explain the authority's policies and actions to those whom they represent.
(b) The capacity to understand technical, economic and sociological problems which are likely to increase in complexity.
(c) The ability to innovate, to manage and direct; the personality to lead and guide public opinion and other members; and the capacity to accept responsibility for the policies of the authority.[28]

To secure councillors with these qualities, it suggested a number of changes to the then existing practice, including compulsory retirement at seventy, training courses, greater opportunities for release from employment, review of the councils' meeting times, increased co-option, reduction in the number of committees and a reduction in central government controls over local government. Some of these points have been dealt with above; others will be covered in later chapters. Here it is appropriate to comment on two aspects: training and facilities.

There is little systematic training for councillors, though most local authorities provide some form of general induction procedure for new members and perhaps some briefing on areas of special interests, such as housing, social services or the financial aspects of the authority's work. Similarly, the facilities available to councillors to help them in their work vary considerably from one authority to another. In relation to secretarial assistance, the Bains Report said, 'Some authorities already provide some facilities for members, but in very few is there anything approaching a comprehensive service.'[29]

A more recent study suggests that the 'Councillor's role has been perceived as a part-time leisure activity rather than as a professional or career activity. As a result . . . the facilities to support the representational role are limited.'[30] It is further suggested that while the task of local government is becoming more demanding, the officers' needs have received attention to the neglect of members'. Consequently, it is recommended that there should be more systematic training for members (both induction and continuing) and more adequate support services (in the form of accommodation, transport, crèches, secretarial assistance and information services).

Corruption

If the 1960s was concerned with the quality of councillors, the 1970s has been concerned with their integrity – or rather apparent lack of it. Such concern, however, is by no means a modern phenomenon: in 1834 the Royal Commission on Municipal Corporations (see p. 28) criticized the way members enjoyed rent-free use of municipal property, held entertainments at public expense and misappropriated corporation income. Throughout the nineteenth century there were numerous scandals involving the Boards of Guardians (see p. 27) and rumours of 'jobbery' in the granting of contracts. In 1888 the allegations of corruption in property development by the Metropolitan Board of Works were such that they led to the appointment of a Royal Commission of Inquiry. Then, in the 1920s and 1930s there was another upsurge of rumour and suspicion about the activities of elected Guardians and councillors – partly due to the supposed vulnerability of the growth in incumbents from poorer backgrounds.

In an attempt to prevent such abuses, the central government used the system of inspection (originally developed to improve efficiency in certain services – see p. 226), and local authority finances became increasingly subject to the professional audit (of their accounts) by the district auditor (see p. 216). Parliament has increasingly required local authorities to open their meetings to the public and press, and it has established local commissioners to investigate complaints of maladministration. Local authorities themselves have laid down codes of conduct in standing orders (see p. 149), and to promote greater openness they have established a number of public relations activities (see p. 267).

In addition a number of legal restraints have been placed upon councillors – notably (a) the disqualification of being an employee of the authority or for unauthorized expenditure exceeding £2,000 (see p. 98 and p. 327); (b) the duty to make a 'declaration of pecuniary interest'; and (c) the regulations against corrupt practices. As the other points are dealt with elsewhere, we shall briefly deal with the last two points here.

Pecuniary interest

Councillors are unique in public life in that their duties are of an executive nature and yet they are not responsible either to an employer or to an appointing authority: their responsibility to the electorate is tenuous to say the least. On the other hand, by the very nature of local government's functions, councillors are likely to encounter a conflict of interests between their own private interest or benefit and those of the community they represent (especially in such areas as planning decisions, awarding building contracts or allocating council house tenancies). To help to guard against the temptations of such situations, it has long been a requirement[31] that councillors who have a direct or indirect financial interest in any matter which is before the authority must at the meeting where the matter is under consideration disclose the fact that he has an interest (except in certain cases – see below) and thereafter refrain from speaking or voting on the matter. The member must declare an interest as soon as practicable after the start of the meeting. Alternatively, where his interest arises because he or his spouse is a member, partner or employee in a business which has dealings with the authority, or is the tenant of authority property, he may give a general written notice of his interest; he need then make no oral disclosure at the meeting. A record of such notices and of disclosures made at meetings is kept by the authority and is open to inspection by members of the council (in England and Wales) or by local electors (in Scotland). Breach of this provision is a criminal offence, and between 1964 and 1974 some twenty members were prosecuted for failing to disclose a pecuniary interest in the business before their council.

However, the law is not totally rigid in this matter, and the Secretary of State has the discretionary power of dispensation. He can (and does) remove from individuals or groups of members the ban on speaking and/or voting in council or committee, usually where the pecuniary interest is somewhat remote or where the incidence of disabilities would be such as to decimate the council or committee concerned. Such general dispensation has been granted, for example, to councillors who are tenants of council houses or have children at state (LEA) schools.

Corrupt practices

The Prevention of Corruption Acts 1906 and 1916 (and their predecessor, the Public Bodies Corrupt Practices Act 1889) were the product of the report in 1888 of the Royal Commission on the Metropolitan Board of Works (see p. 87 above). This report had stated that

it might have a wholesome effect if it were distinctly made a criminal offence to offer to any member or official of a public body any kind of payment, fee, or reward having any relation to the affairs of the body of which he was such a member or official, and also to make the person accepting any such payment . . . amenable to the criminal law.

This legislation has no doubt had the desired salutary effect, but it has not of course eliminated corruption. In recent years, much publicity has been given to cases in which councillors have been convicted under that legislation for taking bribes in respect of the allocation of council houses or the granting of planning permission. The penalties include imprisonment, fine, surrender of the corrupt gift and disqualification from office. Between 1964 and 1974, sixteen members (and twenty-two officials) were convicted for such offences, or similar ones.

The most notorious prosecutions occurred in 1974, when a number of leading councillors in the North of England were imprisoned for corruptly securing lucrative contracts for a private architect, John Poulson. It was this 'Poulson affair' which jolted public opinion and gave rise to several official inquiries into standards of conduct in public life.

The first of these reported in May 1974,[32] the second in July 1976.[33] Neither was unduly concerned at the extent of corruption. 'Our own judgement . . . is that standards of conduct in local government are generally high.'[34] 'We have heard no evidence to give us concern about the integrity and sense of public duty of our bureaucracy as a whole . . .'[35] But they do admit that corruption is difficult to measure. 'There is no objective way of making a true assessment of the amount of public sector corruption that exists now or whether the amount has changed over recent decades.'[36]

However, this view was not entirely supported by at least one member of the Royal Commission, who suggests that certain recently changing factors 'may have enabled corruption to creep into bodies which have rightly enjoyed a long standing reputation for very high standards of honesty and unselfish service'.[37] These factors include:

(1) the growth in power of certain councillors and committees as a result of changes in the planning and building functions of local government;

(2) the emergence of one-party domination in many authorities;

(3) the uncertain tenure of chief executive officers (in contrast to the older-style clerks), which might inhibit their pursuit of a suspicion of corruption by councillors, his employers;[38]

(4) the diminution in the degree of central government control of local government;

(5) the emergence of a 'Robin Hood syndrome', whereby, with the aim of providing services 'in the public interest', more quickly or adequately, members lose their patience with the ordinary processes of government and start to cut corners;

(6) councillors' lack of training, and their inadequate remuneration.

Despite their belief that 'the picture is still of an essentially honest service', the reports themselves saw no room for complacency, and they recommended a number of changes to improve the situation and reduce that minority who 'do not measure up to acceptable standards of probity in public life'. Broadly they sought to do this by (a) further discouraging corruption, for example by suggesting stronger penalties and recommending that, in charges of corruption, the burden of proof should rest on the defence (thus implying the presumption of guilt rather than innocence[39]); (b) making it easier to investigate suspected corruption, for example by increasing police powers of access to information, including information held by the Inland Revenue and other official agencies.

For local government, the more comprehensive recommendations are to be found in the report of the Committee on Conduct in Local Government (1974). This made the following proposals:

(1) Councillors (and officers) should be required to disclose a pecuniary interest orally whenever it arises (that is, exceptions would no longer be allowed).

(2) Such councillors should be required to withdraw completely from the meeting (except where they had a dispensation from the Secretary of State).

(3) Such disclosures, withdrawals and dispensations should be recorded and be open to inspection by local electors (by councillors in the case of officers' disclosure).

(4) There should be a compulsory register of certain pecuniary interests of councillors (paid employments, local land holdings, company interests and tenancies of council property), to be annually revised and open to inspection by electors.

(5) The use for private gain of information received through membership (or employment) in a local authority should be a criminal offence.

(6) Central government departments should consider giving further advice to local authorities on procedures for the award of contracts and the management of comprehensive development.

(7) Consideration should be given to extending the power of local commissioners ('ombudsmen' – see p. 260).

(8) Local authorities should have clear arrangements for the systematic review of their internal procedures from the point of view of probity.

(9) Local authorities should have clear and well publicized arrangements for receiving and investigating complaints.

(10) Local authorities should pursue vigorous policies of public communication, especially to publicize their policies and procedures.

(11) In conjunction with the central government, local government should establish a national code of conduct based upon those principles which already govern the best practice among individual authorities.

(12) Political parties should ensure that rules of conduct in local authority party group meetings are no less strict than in those of the authority itself.

(13) Councillors (and employees) should treat their non-pecuniary interests (such as family ties) on the same basis as the law requires them to treat their pecuniary interests.

(14) Councillors (and employees) should ensure that hospitality given or received in connection with their official duties can always be justified in the public interest; and that official facilities or allowances to which they are entitled are used strictly for the purposes of their official duties.

(15) Members of the public should take action if they have evidence of misconduct on the part of any member or employee of a local authority.

The most immediate result of all these inquiries and suggestions has been the publication of a national code of good behaviour in local government. This reiterates a number of the recommendations and seeks specifically to guide the conduct of councillors and more generally to provide an explicit public standard by which local government can be measured by those outside it.[40]

That such action was desirable was not doubted by Richard Crossman, who wrote, 'The truth is that the moral standards of local government have declined until the relationship between members of public bodies and outside business interests are freely tolerated' (*The Times*, 20 June 1973).

It is difficult to judge its success. If corruption has dimished in scale, it may be the result of other factors. As Doig says, 'The fact that there have been no large corruption cases since the mid-1970s is less the consequences of locking up a handful of rotten apples than the steady decline in the big spending and the relationships of the previous decade.' (A. Doig, *Corruption and Misconduct in Contemporary British Politics*, Pelican, 1984. This book provides a number of useful case studies of corruption in local government.)

The complete elimination of corruption in local government is impossible – after all, corrupt dealings are conducted in secret and are therefore difficult to prove. Codes of conduct and declarations of interest will have little impact on the dishonest, though they may dissuade the pliant. And there is one fundamental dilemma: the introduction of greater scrutiny and regulations can seriously damage the morale and feeling of mutual trust within an organization. In particular, it may inhibit the leadership and initiative of management. Before we turn to management, in the next chapter, perhaps we should conclude by putting local government corruption into perspective: local authorities are local, their activities are watched by the press, they are in many ways more open and exposed to public scrutiny than are government departments, 'quangos', political parties, charities and private enterprise. There may *appear* to be more corruption in local government simply because there is more light and more detection.

9. Internal Organization: The Council and its Committees

How local authorities organize themselves to carry out their responsibilities varies from one authority to another. But they all follow a broadly similar pattern, and certain forms or procedures are universally adopted where they are required by law. Briefly it can be stated that all local authorities will conduct their activities through a council of all members, aided by a number of committees (comprising small groups of members), which work in close collaboration with senior officers, who are employed by the council and head the various departments of the council. This is illustrated by Figure 10. In this chapter we shall be mainly concerned with the work of the council and its committees. The officers and staff of local authorities are more fully examined in Chapter 10.

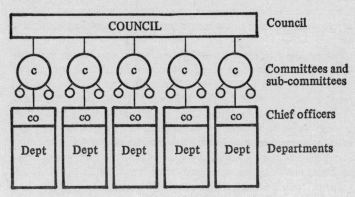

Figure 10 *Basic structure of a local authority*

The council

By 'local authority' we mean those groups of people who are elected to be councillors and form councils, the bodies which take authoritative decisions for their local areas. But all councils delegate much of their work to smaller groups (committees) or to individuals (officers). Such delegation occurs because councils are too large to be effective decision-making bodies (some have over a hundred members) and council members, meeting only as a whole group, would not develop sufficient expertise. Further, most councils do not meet frequently (many meet only five times a year) and their meetings (of perhaps three hours' duration) do not give them enough time to exercise close supervision of the work of the many departments and employees of the council.

Consequently, most of the activity at full council is concerned with (a) the ratification (through voting) of decisions and actions which committees have taken since the last full meeting of the council, and (b) the discussion of committee reports, analyses and recommendations which may then be approved, amended, rejected or 'referred back' for consideration to the committee concerned.

The council itself will determine what or how much is delegated to committees and will often reserve to itself the more important policy matters. It thus remains the ultimate decision-making body. However, as the Bains Report (see below) pointed out, the way councils exercise that role differs widely from one authority to another. At one extreme the council receives and considers the reports and minutes of every committee: at the other extreme, members individually may receive the relevant papers but very little may go before the full council unless members specifically request it. In between these two types are those councils which receive and consider summary reports and may as a consequence debate major matters arising from them.

Council meetings are presided over by a chairman, who may be variously entitled chairman or mayor (in England and Wales), provost or convenor (in Scotland), according to the type of local authority. However, most of the council discussion is led by the chairmen of the various committees. Officers also attend council meetings, but they do not normally speak: their role on these occasions is mainly a consultative one – to be 'on tap'. The other officials present are the clerks. They are responsible for distributing any relevant papers and for taking the minutes (a written summary) of the meeting. These minutes are subsequently open to inspection by the public.

One type of council setting is illustrated in Figure 11.

Council meetings

The frequency and timing of meetings are matters which are left largely to the local authorities themselves to decide. By law, all principal councils (that is, all except parishes and communities) must hold an annual meeting. Some authorities, the GLC for example, meet monthly or even more often; others meet only quarterly. The timing of meetings is an important consideration, as it can affect attendances. Urban authorities tend to meet in the evening; other authorities meet in the daytime for the convenience of councillors who have to travel long distances (e.g. the Western Islands council in Scotland meets for four days at a time), though this may present problems in getting release from employment.

Council meetings are formal affairs, and much ceremony may attach to them – the civic mace may be carried and the chain of office worn. Meetings may start with prayers. Speech-making, the conduct of debate and other procedural matters are quite closely controlled, usually in what are called 'Standing Orders'.[1] Members of the public may attend as observers. In all these respects, council meetings resemble those of Parliament.

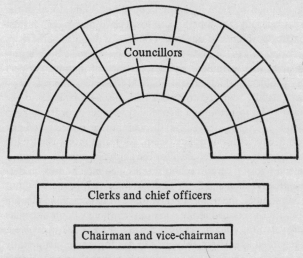

Figure 11 *A council setting*

The leader of the council

In Britain, the *chairman* of the council is elected by councillors from among their number. He is not therefore elected directly by the people, as in the USA. Consequently (and partly because of the tendency to rotate the office) the office is ceremonial rather than effective: he is a figurehead rather than a political force, unlike the council *leader* (normally head of the majority party). However, in some local authorities, the chairman acquires a pre-eminence by way of his social standing, hard work, experience or sheer ability. As a result, he may develop a permanence and so combine chairmanship with leadership of the council. In many local authorities, usually those where parties are strongly developed, council leadership is openly and formally acknowledged (perhaps in standing orders). However, in these circumstances it may be difficult to combine this role with that of chairman, since the latter requires a non-partisan approach, so that the roles of leader and chairman will be separated and come to resemble that of (political) Prime Minister and (non-political) monarch. (The Speaker of the House of Commons plays such a non-political role; so do a number of national presidents, as in West Germany or Italy.)

Committees

The number, size, composition and powers of committees in any local authority are determined by each individual council and laid down in the Standing Orders. Generally, the functions of local government committees are to: (i) take particular interest in one aspect or area of the local authority's work (education or highways for instance); (ii) closely supervise the administration of that area; (iii) formulate policies or lines of action; (iv) deal initially with any problems which arise in its field of special interest.

Committees are usually required to report their discussions back to the full council. This may be something of a formality, simply in order to keep the council informed, as in cases where the committee is delegated the power actually to decide issues of policy (see p. 333). But more usually the purpose is to gain approval of the council for the actions which the committee may recommend (closing certain schools, selling council houses, undertaking a redevelopment scheme etc.). And, by law, certain matters cannot be delegated to committees: the power to raise loans or to determine the rate (poundage) rests with the council alone. Obviously, where a committee has to await the approval of the council before it can act, there is delay involved, but this may be regarded as a reasonable price to pay for greater democratic control. In such cases, the committees are advisory rather than executive in nature. Nevertheless, they do a lot of the detailed groundwork and sifting on behalf of the council and have been aptly described as the 'workshops' of local government (though of course much of the work of local government occurs in the departments and among senior officers).

Types of committee

There are many different kinds of committee in local government. The most usual categories are as follows: (a) *Horizontal* and *vertical*. Those committees which concentrate on the administration of a single service (such as education or housing) are usually called 'vertical' (or service) committees. Other committees may be concerned with a particular function which directly affects many or all other council activities (though often having little contact with the general public), and because they cut across other services these are known as 'horizontal' (or functional) committees – finance or staffing, for example. (b) *Special* and *standing*. Special (or *ad hoc*) committees are formed to deal with a particular problem (for instance, flood) or event (for instance, Jubilee celebrations) and are disbanded when circumstances permit. Standing committees are more permanent, being re-appointed annually to fulfil the roles outlined in (a) above. (c) *Joint* committees are formed by two or more local authorities when they share an interest in some activity or problem (a national park or other amenity). In many instances these committees are called 'boards' or 'authorities' – the Somerset and Avon Police Authority is an example. (d) *Statutory*. While local authorities have considerable discretion as regards the committees they appoint, they are nevertheless required by law to appoint *certain* committees. The most important of these are police, education and social services. (Before the reorganization legislation of 1972/3, the list of such committees was considerably larger, though in all cases only the relevant local authority was affected.)

Size and membership of committees

For the most part, membership of committees in local government is confined to currently elected members of the council, the councillors. (Co-opted members are an exception to this rule – see p. 136.) These members are allocated to committees by the full council, though much of this work is often done in advance by a special 'selection' committee (which usually consists of more senior councillors). In this allocation process, arrangements vary among local authorities. Statutory committees may have certain constraints on their size or composition – police committees must comprise two thirds councillors and one third magistrates, and education committees must contain members who have experience in education. It is normal for some account to be taken of councillors' own preferences, the balance of the parties, the representation of wards or districts and the balance of age and experience of members. Where a party dominates the council, it may well use its advantage to predominate in each of the important committees.

The size of committees is a matter for the individual council to determine and there is wide variation. The desirability of having small and workman-like committees needs to be balanced with the democratic desire to have a proper representation of areas and interests. The importance and even perhaps the popularity of a committee is likely to affect its size. As we have seen (p. 136), some committees will find it necessary to co-opt members from outside the elected membership of the council.

The operation of committees

Usually the first task of a committee is to appoint a chairman, though often this may be done for it by the whole council, and where there is a majority party the allocation of chairmanships is often a foregone conclusion.

Naturally, committees are usually smaller in membership than the full council. Committee meetings are less formal occasions than full council meetings, and officers are expected to play an active role by answering questions and giving advice. Indeed, a lot of committee time is spent hearing and reacting to the reports by chief officers on such matters as the council's budget, a housing development scheme or the planned closures of certain schools. From such questions and discussions will emerge the committee's views, and these views, or 'resolutions', together with the 'minutes' (written summaries of the committee's proceedings) are usually submitted to the next meeting of the full council.

Just as the full council meets at regular intervals, so do committees – they go through a regular 'cycle' of meetings (though, like the council, they may have special or emergency meetings). By law, their meetings are open to the public, but for certain items a committee (and indeed the full council) can exclude the public and press by going into 'closed' session (meeting 'in camera'). These items are usually of a confidential nature, such as a discussion by a housing committee on rent arrears or evictions. On occasion, a member of the public may be invited to address a committee. A number of sub-committees may also be open to the public, but this is left very much to the discretion of the local authority. A government circular merely states that 'councils should bear in mind the advisability of making their proceedings as open as possible'. Whilst local government has no Official Secrets Act such as that operating in central government, local authorities usually have a clause in their standing orders which prohibits the disclosure of council or committee matters until this is authorized by the council. For many matters this occurs in the normal course of events, e.g. in open council or committee meetings; and council minutes are made available for public inspection at the council offices or public libraries.)

As we have seen (p. 141), when items occur at committee or full council meetings in which any councillor has a pecuniary interest, such as owning a property which the council may wish to acquire or running a business which it may wish to employ, he must declare his interest and take no further part in the discussion or voting on that item.

The role of chairman

Chairmen of committees do not merely control the conduct of committee meetings and speak on behalf of their committees at council meetings (like Ministers speaking in Parliament). Between meetings of his committee, a chairman may have to deal with urgent issues – on lesser issues this power may be delegated to the relevant official – and take decisions on behalf of the committee (which he will subsequently have to get its approval for). For this and other reasons he will be in regular contact with the departmental chief officers, especially prior to committee meetings. Occasionally he may call emergency meetings of the committee. And he may also, as its chairman, meet members of the public – to explain the council's policy on school closures or housing rents, for example. The precise role of chairmen will vary among local authorities and may or may not be set out in their standing orders. Generally speaking, a committee chairmanship is a responsible and onerous task.

The pros and cons of the committee sytem

Historically, committees exist in local government because the modern local government system was largely preceded by a collection of *ad hoc* authorities (Boards of Guardians, Boards of Health, School Boards) which were more or less simply amalgamated when local authorities were created, so that the latter became a system of ready-made committees and departments. Furthermore, it has been convenient (and sometimes mandatory) for local authorities, on the acquisition of an extra responsibility, to create a committee (and a department) to administer that function.

There are however some more positive reasons for setting up committees:

(1) They off-load the full council, which can consequently spend less time on details and greater attention to overall policy matters.

(2) They can save the time of councillors, since different matters can be considered at the same time in the different committees – they can be dealt with in parallel rather than in series.

(3) Their existence can simplify the tasks facing the council through the division of labour and the specialization of responsibilities.

(4) Such specialization should facilitate greater knowledge and expertise by councillors (aided where appropriate by co-opted outsiders).

(5) Further, such specialization should produce more effective supervision and control of the local authority's administrative areas.

(6) Committees are generally smaller in size and their procedures are more informal, which may encourage councillors to speak more freely.

(7) Finally, committees provide a useful point of contact with the officials and help to keep them in touch with public opinion (though see p. 185–6).

It is difficult to envisage local government trying to operate without committees, and many councillors would feel that they are not sufficiently involved unless they are a member of at least one committee.[2] However, committee systems can be abused and thus create problems. Among the principal dangers are the following:

(1) Rather than save time, committees may actually waste it. They may do this in a number of ways – by going into excessive detail and talking endlessly, by creating unnecessary sub-committees and working parties, by delaying decisions while waiting for another committee to make a decision which affects its work, and so on. Besides, there may be simply too many of them. In the past, they often grew without regular review, and as a result there was overlapping and duplication of function. Committees may also be accused of dispersing or clouding responsibility.

(2) While committee members may become experts in the field of administration covered by their committee, they may also become narrow-minded and fail to see the work of the council as a whole. Indeed, there is the real danger of insularity (especially among vertical committees and their related departments), with members (and officers) identifying too closely with 'their' service: rivalry, jealousy and protectiveness may follow. Councils have usually tried to secure some co-ordination in the work of their committees and departments by various means, for instance through horizontal committees, such as finance, or by ensuring that there is cross-membership within the vertical committees, (some members sitting on several committees). Some relied on the machinery of the political parties, and perhaps most assumed that the chief administrative officer – the clerk – would provide a sufficient overview of the local authority's affairs. But in the 1960s these arrangements were increasingly felt to be inadequate – hence the setting-up of the Maud Committee (see p. 139).

The Maud Report

Such criticisms were most stridently and tersely stated in the Maud Report (*Report of the Committee on the Management of Local Government*, 1967). That inquiry found that many of the principal local authorities had thirty or more committees and forty or more sub-committees.[3] The same report showed that one large local authority sent out 700–1,000 sheets of official paper (agenda, reports etc.) each month to committee members. Consequently, preparation for, travel to and from, and attendance at meetings were making considerable demands on the time of members and officers. The Committee also expressed its concern that 'the association of each service with a committee, and of a department and a principal officer with both, produces a loose confederation of disparate activities, disperses responsibilities and scatters the taking of decisions'. It concluded:

The virtues of committees are, at present, outweighed by the failures and in-adequacies of the committee system . . . It becomes increasingly difficult for committees to supervise the work of the departments because of the growth of business, lack of time and the technical complexity of many of the problems. The system wastes time, results in delays and causes frustration by involving committees in matters of administrative detail. The system does not encourage discrimination between major objectives and the means to attain them, and the chain of consequential decisions and action required. We see the growth of business adding to the agenda of committees and squeezing out major issues which need time for consideration, with the result that members are misled into a belief that they are controlling and directing the authority when often they are only deliberating on things which are unimportant and taking decisions on matters which do not merit their attention.

Some local authorities had become aware of the deficiencies of their committee structure and their internal arrangements generally, and some had undertaken interesting and sometimes controversial reorganizations (in Newcastle and Basildon, for example). Other local authorities had more conventional arrangements, but sought to achieve greater co-ordination through the creation of special 'policy' or 'management' committees or by enhancing the role of one of the horizontal committees.

The Maud Committee may have been influenced by some of these developments. It was not only outspoken in its criticisms, but radical in its recommendations. It proposed that:

(1) Each local authority should create a small 'management board' of councillors with considerable delegated powers. Its functions would be to develop policy, review progress and generally co-ordinate the work of the council (rather like the Cabinet at central government level).

(2) Committees and departments should be drastically reduced in number (a figure of six was suggested) and certain separate functions should be grouped.

(3) These committees would have deliberative rather than executive responsibilities.

(4) There should be a chief officer for each local authority who should have general management abilities which he should use to supervise and co-ordinate the work of other principal officers and their departments.

(5) More responsibilities should be delegated to officers, and members should generally become less involved in the day-to-day administration of services, decisions on case-work and routine inspection and control.

The Maud Report stimulated a great deal of interest and discussion. But it also provoked much hostility: in whole or in part it was regarded as too radical by many local authorities, who believed that their particular system was adequate to the task. Some argued that the proposed management board would not only be undemocratic but would clash with the principle of the 'collective responsibility' of all councillors. Apart from this, many councillors were afraid of 'losing control' to the officials or of becoming second-class councillors in contrast to the 'elite' appointed to the management board.

However, the Maud Report did cause some local authorities to review their internal organization and procedures, and certain councils began to introduce a number of diluted Maud-type reforms.[4] They received added impetus from the publication of the two Royal Commission reports – the Redcliffe-Maud Report for England and Wales and the Wheatley Report for Scotland – in 1969. Thus there was a reduction in the number of committees and sub-committees[5]; central or 'policy' committees were established; chief executive officers were appointed or clerks had their positions enhanced to give them some formal authority over other chief officers in the authority, who were formed into management teams; departmental functions were amalgamated or grouped and the 'directorate' approach was adopted, chief officers becoming responsible for several areas of activity (such as planning and transportation, or leisure and amenities).

Such moves were encouraged in the 1970s as a result of the reorganization of the local government structures and in particular by the tide of support which accompanied the Bains Report and the Paterson Report. These were the product of two committees set up in 1971 to produce advice on management structures for the new local authorities which were to be established under the reorganization Acts of 1972 (England and Wales) and 1973 (Scotland). These reports were more favourably received than was the Maud Committee Report of 1967, for a number of reasons. In the first place they were not as radical as Maud: all councillors would continue to be substantially involved in the work of the council, as committees were to continue to play an important part, and the controversial idea of a high-powered (some called it 'oligarchical') management board was dropped. Secondly, their recommendations were less dogmatic and presented local authorities with a number of alternative schemes (for the grouping of services, the number and role of committees etc.) from which to choose. Thirdly, the Maud Report had educated (or 'softened up') local authorities to the idea of reform in their internal arrangements. Fourthly, local government was to be comprehensively reorganized and new internal structures would be required: experience of reforming Greater London (1963) has indicated that merely modifying existing structures would not be sufficient to meet the changed circumstances. This view was endorsed by both of the Redcliffe-Maud and Wheatley Royal Commissions (1969). Finally, the Local Government Acts of 1972 and 1973 removed a number of the legal constraints on local government (concerning the compulsory appointment of officers and committees or the scope of delegation), which made it easier for the new authorities to adopt new management structures. However, it has been remarked that 'the extent to which the Bains Report has been accepted is in its own way both exciting and disturbing.'[6]

Bains, Paterson and the 'corporate approach'

The Bains and Paterson Reports of 1972 were very similar both in their general approach and philosophy, and in their detailed recommendations. Similarly they reflected many of the sentiments expressed in the Maud Report and in the Redcliffe-Maud and Wheatley Reports, though they provided more in the way of detail. Above all they emphasized the desirability of a 'corporate' (or integrated) approach to the management of local authority affairs, in contrast to the traditional, departmental approach (so strongly criticized by Maud – see p. 154), which lacked a sufficiently unified attitude towards the development of policies for the locality. Despite the co-ordinating role performed actually or potentially by senior officers (such as the clerk or the finance officer) or by committees (such as the finance committee), the Paterson Report concluded:

In general, the process of formulating policies and devising plans to implement these policies is carried out independently within the various service committees and their respective departments, each making separate recommendations to the full council. Although there is now widespread recognition that the activities of any one committee or department interact to a substantial degree with those of other parts of the organization, particularly in terms of their end-effect on the public, there is still very little in the way of formal co-ordination across the whole range of an authority's activities. (para. 3.5)

Furthermore, although the finance committee could exert some overall influence, its effectiveness was limited because

its members are in no position to assess whether the sum total of the various departmental spending proposals really represents a cohesive programme geared to achieve the authority's objectives; they lack guidelines to assist them in reconciling the competing claims for the services for finance; they are concerned only with the financial implications . . . and not with the deployment of other important elements of resource necessary for the implementation of the programmes. (para. 3.6)

The two reports, then, are concerned with co-ordination, not merely to provide better services and prevent errors (such as housing estates lacking community facilities, or education and housing provisions being out of phase), but also to promote efficiency, avoid wasteful duplication and ensure value for money.[7]

However, there is a third reason for seeking the corporate approach in local government management. The perception of local government should not be

limited to the narrow provision of a series of services to the community ... It has within its purview the overall economic, cultural and physical well-being of the community and for this reason its decisions impinge with increasing frequency upon the lives of its citizens ... Local government is about, and more important, for people. (Bains, paras. 2.10, 2.13)

Such overall responsibility and the interrelationship of problems in the community calls for the wider-ranging, less mutually exclusive, corporate approach. Such an approach is unfortunately limited by the fact that *other* public bodies are responsible for such matters as income maintenance, health services and (except in Scotland) social work with offenders and water supplies.

Corporate management

Both the Bains and Paterson Reports take as their basis a corporate approach to the mangement of local authorities. Management, generally, has been described as consisting of forecasting, planning, organizing, commanding, co-ordinating and controlling.[8] Corporate management aims at securing a unity to these processes, both individually and collectively. For local authorities this implies the development of comprehensive policies and cohesive programmes of action – a unified approach to the formulation and implementation of policies and plans to meet the needs of the community. As the Paterson Report puts it,

The ultimate objective of corporate management is to achieve a situation where the needs of a community are viewed comprehensively and the activities of the local authority are planned, directed and controlled in a unified manner ... (para. 5.3)

The Bains and Paterson Reports both outline management structures to support such an approach, and despite some differences of detail[9] the two sets of proposals are very similar. Thus they recommend that at *councillor* level:

(1) The number of committees should be reduced by organizing them as far as possible on a 'programme area' basis, grouping together those activities which are closely related in terms of their purpose or end-result (such as education, libraries and amenities, or transport, highways and planning).

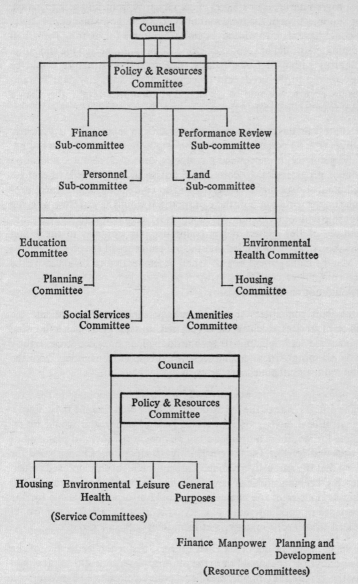

Figure 12 *Sample committee structures proposed by Bains* (upper) *and Paterson* (lower)

These programme areas or spheres of activity arise from, and seek to match, the broad objectives of the local authority. Each of these spheres of activity thus would have its own objectives and programme for meeting them, and the committees would be responsible for each programme and the allocation of resources within it. Consequently, the committee structure would be directly geared to the needs and objectives of the authority, and a 'mini-corporate' approach would be developed at committee level rather than a single-service or departmental view.

(2) A central management committee, which the reports call a Policy & Resources (P&R) committee, should be established to provide co-ordination and guidance to the council on policies, priorities, resource allocation and major programmes, to co-ordinate advice to the council, to exercise overall control over major resources and to co-ordinate and control programme implementation. For these purposes, it would have a close working relationship with other committees, some of which might actually form sub-committees of this central policy committee. (In contrast to the Maud Report, here it is recommended that the pre-eminence of the policy committee – Maud's management board – shall be moderated or balanced by the service committees continuing with a policy-making and executive role: they would not be merely advisory.)

(3) Area joint committees should be set up to plan and co-ordinate the provision of services which are closely related but separated (such as housing and social services in non-metropolitan areas) or provided concurrently (such as planning). These committees would consist of members from the county and district councils in the areas.

(4) At *officer* level, a chief executive officer should be appointed to head the full-time officers' side of the local authority. He would become the council's principal official adviser on matters of general policy and would be responsible for securing co-ordination of advice on the forward planning of objectives and services, for the efficient implementation of policies and for ensuring that the authority's resources are most effectively employed (which implies his keeping under review such matters as the organization and manpower policies of the council). He would also be responsible for the maintenance of good internal and external relations.[10] His key role would be to lead the officers' management team (chief officers' group).

(5) A small group of about six chief officers, under the leadership of the chief executive officer, should form the officers' management team. It would act as the counterpart of the members' policy committee,[11] providing a forum in which chief officers would develop a corporate identity. This team would be responsible for the preparation of plans and programmes in con-

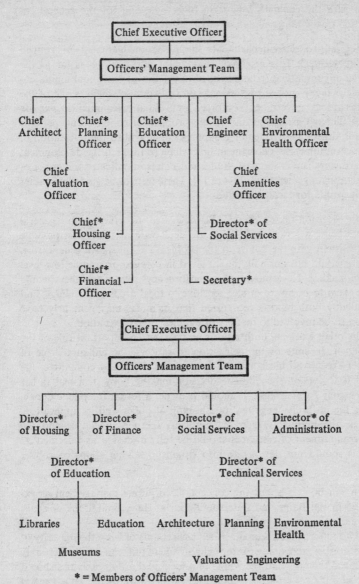

* = Members of Officers' Management Team

Figure 13 *Alternative departmental structures (adapted from the Bains Report)*

nection with the council's long-term objectives, and for the general co-ordination of the implementation of those plans.

(6) Where appropriate, departments should be amalgamated or grouped into 'directorates'. This grouping should not normally go as far as the grouping of committees (recommended in (1) above), since that might jeopardize the highly prized professionalism or expertise which is one of the strengths of local government. Enforced amalgamations might also give rise to some illogical groupings and to the problem of control. But, perhaps above all, drastic departmental groupings might lead to the re-creation of the one-committee/one-department link which so fostered the development of departmentalism in the past. Bains and Paterson indicated a number of alternative arrangements (see Figure 13). These were to be guidelines rather than blueprints for local authorities.

(7) More decision-taking should be delegated to officers, the general principal being asserted that 'issues are dealt with at the lowest possible level consistent with the nature of the problem'.[12] Thus, as a general rule, members would not normally be involved in detailed or routine low-level decision-making. Nevertheless, the 'constituency' role of members would require them to be aware of and sensitive to local needs and feelings, and consequently both reports recognized that members may genuinely have occasion to be involved in matters of detailed policy execution.

At the other extreme, both reports emphasize the important role of the full council. In spite of the delegation to officers, the enhanced role of the chief executive officer and the key role of the policy committee, the council is to remain the ultimate decision-making body in a real rather than a merely formal sense. It should provide 'a forum for public debate and for the open challenge and questioning of policy and its application' ... it is 'the body in which the authority's broad objectives and the major commitment of resources should be fully discussed and decided'.[13] Councils should not degenerate into ritualistic talking shops or rubber stamps.

Much can be said about the concept of corporate management as exemplified in the Bains and Paterson Reports. Here, limitations of space forbid more than a brief comment.

The two reports have been described as accounts of what the minority of local authorities were doing for the enlightenment of the majority. Certainly their central theme – that the whole of a local authority's activities should be carried out by a group of people all working towards the same general end – seems convincing and desirable, and seemed especially so at that time, when local authorities were about to become bigger and cover more diversified geographical areas. Furthermore, in a period of scarce resources, there is an obvious need for their rational allocation, for determining objectives and ordering priorities, and subsequently monitoring results for effectiveness. Not that this necessarily implied restraint or retrenchment: financial management, planning, personnel management and policy in general were to become much more positive and forward-looking instead of simply reacting to events on a piecemeal basis. In short, the multifarious roles of the local authority were to be seen in the round, as a totality. 'Problems do not arise in neat compartments or individual packages, but rather as a tangled, interrelated mass needing a corporate approach to solve them.'[14]

However, some critics quickly denounced the proposals as a 'bureaucrat's charter' and feared that members might become overawed with the new language and procedures and would find it difficult to counter the collective advice coming to them from the officers' management team and the chief executive officer. And there was the fear that the new corporate structures and processes might lead to the general public's becoming further mystified and confused about local government.

Others foresaw the danger of the new approach being implemented because it was fashionable, with local authorities setting up the machinery of corporate management without a proper understanding of how it should work. As Paterson says, 'We would stress that the corporate approach is not merely a question of structure – equally important are the processes needed to sustain it and the genuine willingness of all concerned to make it work . . .' (para. 4.35). Corporate management is 'a total style of management, not merely an isolated technique' (para. 5.1). In particular, there was a fear that old attitudes would persist among committee members and officers, who would identify too closely with *their* service, neighbourhood, political party or interest. In contrast to the Maud Report, the Bains and Paterson Reports had made this more likely by compromising on the matter of committees and giving them an executive rather than a merely advisory or consultative role.[15] In so far as the policy committee consists of service committee chairmen, and the officers' management team of departmental chief officers, effective corporate management would be severely jeopardized, as it would be difficult for these individuals to act otherwise than in a representative or partial capacity.

Similarly, the position of the chief executive in relation to the other chief officers was stated in somewhat ambiguous terms. Paterson says he was to be 'head of the authority's paid service . . . with direct authority over and responsibility for all other officers except . . . where they are exercising their professional judgement'. The Bains Report gives the chief executive the same initial description, but qualifies it by adding:

the range of issues and problems facing any local authority is too numerous and varied for the Chief Executive to grasp in detail, and Heads of Departments must therefore retain the responsibility for the effective and efficient running of the services for which their departments are responsible. (para. 5.13)

This leaves open the question of the relationship between the chief executive and the other chief officers. As head of the paid service, how authoritative is the chief executive to be? Equally uncertain is the relationship between the chief officers and the management team, and, in particular, just how binding upon the officers the decisions of the management team should be.

Local authorities had many decisions to make about how far they would adopt the corporate approach and the ways in which they might adapt the Bains and Paterson models to their particular circumstances. Before we turn to see what has happened, it should be noted that in some respects the work of the two reports was pre-empted by government action. The Local Government Acts of 1972 (England and Wales) and 1973 (Scotland) *required* the appointment of certain chief officers and committees (for education, social work, police etc.). The same legislation also allocated related functions (such as housing and social services or structure and local planning) among different tiers of local authorities (see p. 53). This introduced some constraints and precluded certain organizational possibilities which Bains and Paterson may have considered desirable.

The corporate approach since 1974/5

On a very wide scale, especially in Scotland, local authorities adopted the management recommendations of the Bains and Paterson Reports.[16] Some made adaptations, but others adopted corporate forms without a clear understanding of the requisite relationships and operations for it to work successfully. One study[17] of a sample of local authorities has discovered three broad types of management system in operation:

(1) The 'professional departmental approach' which, while perhaps having the outward appearance of a reformed, corporate system, actually operates in the older, more traditional ways, with policy ideas emerging from the departments and the service committees, the policy committee and management team playing a relatively small co-ordinating role, and the chief executive liable to operate rather like his predecessor (the clerk) and seeing himself as no more than 'first among equals'. Within this arrangement, there is a tendency for the department and committee system to be in a one-to-one relationship, though some inter-departmental working parties may exist. Such arrangements are most likely to be found among the non-metropolitan authorities.

(2) Local authorities with the 'developed corporate approach', as the title suggests, have established corporate structures and operate them in an appropriately corporate fashion, with each part of the machinery fulfilling its proper role – the chief executive acting as policy adviser and director of the officers' management team, which resembles a corporate planning unit and acts in a directing relationship to the individual departments. Similarly, the policy and resources committee sees itself as 'custodian of the corporate plan' and will seek to assert itself over the service or programme committees. Such arrangements are mainly to be found among the urban or metropolitan authorities.

(3) The 'collaborative approach' is found among those local authorities which had developed some corporate processes and were working towards the 'developed' system. These authorities thus exhibit features of the other two systems. Being new authorities based, for the most part, on amalgamations of former councils, they are trying to evolve cautiously and incrementally. Their constituent elements (the policy committee, the chief executive, the management team, the service committees, the interdepartmental working groups) are composed in different ways and exercise varying roles and degrees of ascendancy.

The existence of such variations is in no way surprising. As the research report says, corporate management 'is a phrase to which people react in emotional rather than rational ways' and it is pointed out that many members exhibit a great deal of suspicion of corporate management. The same is true of many chief officers, particularly education officers, some of them believing that their particular service suffers as a result of the corporate approach. Consequently, the assumption of a corporate form of management may be a façade hiding regular inter-committee or departmental battles. Indeed, corporate management has been applied in so many different ways and with so many different levels of understanding that it has 'become a phrase to which it is increasingly difficult to give a real meaning'.[18]

There appears, in fact, to have been something of a retreat from corporate management. Some local authorities unthinkingly adopted the form or machinery of corporate management without the appropriate attitudes and processes. Subsequently, when it did not appear to be working, it was deemed a failure and partly or wholly abandoned. A number of chief executives have either been dropped or have assumed departmental responsibilities. It is perhaps unfortunate that the 'corporate revolution' should have coincided with restraints on public expenditure and strong pressures on local authority resources. Political pressures have compounded this situation, as the opposition parties (usually Conservative) took up the cry of inefficient structures and too much bureaucracy. Thus by the election swings of 1976 and 1977 a head of steam had been built up in many local authorities for change and change away from the existing (corporate) structure.[19]

Other local authorities seem to be weathering the storm, continuing their development of a corporate system. This seems to be due to their having a strong initial commitment to a corporate approach and some early experience of working that system.[20] Thus we see once again the influence of local politics and of the local political culture in shaping the operation of local government.

10. Internal Organization: The Officers

The local government service is the local government equivalent of the civil service, consisting, that is, of paid employees whose job it is to carry out the policy decisions of the elected politicians. Local government officers are therefore 'bureaucrats' in the sense that, in the interests of efficiency and fairness, they are appointed and promoted on merit rather than fear or favour, and they do their work (such as allocating school places, grants or council houses) impartially and in accordance with the council's declared policy and rules of procedure. This is not to deny that they may become 'bureaucrats' in the pejorative sense of becoming slow, rigid, unsympathetic and, above all, exercising power without being held to public account. As we shall see, there are mechanisms and procedures which seek to minimize such undesirable tendencies.

Like the civil service (of 600,000 members), local government employment is large, with 2⅓ million members (see Table 15). Unlike the civil service, however, it is not really one single service: each local authority recruits and employs its own staff. There is no single employing body, and local govern-

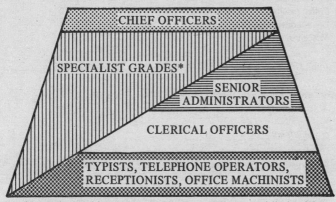

*Includes architects, accountants, engineers, public health inspectors, social workers, technicians

Figure 14 *The structure of local government service*

ment officers cannot be posted from one part of the country to another, as a civil servant can. In practice, however, salaries and conditions of service have become substantially standardized throughout the country as a result of the emergence of national negotiating machinery, trade unions and the Local Government Training Board (see p. 172).

Table 15 shows the large number of different kinds of employee in local government. Traditionally, they are divided into 'officers' (professional, technical and clerical staff, or 'white-collar workers') and 'servants' ('blue collar', or manual workers, including refuse collectors, gardeners, cleaners or road workmen). Each group has its own conditions of service, superannuation provisions and negotiating machinery.

Table 15. *Local authority manpower, 1979 (full-time or equivalent)*

Education: teachers	629,312
others	467,058
Construction	155,336
Transport	31,688
Libraries and museums	37,453
Recreation, parks, baths, tourism	97,767
Environmental health	25,200
Cleaning, refuse collection and disposal	60,852
Housing	54,256
Social services	234,653
Town and country planning	24,369
Fire service	45,892
Police (including cadets, wardens etc.)	172,521
Local courts and probation staff	17,599
Miscellaneous	303,876
Total (= 9% of national workforce)	2,358,686

Source: *Department of Employment Gazette*, January 1980.

Occupational groups	
Chief officers	0·2%
Administrative, professional, technical and clerical	20%
Teachers, police, firemen	30%
Manual	50%
	100

However, there is a third group of employees whose existence is crucial to local government but who are classified neither as officers nor as servants. These are the teachers, firemen and the police. In this chapter we are primarily concerned with the first group, the officers: it is they (about ½ million) who form what is known as the 'local government service'.[1]

Negotiating machinery

Since 1944, local government has developed a national negotiating machinery known as the National Joint Council for Local Authorities Services. This comprises a number of separate committees, about forty in all, covering such occupational groups as firemen, youth leaders, manual workers, engineering craftsmen and teachers. Their function is to negotiate national salary scales and conditions of service. There are thus two 'sides' involved – the employers (or management side) and the employees (the staff side). In practice, the employers' side is drawn from representatives of the local authorities' associations (such as the Association of County Councils – see p. 246) and the staff side from the trade unions such as NALGO and NUPE.

The multiplicity of negotiating bodies makes the negotiating machinery very complex and liable to create inconsistencies and unfairness, as well as being difficult to operate. However, the problems have been reduced by the creation in 1948 of an advisory and co-ordinating body, the Local Authorities Conditions of Service Advisory Board (LACSAB). Apart from advising on pay and conditions and giving guidance on implementation, it also provides such services as information and recommendations on general legislation, reports on how national decisions are working out in practice and responds to requests for advice on specific issues. In addition, at regional level, there are Provincial Councils which keep the national bodies in touch with local opinion on conditions of service matters. They also oversee and assist with the local implementation of national agreements and hear local disputes and staff appeals.

The terms and conditions of employment resulting from the negotiations – sometimes called 'Whitleyism' – are implemented by individual local authorities (except parishes and community councils, to which the agreements do not apply), although the agreements only provide guidelines for minimum rather than necessary conditions, and local authorities are free to improve conditions where they see fit. Where a local authority fails to meet the minimum agreed provisions, employees can appeal through the well-established machinery. It is perhaps ironic, though probably inevitable, that individual councils are advised on matters of implementation by their officers, that is their employees.

Officers and conditions of service

In this chapter we are primarily concerned with the administrative and professional staff of local government – the officers. These comprise various grades and statuses: the professional and specialist officers; general (or 'lay') administrators; technicians; and clerical and other office staff. These are generally referred to as 'the APT & C' grades. Under the Local Government Acts of 1972 and 1973 local authorities are required to 'appoint such officers as they think necessary for the proper discharge by the authority of such of their . . . functions as fall to be discharged by them'. Certain officers are however required by law to be appointed: these include Chief Education Officers, Directors of Social Services, members of fire brigades and Chief Constables.

All such officers 'hold office on such reasonable terms and conditions . . . as the local authority think fit' (Section 112). Some – the chief officers – have their own separate national negotiating machinery. But for the majority of local government officers their conditions of employment are determined by the National Joint Council for the Administrative, Professional, Technical and Clerical staffs, and these conditions are set out in a detailed scheme [2] sometimes called the 'charter' or 'purple book'. This originated in 1946 and represented a breakthrough in the establishment of the principle of equal pay for equal work throughout the country (except for the GLC, which has its own scheme). Previously the rates of pay varied haphazardly among local authorities, partly as a result of local trade-union pressure and partly as a consequence of local party politics. However, variations will still occur, partly because of local authorities' differing management structures and partly because of variations in the local employment situation.

The National Joint Council for the APT & C staffs is regularly negotiating and reviewing the scheme of conditions of employment. As a result there will be regular adjustments in hours, holidays, leave of absence, sickness payments and above all salaries.

Salaries and grading

Apart from certain (designated) chief officers, the scheme divides the staff of the local government service into three groups (there were five up to 1983), each with a number of salary scales:

(1) *Administrative, professional, technical and clerical (APT&C)*. The salary (over six scales in 1984) ranges over £2,703–£8,712 for those doing *clerical* work (such as filing, checking documents, processing claims for grants or other payments) or *technical* work (such as that of draughtsman, building inspector and engineering, laboratory, planning or accounting technician).

There is also a *trainee* grade and scale (£2,703–£6,135). The actual salary scale will vary according to degree of responsibility and level of work undertaken. Thus there is a salary range for *senior officers* of £9,060–£10,539 and for *principal officers* of £9,945–£15,357. These latter posts are available for the more experienced and qualified officers, and it is here that we find education officers, housing officers, planners, lawyers, accountants and engineers. Their work often involves controlling large or important sections of a department and the leadership of teams of officers. At the top are the *chief officers*, whose work involves giving advice on policy and managing whole departments or groups of departments. Their salaries can range over £11,922–£27,711, but the actual levels will depend on the size of the local authority and its population. In England and Wales, chief executive officers have a separate salary scale from other chief officers, currently £15,426–£35,478 (the Director General of the GLC receives £40,000).

(2) *Special classes*, which comprise a variety of occupational groups – librarians, careers officers, public health inspectors, weights and measures inspectors, social workers, shorthand-typists, machine operators and secretaries. Each has its own grade and salary scale e.g. social workers £6,264–£9,660.

(3) *Miscellaneous*, which comprises another range of occupational groupings such as meals supervisors, telephone supervisors and traffic wardens whose duties are neither wholly clerical nor wholly manual. The range is £3,849–£7,404.

Generally speaking, grading in all posts depends on such factors as experience and level of responsibility as well as qualifications. This gives each local authority some discretion in grading posts in relation to the national scheme.

Recruitment, appointment and promotion

Recruitment to local government has traditionally relied on the grammar school leaver. Before the Second World War local government provided an occupation opportunity with some status and security. Entrants were expected to study and gain professional qualifications (in law, engineering, housing administration etc.). Since the war (at least until recently), local government has faced competition from other employers and as a consequence has either had to lower its entrance requirements or has moved 'up market' to recruit A-level students and graduates.[3]

Appointment is based on (desirable) bureaucratic principles: the aim is to appoint on the basis of merit and eliminate the possibility of nepotism or favouritism. Any relationship between a candidate and a councillor or

officer of the authority must be disclosed, and canvassing for an appointment is prohibited (though it still occurs[4]).

Promotion too is based on merit or performance as well as qualifications.
Officers, especially young clerical entrants, are encouraged to move among
departments in order to obtain a wider administrative experience. Officers
are also generally encouraged to undertake approved courses of education
and training to obtain qualifications, especially those in the administrative
and professional grades: the aim is to develop certain skills and promote in
officers a broader and more positive interest in their daily duties.

The education and training of local government officers has long been
exhorted by NALGO.[5] And, although well developed (e.g. the Local
Government Examinations Board was established in 1945), it was given a
substantial impetus with the setting-up of the Local Government Training
Board in 1967. By helping to spread the costs of training among local
authorities, the aim was to deal with the problem of the small authorities
which had difficulties in financing the training of their staff; it also aimed at
stopping the less training-conscious authorities 'poaching' trained staff from
other authorities.

The underlying purpose of this training is to increase the effectiveness of
local government manpower. Training courses include induction, training
in clerical skills, training for supervision, preparation for administrative
and professional qualifications, and instruction in the principles of
management. Some training is carried out at work itself or at home
(through correspondence courses), but a great deal is given in colleges and
polytechnics on a day-release or block-release basis. A number of higher
management courses are provided by the University of Birmingham's
Institute of Local Government Studies (INLOGOV). However, while
education and training have much expanded over the past fifteen years, its
cost is now being more carefully counted, and there is a growing insistence
that training should be job-related and effective.

Security of tenure

The substantial security enjoyed by local government officers is well known,
and in the past has proved an attractive feature of local government employment. However, local government officers can be relegated, suspended
or dismissed on grounds related to discipline or efficiency – for example
persistent lateness or absenteeism. And an officer's employment can be
terminated where a 'closed shop' (trade-union monopoly) exists, as it does
in a number of local authorities (though much depends on the political
composition of the council). Local government employees can also be made
redundant – no longer an empty threat in these days of expenditure cuts.

Local government officers must not only behave properly, but they must be seen (by the public) so to behave. The APT & C scheme (p. 170) states:

The public is entitled to demand of a local government officer conduct of the highest standard and public confidence in his integrity would be shaken were the least suspicion ... to arise that he could in any way be influenced by improper motives.

As a consequence and to reinforce this general goal a number of precepts are laid down:

An officer's off-duty hours are his personal concern, but he should not subordinate his duty to his private interests or put himself in a position where his duty and his private interests conflict.

An example might be taking on an inappropriate part-time job such as a local authority planner or architect undertaking technical or presentational work for an applicant for planning permission.

No officer shall communicate to the public the proceedings of any committee meeting etc., nor the contents of any document relating to the authority unless required to do so by law or expressly authorized to do so.

If it comes to the knowledge of an officer that a contract in which he has any pecuniary interest ... has been, or is proposed to be, entered into by the authority, he shall ... give notice ...

It is difficult to know how far employees live up to these standards. Statistics for the period 1965–75 show that ninety local government employees (including forty dustmen and seventeen policemen) were convicted of offences under the Prevention of Corruption Act (see note 4),[4] and for the period 1967–79 about 1,000 cases of fraud were reported, though this 'does not indicate extensive dishonesty having regard to the scale of local government operations, and many of the sums [frauds] include very small sums'.[6] (Most of the offenders here were those who generally handled small amounts of money. The (illegal) offering of gift vouchers as inducements to local officers who order products for councils appears to be quite widespread among major firms.) Furthermore, officers can be placed in awkward situations when they suspect or allege corruption among their colleagues or councillors: they risk possible victimization and pressure to resign.[7]

Politics

Another potentially hazardous area for local government officers is party politics. The APT & C scheme declares that the officer

... should not be called upon to advise any political group of the employing authority either as to the work of the group or as to the work of the authority, neither shall he be required to attend any meeting of any political group.

A similar provision exists in the conditions of service of chief officers. The aim is to reinforce the political impartiality of the local government service, which, like the civil service, is expected to show disinterested loyalty to whichever political party group controls the council. The situation can be more difficult in local government because parties are a new phenomenon for many authorities, and because local government officers are responsible to the council as a whole rather than to the council chairman or committee chairmen. (Civil servants are responsible to individual Ministers, not to Parliament as such. However, the question is sometimes raised there whether the Opposition, or indeed M Ps generally, should be briefed by officials: see *The Times*, 21 August 1984.) Meanwhile, for local government the questions remain to be decided among the local authorities: should (chief) officers develop special relationships with the majority party and its leaders? Should they appear at party caucus meetings, as a growing number appear to be doing, and if so on what conditions? How should they balance this relationship with the minority parties and the council as a whole?

There is a strong convention that local government officers, especially more senior staff, should refrain from open support of political parties. Otherwise members might lose confidence in the impartiality and objectivity of professional advice and may doubt the speed, enthusiasm or even the direction with which their decisions were being implemented by the officials. Similarly members of the public might come to suspect that they were not receiving fair treatment from their local administrators.

However, while we as a society restrict the political rights of local government officers, we compensate them with security of tenure: we do not (as in the so-called 'spoils system') change our officials when we change (by election) our council. Nor do we elect our officials (as in some parts of America, where they may elect their 'strong' or executive mayor). Like civil service employees, British local government officers are 'permanent' (subject to what has been said on p. 172).

The law also intervenes to keep officials away from party politics by making membership of a local authority legally incompatible with paid employment by that authority.[8] This does not altogether prevent an officer from becoming a councillor, since he is free to stand for election and serve as an elected member for *another* local authority. Clearly this may jeopardize the principle of official impartiality, especially where the candidates fight the election under party banners. However, a concerned local authority can insist that an officer does not 'put himself in a position where his duty and his private interests conflict'. Indeed, under the scheme senior officers must obtain the consent of the council before 'engaging in any other business or take up any other additional appointment'.

It has, however, been argued that this disqualification for council membership is no longer valid, particularly for the majority of the two million employees in local government who play no part in policy advice or formulation. Apart from depriving employees of their rights as citizens to take part in the civic life of their community, it denies both to local government and the public the benefits of the pool of skill, experience and enthusiasm which such employees may possess. In addition it is argued that local government should follow the tendency of other forms of employment towards greater participation by employees in decision-making. (In practice, some local authorities such as Basildon, Slough and Hampshire have allowed manual and staff workers speaking rights at council and committee meetings.) The Committee on Conduct in Local Government (HMSO, 1974) considered these arguments but concluded that it was in the public interest that the law should remain unchanged. However, the issue is being kept alive by the trade unions and by the publication of the Bullock Report on industrial democracy.[9]

The role of local government officers

The primary task of local government officers is to implement the policy decisions of the council. In the Middle Ages everyone was expected to spend a few days in the year making up the local roads, whereas highway engineering today requires skill and training, as do all modern local government services – social work, housing maintenance, planning, architecture. Elected councillors themselves lack both the experience and the time: hence they employ full-time paid officers.

Not all officers are directly concerned with the delivery of services. Many are providing back-up or support services. Just as local authorities have 'vertical' (or service) and 'horizontal' (or functional) committees (see p. 150), so they have vertical departments (such as the education department and the social services department) and horizontal departments (such as finance). Officials in the latter departments help only indirectly to implement policy. Their immediate function is to provide support services for the other, 'delivering', departments.

A third and perhaps less obvious role of officials is to advise on policy. It is no longer possible these days (if it ever was) to say that members make policy and officers merely carry it out. Officers, especially senior officers, not only have experience and professional training: they also have a commitment to their service – whether in education, social work or engineering. As a result they will have ideas, pet schemes and ambitions which will inevitably be communicated to councillors, especially committee chairmen. In some ways it is true to say that the members' task is to keep a rein on officials' enthusiasm and tell them what the public will not stand! Apart from the fact that ideas will emerge from the administrative process itself, administrative experience provides other lessons. Officers too will exercise a negative influence, checking members' exuberance and advising them what is not feasible (for legal, financial or other reasons) or warning them of possible snags and suggesting alternatives. This officer–member relationship is explored further below (p. 183).

The chief officers

Chief officers head the departments, or, in some cases, as 'directors', groups of departments. (The exception is the chief executive officer – C E O – who, following the Bains recommendation, in most local authorities does not have a department. See Chapter 9 and p. 178.) Although in any one day most of the work of chief officers is totally unpredictable, their work generally falls into four general areas or directions, each of which involves a combination of administration and politics, in the non-party sense of the word.

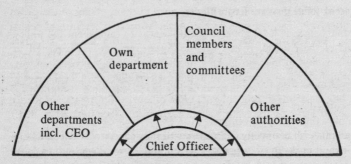

Figure 15 *A chief officer's domain*

(1) Working within their own department. Here they exercise an administrative or managerial role – overseeing the execution of policy, being responsible for the allocation of work and the general standards and efficiency of working methods, staff appointments, discipline and general morale and leadership. Apart from managing the current work of the department, chief officers also see their role as a policy-formulating one (see pp. 185–7). When the chief officer is heavily involved in working outside his department, some of this work, especially the management aspect, is likely to be shared with or devolved upon their deputies, who are most frequently appointed in the county authorities.[10]

(2) Working with other departments. This is likely to involve a lot of the chief officer's time in councils where the corporate approach has been

developed and inter-departmental mechanisms have been instituted (such as officers' management teams and inter-departmental working parties – see pp. 160 and 178). This is particularly likely in the case of the larger authorities, but there are differences among the departments, especially between the service (vertical) departments and the function (horizontal) departments such as the chief executive's or treasurer's. A particular problem for chief officers is balancing the claims of their individual departments with those of the authority as a whole (as represented by the CEO).

(3) Working outside the department with other authorities. This would involve relations with other local authorities (such as district councils) and liaison with government departments (such as the local DHSS or MSC Job Centre) and semi-government bodies (such as the Health Authority or the Forestry Commission). Some chief officers have direct links with Whitehall departments or their regional outposts in, for example, discussions over educational matters, building programmes or local government finance. In addition many chief officers act as advisers to the local authority associations (see p. 246), they are frequently engaged in the activities of their own professional associations such as the Association of Directors of Social Services (ADSS) or the Society of Local Authority Chief Executives (SOLACE) and all of them are expected to play some part in the public relations side of their department, including relations with the media and pressure groups. The actual amount of time involved here will vary, especially among departments and different types of local authority (the incidence being heaviest among the metropolitan authorities). (See note 10, p. 334.)

(4) Working with councillors. This occurs mainly in the formal setting of committees, but involves a considerable amount of time in preparations for committees, including the briefing of committee chairmen before meetings. Again certain officers are more heavily involved than others: the treasurer or secretary are called on to attend many committees. The Maud Committee (1967) was critical of the extent to which members were involved in the detailed aspects of administration (for instance, choosing furniture or colour schemes for homes or constituting selection committees for minor posts such as junior library assistant). The Committee urged greater delegation of authority to officers, with members concentrating on broader policy matters (especially in the management board – see p. 155) and on their representative or constituency roles (especially in their non-executive committees). As we have seen (p. 157), the general tenor of the Maud Committee was endorsed by the Bains and Paterson Reports, but they were less radical (and arguably more persuasive) in their detailed recommendations. Consequently, it is interesting to observe that there is a feeling among some officers that members are becoming increasingly involved in departmental administration

(with more regular visits to the departments etc.) to the extent that some of them, especially committee chairmen, are becoming virtually full-time.[11]

Departmental reform

Despite the strictures of the Maud Report and the recommendations of the Bains and Paterson Reports, the number and form of local authority departments have not changed greatly, especially in England and Wales. Few local authorities have adopted a thoroughgoing directorate approach (of grouping departments). Most have retained the traditional departmental/professional structure, but with some inter-departmental links such as programme teams (sometimes known as the matrix system).[12] Where the directorate form has been adopted in substance (not merely in change of title), it has been mostly in the areas of technical or recreational services.

Change has been much more dramatic in the formal designation of a head of the officer structure. By 1975 only one major local authority in England and Wales had not appointed a chief executive officer.[13] Most of them had been given, at least formally, the responsibilities recommended by Bains and Paterson, with the important exception that a large minority had given their chief executive a department. These local authorities argued that a non-departmental chief executive officer would become too detached and isolated. For the most part, their departmental responsibilities involve such central support services functions as personnel, management services, public relations, corporate planning and research. This is in contrast to the functions of the traditional and largely superseded clerk's department, which was responsible for legal services, committee administration and electoral registration. The latter responsibilities are now usually in the hands of the local authorities' secretary or chief administrative officer.

In the appointment of chief executives, local authorities were urged[14] to have regard to managerial ability above all. Professional and technical expertise and background should no longer be the main criterion (as in the appointment of other chief officers and as traditionally in the appointment of lawyers as clerks). The top local government post therefore was to be an open field to officers from any background. The Mallaby Committee in particular envisaged a place for 'lay' administrative officers (that is, officers whose work in local government is of a general administrative nature, like that of the top civil servants, rather than those who specialize in education, finance or engineering). In practice, local authorities have tended to appoint their former Clerk (or Town Clerk) to the post of chief executive, although some have appointed treasurers. Only a few have gone outside local government (for instance to the civil service, the water industry or the district audit service) for their appointments.[15]

A third area of change in the administrative arrangements at officer level is in the universal creation in the 1970s of officers' management teams (OMTs) or chief officers' groups (COGs). In the early 1960s these were rare; by 1970 more than half the local authorities had them; by 1975 all local authorities had them. There are, however, variations in the size of these teams, in the proportion of chief officers included and in the frequency of their meetings.[16] A few councils have developed joint councillor–officer management committees.

Management services

(a) Personnel management

The Bains Report argued that local government tended to lag behind industry and other areas of the public service in its recognition and development of the personnel management function:

> There must be a greater awareness of the importance of personnel management in local government. Manpower is a leading resource of any authority and must be properly deployed. The appointment of the senior officer responsible for personnel management is crucial . . . (p. xv)

Personnel and establishment officers had traditionally confined themselves to the oversight and administration of salaries and conditions of service. Bains and Paterson emphasized that they should take a wider and more positive approach to promote the effectiveness of (costly) human resources and to create opportunities for flexibility and change when it becomes necessary. Thus personnel management should encompass manpower planning, recruitment techniques, training, career development and industrial relations.

In practice, while the personnel function has received greater recognition by local government, it has not achieved the important role envisaged by Bains.[17] This is partly because it is new to many councils and is having to establish itself at a time of economic restraint and expenditure cuts. But it is also due to the distrust shown by many chief officers who

> . . . see it as negative rather than positive . . . as being there to stop them doing what they want to do, and what they are there to do. They feel that personnel does not understand the professional needs and difficulties of the departments.[17]

Furthermore, the personnel function tends to react to events rather than initiate activities:

> Frequently it has to wait to be consulted by other officers on questions of staffing, or possibly even industrial questions. Frequently also O & M and work study are dependent on requests from chief officers, committees or the unions. These problems

are heightened where employees are seen as being employed by the department rather than the authority.[17]

(b) Management techniques

The Maud Report recommended that local authorities should adopt 'a systematic approach to the processes of management'. Subsequently local authorities have taken an increasing interest in management processes, techniques and services. Impetus was added by the creation of the Local Authorities Management Services and Computer Committee (LAMSAC) in 1967. (This body's function is to co-ordinate research, development and training, to establish a central information library and to act as a clearing house for local authorities. It co-operates with the government and other bodies and advises local authorities on latest management services.)

Management services help management to plan, control and improve the activities of the organization. Broadly their role is either to assist the planning and decision-making process or to promote the efficiency of execution. Some of the services will be grouped and centralized in a Management Services Unit; others may be dispersed and utilized in individual departments. The following is a brief description of the main management techniques.[18]

Planning, Programming and Budgeting Systems (PPBs) have been defined as a method of analysing programmed expenditure by reference to particular objectives rather than under input headings such as staff, buildings and equipment. It is thus concerned with the scheduling and measuring of the 'output' of local government (such as the number of old people rehoused or the miles of road re-surfaced) in relation to expenditure.[19] A similar technique is *management by objectives* (MbO), which generally seeks to pinpoint key tasks and set work targets for officers.

More measurable or quantifiable forms of work may be set targets as a result of *work study*. As the name implies this involves the investigation of work processes and the various factors which affect their operation (such as the layout of the office) with a view to improving their efficiency. It is often used as the basis for incentive bonus schemes, in refuse collection for example. It may also be used for job evaluation and the grading of posts.

Organization and methods (O & M) is concerned with the structure of an organizational unit and the way in which that unit operates to achieve its objectives. It is often applied to administrative arrangements to secure more efficient methods, for example by simplifying procedures and delegating more routine clerical operations so as to enable the professional staff to devote more time to their professional work.

Operational research (OR) is used to establish a more rational or scientific basis for management decision-making. It uses complex mathematical techniques, and local authorities receive information and guidance from the Local Government Operational Research Unit (established in 1965). The technique has been applied to operations such as refuse disposal, purchasing methods and urban planning.[20]

Another decision-making technique is *cost-benefit analysis* (CBA). This attempts to go beyond the immediate direct (or primary) costs and benefits of a service or project by taking into account the indirect or 'external' costs and benefits. Many of the latter are intangible and difficult to measure, since they involve social considerations. For example, the relative financial cheapness of high-rise dwellings may be offset by the social costs of the possible family distress they cause. But this analysis does have the merit of extending perspectives, of reducing to statistical terms matters which would otherwise be the subject of unscientific value judgements and of facilitating detailed consideration of alternative courses of action.

Network analysis may be used once a new project has been approved. It aims at providing a plan of action by analysing the project into component parts and recording them on an arrow network diagram. The implementation stages and the inter-relationships of the various activities then become clear and the work – such as school building or engineering projects – can be programmed. This procedure can give rise to a number of ancillary techniques such as *critical path analysis* (CPA), *programme evaluation and review* (PERT) and *resources allocation and multi-project scheduling* (RAMPS).

Many of these procedures will involve substantial use of the *computer*. Its advantages stem from its ability to store masses of information and solve very complex problems with speed and accuracy.

How efficient is local government?

It is not easy to measure local government efficiency, since there are no indices of success as there are in the business world (such as profits or market penetration figures). Local government has to satisfy three criteria;

(1) *Relevance:* Is the local authority doing the right thing, pursuing the right policies, providing the appropriate service? A local authority's operations may be highly efficient but they may be irrelevant to the problems to be solved. Should local authorities engage in such activities as housing, refuse collection or transport services or should these be left to private enterprise or other public bodies? The answer to this will depend on one's moral and political values as well as economic considerations. There is no simple test of what is 'right' for local government.

(2) *Effectiveness:* If it is accepted that local authorities should provide certain services, such as welfare for children or the elderly, they may still be wasteful of resources even if they are efficient in making such provision. This may be due to their pursuing the wrong policies which limit the effectiveness of the operations. For example, a local authority may be building residential homes more cheaply than ever before or more cheaply than other local authorities, but residential care may not be contributing much to the needs of deprived children or the elderly.

(3) *Efficiency:* Having identified a correct course of action, the local authority must seek to operate efficiently so that its actions are in themselves not wasteful, extravagant or incompetent. There is certainly a danger of inefficiency in this sense, since local authorities do not have the financial discipline of the market: they cannot make losses since they have the power of taxation. Furthermore, how does one measure inefficiency or extravagance? How much time should a social worker spend with a client? How many hours per week should a GCE student receive in tuition? Some guidance can be obtained by making comparisons with other authorities, but such comparisons are difficult because local authorities vary considerably in their physical, social and economic characteristics. Local authorities' internal audit (see p. 216) and the government's external audit [21] may provide a check, as they detect unreasonable expenditure. But traditionally their function is to investigate the legality of financial transactions (for example that the correct fees have been charged and collected).

The various management techniques outlined above all seek to improve the efficiency of local government operations. But many people are sceptical of the progress in this field,[22] pointing to the growth in local government manpower and rising local government costs (reflected in the rates). Much of this is, of course, due to inflation (labour costs absorb some 70 per cent of local government expenditure) and part is due to the increased responsibilities which the government has until recently placed on local authorities. Undoubtedly some is also due to improved conditions of service (itself enhanced by the growth in trade-union activity in local government). Reorganization in the 1970s, with its widespread upgradings and golden handshakes, also added to costs, at least in the short run.

Perhaps the most significant change which is taking place is in the area of programme or output budgeting. Traditional indicators of performance in local government have been in terms of inputs: in the size and funding of the authority and its services (and so to a large extent local authorities have been more interested in improving – that is, expanding – services than merely reducing rates). Much more attention is now being given to performance and output measurement. This involves the clarification of objectives and the devising of techniques to measure the achievement of those objectives. Expenditure is thus considered in terms of its purpose or the activity it finances, for example the tons of rubbish collected per dustman, or in housing, the number of dwellings improved to a planned standard, or in education, the number of children acquiring basic skills by a given age.[23]

However, useful as such steps are, there are problems, especially in defining suitable output measures for many services and in particular those of administrative personnel. (Bains suggested that their performance should be subject to an annual review.)

Local authorities face other problems in trying to give value for money. Councillors, as elected politicians, may wish to see reductions in overall expenditure and rates, but will urge particular expenditures, especially for their own localities. And unlike their opposite numbers in the business world, the top managers (chief officers) are not autonomous: the chief executive officer does not have the authority of a managing director of a company or an American 'city manager' to 'hire and fire', and the chairman of the council or of a major committee has nothing like the authority of the chairman of a public company. Besides, broadly speaking local authorities are anxious to avoid redundancies; as good employers, they are normally conscious of their responsibilities as regards the employment situation in their areas. But perhaps the biggest contrast to the business world is local government's system of dual management. We consider this below.

Member-officer relationships

The traditional view of the relationship between members and officers is that of master and servant: the council issues orders and the officers carry them out. Such a view is based on the rational, democratic principle that councillors are elected to make policy decisions and the expert is engaged to execute those decisions. Furthermore, the law appears to support such a view: in the Bognor Regis case (1965) the Q C conducting the inquiry concluded that

. . . if a Clerk is not answerable to his council he is answerable to no one. In my view he is the employee of his council and it is to them that his primary loyalty and duty lie and it is to them that he is answerable for his actions.[24]

In practice, the notion that the council formulates policy is substantially qualified by the fact that many responsibilities are delegated to officers (especially since the Local Government Acts of 1972 and 1973). But a more important modification lies in the long-standing fact that local government officers advise the council and its committees. This is both inevitable and desirable: after all the officers are full-time and permanent, and with training and experience acquire considerable expertise. Members can therefore scarcely avoid placing considerable reliance on their judgement: the range of policy and individual matters of administration is too great to be managed by part-time members. According to the Maud Report:

> In nearly two-thirds of the authorities we consulted officers were said to make a significant contribution to the initiation of policy and in nearly a quarter they were said to play the major part.[25]

It is this advisory role which was clearly articulated in the Maud Report, which consequently, in the words of the Bains Report, 'exploded the myth of policy being a matter for the elected members and administration for officers'.

> We do not believe that it is possible to lay down what is policy and what is administrative detail; some issues stand out patently as important and can be regarded as 'policy'; other matters, seemingly trivial, may involve political or social reaction of such significance that deciding them becomes a matter of policy and members feel that they must reserve to themselves consideration and decision on them. A succession of detailed decisions may contribute, eventually, to the formulation of a policy . . . policy making can arise out of particular problems when consideration of a new case leads to the determination of general guides to action which have a general application.[26]

Thus administrative details shade imperceptibly into policy and both officers and members therefore play a part in policy-making and in detailed administration. Bains refers to it as the 'dual nature of management' and likens it (in the words of one witness to the committee) to a scale or spectrum, with the setting of objectives and allocation of major resources at one end, moving through the designing of programmes and plans, to the execution of those plans at the other end. At all points on the scale, both the elected and the official elements are involved, but to varying degrees. This may be illustrated as follows:

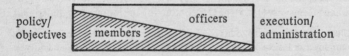

policy/objectives | officers | execution/administration
members

Points of contact

This duality appears in a number of settings. Some of these are *formal*, such as council meetings, committees, joint meetings with other local or regional and central authorities, and ceremonial occasions. There may, for example, be joint meetings of the officers' management team and the P & R committee, and many chief officers attend meetings of the P & R committee as a matter of course. *Semi-official* meetings take place at site visits, disaster areas (such as those damaged by flood), party caucus meetings or in departments when a councillor calls in to discuss a constituency matter. Finally, officers and members may meet *informally* at the club, in the pub or at civic socials. It is usually assumed that the most important of these is the first, particularly committee meetings. At this level there is a close relationship between chief officers and committee chairmen (and vice-chairmen). This situation may be changing somewhat in so far as councils are setting up panels or 'working groups' of officers and members with the task of examining particular issues or areas in order to discover the facts or possible courses of action rather than make any decisions. In addition, in so far as programme committees have been formed, the committee chairmen will each have to relate to a number of chief officers rather than develop a close working relationship with just one.

In the traditional setting, this close relationship between the chairman and the chief officer was the result of their working in their particular service area (education, social services, finance etc.). The chairman would be in regular contact with the department; he may have had an office there; he would attend pre-committee briefing meetings (and perhaps agenda meetings) so as to be kept informed of latest developments before the formal committee takes place. And in the meantime he may be called upon to make decisions or approve the actions of the senior officers.

Where the power lies

Sir John Maud, himself an ex-civil servant, was concerned that members were getting too involved in matters of day-to-day administration at the expense of the officers, whose capacities were thus being under-utilized. Consequently the Maud Report recommended:

It is members who should take and be responsible for the key decisions on objectives, and on the means and plans to attain them. It is they who must periodically review the position as part of their function of directing and controlling. It is the officers who should provide the necessary staff work and advice which will enable the members to identify the problems, set the objectives and select the means and plans to attain them. It is the officer who should direct and co-ordinate the necessary action, and see that material is presented to enable members to review progress and check performance.[27]

However, more people see the problem not as one of too much interference in administration by members but rather as one of too much influence on policy by officials: that is, they see the problem as one of 'bureaucracy'. After all, members are amateurs (non-experts), they are part-time and they are (largely) unpaid. They can therefore be easily dominated by the full-time professionals, especially when they adopt the corporate approach, with its seemingly conspiratorial groupings, its somewhat alien language and its co-ordinated advice which is so plausible and persuasive.

Such dominance by officials may occur because of their superior knowledge, and this may be the product of the way central government relates to local authorities, i.e. dealing with officers rather than councillors, even to the latters' exclusion. For example, in 1982 government inspectors' (H M Is) reports on the effects of expenditure cuts on education provision in certain LEAs were sent to chief officers under conditions of such confidentiality that in some cases elected members were not given the information.[28] (In February 1982 a councillor was denied access to council records by Lord Denning in the Court of Appeal[29] – which is similar to, but not the same as the position of M Ps since the latter have no responsibility for administration as councillors have.)

Sir Horace Cutler, a former Conservative leader of the G L C (1977–81) recently declared that 'it is because we have not enough people with discernment that officials are able to take advantage of elected members and do very much as they please . . . Paper is useful in baffling councillors when bureaucrats want to get their own way. Documents go on endlessly when it would be perfectly possible to reduce them to the important facts. As a result, policies can be manipulated and distorted so that they slip through in a totally different fashion from what was intended.'[30]

A more striking lack of trust between members and officers was vividly revealed in Walsall Borough Council in 1980. Here the Labour members suspected that when they gained office after the elections officials would undermine or thwart their policies. Consequently, to help secure the achievement of their manifesto objectives, they declared their intention of appointing only officers whose social awareness was 'akin to Labour philosophy'. (Such 'politicization' of officials is similar to the 'spoils' system operating in the USA whereby the top levels of the civil service are replaced when a new party gains the Presidency.) A more moderate approach (which models itself on recent central government practices in Britain and longer experience in France) is being tried in some local authorities: here, special advisers are brought in to advise the council (the majority party) on policy or to help keep policy running in line with party ideology or plans.

The general premise here then is that local government is run by officials; they are 'statesmen in disguise', and the existence of elected members merely provides a democratic veneer.

Such a view is no more tenable than that of the ever-meddling councillor. However, to say that the true situation lies somewhere in between is too simple. There may well be authorities which are substantially run by the officers; and there may be those in which weak or intimidated officers push upwards to councillors trivial administrative decisions. However, it is quite possible to have a combination of these situations so that councillors become heavily involved in routine administrative decisions (see p. 155) while effective control and initiation of major policy decisions rest with the officers. A chief officer has suggested that 'Local government is full of transvestites, members who want to take control of detail and officers who want to make policy.' (See note 10.) Furthermore there can be variations among departments within the same authority. In one authority, although the housing manager could himself sanction all repairs and maintenance work below a total of £3·5 million, the children's officer could spend only £10 per case without reference to the committee.[31]

Undoubtedly officers can and do exert substantial influence, since most of the discussion at committee meetings is based on the reports drawn up by senior officers. Most of these reports are well-informed and often based on the guidelines of statute law or central government advice (circulars and official memoranda) which is the familiar province of officers. And although the reports often point out the implications of following certain policy lines or provide a number of options from which the committee may choose, the main themes underlying the reports are influential in the sense of tending to focus discussion and thus limit the range of thinking (especially if there is no alternative paper to consider). In this and other ways, officers, perhaps unconsciously, will filter the information which comes before members. In addition, officers attend committee meetings and they normally speak: indeed some may insist on speaking[32] – they might even have a greater moral claim to local knowledge than the more mobile, less native members. But they need not even speak in order to exercise some influence:

> The reality of the formal proceedings of council and committee meetings is that the elected members meet in the presence of officers to consider reports prepared by the officers containing recommendations for action made by the officers. The meetings thus differ from other meetings . . . in that information and advice from experts is rendered in person whilst the process of decision making is under way. This . . . offers to the officers the opportunity for the well-timed remark, the cautionary aside to the chairman, even the occasional sigh or grimace, which might prevent the councillors taking a decision unwelcome to the officers.[33]

As one chief officer has stated, councillors 'should be led to the right conclusion under the impression that they are arriving at it under their own steam'.[34]

Not all officers, however, are strong-minded or have a 'line' on policy: there may not exist a departmental view on policy, and still less likely is there to be a monolithic official view. Corporate management tends perhaps to encourage such a development, but it is far from being achieved, and it is by no means unknown for differences of opinion among officers to be displayed at committee meetings,[35] which can place the chairman in an awkward situation.

The extent of official influence on policy-making is significantly determined by the role played by the committee chairmen. They work closely with the senior officers, though how much one will influence the other will depend on personality, on mutual respect and on whether theirs is a close or an arm's-length relationship. In practice there is a range of such relationships, with some committee chairmen taking a strong lead and severely limiting the officers' contribution while others are prepared to play a backseat role, perhaps to the extent of appearing as mouthpiece or ventriloquist's doll to the chief officer. Some chairmen surrender, others are captured.[36] Whether the chairman himself carries influence with his committee will also vary. Some are respected, popular, acknowledged as leaders. Others are seen as party placemen. And in some authorities, chairmen will tend to carry less weight if they have achieved office merely on the basis of 'Buggins' turn next'.

It used to be said that county councils are run by the officers and town councils by the members. The evidence for such a view was related to some extent to the existence or non-existence of political parties.[37] However, in so far as it was ever true, recent events will have an impact in that party politics are now more pervasive and reorganization has diluted the town–country distinction.

However, it may be dangerous to try to make any sort of general statement about the relative importance to decision-making of officers and members. It is 'a fundamental error to believe . . . that one set of relationships exist throughout our infinitely variable local government system'.[38] That author goes on to suggest that the relationship depends on a number of characteristics:

(1) the range and size of the authority's service provision,
(2) the degree of professionalism among its officers,
(3) the existence of political party arrangements,
(4) the sensitivity to local public opinion and
(5) the extent of central government involvement.

On the basis of these factors a range of possible situations is suggested, from those where 'the officer runs the show' to others where 'the party rules and officers do what they are told – or get out'.

Furthermore, within any particular authority the relationship of officers to members will vary with local custom, convention and local political culture: in some authorities, officers will grow up with (or be sharply taught[39]) the notion that policy is councillors' business and officers must keep clear. The relationship will also depend on personality, since, in practice, power is not shared equally even among members themselves. Chairmanships, council leadership, policy committees, in- and out-groups etc. all have variable effects, and there are individual differences in members' sense of justice or mission, in their tenacity, in their time and devotion to duty. And there are also differences in their 'legitimacy' (their claim to act as decision-makers), especially since some councillors are barely elected and others not elected at all (see p. 105).

Finally the relative importance of members and officers will vary with the nature of the issue. Matters involving delicate human problems (such as rent arrears by single-parent families) may require the members' common sense rather than the officers' specialized knowledge. Similar considerations apply in controversial matters, likely to arouse strong feelings in the locality, such as the use of the Welsh language in Welsh schools. If, on the other hand, the question is highly technical in character, such as a flood-relief scheme or the purchase of a computer, the tendency is for members to accept the recommendations of the officers.

It is clear from these remarks that power does not lie at any given point in the British system of local government. Instead there are a number of actual or potential centres of power – the policy committee, the officers' team, the individual chief officers or committee chairmen (or both together), the party group, the whole council etc. So, rather than seeing power as consisting of a hierarchy or series of concentric circles spreading from a small apex or central point, it might be more accurate to see local government power-points as consisting of a series or cluster of more or less influential groupings, varying in size in relation to time and issue. If, in general, councillors feel themselves to be somewhat at a disadvantage in their relationship to officers, perhaps they should do something about it by improving their own back-up services and procedures, using such means as properly organized training and secretarial services.[40]

The payment of allowances to members since 1974 and the introduction of special responsibility allowances to committee and council chairmen in 1980 provides some recognition of the fact that the work can no longer be left on an amateur basis in the hands of relatively few councillors.[41]

11. Finance

The scale of expenditure

Local government is big business. Local authorities spend over £30,000 million a year (£500 per person). This amounts to 30 per cent of all state spending and about one eighth of the National Income (GNP). Local authorities manage a total debt of over £40,000 million (£700 per person) and, as we saw in Chapter 10, local government employs nearly 2½ million people (about one person in ten in Britain works for local government). Local authorities are also big landowners, landlords and shareholders.

However, local government has not always been so important in economic terms. In 1951 it was responsible for spending about £1,300 million (about 9 per cent of GNP) and at the beginning of this century the figure was only about £100 million (5 per cent GNP).[1] Local government has grown as Britain committed itself to the idea of the Welfare State and as legislation has extended the responsibilities of local authorities in the fields of education, housing, social work, transport and the protective services.

Much of local government's expenditure is therefore a result of decisions by the central government and Parliament. For example the Education Act 1944 requires local education authorities to provide schools and teachers, and since the Children's Act 1948 they have been obliged to provide a service for deprived children. In addition the central government may lay down certain standards for those services which may be scrutinized by means of inspection (as in the education, police and fire services). But local authorities also spend money in response to local demands and needs, whether expressed through elections and pressure groups or discerned by professional judgement. Certain services are optional and local authorities decide whether and at what standard to provide them.

But even then local authorities do not have an entirely free hand to determine their levels of spending. They are faced with pressures which arise from their own local economic and social conditions (they may have a backlog of slums to be cleared or a growing number of old people to be accommodated), or from public expectations and aspirations about the appropriate levels of service (for example, as regards traffic congestion, street cleaning or school crossing patrols). Furthermore local authorities are committed to certain expenditures under national pay agreements (see

Chapter 8) and by joint financing (or 'pooling') schemes, such as for teacher training and advanced further education courses.[2] Finally, there is the legacy of previous spending decisions: if a local authority opens a new school or welfare home, it will be committed to paying for it for many years, for, even if it were closed down in order to save the running costs (staff wages, lighting, heating etc.), loan charges would still have to be paid.

Capital and revenue expenditure

Expenditure on school buildings and residential homes are examples of what is called 'capital' expenditure. Such expenditure implies that the object of expenditure has a long life: it is an asset. Such items are usually very expensive: they involve a heavy outlay and for that reason they tend to be financed largely from borrowed money (and so repaid over a long period). Short-lived items – fuel, typing paper, the manpower services of teachers, cleaners or social workers – are known as 'revenue' (or current) expenditure. They are consumed as soon as they are purchased or a short time afterwards, and thus have to be regularly re-purchased. Such items are paid for out of current revenues rather than borrowed money.

The distinction between capital and revenue items is not always clear-cut: some items could be classified either way (school books for example), but the distinction is important, for in general it is felt that an expensive asset – such as a sports centre or swimming pool, or a fleet of vehicles (refuse wagons or buses) – should in fairness be paid for by the beneficiaries – those who do or could use them. It would be unfair to spend £1 million on a new swimming pool and charge the full cost to the rate-payers in one year: many of those ratepayers will move away from the area or die while the asset continues to give service, and new residents (who will not have paid anything towards the pool) will move in and be able to make use of it. By borrowing money to purchase a capital item, a local authority can spread the cost (of repayment plus interest) over a number of years and so among the actual or potential beneficiaries. Consequently, notwithstanding the high interest charges, a large proportion (normally about 70 per cent) of capital expenditure is financed by borrowing (though the figure has fallen substantially in recent years), and local authorities have a collective outstanding loan debt of £40,000 million (which itself costs them about £4,000 million a year – see Table 16).

A high proportion of local government expenditure is thus committed in loan charges. As a result any move to cut government expenditure cannot be made 'across the board' (say 10 per cent off all items) because the debt interest expenditure is protected: it *must* be paid or local authorities will be defaulting on their creditors. The cuts must therefore fall more heavily on

Table 16. *Local government expenditure (by service category), 1980*

Current/Revenue items			Capital items	
£m	%		£m	%
		Education, libraries, arts, museums,		
10,521	41	milk and meals	624	15
1,876	7	Environmental services	592	14
1,589	6	Roads, lighting, transport	470	11
869	3	Housing (incl. subsidies and rebates)	1,574	37
2,133	8	Personal social services	109	3
2,569	10	Police, fire services, justice	104	2
4,233	17	Debt interest	.	.
1,840	7	Others, including trading (harbours, aerodromes etc.), administration, grants	744	18
25,630	100	TOTAL	4,217	100
1,118		*Surplus* of income over expenditure (before depreciation) (Table 17)		
26,748				

Source: *National Income and Expenditure 1982*, HMSO.

the other items of expenditure, that is on the services provided by the local authorities.

Local government expenditure

Tables 16 and 17 show that local government is spending some £30,000 million a year. Within this total, the principal item of capital expenditure is housing (comprising 37 per cent of that total), followed by education (15 per cent), with environmental services and roads and transport at the same level (14 and 11 per cent). Revenue expenditure is dominated by education (41 per cent), followed by debt interest (17 per cent).

There are, in addition, considerable differences in the magnitude of expenditure among the different types and tiers of local authority. In England and Wales, county councils are responsible for spending 85 per cent and the district councils for 15 per cent of their combined total expenditure. In the metropolitan areas, the proportions are reversed – the metropolitan counties spending 20 per cent, the metropolitan districts 80 per cent. In London (itself responsible for 20 per cent of all local government expenditure in Britain) the ratio of spending is 45 per cent for the GLC (together with the ILEA and the Metropolitan Police), 40 per cent for the outer London boroughs and 15 per cent for the inner London boroughs. In Scotland, the regional councils spend 85 per cent and the districts 15 per cent of the

Table 17. *Local government income, 1980*

Current/Revenue			Capital	
£m	%	Grants from central government	£m	%
10,759	40	– *unallocated*	.	
697		– *specific*: education	32	
374		roads, transport	34	
320		housing	.	
1,196	10	police and justice	.	
.		environmental	86	
146		other	222	
13,492	50		374	8
8,244	31	Rates	.	
202	1	Trading surplus	.	
3,021	11	Rent (including housing subsidies)	.	
686	3	Interest		
		Borrowing – from central government	1,230	71
		– from other sources	1,793	
1,103	4	Other (incl. loans to tenants etc.)	−298	−6
.	.	Surplus from current account (Table 15)	1,118	27
26,748	100	TOTAL	4,217	100

Source: *National Income and Expenditure 1982*, HMSO (adapted).

total.[3] Similarly local authorities' income patterns vary considerably, with the shire counties for example depending a great deal more on grants than rate (precept) revenues.

Local government income

Local authorities derive their income from three main sources: (a) from the rents and fees they charge for services (car parks, bus fares etc.), (b) from grants or subsidies which they receive from the central government (housing subsidies etc.), and (c) from local taxation (the rates). In addition they receive a number of miscellaneous revenues, such as interest and dividends, the proceeds of sales of land and property (such as council houses) and, for the purpose of capital items, by borrowing. Each of these is dealt with in some detail below, and their relative importance is shown in Tables 16 and 17, and Figure 16. What the tables do not show is how the pattern is changing over the years, notably the rise in the importance of government

Capital account (£4,217m., excluding £298m. lending etc. = £4,515m.)

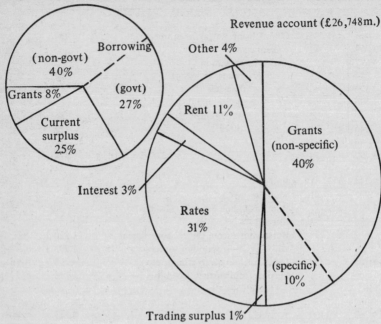

Figure 16 *Local government revenue (1980 figures)*

grants (for example from less than 30 per cent in 1951 to over 50 per cent today), and the recent fall in local authority borrowing.[4]

(a) Charges and miscellaneous incomes

Local authorities receive small sums of money from a variety of sources – licence fees (dog licences, births, marriages and death certificates etc.), interest on its loans to house purchasers and dividend receipts from its investments (of superannuation funds for example). Since the Lotteries Act 1976 local authorities have been able to run local lotteries for particular purposes or projects. These have been described as an 'instant success', their turnover increasing from £9¼ million in the first year to £21 million in the following year, and by 1979 about 350 had been registered with the Gaming Board. However, there are significant restrictions involved in their actual operation, such as the permitted amounts to be raised, and a number of local authorities have demurred on moral grounds.[5]

Larger sums are derived from the sale of land and property[6] and from loan repayments from those who borrow from local authorities. But above all they receive substantial revenues from their charges on a whole range of services. Broadly speaking there are three groups of charges: [7] (i) For *trading* or commercial services, which include industrial waste disposal, passenger transport, harbours and docks, civic aerodromes and markets. Theoretically, as trading undertakings these should raise sufficient revenue from charges to cover costs, but in practice many do not achieve this and have to be subsidized. (ii) For *personal* services, such as charges for home helps and for maintaining children or old people in care, or fees for adult and further education classes. Such fees will often take account of the individual's ability to pay [8] and seldom cover the full economic cost of the service. Some critics wish to see such charges abolished altogether on the grounds that they deter those in need, that they often involve high collection costs and that there are considerable inconsistencies and inequities in the various means tests for the different services. (iii) For *amenities* such as baths, sports facilities and car parks. The level of charges here will depend on how far the local authorities take account of social criteria: should the ratepayer subsidize a laundry service, in the interests of the needy, or sports facilities, in order to encourage healthy pursuits? Equally, subsidized facilities may, by helping local business, encourage tourism and local prosperity. (Some socialists are critical of this arrangement, as it suggests the deliberate subsidizing of capitalist enterprises, in the same way as the nationalized industries have perhaps provided private enterprise with low-cost supplies.) Alternatively, hefty car-parking fees (for example) may be used as a deterrent to traffic congestion or too rapid a deterioration of the highways. Each council has to make up its own mind about charges.

The single most important charging service is housing. However, for social reasons housing is a service which is (or has been until recently) substantially subsidized both by the central government (via subsidies) and by local authorities (from their rates). In 1976 council rents were meeting only 45 per cent of costs, compared with 75 per cent ten years earlier.[9]

Table 18. *Local authorities' charges and miscellaneous incomes*

Rents and trading (especially transport)	50 per cent
Superannuation investment income and interest	25 per cent
Sales, other fees and charges	25 per cent

It is sometimes suggested that more income could be derived from charges either by raising their level or by extending their scope.[10] Alternatively, to achieve the same net result local authorities could 'privatize' or 'hive off' some of their services to private firms. Councils could then collect rates to cover the costs of the contracted-out services; or they could allow the firms to collect normal commercial charges from the public. The Minister for Local Government (in 1980, Tom King) suggested that such things as office cleaning, refuse collection, parks maintenance and architectural design should be contracted out to private industry (though others are sceptical[9a]).

Such charges would perhaps help to sort out those who really need the services from those who use them because they are free. Furthermore a review of local authority charging policy might help to remove some apparent anomalies, such as charging for day nursery care (under the social services department) but not for nursery schooling (provided by the education departments, the LEAs).

The present (Conservative) government has much sympathy with the notion of charges and (under the Local Government, Planning and Land Act 1980) allows councils to charge for planning applications and appeals and for building regulations enforcement as well as allowing LEAs a free hand in deciding their charges for school meals (under the Education Act 1980) – though not for their lessons.[10] (It had also planned to allow LEAs to introduce charges for school transport, but this was defeated in the House of Lords on the grounds that the legislation would discriminate against rural families and religious groups.) The more general argument against increasing charges is the hardship it might cause to the low-income groups (although this could perhaps be overcome by government grants, such as those paid on a means-tested basis for housing rent allowances). Also there may well be wider social benefits from having, say, a community with general access to low-cost housing and transport.

The issue of 'privatizing' local services involves the political question of the proper role of government in society; it is also very much a matter of economics and efficiency. Some councils have adopted the working methods of the commercial world (such as incentive bonus schemes in refuse collection) so that transfer to the private sector may involve no great advantage to the economy as a whole. But there is a widespread feeling, especially in Conservative circles, that much of the work conducted by local authorities could be more effectively undertaken by the private sector. Consequently, the Local Government, Land and Planning Act now requires councils to scrutinize and justify their use of direct labour (or DLOs – that is, where they employ their own staff rather than outside contractors for building or maintaining roads, parks and housing). DLOs must now submit tenders (i.e. competitive estimates) and must achieve given rates of return (or 'profit') or face closure: in effect they are now trading undertakings.

(b) Government grants

The central government has been helping to finance local authorities since 1835, when grants in aid were introduced to assist local authorities in the cost of transporting prisoners. Subsequently grants were developed for local services such as police and education. Since they helped to finance the cost of particular services, they were known as 'specific' grants. One interesting and notorious form of grant was based on the 'payment by results' system, whereby teachers got paid according to their success in drilling their pupils in the 'three Rs' and getting them through their exams!

Another unusual form of grant was the system of 'assigned revenues'. In 1888 local authorities were empowered to retain and utilize the proceeds of certain taxes (mainly licence duties) collected in their area. Thus tax revenues (sometimes known as 'whisky money') were diverted from the central government to local government. However, this form of financial aid proved to be too erratic in its distribution and insufficiently expansive to keep pace with local authorities' growing expenditures.[11] Consequently, local authorities continued to draw upon government grants.

The character of these grants began to change in the course of the twentieth century. Under the Local Government Act 1929, assigned revenues ceased (apart from a few licence fees, which still exist), and a number of specific grants were replaced by a 'block grant' – a sum of money not tied to any particular service and which the local authorities could use for spending as they saw fit. The aim of this new grant was to place a limit on the government's financial commitment to local government. From 1948 onwards, the block grant was paid only to those local authorities whose means (or rate resources) were below the national average. It was known as the 'exchequer equalization grant'.

In the meantime, specific grants[12] continued to grow in magnitude as services (such as education, housing and roads) expanded. Consequently, in 1958 the government replaced many of them with a new form of block (or 'general') grant. The equalization grant continued under the name of the 'rate deficiency grant'. Finally, in 1966 these two block grants, together with some of the remaining specific grants (for school meals and milk), were incorporated into a single 'rate support grant' (R S G) which forms the basis of our present system of grant aid. Before we examine the details of current grants, some general aspects must be considered.

The justification for government grants

Government grants to local government may be justified on a number of grounds. In the first place, the central government will wish to encourage the development of certain services which are felt to be in the national interest (education, for example), and it may feel a moral obligation to assist local authorities financially where national legislation compels the latter to provide certain services. Secondly, government grants can help to even out the differences in resources between rich and poor authorities. Thirdly, grants may seek to compensate local authorities for their varying needs to spend, either because of the amount of need in their area (they may have many schoolchildren or old people) or because of the costs involved in meeting those needs (the population may spread thinly, for instance). Fourthly, government grants may seek to reduce the impact of rates (the local tax). The latter is often said to be 'regressive' or unfair to the lower income groups. In so far as central government taxation is 'progressive' (taking proportionately more from the better off), government grants can partially help to balance the tax burden on the local taxpayer. Finally, the central government may pay grants to local authorities to compensate them for any restrictions it may have placed on their other sources of income: thus in 1929, when the government ceased to allow local authorities to collect rates from agricultural property, their lost income was made up to some extent in the new block grant. Since 1966, government grants have been used for the explicit purpose of keeping the rates down, at least in the case of the domestic ratepayer (see p. 200).

There is, then, a strong case for grants. But some would doubt the wisdom of local government's being so dependent on the central government. Grants to local government have increased substantially in this century: as a proportion of local government income they have increased from 15 per cent in 1913, to 34 per cent in 1950 and to 50 per cent in 1980. Ignoring income from fees, charges and other sources, the ratio of grants to rates changed from 51:49 in 1966 to 65:35 in 1980, but has fallen since to 55:45 in 1984.

One consequence of such grant aid is that the central government increases its control over local authorities. This appears to be a world-wide phenomenon and is perhaps an inevitable feature of modern society. It is not necessarily or totally undesirable (see p. 244), and for the most part it is not the principle which is in question but the lengths to which it has been taken. In some respects this has been recognized by the government, which has sought to ameliorate the problem by changing the nature of its grants. It is widely felt that grants in the specific form bring closer central controls [13] and they certainly appear to encourage the provision of particular services, which perhaps distorts local authorities' patterns of spending. It was partly for this reason – to give authorities more discretion – that specific grants have largely been replaced by the block form.

The present grant system

Current grants to local authorities take four forms: (a) the rate support grant, (b) specific grants (for police, etc.), (c) supplementary grants (for transport, for instance), and (d) housing subsidies (which, like student awards and rate rebates, are a special form of specific grant and are subject to a separate procedure).

Table 19. *Grants to local government, 1984–5* £ million

	England	Wales	Scotland
1. Relevant expenditure	22,883	1,440	3,206
2. Total grant	11,872 (51·9%)	996 (69·2%)	1,930 (60·2%)
3. Specific grants	2,144	138	217
4. Supplementary grants	405	33	—
5. Rate Support Grant [= 2 − (3 + 4)]	9,323	825	1,713
Domestic Rate Relief Grant	692 (18·5p)	25 (18·5p)	14 (3p)
Block Grant	8,631	800 { Resources / Needs	212 / 1,486

Sources: *Rate Support Grant Orders; Public Finance & Accountancy* February 1983

The rate support grant (RSG)

Every year, central government departments and local authority associations meet to agree a forecast of total 'relevant' expenditure[14] for local authorities for the coming year. This comprises all local government expenditure except mandatory payments such as student awards, rate rebates and housing subsidies (which are subject to separate arrangements). The government then decides what proportion of this total it is going to finance by grant: from 1977 to 1981 the figure was 61 per cent for England and Wales, and 68·5 per cent for Scotland;[15] for 1983–4 the percentage figures were 52·8 for England, 70·4 for Wales and 61·7 for Scotland; for 1984–5 the figures are 51·9, 69·2 and 60·2 respectively. The resulting grant total is the 'aggregate exchequer grant'. From this total figure are deducted the various small, specific grants (for police, housing improvement etc., amounting to only about 10 per cent of the total) and supplementary grants (for transport and national parks, amounting to 5 per cent of the total). The remainder (85 per cent) constitutes the rate support grant (RSG), which is distributed as a block grant and is not therefore tied to particular services.

For distribution purposes, the RSG has been divided into three elements: (i) the 'needs' element, which was designed to compensate local authorities for differences in the amounts they need to spend per head of population to provide a given standard of service. It was calculated by reference to a complex formula prescribed annually by the government and based upon an analysis of each local authority's past expenditure, together with some objective indicators of their expenditure needs (factors such as population, number of children, density etc.); (ii) the 'resources' element, which sought to compensate for the disparities in local authorities' tax (rate) resources. The government would prescribe annually a 'national standard rateable value per head' (in 1981 for example it was £178) and those rating authorities whose rateable value (see p. 203) fell below this figure (the majority) would receive payment in proportion to their rate deficiency. Taken together, and assuming local authorities to be providing some given standard of services, the 'needs' and 'resources' elements were to lead to an equalization of rate poundages (the standard rate in the pound which ratepayers have to pay). In other words these two elements should have enabled local authorities to provide similar levels of service without widely different rate burdens; (iii) the 'domestic' element, which is a form of rate relief for domestic ratepayers: householders thus pay less than industrial and commercial ratepayers, and the difference is made up to the local authorities in the 'domestic' rate relief element of the RSG (a grant amounting to some 18·5p. in the pound for the householder in England and Wales and 3p. in Scotland).[16]

The RSG is clearly the most important financial aid to local authorities, and while the needs and resources elements were largely a continuation of what existed before 1966 when this grant was introduced, the domestic element – a response to the then growing concern over the rises in rates – was new. The result now is that, while rates appear to be rocketing, their impact on householders in real terms has barely altered since 1966 (see p. 206). This (domestic) element may be criticized on the grounds that it is

Figure 17 *Grant structure* (*1984–5*)

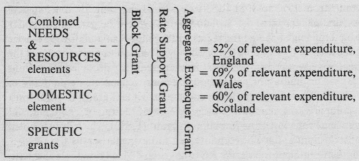

inequitable, being paid on a flat-rate basis regardless of ratepayers' ability to pay. A second criticism is that, by disguising the true cost, it may be wastefully drawing resources into the housing sector.

However, in general it is the other elements of the RSG which have come in for criticism. In particular, the needs element has been held to be unduly influenced by local authorities' past expenditure patterns, which may not be an accurate guide to local needs.[17] The resources element has been criticized on the ground that rateable values (upon which this element is based) are not a fair reflection of property values.

Another more general criticism is that the formulae on which the RSG distribution is based can be manipulated by the party in government to suit its own purposes or in response to community pressure groups, with, in general, Labour diverting financial aid to urban areas at the expense of rural, and Conservative governments doing the opposite.

The present government however has sought to change the RSG for another reason: to contain local government expenditure. Under the *Local Government, Planning and Land Act 1980*, a new block (or 'unitary') grants system has been introduced (for England and Wales only) whereby local authorities which spend in excess of their 'true needs' would not receive the same proportionate level of grant support as authorities which exercise restraint on their spending. The idea of a 'unitary' grant, combining into one the *needs* and *resources* elements, was commended by the Layfield Committee on Local Government Finance and was accepted by the government in 1977.[18] It is seen as a means of penalizing the 'spendthrift' authorities without harming the others, for under the old RSG system, if some councils spent more than the government wished, the latter could take action only by reducing the whole level of its RSG (thus shifting the burden on to the rates of *all* local authorities). Under the new scheme a 'block grant' is calculated for each local authority to cover the deficiency or gap between the cost of providing services comparable with those of similar authorities and the local rate revenue assuming it to be set at a particular level (determined by the government). In effect, the government calculates what the local authority should spend; it then deducts what the standard (or national) rate would produce, and the difference is paid in grant. A local authority spending above its 'norm' (officially known as Grant Related Expenditure Assessment or GREA) will have to find more from the rates as its grant is reduced or tapered away. (For 1981–2 the average rate 'norm' figure was set at 134p.; and for 1983–4 it was 160p.)

Local authorities have reacted strongly to this legislation. While perhaps having some general sympathy for the general aim of the proposal (to restrain overall local government spending), many authorities feel that extensive powers are being taken to control all local authorities for the sake of a few who act irresponsibly. And in general it is felt that this is a dangerous attempt to substitute a 'national judgement' about local spending for the 'local accountability' of the authorities themselves (see p. 238). Subsequent developments have increased these anxieties (see p. 283ff.).

(c) Rates

Rates are a form of local property taxation levied on property (real or fixed rather than personal) according to its value. They originated in the Middle Ages, and over the years new and separate rates were established to help to pay for separate services (public health, schools, the poor, highways, water etc.). These were finally consolidated into a single general rate in 1925 (although in England and Wales water and sewerage rates are still separately assessed and collected). Under the Rating and Valuation Act of that year certain types of local authority were classified as 'rating authorities'. Those which were not so named (counties and parishes) were to raise their finance by 'precepting' the rating authorities (the district councils): in effect this means that the rating authorities collect the rate for the other authorities (and, since 1981, also bear the cost of administration).[19] In Scotland, both regional/island and district councils are rating authorities, although the regions actually collect them.

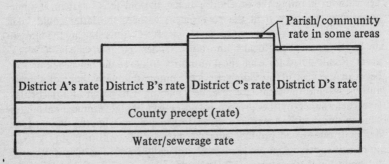

Figure 18 *Components of the rate demand (England and Wales)*

Liability for rates

There are about 18 million ratepayers in Britain. Technically, to be liable for rates, property (or 'hereditaments', as they are called) must be occupied (though not necessarily in a personal sense: a house may be liable for rates if it is empty but contains furniture). However, since 1967 rating authorities have had a discretionary power to rate empty properties if they are continuously empty for a given period, usually three or six months. (From 1981 the maximum rate on empty commercial property was 50 per cent; since 1984 empty industrial property is de-rated, see p. 281.) Whether they decide to rate empty properties and whether they charge full or partial rates will depend on such factors as the administrative costs, the revenue product and whether they think such an action will encourage owners to utilize the property more quickly or whether it may deter further development.[20]

Certain properties are statutorily exempt from the payment of rates. The main ones include: (a) Crown property, such as government building, military premises, royal parks etc. (in practice, the Treasury compensates rating authorities with 'contributions in lieu'); (b) agricultural land and buildings (except the farmhouse), which have been exempt since 1929 (worth some £250m. p.a. today), when they were de-rated partly in order to lighten the farmers' burden at that time of economic difficulty; (c) churches and other buildings used exclusively for religious purposes, charities and related organizations, public parks, police properties, lighthouses, sewers and pumping stations and foreign consulates. Recently, disabled persons have been granted rate relief on their properties where these have been specially adapted and where they house their vehicles. In Scotland, industrial property is rated at only 50 per cent, in order to offset the generally higher rate poundages than in England and Wales.

The calculation of the rate

The basic idea of the rating system is quite simple. All property in the area (apart from the exemptions) is given a valuation: this is the 'rateable value'. Every year the rating authority fixes a rate in the pound (per pound of rateable value) and the occupier of that property has to pay rates at that poundage. Thus, if the rate is 80p. and the property's rateable value is £200, the rates due are £0.80 × 200 = £160. The key elements therefore are rateable value and the rate poundage.

The valuation of property is undertaken by the Inland Revenue (England and Wales) and by the Scottish Assessors' Association. Since the 1939–45 war regular revaluations should have taken place every five years, but in practice they have occurred at very irregular intervals except in Scotland[21] and the government has now decided to change the law and allow the Minister to determine the dates for revaluation at his discretion (under the Local Government, Planning and Land Act 1980).

The valuation of property is based essentially on the market rent which the property could earn in the course of a year. From this gross or rental value is allowed the deduction of the notional cost of repairs and insurance etc. For some properties (such as a town hall, school or cinema) it is extremely difficult to assess a rental value and so other bases may be used, such as capital values or profits records. Indeed the rental basis for ordinary purposes may be substantially distorted (for example, because of statutory rent controls under the Rent Acts) and the use of alternative criteria have been proposed, such as capital values or site values.[22]

Information on the valuation of properties is publicly available in the form of a valuation list (England and Wales) or roll (Scotland), which is usually held at the council offices. Individuals may appeal against the valuation of their property to the valuation court and beyond that if necessary to the land tribunal. Any structural changes affecting a property's valuation will come to the attention of the local valuation officer normally as a result of the planning permission process.

The rate poundage (or simply 'the rate') is the amount per pound of rateable value which is collected from occupiers of property. This rate is determined annually by the local authority (some being issued in the form of 'precepts' on the rating authorities – see p. 202). The basis of the calculation is as follows: each local authority estimates its expenditure for the coming year. (The financial year runs from April to April. Until recently the financial year in Scotland ran from May.) It deducts from this figure its known or estimated revenues from charges and grants. This leaves a sum – known as the 'rate-borne expenditure' – which has to be financed from the remaining source of income – the rating of property. The proportion of that rate-borne expenditure figure to the total rateable value in the local authority area (say 80 per cent) shows the poundage (80p.) or 'rate' of tax necessary to raise the sum required. (An illustration is provided on p. 338.)[23] Thus for the individual ratepayer his property's rateable value multiplied by the rate produces his rate demand.

The rating system is unpopular because it requires lump-sum payments (usually twice a year) rather than regular (and smaller) weekly or monthly payments such as we use to pay income tax ('pay as you earn'). However, since the General Rate Act 1967, the system has been modified to allow some rates to be paid in instalments of not more than ten monthly payments. From 1981 this facility has applied to all ratepayers except (in England and Wales) for business properties over £2,000 (£5,000 in London) rateable value – £5,000 and £10,000 in 1984/5 after which date the limits cease. The same Act provided an incentive to the ratepayer to pay in full by allowing local authorities to give discounts to those who paid promptly.

Table 20. *Rate yields, 1976 (£m) and 1981/2 (£bn)*[23a]

	England and Wales	*Scotland*	*Total*	*1981/2*
Domestic	1,565	179	1,744	4·8
Commercial and industrial	1,985	150	2,135	5·0
Other (schools, hospitals etc.)	450	73	523	1·1
	4,000	402	4,402	10·9

Criticisms of the rating system

No tax is popular, but rates appear to be more unpopular than most others. This is partly because they are often paid in advance and in a lump sum (even if they are paid in instalments, the demand arrives initially as a lump sum). But rates are also unpopular because the rate (poundage) receives a lot of media attention when it is fixed (which these days means increased) each year. So rates are an overtly painful form of tax. In this respect they differ from income tax and indeed most other taxes which ratepayers have to pay: the total yield from other taxes increases automatically as incomes or prices rise, but that from rates increases only when there is an appreciation in rateable values (following an infrequent, and well-publicized, revaluation survey). Consequently rates lack 'buoyancy' and the rate has to be altered regularly in order to increase the yield.

Rates are also unsatisfactory, as we have mentioned above (p. 203), because their basis (the annual rental value) is inadequate or distorted. Furthermore, it is suggested that they may act as a brake on property improvement, householders, for example, being deterred by a threatened rise in their rates through increased revaluation.

However, the biggest criticisms of the rating system relate to its unfairness. In the first place, rate resources are very unevenly distributed among local authorities and are quite unrelated to their varying needs: hence the 'resources' element of the rate support grant (see p. 199). It may be added, however, that no known form of local taxation could easily secure an even or fair distribution of resources. Secondly, rates are said to be 'regressive', that is, relatively they bear most heavily on those with low incomes, since the rate demand is applied to the value of property, not to the occupier's ability to pay. One household may depend on a small income (say a pension), while another identical house, subject to the same rate demand, may enjoy the benefit of several larger incomes.[24] (There are 10 million fewer ratepayers than income-tax payers.)

This last criticism has lost much of its force in recent years. This is partly because incomes are taxed nationally (some on a 'progressive' basis) and part of the proceeds help to finance local government in the form of government grants. But mainly it is because since 1967 lower income groups have been able to claim rate rebates. Such relief varies with income and family circumstances, but it can amount to as much as £381 per annum (£470 in London).[25] The average rate rebate is about £100. Rate demands should now therefore bear a closer relationship to incomes, and recent evidence confirms this.[26] However, there is strong evidence that many groups in society (especially private tenants) are not claiming this benefit, although they are entitled to it. In 1980–81 some 1·45 million eligible householders did not claim, compared to the 3·35 million who did. And there are others who are outside the rebate scheme although they may be on low income (such as owners of small commercial premises). Also, there is no provision for rebates on water rates since the separate collections in 1980/81.

Merits of the rating system

The rating system has a number of strengths. As a tax, it is simple to administer, difficult to evade and cheap to collect. The total yield of rates is substantial (equivalent to about a 10p. income tax) and, being stable from one year to the next, it is reliable and predictable. In addition, since it is truly local in nature, it makes an impact (sometimes very painful) on the ratepayer, and is commonly seen (rightly or wrongly) as the payment for local services. It may thus have the merit of arousing an interest in local government affairs and promote the accountability of the councillors and officers who spend it. This is enhanced by the requirements under the General Rate Act 1967 that local authorities provide certain specified information with the rate demand, such as description of the property, its rateable value, the amounts in the pound for each principal service etc. Such information is to be expanded under current legislation (see p. 238).

A further advantage of the rating system is that, by encouraging a fuller utilization of the household stock and discouraging households from occupying premises which are larger than they need, it helps to mobilize the supplies of housing. A small family or business occupying unnecessarily large premises will be inclined to move to a smaller property because of the relatively heavy rates which large premises attract, and thus make space available for those better able to use it.

Apart from these technical advantages, there is also the perhaps surprising fact that domestic rates in general remain a small and steady proportion of households' disposable incomes – between 2 and 3 per cent, which is roughly what it was in 1939[27] (national taxes are some 47 per cent). This may help to explain why rates are not as unpopular as many people believe.[28] However, while domestic ratepayers have been protected by the 'domestic' element of the RSG and by rebates, industrial and commercial ratepayers (especially in England and Wales) have been less fortunate. While for the period 1966–74 the overall rate bill rose by 120 per cent, domestic rates payments rose by 80 per cent and non-domestic by 150 per cent. And among the 2 million non-domestic ratepayers businesses as such since 1969 have no local vote (although arguably business is well represented among the membership of most councils). On the other hand, businesses can offset their rates against other taxes (assuming profits are being made) and perhaps pass it on (in whole or part) in higher prices for their product.

Reform of the rating system

While many people (including, officially, the two major parties) would wish to see domestic rates abolished, others would be content with a reform of the rating system. One group of reforms seeks to increase the yield of rates, in particular by shifting the burden of de-rating from local authorities to the central government. Thus if the government sees fit to exempt agriculture or charities from rates, it should re-imburse local authorities for the revenue foregone.[29] In effect this already happens indirectly through the resources element of the RSG, and in Scotland there is some direct recognition through the payment of a higher RSG (at 60·3 per cent in 1984/5) to cover the rate relief of charities. However, what some critics seek is 100 per cent rate liability of all properties; anyone claiming hardship should then be able to approach the central government for financial assistance in the form of grants. A further suggestion is that property revaluation should occur more frequently (the Layfield Committee suggested three-yearly intervals) and that perhaps capital values should be used, in view of the narrow base which exists for rental comparisons (see p. 204).

These seem sensible suggestions, but there are technical problems in trying to value agricultural property or undertake more regular revaluations. And the yield may be rather insignificant. But above all are the political problems involved in trying, for instance, to re-rate agriculture or charities. More generally, it is suggested that local authorities which rely heavily on local incomes tend to be parsimonious.[30]

Alternative sources

A second group of reforms have, over the years, been put forward to supplement, or to replace, the rating system.[31] These proposals have comprised a selection of local taxes, including petrol duties, sales tax, employment tax, vehicle duties and above all a local income tax. They have been regarded as unacceptable on various specific grounds, including the problems of collection, the scope for avoidance, the small yield, their regressive nature, their intrusion upon the government's revenue sources, their uneven distribution among local authorities or the fact that such new forms of taxation would confuse the public and so jeopardize the delicate thread of accountability which runs between the council and the people.

Governments have rejected such proposals on the grounds that the time was 'not appropriate' for the introduction of new taxes.[32] A recent example of this was the (Labour) government's response to the report of the Layfield Committee, which dealt thoroughly and comprehensively with the subject of local income tax (LIT) – widely regarded as the most realistic potential source of local revenue. The Committee was set up in June 1974 in response to widespread public protest over the rises in rates that year: local government was seen to be particularly susceptible to the effects of inflation (some 70 per cent of its expenditure going on wages and salaries), while its rate revenues tend to be rather sluggish (i.e. they lack buoyancy – see p. 205). However, the Layfield Committee did not consider it feasible to abolish rates. Instead they proposed that a local income tax should be instituted as an additional source of local revenue. The objective was to 'foster the autonomy of local authorities by reducing their dependence on government grants and giving them sources of revenue they can more easily vary under their own control to meet their expenditure requirements'.

The government's response was to deny that a large central grant did undermine local discretion over expenditure: the block grant (RSG) allowed local authorities the freedom to decide their own expenditure priorities. Consequently it saw no need to introduce LIT, and indeed it went further and positively rejected it on the grounds that

the freedom of local authorities to vary the LIT rate would have to be closely constrained so that it did not unduly complicate central government economic and financial management . . . it seems highly questionable whether the majority of electors could be made aware of the LIT element in their normal PAYE deductions as to achieve the [Layfield] Committee's objective of securing an effective local discipline on local authority expenditure decisions.[33]

The present Conservative government pledged itself to abolish domestic rates and considered a number of alternative local revenue sources – only to reject them all (see p. 220). But in the meantime, instead of finding new revenues for local government, the government has adopted the alternative policy – that of taking an even bigger say in how money is raised and spent by councils (see pp. 238–9). In the interests of the management of Britain's economy (by whichever political party) regulation rather than greater freedom of local government finance is likely to predominate, so that even if local government did find new revenues, their expenditure would still be controlled. (In so far as this cuts public services it effectively transfers some costs to families, neighbours and voluntary organizations.)

Alternative strategies

A third area of possible reform is the transfer of some local government services (such as the police) to the central government or alternatively the transfer of the cost of certain services (such as teachers' pay). The examples quoted are felt to be particularly appropriate because they are already subject to considerable government intervention. The latter proposal also features in the 1979 election manifesto of the Conservative and Liberal Parties. However, there are a number of serious objections to such a transfer. In the first place it would lead to a further erosion of local government responsibilities or discretion, and if it were the costs that were transferred it would make local authorities appear even more as the agents of central government. Furthermore, it might be damaging to the service to have a divided responsibility (and it would inhibit local corporate management). The likelihood of greater public confusion would again endanger account-ability. And in the end there might be no net financial gain for local govern-ment if the central government simply reduced its grants to compensate. Above all, however, the decision about whether a service should be admin-istered locally or centrally ought to be decided on its own merits; it should not be seen merely as a device for easing local authority financial (especially rating) problems (see p. 220).[34]

Capital finance

Capital expenditure is spending on items which have a long life, such as houses, vehicles, roads and schools. Such expenditures are tradition-ally financed by borrowing, but there are other sources (see Table 17, p. 193).

Table 21. *Sources of local government capital finance*

	£m 1980	%	1970%
Capital grants	374	8	8
Borrowing – from government	1,230	27	37
– from others	1,793	40	26
Other	−298	−6	5
Surplus on current account	1,118	25	24
Total	4,217	100	100

Source: *National Income and Expenditure 1982*, HMSO. See Table 17 and Fig. 16 above.
NOTE: Total outstanding local authority debt = £32,000 m. Annual debt interest = £3,000 m. The above are national figures; as with current expenditure, the actual pattern of revenues for individual authorities will vary considerably from one to another.

These include *sales* of assets (such as land or houses), money received in the *repayment* of loans by those who have borrowed from local authorities (for house purchase etc.) and revenue from *grants*. The central government provides (capital) grants to local authorities for such purposes as road construction, the purchase of derelict land and the adaptation of properties in smoke-control areas. Local authorities also receive grant-aid from the European Economic Community (EEC) for such purposes as industrial redevelopment or school milk. In addition to these, they can, and substantially do, finance their capital expenditures from *current revenues* (rates, charges and sale of assets etc.); in recent years there has been a trend in this direction, partly because it is cheaper (as a result of inflation and the high-interest costs of borrowing) and partly for political reasons.[35]

Borrowing

Local authorities (except the GLC, which must promote a Bill through Parliament each year to gain approval for its proposed borrowing) are empowered to borrow under the Local Government Acts of 1972 and 1973. There are many ways in which they may raise loans; which precise method they decide to adopt will vary according to current legislation[36] and policy, current financial conditions and the individual judgement (and politics) of the local authority. A large proportion of local government borrowing takes the form of loans from the Public Works Loan Board (PWLB), a government agency comprising twelve Commissioners (originally established in 1815) to lend to public authorities. Under this arrangement each local authority is given a quota which it may borrow from the PWLB (and which it may exceed but at higher rates of interest). Otherwise local authorities raise mortgage loans from the public, or they issue stock and bonds (these are regularly advertised in the press), or they can raise temporary loans (which do not need loan sanction – see below) such as bank overdrafts. Such borrowing may be expensive when local authorities have to compete with other borrowers and offer attractive interest rates. It can also, on occasion, be rather embarrassing, as when, in 1980, being in dispute with their local authority employers, the National and Local Government Officers' Association (NALGO) threatened to withdraw £2 million of short-term loans from fifteen councils which had borrowed from it! It may be safer and cheaper therefore for local authorities to build up their own reserve funds (for specific capital items) and balances, as indeed most do. Many of them also utilize their superannuation funds. Thus, in effect, local authorities 'borrow' from themselves.

Loan sanction

Before 1980, the central government placed strict limits on the amounts which local authorities could borrow. This system of control was known as 'loan sanction'. Under this system local authorities had to obtain explicit permissions from the relevant government department (such as the DES or DHSS) before they could borrow money, so that, for example, before raising a loan to finance the building of schools, an LEA had to apply for loan approval. In the early days, such applications were often for individual projects such as a single school, but increasingly approvals were being granted for whole programmes of expenditure, especially in the fields of housing and transport in England and Wales, and more generally in Scotland (where the approvals are given for programmes of expenditure rather than for borrowing as such).

Under the Local Government, Planning and Land Act 1980, local authorities in England and Wales moved closer to the capital control system operating in Scotland (though it was already operating for housing investment – HIPS – and transport policies). Thus under the system now operating central approvals apply to programmes rather than individual projects; relate to expenditure as such rather than borrowing; and relate to one year at a time (though they are accompanied by an indication of the figures likely to be approved in subsequent years). Local authorities thus receive annual capital allocations for capital expenditure, known as prescribed expenditure allocations, under five blocks – housing, education, transport, personal social services and all other services (excluding police, probation and magistrates' courts). Authorities are free to aggregate these allocations into a single block and then decide their own levels of expenditure (up to the total) among the different services. They can raise the finance for this total in any way they wish, and they can even go some way beyond that figure by using capital receipts such as the proceeds of sales. Specific government approval will still be necessary for capital projects of regional or national importance. The new controls are intended to enable central government to ensure that the total of local authority capital spending each year is consistent with national expenditure plans (in recent years such planning has been too often frustrated[37]), while reducing central government involvement in detailed local capital spending decisions. Many local authorities, however, remain suspicious and sceptical about this enhanced freedom from central surveillance (see p. 238).

Financial organization and procedures

Local authorities differ in their internal arrangements for dealing with financial matters. By law they are merely required to 'make arrangements for the proper administration of their financial affairs and ... secure that one of their officers has responsibility for the administration of those affairs'.[38] However, in practice local authorities have adopted a number of common procedures from which it is possible to generalize.

As we saw in Chapter 9, local authorities generally have appointed a policy or Policy & Resources (P & R) committee. This committee plays a key role in the co-ordination and control of the local authorities' financial decisions and actions (for an illustration, see p. 304). However, it is also common practice for the council to create a separate finance committee which works closely with (and is often a sub-committee of) the P & R committee. To facilitate control and co-ordination, members of the P & R committee (and the finance sub-committee) are drawn from (and are often the chairmen of) the service or 'spending' committees.

The chairman of the finance committee is a key figure in the local authority, acting in the capacity of a minor Chancellor of the Exchequer and often making a dramatic 'state of the economy' speech at the council's annual budget and rate-fixing meeting. He is almost certainly a member of the P & R committee and as chairman of the finance committee he will have the power to authorize actions (by officers) on behalf of the committee between its meetings. In this respect he has a close working relationship with the chief financial officer of the authority (variously entitled the Treasurer or Director of Finance). The latter is the head of the Finance (or Treasurer's) Department, which comprises the senior officials who are professionally qualified in accountancy, together with the more junior staff who undertake the more routine processes of collecting money, checking bills and making payments on behalf of the authority.

Preparing the budget

The budget is a statement containing the details of the local authority's recent current and capital incomes and expenditures, together with plans for the coming year. While traditionally the budget is drawn up for one year at a time, it has become common practice to develop forward plans or 'continuation budgets' for several years ahead,[39] based tentatively on the authority's long-term corporate plans (and rolling programmes), together with population forecasts and estimates of need in the local community.

There are broadly two methods of preparing the budget:

(1) The traditional method, which involves the chief officers and the finance officer calculating the costs of the authority's current activities and making an addition for any expansion or new developments. These estimates are then submitted to the relevant committees (education, social services etc.)

for their approval or amendment. All of the agreed estimates then go to the finance committee, which may make adjustments for inflation and other contingencies. The finance committee will then deduct from the total figure its estimates of incomes from grants and charges (and other incomes such as the use of internal reserves) and make the rate (or precept) for the coming year (see p. 203). The P & R committee will also have a part to play here, especially when the finance committee is a sub-committee of P & R.

(2) Rate rationing, a process which begins by deciding what is the possible or appropriate level of the rate. The total product or yield of that rate is then divided among the various services of the authority. It is sometimes held that this approach is more in keeping with the corporate planning system of management (see Chapter 9). In practice, many local authorities these days adopt a combination of the two methods: the finance or P & R committee sets targets or guidelines upon which the service committees base their estimates, but with more or less room for variation.

The budget cycle

Local authority procedures differ in detail, but broadly the budget cycle operates as follows:

(1) In about mid-March, the P & R or finance committee will start to devise expenditure targets or guidelines for the service committees.

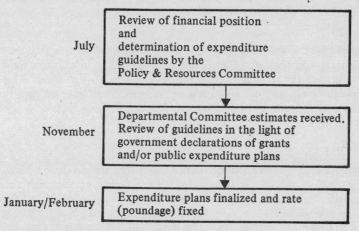

July   Review of financial position and determination of expenditure guidelines by the Policy & Resources Committee

November   Departmental Committee estimates received. Review of guidelines in the light of government declarations of grants and/or public expenditure plans

January/February   Expenditure plans finalized and rate (poundage) fixed

Figure 19 *Outline of the budget cycle*

(2) In early autumn the service committees, in drawing up their estimates of expenditure for the next year, will relate the cost of existing services, together with any proposed developments, to these guidelines. This can be a painful process, as committees may have to abandon some of their cherished schemes in order to conform to the target figures. There may be much negotiation, manoeuvring and haggling at this stage between the service committees (and sub-committees) and the P & R and finance committees, and especially within the latter committees, where representatives of the service committees will seek to protect 'their' service. (This may well also have occurred earlier at the target-setting stage.)

(3) In November the central government announces the details of its grants (the RSG) to local authorities. This, plus the 'cash limits', may be more or less than the local authorities expected[40] and they will have to adjust their estimates. For example, service committees may be asked to make a 5 per cent reduction or find equivalent savings.

(4) In February more detail becomes available on government grants, so that service committees are able to complete their budgets and submit their estimates to the P & R or finance committee for adjustment and approval. At this point the P & R or finance committee will take account of the aggregates of income and expenditure and thus determine the rate (unless it is operating the rate rationing scheme – see p. 213). The complete estimates and recommendations for the rate (precept) then go for approval before the whole council at its annual budget meeting. This is usually in February, in good time for the start of the new financial year (1 April). From that date, the local authority starts collecting its incomes and spending on the various approved services.

Soon the cycle will start again for the next financial year, though it may be interrupted or influenced by events (such as strikes, inflationary wage settlements or the announcement of new government targets) which cause the authority to levy an additional or 'supplementary' rate or precept midway through the year (but these are now banned see p. 284).

Control

The most important financial decisions – fixing the rate and deciding borrowing policy – rest with the council: by law they cannot be delegated. Yet, in practice, it often appears that the financial control exercised by the council as a whole is little more than a charade, since the estimates always seem to go through 'on the nod', without discussion or alteration. This may in part be due to their complexity and perhaps to the obscurity or esoteric nature of some of the language. Few councillors are financial experts and many feel somewhat at a loss.

However, many of the figures merely represent in money terms the nature of most of the local authority's activities: changes tend to be marginal (or 'incremental') and are usually well understood by members of the service committees. And members of the P & R or finance committee build up a familiarity and expertise which allows them to guide the council for purposes of control.

Indeed the whole purpose of the estimates and budgetary procedure is to allow the exercise of control from a central point – the P & R or finance committee. This committee will also have responsibility for monitoring progress in the work and expenditure of the local authority. In this respect, at all stages the finance officer and his staff play a leading role – checking that expenditures are in line with targets, that cash flows are running according to plan and reporting on the state of the local authority's finances and any difficulties to the appropriate committee or department.

Control is also exercised through standing orders (see p. 149 and, for illustration, p. 308), which are usually supplemented by special rules known as 'financial regulations'. Together these cover such procedures as the composition and role of the P & R and/or finance committee, the drawing-up and submission of estimates, special notification of proposals for large schemes, rules on virement (transfers of funds from one purpose to another) and on tenders (firms' quotations) and the placing of contracts. Another form of control which itself will be set down in standing orders (at least in part) is audit.

The finance department inevitably has close contact with all the departments of the authority and the chief finance officer has close contacts with other chief officers (especially the chief executive officer) and with the various service committees and their chairmen. It is his job to exercise a general oversight of the local authority's financial practices – methods of payment, timing cash flows, auditing and keeping within guidelines, checking virement etc. In practice, he will devolve much of this work on to his senior officers and he himself will concentrate on his other main role as financial adviser to the council. He will be concerned with the financial implications of the council's overall policy and hence with the specific policies of the service committees and departments. While he may attend these committees or send reports to them, most of his attention will be focused on the finance committee and the P & R committee.

Like the finance officer, these two committees will have two broad roles: firstly, the more routine control function of approving the payment of bills, administration of the authority's superannuation scheme and insurance matters, supervision of the work of the finance department and investment arrangements etc.; secondly, the more creative function of examining the spending plans and proposals (the 'estimates') of the service committees, with a view both to their co-ordination and to assessing their total impact on the resources of the local authority and its broad aims and priorities. The latter process – the drawing-up of the council's budget – is crucial to the operation of the local authority. It requires the close involvement of the P & R and the finance committees with other committees in order to strengthen the corporate approach to the authority's affairs. (A similar and parallel collaboration occurs between the finance department and other departments.) The result of their deliberations is a series of recommendations to the full council.

Audit

This takes two forms:

(1) *Internal*, undertaken by the officials of the local authority's own finance department. They will keep a regular check on incomes from rents, charges and other sources, the receipt of stores, claims for expenses, official receipts etc. They will be checking the accuracy of stocks and accounts, together with the procedures involved, in order to prevent fraud and the misappropriation of council property. The purpose of internal audit is thus to ensure that the financial dealings of the local authority are undertaken in a proper manner. But additionally, such audit will be concerned to ensure that departmental expenditures are being made in accordance with the approved estimates, and that money is not being unofficially transferred from one purpose to another (otherwise the whole idea of the budgetary procedure is undermined).

(2) *External*. By law, all local authorities are subject to external audit. This itself may take two forms.[41] The first is 'district audit', whereby the country is divided into districts and a district auditor is appointed to each to conduct audits of local authority accounts. Formerly – see p. 218 – these auditors were appointed by the Minister, though they remained substantially independent of him. In Scotland, external auditing is the responsibility of an independent Commission for Local Authority Accounts, appointed by the Secretary of State. This Commission recruits its own audit staff, but it also substantially (and traditionally) appoints private practitioners (see below).

The function of the district auditor is to inspect local authority accounts in order to detect financial irregularities (fraud), to promote sound financial practices and procedures and to prevent or uncover unlawful payments. In this last capacity he is in effect re-inforcing the *ultra vires* rule (see p. 65), for when he discovers expenditure which is outside the legal powers of the local authority, he may refer the matter for a judicial ruling to the courts. (He used to have greater powers: see pp. 327 and 340.) The latter can disallow such expenditures and may order repayment by those members and officers who were responsible for the illegal expenditure (or for failure to collect any incomes due).[42] In the twenty-five years 1947–72 the number of cases of reported fraud or unlawful expenditure amounted to about fifty a year.[43]

Over the years, the district auditor (and internal auditors) have been focusing attention on wasteful expenditures or procedures (mode of borrowing, fuel consumption, cost controls over repairs expenditure etc.) and increasingly on value for money. In the three years 1970–73, suggestions by the district audit saved an estimated £1·5 million.[43] For the latter purpose, district auditors have started devising 'performance indicators' (output divided by input) for comparing different services and different authorities.[44] And in 1979 the Advisory Committee on Local Government Audit was established, to consider the annual report of the Chief Inspector of Audit[45] and any questions arising from it which were of general interest, and to make recommendations to local authorities in respect of value for money. (Such a body was recommended but some critics see it as a move to exercise greater central control.)

The second form of external audit was the 'approved audit'. Here the auditors, usually local firms of professional accountants, had to be approved by the Minister. Where the approved auditor found cases of illegal expenditure or losses due to failure to collect revenue, he had to report the matter to the Minister, who could order an extra-ordinary audit by the district auditor.

External auditors issue a report when they have completed their work, though if a matter is sufficiently important it may be issued beforehand. Audit is announced in advance in the press or public notice boards, and by law the local authority's accounts must be made available to the public (public access in Scotland is no longer more restricted[46]). Members of the public are entitled to raise questions about the accounts with the auditors, and this can be an important aspect of local government accountability (seemingly under-utilized).[44] Furthermore, if an elector makes objections to the auditor about the accounts, the district auditor may refer the matter to the law court to rule on the lawfulness of expenditure. (In the Camden case, 1982, two members of the council's Conservative opposition party complained to the district auditor that the council had been 'illegally generous' in their pay settlement to striking workers during the 'dirty jobs' dispute in the 1978–9 'winter of discontent'. The auditor took the case to the High Court. The case was dismissed on the grounds that the settlement was within the council's discretion.) Alternatively, the Minister could order the district auditor to hold an extraordinary audit, as in the Clay Cross case (see p. 226). If the district auditor refuses to submit an elector's objection to the court, the latter may himself go to court for a declaration and if necessary an injunction against the unlawful expenditure.

Under the Local Government Finance Act 1982, local authorities in England and Wales are now subject to the 'Scottish system' of audit. An Audit Commission (comprising sixteen members appointed by the Secretary of State) is now responsible for local government audit. It appoints auditors for local authorities, drawing on the District Audit service or, for 40 per cent of councils, from the private sector: local authorities no longer have a choice. It is specifically charged with promoting more value-for-money auditing (for which purpose absorbed the Advisory Committee). The aim of the change was to increase the apparent independence of audit, to bring in more private auditors and to increase the value-for-money approach. But some see it as a further step to centralization (and 'privatization'), with auditors being politicized and used as instruments of central government control; others say it uses too many irrelevant business criteria.

In addition to the procedures for the audit of accounts, each local authority must supply annual financial returns to the Minister. These cover income and expenditure and details of rating matters, and they provide an additional safeguard against improper financial activities and a source of national statistics on local government finance.

Value for money

The question of local government's efficiency was raised in Chapter 10. Efficiency may be defined as the maximum output from a given input of resources. But since the ultimate goal of local government is to enhance the general welfare of society, there can be no easy measure of its 'output'. And even if there were such a measure, allowance has to be made for political factors, both in the narrow (party) sense and in the broader (democratic) sense. Thus local government is subject to regular election, public funds must not be subject to risk, local authorities are subject to public accountability through open committee meetings and the publication of accounts (see above and Chapter 9) and to considerable oversight by the central government (see Chapter 12). On top of all this, local authorities are urged to encourage and facilitate popular participation.

Such features are in many ways very desirable, but they are not without some cost – such as the sudden reversals of policy following elections or the slowing-down of the decision-making process. Perhaps the best example of the latter is the two-tier structure of local government, which could be viewed as a deliberate sacrifice of efficiency for democracy (see Chapter 3). However, as the Layfield Committee pointed out, the public are increasingly concerned at local government's efficiency and effectiveness in view of the steep rises in rates, while standards of service fall in spite of the fact that manpower levels appear to be stable. Consequently there have been calls for greater information to be made available to the general public about local government services.[47] And under recent legislation (the Local Government, Planning and Land Act 1980) local authorities are required to publish annually their financial and manpower figures, together with information on performances, in order to strengthen local government's accountability to their electors and ratepayers.

Constraints

In the pursuit of value for money, local authorities should at least begin with a set of objectives, ranked in some sort of order of priority (based on rational criteria, such as need or expressed demand). Various ways of achieving those objectives should be considered and the most effective projects (those which maximize benefits) chosen and pursued. In Chapter 9 a number of management techniques which could help in this respect were outlined. In addition, local authorities are advised by their own management services units and by outside bodies such as LAMSAC and LACSAB (see p. 169) or private consultants. And apart from the work of internal audit and budget monitoring techniques, many local authorities have established performance review committees.[48]

All of this, however, requires planning and reasonable stability. In practice, local authorities do not have this stability, partly as a result of local elections and changing party fortunes, which are paralleled at national level (with the consequence of significant changes in economic policy which can vitally affect local government), but also partly as a result of inconsistencies within central government (or at least a differing view on priorities) with some departments urging major local government restraint (e.g. the Department of the Environment), while others urge greater provision (e.g. the DHSS seeking greater local authority community care of hospital patients; or the Department of Energy urging more expenditure on housing insulation grants by local housing authorities). Perhaps the area of greatest paradox is within the DOE itself: on the one hand it is urging expenditure restraint through grant penalties, and on the other it is seeking inner-city regeneration through 'partnership' schemes and special grants (or, in some cases, through the creation of special urban development corporations – UDCs – as in Liverpool and London: see Hackney case, p. 338).

Furthermore, the central government can also regulate local authority charges (for instance, for old people's homes, car parks and even library fines), and they can impose schemes on local authorities (such as rent and rate rebates, sale of houses, new charges for old services) which have significant manpower implications for the authorities concerned. In this chapter we have seen how local government is subject to considerable financial control and influence, in particular through the RSG settlement and cash limits (both of which appear rather late for local authority financial planning purposes), loan sanction and public expenditure plans. In terms of value for money, therefore, local authorities are not entirely masters of their own fate. As the Layfield Committee commented, 'Our Report finds a lack of clear accountability for local government expenditure, which results from the present confusion of responsibilities between the government and local authorities.' This central–local relationship is considered in the following chapter.

'Alternatives to Domestic Rates' Cmnd 8449 (HMSO 1981)

This Green Paper outlines the possible sources of income for local government which could replace or supplement domestic rates. It explains the problems of rates (unfairness, lack of buoyancy, etc.) and suggests reforms which could overcome some of those defects (such as a levy on earning non-householders, offsetting rates against income tax and capital valuation).

For reasons of cost and practicability, it *rejects* local duties (on petrol, tobacco, alcohol), local vehicle excise duty and a local payroll tax. It regards the following as *feasible*, either on their own or in combination: a local sales tax, local income tax, a poll tax and assigned revenues. But it does point out the problems inherent in some or all of these including the unpredictability and/or lumpiness of yield; the lack of perceptibility (and thus the accountability impact); danger of encroachment on national taxation; possible impact on businesses; and the risk to local government independence.

A further suggestion is that of a separate block grant for education (a kind of specific-block grant). This has been welcomed in some education circles as a means of protecting or strengthening the education service. But some fear greater centralization, and others see such a development jeopardizing the corporate approach to local government management (see p. 158) especially if other services, such as social services, follow suit.

Since the Green Paper the Government has modified the rating system by abolishing supplementary rates (see pp. 214, 284). It is also implementing a modest measure of (discretionary) specific grants for selected educational purposes (under the Education (Grants and Awards) Act 1984). But above all it has completed its reflections on the rating system and published the White Paper 'Rates' (Cmnd 9008 August 1983) which declares that the rating system is to be retained after all, but it is to be radically (and controversially) reformed. This became law with the Rates Act 1984 (see pp. 284–5 below).

12. Controls and Influences

Local authorities are political institutions: they exercise power. But they themselves are, of course, subject to a substantial degree of control and influence. Such control takes a number of different forms: some of these are widely accepted and cause little offence; others are regarded as exceptionable and give rise to substantial controversy.

(1) Legislative/parliamentary control

In our system of government, Parliament is sovereign: an Act of Parliament becomes the law of the land and cannot be gainsaid. As a consequence, Britain has a 'unitary' constitution, in contrast to those 'federal' systems such as that of the USA, where power is divided and exercised co-ordinately (or in parallel) by both the central (federal) government and the individual states. In Britain legal authority emanates from Parliament and it may be convenient for Parliament to devolve power on to other bodies (such as local authorities or to regional assemblies like the old Stormont Parliament in Ulster). It may at any time rescind or withdraw that power from them (as indeed it did in the case of Stormont, returning Ulster to 'direct rule' from Westminster in 1972).

Local authorities in Britain therefore exist by virtue of Acts of Parliament: legislation brings local authorities into existence, as the Local Government Act 1888 did (see p. 29), it gives them powers and duties, as the Education Act 1944 did (see p. 76), it will shape their composition and constitution, as the Local Government Act 1972 did and it may pre-determine their internal arrangements, as the Local Government Social Services Act 1970 did. Local government – with the exception of the City of London, which is technically a common law corporation rather than a statutory one – is thus the creature of Parliament.

(2) Legal/judicial control

As a consequence of their being statutory bodies, local authorities are subject to a high degree of judicial control; that is there are special remedies against local authorities because they themselves have special rights, powers and duties conferred by statute. We have already seen how they are subject to the principle of *ultra vires* (see p. 65) and how this is reinforced by the scrutiny of external audit (see p. 216). Where the auditor or an individual citizen believes that the local authority is acting *ultra vires* (including unreasonable expenditure) he can seek a declaration and injunction from a court of law, which might subsequently impose the requirement of recompense by repayment. See the London fares case p. 93 above.

However, the remedy of a High Court declaration or injunction is not confined to cases of *ultra vires*[1] or illegal expenditure: it may indeed be used where an individual's private right suffers particular damage or infringement, for instance against a local authority which erects a hoarding and blocks the light from a person's windows. Where an individual is involved he will usually conduct his own case. Where the aggrieved persons consist of the general body of ratepayers, as in the Fulham case,[2] court action is normally taken on their behalf by the Attorney-General.

Alternatively, certain kinds of local authority action or decision may be challenged in the courts by means of what are called *prerogative orders*. These are High Court orders usually initiated by an aggrieved individual but pursued by the Crown. They take three forms: (i) the order of *mandamus* (the most frequently used) will require a local authority to carry out a duty imposed on it by law (for example, to require an authority to issue a precept or to permit the inspection of its records); (ii) the order of *prohibition* will restrain a local authority from proceeding further in a situation where it appears to be exceeding its jurisdiction, has disregarded the principles of natural justice or has not followed prescribed procedures (e.g. such an order was made to prevent a police doctor from determining the question of whether a police officer should be retired as disabled, as the doctor had prejudiced the issue in an earlier report[3]); (iii) the order of *certiorari* applies, as does prohibition, in those situations where the local authority is acting in a judicial or semi-judicial – as opposed to purely administrative – capacity (as where it is hearing objections to one of its proposals, such as slum clearance). Under this order the action or decision-making procedure does not simply cease, as with the prohibition order. Instead the record or the decision of the authority is sent to the High Court to have its legality inquired into and if necessary to have the decision quashed. The decision of a rent assessment committee for example, might be quashed on the grounds of bias by its chairman.[4]

The procedure involved in these prerogative orders is somewhat involved and cumbersome; as a result there has been a tendency for aggrieved persons to seek judicial redress through actions for a declaration and injunction (see p. 218) or through statutory remedies.[5] The latter may take the form of appeals to the Minister (see p. 226) or statutory appeals.

Since many of the powers conferred on local authorities may affect the interests of individuals, a safeguard is provided in the appeals machinery. In contrast to the procedure for injunctions or prerogative orders, *statutory appeals* are relatively simple and accessible. Under this procedure the individual has the right of appeal, stated in individual Acts of Parliament, against the improper or inequitable use of powers conferred on local authorities by the legislation, such as the granting of licences. Thus, under the Highways Act 1959 owners of properties abutting private streets may appeal to the Magistrates Court against the specification of works served on them by the council for making up the paving and drainage of the street. Similarly, under Housing Acts, property owners may appeal to the county court against a local authority's order requiring the repair, demolition or closure of insanitary property. Finally, appeals may go to the High Court over such issues as clearance orders and compulsory purchase (cpo's). In some instances, the court's powers will be limited, but in many cases it will be empowered to substitute its own discretion for that of the authority.

Local authorities are, in addition, subject to the control of the courts in much the same way as other organizations or individual people, so that if they are in breach of contract they may be sued (in tort or contract) and if they (through one of their employees) commit a criminal offence proceedings will be taken against them.

Despite their vast powers and responsibilities, however, and not withstanding the recent spate of notable cases, local authorities are not often taken to court, though there are mounting threats of actions by parents on the grounds that expenditure cuts are causing LEAs to fail in their statutory duties to maintain minimum education standards.[6] This is because they are normally law-abiding bodies who keep careful track of the legality of their actions by appointing a solicitor or other legal staff to advise them. In addition, much control is exercised over them administratively (by the Minister – see below), which reduces the need for judicial control. And finally, judicial intervention occurs only when an aggrieved party (a citizen) institutes the necessary action, and this is not always easy: in spite of the apparently wide-ranging opportunities for redress, the judicial remedies for review and control of local government actions have long been the subject of criticism. The system is held to be confusing and the procedures complex. It is sometimes suggested that they should be consolidated and simplified. It is also felt that the ordinary courts of law are not always well suited to consider the technical issues which may arise in matters such as house repair or demolition. (An alternative system would be a series of courts or tribunals which specialize in administrative justice, such as they have in France.)

Notwithstanding these criticisms, judicial control can be justified on the grounds that it is impartial and not tied to policy matters. Consequently, it helps to secure public confidence that bias and corruption are not present in the administration of local government business. Such suspicions may linger where administrative control alone is involved. However, these suspicions may be assuaged by the introduction (in 1974) of the Local Government Commissioners ('ombudsmen') whose role it is to investigate and remedy maladministration (see p. 260).

(3) Administrative/governmental control

The closest and most continuous form of control over local authorities is that exercised by government departments. Such controls have come into existence piecemeal, as convenience and expediency required. Consequently, they are not uniform in their application and their scale varies from time to time and among the different services.

Government supervision of local authorities has always existed in some form – from the JPs of the Middle Ages, the Poor Law Commissioners of the 1830s and the school inspectors of the 1860s to the powers exercised by the modern Secretary of State. However, although the scale of this control appears to have fluctuated, there has been a more sustained increase since the 1920s and especially since the war of 1939–45.[7]

Justification of government control

Central control of local government may be justified on a number of grounds. Firstly, many of the services for which local authorities are responsible (education, housing etc.) are national in character and need therefore to be sustained at some minimum standard at least. Secondly, in the interests of social justice the government will try to secure equality of standards and the avoidance of disparities. Besides, many local needs – traffic, fire safety, building controls, food safety, children's services etc. – are common throughout the country. Thirdly, councils are substantial spenders and taxers (see Chapter 11) and they control too many of the nation's resources to be left alone by the central government, which is generally held responsible for the management of the economy as a whole.

Thus, in general terms, the role of the central government is to secure the national interest over and above the purely local. For example the Minister may intervene in matters of land use or development. It is sometimes held that central government control is justified because it is more efficient than local government ('auntie knows best'). This may have been true in the last century, when local authorities were far from honest or were often reluctant to spend ratepayers' money, but it is by no means demonstrably true today.

What is true is that the central government can act as a clearing house for useful ideas and good practices which it can disseminate among local authorities. Furthermore it is generally accepted that individuals and local authorities themselves need to have an accessible point of reference in cases of dispute (for example, between two local authorities regarding an overspill or development project or liability for homeless persons). In such cases the Minister can act as a referee.

These are the justifications for central government intervention in the affairs of local government. Whether they justify the present degree of control is another matter. But before examining the various forms which this intervention may take, it is worth pointing out that central intervention is inevitable, partly because the central government substantially finances local government (see p. 179), which provides a means of intervention; but also because political parties seek to apply their principles throughout the country and, since parties exist at both the national and the local levels, this will provide the necessary motive for intervention.

The forms of control

Acts of Parliament establishing local authority services give Ministers certain general powers to control the way in which councils act, and in some cases these powers may be quite sweeping. Thus the Education Act 1944 makes it the duty of the Secretary of State for Education 'to secure the effective execution by local authorities, under his control and direction, of national policy for providing a varied and comprehensive educational service in every area'. In fact, however, such broad, almost autocratic, powers are rarely found. Furthermore it appears to be a convention that where they do exist they are rarely exercised. (This is not to deny that their mere existence and potential use may be a powerful influence. But see pp. 230–31.)

It is more usual for the legislation to specify the Minister's powers, and these specific forms of control are much more likely to be used. In many cases Ministers have conferred on them the power to issue regulations and orders (generally called 'delegated legislation' or 'statutory instruments') to fill in the details of a service outlined in legislation or to bring in new elements and add to that service when circumstances suggest. For example, the Home Secretary issues regulations for the administration and conditions of service of police forces, and the Secretary of State for Social Services does the same for local authorities' arrangements for fostering children or for charges in old people's homes. It is usually by means of such regulations that Ministers try to secure the maintenance of standards in many local government services (as in the regulations concerning school buildings[8] or the qualifications of teachers or housebuilding).

Alternatively, the government may vet and perhaps modify local authority schemes. Many Acts of Parliament require local authorities to submit their schemes for the development of certain services. In the 1960s and 1970s a number of L E As' schemes for 'going comprehensive' in their secondary schools were rejected as unsuitable by various Secretaries of State for Education. Similarly local authorities' structure plans (see p. 75) have to be approved by the Minister, and they may be altered.[9]

Planning is an example (making by-laws is another) of an area where the Minister's consent or approval might be required for individual actions by the local authority. It is regularly needed for compulsory purchase orders and appeals over planning refusals. In the latter cases, an inquiry is usually conducted by a government official (or someone appointed by the government), known as the inspector. Inspectors' reports go to the Minister for his final decision, which in practice normally, but not always, endorses the recommendation of the inspector.

In this respect, the Minister is acting as an arbitrator or judge in a dispute between the local authority and its citizens, such as there might be when parents object to the L E A's closure of a school. Or he may act to resolve a dispute between local authorities themselves, for instance over planning or overspill issues or financial liability for students or welfare clients. Similarly he may be called in to deal with disputes between a local authority and its staff over such issues as superannuation rights or conditions of service.

Some legislation gives Ministers important default powers over an authority which is failing to provide a service satisfactorily. If a Minister is dissatisfied with an authority's provision of a particular service he may remove the responsibility from that authority, either taking it over himself (for instance by his appointing a school's board of governors, or issuing new street by-laws, where the authority has failed to do so; a recent case involved Norwich council-house sales[10]); or, more frequently, transferring responsibility to another local authority or to a special body, as in the Clay Cross case (see note 10). In each case, the financial liability remains with the defaulting authority. (The alternative procedure is for the Minister to issue directions or a default order enforceable through the courts – see p. 222). In practice, such events are rare, though the tendency of modern legislation to confer default powers on Ministers is increasing.[11]

Influences and informal controls

Besides these formal controls, there exist a number of other points of contact and influence between central and local government. They are less dramatic, but they are equally if not more influential on the operation of local authorities.[12] Thus Ministers may intervene in the appointment (or dismissal) of certain chief officers. For example the appointment of chief constables, fire officers and directors of social services requires ministerial approval and normally the local authority is obliged to submit its short list of candidates, many of whom may be vetoed by the Minister as unsuitable in an attempt to safeguard the quality of the service.[13]

Ministers will also seek to maintain the standards of certain services by means of inspection. The police, fire and education services are subject to regular inspection by Her Majesty's Inspectors (HMIs) from the Home Office and the Department of Education and Science, and social service departments are reviewed by the 'Advisory Services' of the Social Work Service of the Department of Health and Social Security. In Scotland the relevant departments are the Scottish Education Department and the Scottish Home and Health Department (in effect they are sub-departments of the Scottish Office). These departmental inspectorates act as the 'eyes and ears' of the central government, and they collect and disseminate information and advice – 'local good practices' – on a large scale. Examples include educational organization and teaching methods, and sheltered housing schemes.

However, much of this information is collected from local government directly by the central government departments, for local authorities are required by law to 'send the Secretary of State such reports and returns, and give him such information ... as he may require ...'[14] Innocent as such data collection may seem, it might nevertheless have some influence on the methods and standards of council services, even if it only causes local authorities themselves to analyse and utilize their own findings.

Local authorities have the power (and in some cases the duty) to make by-laws. These must receive ministerial approval before they are valid and enforceable (e.g. in 1980 a number of councils failed to get Home Office approval of by-laws banning dogs in parks), but Ministers will usually short-circuit the process by issuing 'model' by-laws, which tend to be adopted by local authorities if only to save them time and effort. The same arrangement applies to the requirement that LEAs draw up and submit for approval their Instruments and Articles of Government for schools and colleges.[15]

Local authorities are influenced and persuaded by other central government documents. These include memoranda, research reports, White Papers, Green Papers[16] and statements (for instance, the statement on housing investment plans in 1979, which also said that local authorities would have to raise their rents by 60p. per week in the following year). Some departments regularly publish a news-sheet or bulletin (such as the Treasury's *Economic Progress Report*, the DES's *Reports on Education,* DOE Design Bulletins (for roads, footpaths, etc.), and the DHSS's *Social*

Work Service). All of these more or less help to shape local government activity.

Of particular importance in this respect are government circulars, which are sent out very regularly to local authorities explaining new legislation, suggesting new directions in policy or methods of administration, and perhaps explaining government policy. They vary from the relatively trivial circular concerned with minor matters of detail to the highly significant, such as the DES circular 10/65, which requested LEAs to submit their schemes for comprehensive school reorganization, and the DOE circular 21/79, which explained the government's expectation of a 3 per cent fall in local government expenditure in 1979–80. (Other, less official 'circulars' include those which are issued to local political parties by the party headquarters, and those which are sent to member authorities by the local authority associations.)

Finally, Ministers can exercise influence personally and directly when they meet local government members and officials at official visits or local government conferences. They can also make their views known through articles in local government journals (such as the *Local Government Chronicle*, the *Municipal Journal*, *Community Care*, *Public Finance and Accountancy* or *Municipal Engineering*) or through well-publicized statements. Two recent examples of the latter include Anthony Crosland's declaration in 1975 that (for local government) 'the party's over' and Michael Heseltine's speech at the local government conference in September 1981 that it was 'closing time' for local authority growth – both of which helped to shape the psychological atmosphere in local government for the years ahead.

Financial controls

The financial relationship between local and central government has been described as the iron fist in the velvet glove. It comprises a mixture of controls and influences. It was observed (on p. 216) how the external audit seeks to reinforce the judicial control of local authorities by its concern with the legality of local authority expenditure. Increasingly, however, the Audit Commission is exercising an administrative influence by widening its remit to cover value for money considerations, as a consequence of which it may attempt to guide and advise local authorities.

Stronger and more overt influence is exercised through government grants. This influence may be either particular or general in effect. 'Specific' grants (allocated to a particular service[17]) will tend to encourage the provision of that service, influencing the authority's pattern of service provision (and its corporate plan). It was suggested too (on p. 198) that such grants tend to bring with them rather closer central supervision. The substitution of a 'block' (non-allocated) grant for specific grants, which occurred substantially in 1958, was intended to release local authorities from such close oversight. However, a general grant brings with it the means of a more general control or influence, since all local authorities can be encouraged or discouraged from spending by the central government's increasing or decreasing the proportion of expenditure it is prepared to finance.[18] The government's allowance for cost increases resulting from inflation (the 'cash limits' – see p. 335) is another important factor.

Local resources can be affected by central government in other ways. The government can delay carrying out the revaluation of property. It can determine (through legislation) the de-rating or re-rating of certain categories of property (see p. 207), both of which decisions will impinge on local authorities' tax (rate) resources. It may issue guidelines – even deadlines (p. 284) – for local rate increases. It can exercise some influence on local authorities' other main source of income – charges. In a general way it may seek to regulate all charges through a prices policy. More directly, the government can specify or restrict certain local authority fees, such as those for children in care, old people's homes, library fines, or (using heavy persuasion and altered subsidies) council rents. Recent legislation even tells councils what discount they must offer on their council house sales.

In Chapter 11 we saw how local authority capital expenditure has long been subject to loan sanction. Apart from the control element inherent in such a process, additional influences flowed from the various conditions which often accompanied borrowing approval. Until recently, in seeking loan sanction to build houses, local authorities have had to follow certain building standards and conform to certain cost yardsticks.[19] Or in seeking loan sanction to develop nursery education, LEAs found Ministers more favourably disposed to approve certain kinds of project (such as nursery classes attached to primary schools) than others (such as separate nursery school buildings).[20] Finally central government has an impact on local government's capital finance by changing its policy regarding access to the Public Works Loan Board (see p. 210) and through the interest charged on its loans, and by declaring moratoria on spending (as in 1982 and 1984).

Local authority resources are being regularly committed by the central government when it legislates for new services (for example, the Children and Young Persons Act 1969 introduced the concept of 'intermediate treatment' for young offenders which became the responsibility of the local authority social services departments); or, through the device of inspection or new regulations, when it urges the expansion or improvement of existing services (police recruitment, fire regulations or schools building standards for instance). Equally, the central government is committing local government resources when it sets up pay inquiries and commissions to determine appropriate wage increases, such as the Houghton Committee on teachers' pay in 1974 and the Comparability Commission (Clegg) which was involved in 1979 in the determination of the pay of teachers and other local government employees. It is difficult for local authorities not to be bound by the recommendations of these bodies.

Consequences of control

The vast array of controls and influences outlined above has given rise to deep concern about central domination and the subordination of local government. Professor Keith-Lucas suggests that local democratic self-government in Britain has become a 'romantic dream'.[21] And the Maud Committee (1967) concluded that British local government has, as a result of central government control, less discretion than local authorities in other countries. It also outlined the dangerous consequences of this excessive control, which it saw causing frustration and discouragement among local government officers and councillors (actual or potential). They also believed that public interest in local government was diminished in so far as people perceived local authorities as little more than puppets dancing at the ends of central government strings.

Another consequence of controls is that local authorities' efficiency and corporate planning may be jeopardized, since different government departments could be pulling local authorities in different, even conflicting, directions. This view was confirmed to a certain extent by the government's own advisory 'think tank' in 1977.[22] Furthermore, as the Bains and Paterson Reports pointed out (see Chapter 9), central requirements to appoint certain committees, such as social services, reduce local authorities' flexibility for internal organization; similarly, the requirement to appoint (and perhaps have vetted) certain chief officers, such as the director of social services, but not others, creates inconsistencies.

As a result a number of remedies have been suggested. These are dealt with below (p. 233). But before examining them, it is important to be aware of the danger of exaggerating the central government's control of local government.

It is easy to overstate and distort the image of the relationship between central and local government. Ministers do not have a free hand to interfere in local government affairs: local authorities are created by Acts of Parliament and these give them a substantially independent existence and range of powers. To intervene, Ministers must normally be able to point to a statutory power to do so. The wide powers of the Secretary of State for Education (see p. 225) are perhaps exceptional, but even here there are limits, as was shown by the Tameside case of 1976, when the Court of

Appeal and the House of Lords decided that the Minister's direction to the LEA (which he believed was acting unreasonably in seeking to re-introduce selective secondary education) was invalid. A number of cases have recently gone against the Secretary of State for the Environment.[23]

Secondly, the central government is not monolithic. There is no unity or uniformity in the controls exercised by the various government departments: indeed there is considerable variation, even among the different services within the same department (between the police services and urban programmes within the Home Office, for instance).[24]

Thirdly, while the central government may lay down certain minimum standards, local authorities have a substantial, though not unlimited, freedom to decide higher standards as they see fit. This derives, in part, from the fact that local authorities themselves raise a significant proportion of their income from rates, charges and internal funds, which thus gives them a degree of financial independence (some councils get no grant).[25]

In addition to their financial and legal independence, local authorities have a considerable degree of political independence: they are, after all, elected bodies, which must carry some weight in the mind of the central government.[26] And where the party in power locally differs from that in power at the centre, there is a greater tendency to resist central dictates (in the 1970s, housing finance reform and council house sales policies were resisted by Labour councils, while comprehensive education plans received filibuster treatment – deliberate delay through talk – from many Conservative councils). The 1980s opened with much united hostility among councils of all political colours to the government's expenditure cuts, and the AMA mounted a national publicity campaign ('Keep It Local').

Such open hostility and defiance is rare, for central government and local authorities conduct much of their business informally (by means of letters, deputations to Whitehall, telephone calls etc.) in an attempt to smooth differences and reach compromises. Local authority representatives sit on government advisory bodies (the Housing Services Advisory Group, the Schools Council, the Personal Social Services Council and so on), where they can expound the local government viewpoint. Local authorities (especially through their associations – see p. 246) are in regular consultation with government departments prior to legislation or the publication of circulars (it took six months to negotiate the contents of the circular 10/65[27]). And the local government professional associations, such as the Institute of Housing or the Association of Directors of Social Services (ADSS), are regularly called on to advise the government or participate in a working party which will shape government policy. Indeed, the official Housing Advice Unit in the DOE comprises former local government officers and members of the Institute of Housing.

In addition, local authorities may exercise their own influence on central government through their party machinery. The major parties have regular conferences on local government which provide an opportunity for central and local politicians to get together and exchange views. Both in and out of Parliament, the major parties have local government committees and advisory groups (the latter usually drawing on personnel from local government itself). Ministers are regularly receiving party delegations and deputations from local government (especially in recent years) and they may be similarly confronted when they return to their constituencies at weekends.

Some Ministers may have particular links, past or present, with local government.[28] So too do MPs, who can display their concern about local government through parliamentary questions and adjournment debates. About one third of MPs have had experience in local government, and some of them (24 in 1980, 56 in 1983) have a 'dual mandate' and combine the role of councillor with that of MP. A great deal of MPs' constituency (or 'surgery') matters concern local government, as does a significant proportion of their correspondence.[29] In 1981 Conservative MPs forced their own government to withdraw and substantially revise the Local Government Finance Bill (thereby dropping plans for local rates referenda).

Furthermore, some individual councillors and officers can be quite influential with Ministers and civil servants, on account of their personality, qualifications or expertise.[30]

Local authorities may also exercise influence by forming regional groups and applying collective pressure. In some areas in the 1960s such groups pressed the government to speed up motorway building and reform the Selective Employment Tax (which was adversely affecting the tourist trade). In the 1970s pressure was used in bidding for government economic and industrial aid.

Finally, what of the claim that local authority services are fragmented and their corporate planning undermined by the central government departments' pursuing different policies and pulling local authority departments in different directions? In 1977 the government's 'think tank' (CPRS) did find some evidence for this claim – on occasion, the implementation by local authorities of multi-purpose capital projects had been hindered because different elements in the project received different responses – some approved, others refused – from different departments (see note 12). There was also a more general tendency to contradiction between the central spending departments (DHSS, DES, Home Office etc.) and the control departments (the Treasury and the Department of the Environment) (see note 22).

However, the CPRS report concluded that the claim to lack of co-ordination was exaggerated, and that in many ways the central government was as well forward in the development and application of corporate management as most local authorities were. Nevertheless it did recommend that central government should deal with local authorities more on an inter-departmental programme basis than on a separate service-by-service basis. (In this respect it commended the Scottish system of regional reports.[31] It might be added that the problem is less great in Scotland and Wales because they each have a single department – the Scottish and Welsh Offices – which exercise the responsibilities relating to local government which in England are the functions of the DHSS, DOE, DES etc.) It also suggested that there should be more contact and mutual understanding between the central and the local authorities. And finally it suggested that the central government should reduce its interventions on matters of detail and con-centrate instead on key matters, such as the overall size of capital alloca-tions.

Proposed remedies

Clearly the CPRS report was not content with the state of local–central relations. In this respect the report was echoing the sentiments of the Red-cliffe-Maud and Wheatley Royal Commissions of 1966–9 and of the Maud Committee of 1967. It was the latter which most clearly outlined proposals to improve the relationship of local government to central government. It recommended:

(1) abolition of statutory requirements for the appointment of committees and officers;

(2) abolition of ministerial control over the appointment and dismissal of officers;

(3) abolition of the district auditor's power of surcharge (see pp. 327 and 340), with its inhibiting effect on initiative by councillors;

(4) abolition of the *ultra vires* principle; instead local authorities should be given general competence to do anything they considered to be for the good of their citizens;

(5) freedom for local authorities to fix their scales for members' expenses;

(6) greater financial freedom for local authorities, with additional sources of revenue to be devised and less detailed government involvement in local capital spending;

(7) simplification of Whitehall's machinery for dealing with local authori-ties: one department to be responsible for co-ordinating national policy relating to local government;

(8) the setting-up of a Central Office by the local authority associations to conduct negotiations with the central government.

The Layfield Committee,[32] although appointed to 'review the whole system of local government finance ... and to make recommendations', was very concerned about the state of local–central relations. It declared: 'What has been clearly visible over recent years is a growing propensity for the government to determine, in increasing detail, the pace and direction in which local services should be developed, the resources which should be devoted to them and the priorities between them' (Report p. 65). (It also pointed out that the 'drift towards centralization' was even more marked in Scotland than in England and Wales.) In particular, it found 'a lack of clear accountability for local government expenditure, which results from the present confusion of responsibilities between the government and local authorities' (p. xxv).

The Committee then posed a choice: that either an explicitly 'centralist' relationship should be instituted, giving clear and recognized responsibility to the central government for local government expenditure, both generally and among individual authorities; or a more 'localist' solution should be adopted. The latter was favoured by the Committee. It would involve local authorities taking greater responsibility for the conduct of local affairs, including more powers of decision in services such as education, social services, transport and housing (the government was to exercise reserve powers, but these were to be confined to essential issues of national policy and were to be defined by statute). But above all, under this 'localist' solution, local authorities were to have an additional source of revenue in the form of a local income tax (LIT).

In practice, the central government has not accepted the recommendation of the LIT. Indeed, the (Labour) government did precisely what Layfield feared: it declared for a middle way between the two alternatives posed and argued in favour of a 'partnership' approach to the central–local relationship.[33] (Layfield thought this too vague and that it fudged the issue, and believed that it would only allow the centralist drift to continue.) In the meantime, there have been other developments.

Recent developments

Concern over central intervention in local government affairs is not new: it was expressed strongly in the early nineteenth century,[34] in the late nineteenth century[35] and in the early twentieth century.[36] However, it has been suggested that the situation became worse in the years following the Second World War.[37] In 1956 the government acknowledged the problem and sought to improve it by tidying the structure (via the Local Government Commissions of 1958–65 – see p. 46) and by replacing a number of specific grants by a block grant in 1958 (converted into the RSG in 1966). In 1963 local authorities were empowered to spend up to a 1d. rate on anything which was in the general interests of their area. (Parishes were permitted to spend up to 0.2d. Scotland already had these powers.) In 1968 planning procedures were changed such that local plans (as opposed to the development plans) would no longer need government approval. At the same time there was some relaxation of central control over local authority transport planning, where, with the introduction of Transport Policies and Programmes (TPPs), the government gave approval for whole programmes of expenditure rather than individual projects (see p. 211). A similar development occurred in 1970 in the field of loan sanction for 'locally determined' schemes of capital development.

Further encouragement was given to local authorities in 1970 with the Conservatives' promise to abolish many of the 1,200 or so controls exercised over local government. Yet, in practice, it seemed that control was *increasing*: local authority social service departments were required to prepare ten year plans; LEAs were obliged to stop supplying milk in schools to the over-7s (even if the LEA was itself prepared to pay for it); rate monitoring was undertaken by the central government; and the Housing Finance Act 1972 required local authorities to apply a universal system of rent rebates and to raise their rents in line with government policy (see p. 81).

However the Local Government Acts 1972 and 1973 did remove many controls, including some quite significant ones: indeed one of the purposes of the local government reform was to strengthen and increase the independence of local government by eliminating the smaller and weaker authorities which were often held to be responsible for some of the government's controls (just as the speed of a convoy is dictated by the slowest vehicle).

Thus, apart from the reorganization itself, the legislation reduced the previous mandatory requirements on the appointment of officials and committees, and gave Ministers less power to intervene in appointment and dismissal procedures, including, in 1973, those of chief education officers. Secondly, the power of the district auditor was reduced, so that issues of disallowance and surcharge are now decided by the courts (see pp. 217 and 340). Thirdly, the 'free 1d.' has been increased to 2p. and has a wider application: not only does it apply equally to parishes and communities but it may now be spent in the interests of a part of an area or some of the inhabitants (not all, as had previously been the case). Finally, the Local Government Acts of 1972 (England and Wales) and 1973 empowered local authorities to pay members attendance allowances. (In the meantime, the giant Department of the Environment had been created, and acted, at least to some extent, as the central department for co-ordinating relationships with local authorities, rather as the Scottish Office and the Welsh Office do.)

All this seemed to reflect a new faith in local government. But there was no real consistency, partly because of the impact of party politics. In 1975 the Labour government (1974–9) repealed much of the previous government's Housing Finance Act (freeing local authorities to a certain extent) but in 1976 it passed an Education Act which required all L E As to introduce comprehensive secondary schooling. In addition, economic problems were imposing themselves on the relationship: the government's incomes policy in 1975 led to local authorities being threatened with a reduction in their R S G if they gave pay rises in excess of £6 per week. In 1978 a new form of control was introduced in the shape of 'cash limits' (see p. 229). And since the late 1970s, government inspectors have been becoming more directive (rather than merely advisory) in their approach. In broad terms, therefore, it seems that when national resources are scarce or under pressure the central grip tends to tighten.

In response to the economic and financial problems of 1974–5 (when there were numerous rate protests and sporadic rate strikes) the government established two new and important institutions. The first is the Joint Manpower Watch, whereby local authorities (mainly through L A C S A B – see p. 169) and the central government together collect and analyse information on local government employment numbers and patterns. This does not give the government any greater control, but it does show its concern and possibly leaves room for influence, perhaps through the effect of a well-timed statement acting on public opinion.[38] The second new body is the Consultative Council on Local Government Finance (which technically conducts the Joint Manpower Watch through one of its committees). This Council has brought local authorities into the government's budgetary machinery. It is chaired by the Secretary of State for the Environment and is attended by Ministers and officials from the 'spending' departments (D H S S, D E S, H O etc.) as well as the D O E itself and the Treasury. The local authorities are represented by members and officials from the local authorities' associations. Its purpose is to discuss 'matters of policy affecting local authorities which have major financial implications'.[39] In particular it discusses the local authorities' spending plans, and the government's R S G and its distribution. There is a separate council for Wales for a number of these purposes. In Scotland, there is no such formal machinery: the Scottish local authorities (since reorganization in 1975) all belong to a single association (the Convention of Scottish Local Authorities – C O S L A) and the Secretary of State for Scotland speaks for the central government. Consequently there already exists an ample two-way dialogue between them.

The Consultative Council was a particularly significant step in that it brought together Ministers and the political leaders from local government on a formal and frequent basis for the first time. The essential idea was to let local government make a constructive contribution to government decisions at their formative stages, and especially help to avoid inconsistent and contradictory instructions from government departments. But it is felt that the local authority side is not sufficiently involved in the fundamental public expenditure (PES) decisions, and some local authorities feel sceptical about the consultation, believing that all too often both sides listen to each other but nothing results to deflect the government from a predetermined course. In part this may be due to the local authority associations' having different interests (sometimes reflected in their disagreements over the distribution of the RSG).[40]

The present (Conservative) government has sought to rationalize controls over local government. In a White Paper (see note 13) published in September 1979, it declared:

> Democratically elected local authorities are wholly responsible bodies who must be free to get on with the tasks entrusted to them by Parliament without constant interference in matters of detail by the Government of the day. On the other hand there are certain national policies which it is the Government's duty to pursue even though they may be administered locally; for example, where by statute the responsibilities are shared between central and local government or where the Government of the day may have secured a particular mandate at a general election. It would be inappropriate therefore to abandon all control over local government; to do so would be an abdication of the Government's proper role.

Consequently its intention has been to remove or relax some 300 controls. These include controls over interest rates for various purposes; the hearing of appeals concerning the erection of bus shelters or against bridge restrictions or the provision of street lighting; the prescription of various fees (libraries, testing weights and measures equipment etc. and various licences); the approval of school development plans, of financial assistance to independent schools, of arrangements for the provision of PE clothing, of purchase of equipment for FE colleges; the power to require the submission of housing programmes, control over conditions attached to individual local authority mortgages; the confirmation of noise abatement orders; the consent to disposal of land by non-principal councils; the confirmation of new street by-laws; and the approval of plans for crematoria.

At the same time, the government has reduced the volume of circulars and other papers issued to local government (they have fallen from 1,873 in 1978/9 to 592 in 1981/2) and it has been reviewing its need for statistical information from local authorities. In addition, the government has repealed the Education Act 1976, which means that LEAs are no longer obliged to introduce comprehensive schools and may themselves decide what form secondary schooling will take. In the field of housing (since April 1981) local authorities are no longer bound by minimum (Parker-Morris) standards or maximum (yardstick) costings. And, more generally, the system of côntrol over local authorities' capital expenditure is changed so that less detailed intervention is necessary (see p. 211).

The Local Government, Planning and Land Act 1980

Many people, especially those inside local government, are sceptical about the changes outlined above. Some see them as aimed not so much at reducing the scope of government *interference* in local government affairs but at reducing the scope of *government* generally, in line with current Conservative philosophy. Others see the government as giving with one hand and taking away with the other. As *The Times* put it, 'Where less government means more.' [41] Thus, under the same legislation which removes or relaxes many controls – the Local Government, Planning and Land Act 1980 – local authorities are required to: (i) publish key information about their finances and their performance generally; (ii) to be more publicly accountable for their direct labour organizations, some of which are prevented from under-taking work at the discretion of the Minister; and (iii) prepare a register of unused land (following the repeal of the Community Land Act 1975). In addition (iv) urban development corporations (UDCs) have been set up, at the Minister's discretion, in inner city areas of Liverpool and London, with wide powers to by-pass ordinary planning procedures, and 22 tax- and planning-free 'enterprise zones' are being established in inner city areas. This is in addition to the Housing Act 1980, which now obliges local authorities to sell (at discount) council houses. And while some local authorities are concerned at (v) the new capital expenditure controls procedure (see p. 211), many are particularly incensed at (vi) the new form of the block grant (see p. 201), which is presenting a massive threat to local government's already limited freedom, now reinforced by rate-capping: see p. 284).

As a consequence, the legislation united the various local authority associations in their opposition to the (Conservative) government. This unity was unusual; equally unusual was their hostility to the government, as they were all at the time themselves Conservative-dominated in the composition of their own leadership (see p. 246). The chairman of the Association of Metropolitan Authorities appeared to speak for them all when he said that the legislation presented 'the biggest threat to the constitutional independ-ence of local government in this country since the nineteenth century'.[42]

If this legislation moved many Conservative councils to opposition, anger or anxiety over government policies, others were more favourably disposed because they saw the legislation (especially the new grant procedures) as a means whereby 'spendthrift' or 'profligate' Labour councils could be penalized and checked. Many of the latter, rightly or wrongly, were seen as actively sabotaging the government's economic policy by raising their rates and spending on public services. (In practice many Conservative councils have been hit too – see Chapter 14.)

This argument illustrates the perennial question of 'democracy versus equality' – of how far individual authorities should be allowed to raise service standards above those of their neighbours, and face the consequent judgement of the electors at the next poll.

The relationship between local authorities and the central government has been variously described as that of 'principal and agent' and as a 'partnership'. As *statements* or *prescriptions* of what is desirable or proper, this is clearly a matter of opinion and personal values. There is no formal or constitutional definition of the relationship, and there is no generally accepted theory or philosophy of local government.[43]

Attempts to assess or *describe* the working relationship are very much a matter of individual judgement. Probably local authorities today are neither mere agents of the government nor equal partners: the relationship is somewhere between. But it is difficult to generalize. Politically, the government controls Parliament and thus can normally push through legislation which will affect the shape and substance of local government. Yet, in practice, local authorities too have a mandate (from their own electors), they have their own source of finance (from rates and charges) and they have 'know-how' in the sense that they are 'in the field' and responsible for the delivery of a mass of services. As a result, the central government depends upon local authorities' knowledge, field experience and expertise (particularly that of local government officers). This applies more especially to some departments (education, social services, housing) than to others (the Treasury, energy or trade for example).

While relationships and influences vary among departments and different services, it is generally true to say that what is sought by both sides is agreement and amicable relations rather than hostility and the grudging acceptance of repugnant policies, for ultimately they both share a common concern: the public service. Clashes do occur and some of them become very public (such as those at Clay Cross and Tameside – see p. 230). But the use of 'the big stick' can be awkward and embarrassing for central government (as the Clay Cross and the earlier Poplar cases well illustrated). And in practice, standards do vary considerably among local authorities: in spite of the central government's apparent dominance, local authorities have not been homogenized.[44] Disagreements are inevitable, since local authorities and central government have different perspectives, different party allegiances and different priorities.[45] What is needed is a clearer recognition of these differences and a better mutual understanding (promoted perhaps by a greater interchange of staff between central and local government).[46]

Not everyone in local government wants more 'freedom' from central controls: the removal of ministerial control over charges may cause authorities to turn basically free services into money-making ventures; standards of service may be jeopardized if ministerial intervention were to be removed; and certain controls may be welcomed as a means of sustaining local government employment (the need for ministerial approval may delay school closures, for instance). But above all, both inside and out of local government, is the view that real, local self-government is incompatible with social or territorial justice:[47] that social justice requires a high degree of equality in the standards of service from one part of the country to another. Such a view is widely held by Socialists,[48] though not exclusively or universally. It is the Conservatives who have expressed the desire to 'get off the back' of local government (notwithstanding the financial implications of the Local Government, Planning and Land Act 1980). Paradoxically, the Marxist Left also see a danger in centralization (see p. 57), with local authorities becoming little more than extensions of the capitalist state:[49] hence their advocacy of 'community politics'.

Local government and the EEC

Increasingly, British local government is having to look beyond the central government to the political institutions of the European Economic Community (EEC). Ever since Britain formally joined the European Community in 1973 (under the European Communities Act 1972), local authorities, together with the rest of our society, have become subject to the international laws emanating from the European Commission in Brussels.

For the most part these laws – generally referred to as 'Community law' – take the form of regulations and directives (or 'secondary legislation'). These regulations seek to standardize throughout the Community such things as weights and measures (packaging, labelling, ingredients); vehicle construction (size, weight, safety); public works contracts (advertising, tendering, non-discrimination); and control of pollution (use of pesticides, herbicides, fertilizers). They will have substantial implications for particular local authority departments, such as those concerned with trading standards, and for particular occupational groups, such as those concerned with environmental health.[50]

However, there are other aspects of Community law which have more general implications for local government. The free movement of labour (one of the 'four freedoms' of the EEC) will have an impact on local authority housing policies, especially in relation to the principle of equal access by non-nationals. Other Community laws raise questions about the legality of rate subsidization (e.g. de-rating agriculture). And perhaps hovering in the background is the prospect of scrutiny and control accompanying the financial aid which comes to local authorities from the EEC. These funds take the form of grants or loans, and derive from the European Investment Bank and the Regional Development Fund.[51]

Local authorities, therefore, may obtain substantial material benefit from the EEC. And, as in its relations with the British central government, local government is not without influence: apart from briefing Members of the European Parliament (MEPs) (and perhaps influencing them through the party machinery) and sending deputations (lobbying) to the EEC,[52] local authorities co-operate jointly with the EEC through the International Union of Local Authorities (IULA) and the Council of European Municipalities (CEM – see p. 242). They are also represented on various consultative committees. Evidently 'local government participation in Community affairs is not purely a matter of form. It can and does produce results . . .'[53] But clearly this is not always the case,[54] which may in part be due to inadequate information. Consequently, in 1979 the British section of the IULA and CEM set up the European Information Service.

Information on EEC matters also derives from the consultative advisory machinery on EEC affairs which exists inside many British government departments. And there is a six-monthly meeting of representatives from British local and central government in the European Joint Group, which meets to consider EEC legislation and to act as an information clearing house for local authorities. Together these devices enhance co-ordination, so that lines do not get crossed when local and central governments are in direct but separate contact with the EEC. Thus there is developing another area of common ground between the central government and local authorities.

13. Local Government and the Local Community

We have seen in the last chapter how local government has a close relationship with the central government, and that British local authorities are subject to international (EEC) controls as well as the benefits of financial aid (mainly for industrial development). Local authorities have long had other international links, mainly through the International Union of Local Authorities (IULA), an organization, based in the Netherlands, which acts as a spokesman for local government on the international level, provides a forum for the exchange of views on local government policies and supplies services (training, research, information etc.) for the sixty-three member countries. The latter are particularly useful to the developing countries, but the regular bi-annual conference (which has considered such themes as urbanization, leisure and conservation) is well attended by the membership generally. Similar organizations, though more limited in membership, are the Council of European Municipalities (CEM) and the Conference of Local and Regional Authorities in Europe. More specialized still are the Commonwealth Association of Town Clerks and the International Federation for Housing and Planning. There are similar organizations for recreation administration, for conservation and for public cleaning. Co-operation at a very practical level takes place through the Standing Technological Conference of European Local Authorities (STCELA). This is a new development for the exchange of technical know-how and the benefits of centralized purchasing.[1]

Local government perspectives are thus by no means as narrow as many people imagine. Perhaps the best illustration of this is the involvement of officials from British local authorities in the Zimbabwe (Rhodesia) elections in 1980.

However, in this chapter, our primary concern is with the *local* community and local government's varied relationship with its inhabitants.

Local government and other local public bodies

Apart from government departments, the other form of public authority with which local authorities are likely to have contact is the 'quango' or semi-independent government agency. There are many such agencies and, collectively, they present a vast and rather ill-defined area of government. (Indeed, as many of them are regional or local in scale and character, they might even be regarded as another form of local government.) All local authorities have some working relationships with them, especially the public corporations (gas, electricity, telecommunications etc.), in such fields as rating (or payments in lieu), housing and other development, planning controls and amenity arrangements (such as undergrounding power cables). There are also disputes and even legal entanglements (for instance with the post office, for failing to make good a road it has dug up). And there is substantial cross-membership, with, for example, local authority repre-sentatives sitting on gas or electricity consumer councils.

Some local authorities have especially close relations (and overlapping membership) with particular government bodies such as the tourist boards, the Countryside Commission and New Town corporations. For example, Somerset County Council has had close links with the South West Road Construction Unit, Cumbria County Council with the Lake District Plan-ning Board, and Scottish and Welsh local authorities with their respective Development Agencies.

Health and water

There are two services which are particularly important to local government. The first is the National Health Service. By law the 201 English and Welsh District Health Authorities and the 15 Scottish Health Boards must set aside a certain number of places for representatives from constituent local authorities. Similarly, local authority members must constitute half of the membership of the Local (Scotland) or Community (England and Wales) Health Councils (the consumer 'watchdogs'). There is also local authority representation on the Family Practitioner Committees which exist in Eng-land and Wales. In addition there are day-to-day working relationships, with local authority social workers employed in hospitals or attached to general practitioners; there are close links between the community physician[2] and local authorities' public analysts and environmental health officers; and there is close collaboration between local authority social services and local health authorities – through what are known as 'joint care planning teams' – to plan and finance local health/welfare projects, such as hostels or sheltered accommodation for patients from psychiatric hospitals. These links are facilitated by the common geographical boundaries of local authorities and the NHS boards.

The other public body with which local authorities (in England and Wales) are in regular contact is the water authority. Under the Water Act

1973, existing water boards were grouped into ten regional water authorities. Local authority representatives constituted a majority of the members of these managing authorities (until the Water Act 1983, since when members are appointed by the Minister: see p. 352) and they also have a strong representation on the regional and local drainage committees. Some local authorities also undertake some of the water authority functions on an agency basis (see p. 69).

Close and continuous links between local authorities and these other agencies are crucial for a truly 'corporate' approach to the planning and management of services for the community. But in practice there are deficiencies. Boundaries do not always coincide, budgets are separate, particular interests are pursued rather than the general interest and there is a certain amount of resentment on the part of local authorities who, only a few years ago, were themselves responsible for many of these services.

Local authority inter-relationships

The 'corporate approach' demands no less of a close working relationship among local authorities than it does between local government and other public bodies. Unfortunately, the history of local co-operation has not been an entirely happy one in this respect, partly because of the differences between the all-purpose authorities ('county boroughs' in England and Wales, 'counties of cities' in Scotland) and the counties in which they were located (see Chapter 3). The reorganization of 1974 has eased this problem, but it has not eliminated it: there is still considerable hostility among the several parts of the newly formed authorities – resentment at lost functions, allegations of neglect, squabbles and delays over muddled responsibilities. This point is well illustrated by the uneasy relationships between the GLC and some London boroughs, Greater Manchester and some constituent districts (especially Manchester City), Merseyside County and Liverpool City, and Lothian Region and Edinburgh City Council.[3] A recent survey of local authorities found only 14 per cent of councillors reporting good relations among local councils, and 67 per cent considered the two-tier structure a mistake.[4]

To some extent conflicts are inevitable: old identities and loyalties underlie the new structures; some of the responsibilities are split; precepting arrangements can cause ill-will; and frictions arise from differences in party control. But perhaps above all, each council exists in its own right and will therefore seek jealously to guard its independence. (Although it is usual to refer to the 'tiers' of local government, this does not imply a relationship of authority or power. Counties or regions do not have authority over the district councils, except for emergency planning situations; nor, except for minor matters like filling vacant seats, do the districts exercise any legal authority over parishes and communities.) In such cases of conflict, the Minister may be called in to arbitrate (see p. 226), or another third party (person) may be engaged, for instance to decide which authority is responsible for a particular homeless family. Sometimes the issue is settled in the law courts.[5] Otherwise if it is a dispute of general interest, it may be carried upwards to the local authority associations (see below).

Fortunately, most local authorities seek co-operative and amicable relations with their neighbours: after all, they have in so many cases to work together – where powers are shared (as in planning[6]), or where agency arrangements exist (as in much highway maintenance), or where powers are exercised concurrently (as in the provision of amenities). Even where functions are apparently quite separate, there is much need for close consultation. For example, the county or regional social services departments will from time to time have to consult with the districts – the housing authorities – concerning the nature and extent of the special accommodation (sheltered housing) needed for infirm people.

Liaison, co-ordination and mutual understanding are facilitated by the overlapping of membership among the various tiers of local authorities. This cross-membership at council level, unlike that which occurs at committee level (see below), is not deliberate or consciously planned, yet it does occur on a substantial scale, both between district and county or region and between parish or community and district. Such councillors are said to have a 'dual mandate' (some may belong to three sets of authorities and thus have a 'triple' mandate). In a study of the English metropolitan areas, Stewart has shown that cross-membership of the county and district councils range from 13 per cent in one county to 59 per cent in another.[7]

Local authorities form joint committees to discuss common problems and matters of mutual interest. Typically, there are county or regional joint committees comprising representatives from the county or regional council and from the constituent district councils. Where these committees are responsible for allocating capital expenditure approvals (see Chapter 11), the parish and community councils will also send representatives.

Such joint committees were strongly advocated by the Bains Report[8] as a means to 'co-ordinate the interaction of all county and district functions and policies for the locality' and for 'co-ordination and joint planning of the broad overall policies of the county and the districts within it'. Some of them take the form of 'area' committees or 'district joint committees'. These may comprise district and county councillors for the particular area (together with a team of officers from both tiers) or just the relevant members of the county council. Their purpose is to take a community or corporate approach to the problems of the particular area and the co-ordination of the local services. However, these committees are non-executive and are not directly responsible for the provision of services, but are rather a means of reviewing the services provided and of inviting local public participation, comment and 'feedback'.[9]

Some of these advisory or consultative committees may specialize in a particular service, e.g. education, where many LEAs have established district advisory groups to replace the former divisional executives[10]; these often comprise headmasters and officers as well as county and district councillors. They may also contain representatives from the local schools' governing bodies. And these bodies themselves are another example of inter-authority contact, the LEA appointing members to governing bodies from local district and parish or community councils.

Not all of these joint committees are merely consultative or advisory. Some of them are executive; they may specialize in a particular service, such as planning or highways, and they may appoint staff and be given substantial amounts of delegated power. They may thus come to resemble 'quangos' (see pp. 19–21), the best-known example of which is the Inner London Education Authority (ILEA), which is a statutory body; but more general examples include those joint authorities established for services such as police, airports or crematoria.

More informal groupings may also take place at a local level, particularly among officers, though often on a purely professional rather than a strictly inter-authority basis. Local authorities also frequently share premises and equipment, such as computers, and engage in joint purchasing schemes – in 1970 the Consortium for Purchasing and Distribution, or 'CPD', was formed to provide joint purchasing facilities for a group of local authorities in the south-west of England. The GLC is the main purchaser for London local authorities. There are also a large number of local authority consortia for education system building (such as CLASP), and for housing.

Local authority associations [11]

Local authorities have common interests and common problems. It is therefore not at all surprising that they should join together to consider them. However, their interests and problems are not identical, and as a result they have formed into a number of separate groupings, each representing a different type or tier of local authority though some individual councils do not join.* In England and Wales there is an association for the (non-metropolitan) county councils (the ACC), another for all metropolitan

* e.g. in 1983 the 13 Labour-controlled boroughs broke away from the (Conservative-controlled) London Boroughs Association to form the Association of London Authorities. Bromley has left the AMA, and Avon and Derbyshire have left the ACC.

authorities (the AMA) and a third for the district councils (the ADC). Parish and community councils are represented in the National Association of Local Councils and there is a separate association for 'neighbourhood councils' (see p. 276). In addition to these national groupings, there are some area associations, such as the London Boroughs Association or the Welsh Association of Community and Town Councils, and some specialized bodies, such as the Council of Local Education Authorities (CLEA), the British Fire Service Association and the British Resorts Association.

In Scotland, there is just one association for the various councils: the Convention of Scottish Local Authorities (COSLA), formed at the time of reorganization (1975). It was once hoped that a similar unity might occur in England and Wales, but apart from there being something of a history of disagreements (see below) there were fears over party political domination. (The ACC is usually Conservative-dominated, the AMA Labour-dominated.) It is often said that this fragmentation weakens local government: that a more united voice would be a stronger one. However, some would cast doubt on this assertion[12] and it has been suggested that Scottish local authorities are less free from central control than their counterparts in England and Wales.[13]

The purpose of these bodies is to protect and advance the interests and powers of member authorities, especially as these may be affected by legislation. Some also have the explicit objective of promoting high standards of administration. For these purposes they nominate members to the various staff negotiating bodies (see Chapter 10) and have formed a number of joint bodies to advise on or provide central services, such as training, management, etc.[14] But above all they discuss issues of common concern to themselves, and negotiate with the central government on matters of local government policy and finance. They may sometimes try to promote legislation to enhance the powers of local government[15] and usually establish a special relationship with certain MPs who will be expected to speak on their behalf in Parliament.

Their most important role concerns negotiations with the central government (mainly the Department of the Environment or, for Scotland, the Scottish Office, and to a lesser extent the Welsh Office in Wales). In these negotiations (at the Consultative Council on Local Government Finance, for instance – see p. 236) the associations may present a united front and exercise considerable influence: one Minister has declared that '... the Associations have now virtually become a part of the constitution of the country'.[16] But differences (over the distribution of functions or of the RSG for example) do emerge and they may become quite public. However, it is not easy to assess their impact, since much of their work occurs behind closed doors. Their disputes and disagreements appear to have 'successfully' delayed the reform of local government (see Chapter 3) and they can be said to have lobbied successfully against the 'unitary authority' proposals of the English Royal Commission, with a publicity campaign emphasizing the word 'remote'. However, they are powerless to stop a determined government, as the disputes over the 1980 Local Government, Planning and Land Act have shown. Negotiations gained some concessions in the Bill (e.g. capital allocation) but not in the areas of greatest contention (i.e. financial controls).

In similar fashion local authorities may themselves act in a determined way in relation to the interest groups which *they* have to deal with.

Voluntary organizations and pressure politics

The variety of groups

Most of us belong to a pressure group, though we may not normally think of it as such: it may be the tennis club; the A A; the British Legion; the Church; the Red Cross; the RSPCA; the Old Boys' Association; the WRVS; the Parent-Teachers' Association; the WI; the Embroiderers' Guild ... each going about its own business and not interfering in the pursuits of others. We belong because it is convenient: it helps to meet one of our needs or interests.

Some members, however, will want more than this: they will wish to see their interests not merely provided for but also defended against any threats from outside and positively promoted in terms of facilities and resources. This aspect is perhaps most obviously displayed by such groups as trade unions or professional and business associations (such as the Chamber of Commerce or the Licensed Victuallers' Association), but even seemingly innocuous groups like the Old Boys' Association or the PTA can be stung into 'political action' or protest against a local authority proposal to change a school's status, or the squash club can be moved to write to the local paper about the unreasonable increase in the hall letting charges.

For the latter groups, such political action is an occasional event, a by-product of their existence.[17] For the other groups such as trade unions or commercial associations, protecting and furthering the interests of their members is their *raison d'être* and their use of political pressure as a method is commonplace. Consequently we may refer to voluntary organizations as 'interest groups' where they seek to protect and promote the interests of their members by the use, occasional or otherwise, of political methods, i.e. by bringing pressure or influence to bear on governmental authorities to achieve (or resist) changes in public policy. At local level, common examples include teachers' unions, civic societies, residents' or ratepayers' associations, tenant groups, allotment holders, market traders' groups etc.

A second broad type of pressure group is the 'cause group' – of those who share an attitude and pursue a goal which is not confined to the immediate interests of members of the group but is of more general benefit. Notable examples at national level include Age Concern, CND, the League Against Cruel Sports, Oxfam, the Society for the Protection of the Unborn Child, NCCL, Shelter, the Lord's Day Observance Society and CAMRA. At local level, there may exist branches of these national organizations, and there will be many of purely local origin, for example: a by-pass or motorway action group, a women's aid group, an association for homeless men, an anti-fluoridation group and a host of other amenity and preservation groups.

Some groups may overlap and be difficult to categorize into one broad type or the other: for example the National Union of Public Employees (NUPE) will primarily seek to protect their sectional interests through campaigns against local authority expenditure cuts, but it will also undertake a cause role in so far as it presses (perhaps through the TUC) for better universal retirement pensions or greater priority to be given to the educational provision for the sixteen- to nineteen-year-olds. Other varieties of pressure group may be found locally. Some, such as community groups and Councils of Voluntary Service, are inaugurated by local authorities themselves; others are substantially funded by local authorities or receive material assistance, such as the use of rent-free property. Some 'pressure groups' are no more than a local but important employer (Clarks of Street or Fords at Dagenham). Many groups, such as those formed for rent strikes or school-saving campaigns, are short-lived, temporary 'flashes' which wither away once their goal has been gained (or lost). Others are barely organized at all and hardly amount to a pressure group in the normally understood sense, like the 'Grocks [i.e. Outsiders] Go Home' sentiment-cum-movement in Cornwall.

The spread of pressure groups

Pressure groups, like political parties, are by no means a new phenomenon in local government, although it does seem that their activities have been increasing in recent years. Nearly 500 civic societies were founded between 1957 and 1970; nearly 200 local consumer groups between 1961 and 1970; and some 16,000 charities in England and Wales alone since 1960.[18] Clearly, many of these are only 'partial' pressure groups in that their principal focus of activity is not their relations with local authorities and other public bodies. However, in so far as many of them do try to exercise some influence, it is pertinent to ask why their numbers have grown so substantially. A number of reasons can be suggested, such as greater leisure, affluence and education, or the emergence of new specialist occupations. It is also perhaps a consequence of the widely reported decline in deference or traditional respect for authority. More likely is it a response to the growth in concentration of power as the state assumes greater responsibilities and business units become bigger and more impersonal. Finally it might be suggested the pressure groups are self-generating in that their presence in society has come to be taken for granted and as their activities and successes are given wide coverage in the media, so are other groups encouraged to form.

Because of their volatility and the problems of definition, it is difficult accurately to determine their numbers in any particular area, but it is likely to be substantial. In his study of Birmingham, Newton gave a figure of over 4,000 voluntary organizations[19] operating in that city. Of these about one third were politically active, that is 'making demands on public policy and resources', and most (63 per cent) of these were only involved over a single issue. Since they are usually quite specific and limited in their demands, being mostly concerned with individual decisions, they tend to be more sporadic and less institutionalized than those groups which operate at national level.[20]

A comparison with parties

In many ways pressure groups are like political parties, especially newly founded, local or single-issue parties such as the United Country Party, the Wessex Regional Party or the Campaign for a More Prosperous Britain Party.

However, pressure groups are normally distinguished from parties in that they do not generally seek office but only seek to influence the actions – the authoritative decisions – of those holding office. But with all definitions and classifications there are marginal cases – after all the Labour Party itself is the product of the trade unions' aim to get direct representation for themselves in Parliament, and locally there are close ties between local Labour council groups and trades councils. There may even be factions or pressure groups within the parties, for example CAER – Conservative Action for Electoral Reform. Furthermore there is substantial overlap (some deliberate, some fortuitous) between elected members of local authorities and members of voluntary organizations: in 1967 the Maud Committee showed that 99 per cent of councillors belong to organizations outside the council,[21] and the average councillor belongs to between six and seven such organizations. The Birmingham survey showed that one third of politically active organizations had a member serving on at least one statutory, advisory or other public body in the city, and 40 per cent had at least one council member or MP holding an official position in the organization. Such cross-membership will colour the local authorities' attitudes to organizations, and will influence the way the latter operate politically.

How pressure groups operate

Like pressure groups at national level, local groups can engage in public politics in a variety of ways. They may approach the council as a whole (by letter or petition). They may contact and 'lobby' individual councillors, especially committee chairmen and those who show sympathy with their cause (perhaps members of their organization), and ask them to press the matter at council/committee level. Alternatively, they may negotiate directly with the local authority departments and their officers (again, by letter, petition or delegation). All this implies an initiative by the group itself. In fact, organizations may be approached by the local authority, or they may be automatically consulted in so far as they are represented on advisory bodies: for example teachers' organizations are represented on committees through the process of co-option (see p. 136 above), and amenity groups and the County Land-owners' Association are consulted on development and planning matters.

Some groups will act by seeking the support of other groups ('coalition-building') or the local political parties,[22] especially where the group's cause seems to fit into the party's ideology, or where they can promise or threaten electoral repercussions for the party.[23] Quite often organizations will call on the local MP to intervene, perhaps to prevent the closure of a local hospital or school, and possibly they will appeal to the government (see p. 226), the 'ombudsman' (see p. 260) or even the law courts (see p. 221). At the same time such groups may resort to publicity (via the press, television, leaflets, meetings) and in the last resort take direct action such as de-monstrations, sit-ins, squatting, rent strikes or disrupting council meetings.

Which of these different approaches a group will take will depend on a variety of factors:

(1) Is the group attempting to influence policy or just details of administration? Such a distinction is not always easy to make, but the orientation is likely to have some influence on the group's mode of operation. Broadly speaking, if it is a question of administrative detail it might seem reasonable for the group to approach the administrators (the officials), and where policy is involved to approach the policy-makers (the members).[24]

(2) One would expect pressure groups to operate at those points in the local government system where they will be most effective, that is where the power lies. But local authorities will show variations in the locus and dif-

fusion of power (as between committee chairmen, the majority party group, the officers, particular committees and the council as a whole). And pressure groups will vary in their knowledge and understanding of the mechanics of the local government decision-making, both in local government generally and in their own local authority in particular. Some organizations will therefore know who to approach; others will not and may thus simply focus on the most visible or apparently accessible point in the system.

(3) Knowledge of the appropriate 'pressure points' will be aided by having knowledgeable members, especially 'insiders', such as councillors or officers of the council (see p. 251 above). Newton[25] shows (and the author can confirm from his experience) how these insiders may sometimes find themselves 'wearing two hats'; as members of an outside body they may have to communicate with themselves as members or officers of the local authority!

(4) Effective contact with the local authority need not be confined to cross-membership. The extent to which an outside organization is 'established' or held to be respectable will help to determine the attitude and receptiveness of the authority towards them; that is whether they are regarded as 'in-groups' or 'out-groups'. Their respectability (or 'legitimacy') very much depends on the social standing of their membership, or at least of their officers. Having an MP or other local notable as chairman or committee member is an asset to any group wishing to exercise some influence with the local authority.

In this respect a study by Dearlove[26] suggests that the attitude of local authorities to outside organizations will be based not just on the character of the group, but also on the nature of its demands and its methods of communicating those demands. Some groups are accepted because their membership contains the 'right' people, or because of the moderateness or usefulness of their cause, or because of the propriety of their methods or 'style'. Other groups become alienated and forfeit their chances to influence the council by appearing too radical, supporting questionable causes (such as 'gay lib' or topless beaches) or resorting to unacceptable methods such as direct action.[27] As a result some groups – out-groups – can find themselves in a very difficult position: if they have the wrong 'image' they will not have the 'ear' of the council and will have to use aggressive publicity-seeking methods which will be less acceptable to the council and will thus further diminish the group's standing and frustrate the achievement of its cause.

Apart from their attitude to individual groups, councillors may have a general judgement on pressure groups (see p. 253). This will be coloured no doubt by their experience of particular groups, but it is likely to be generally influenced by the councillor's perception of his own role. We have referred (p. 132) to the 'trustee', 'delegate' and 'politico' types of councillor. One might expect the trustee type to resist sectional interests on principle and conversely the politico to be more accommodating. There is some evidence for this view, but it is not conclusive.[28] What does appear to be more certain is that the older, more experienced councillors are more favourably disposed towards pressure groups than the newer members.

One might also expect Conservative councillors to look quite favourably on pressure groups (especially the welfare, service-providing groups) because they exemplify self-help as well as helping to keep down the rates. Labour councillors on the other hand might well be expected to cavil at the distortions and inequalities which such groups may introduce. The evidence is, however, conflicting.[29]

(5) While councillors have attitudes towards groups, so do groups have opinions about councillors, and this can affect the way they seek to influence the authority. It is evident for example that many groups operate through the official side of local authorities because of their lack of confidence in councillors.[30]

(6) The timing of the issue (whether it is near an election for example) and the stage at which the outside organization comes to hear of it (whether before or after the relevant committee meeting) will obviously have a bearing on the group's approach. And the nature of the issue itself can be critical: for example, if there is conflict over a local authority's promotion of a Private Bill (see p. 67), pressure groups may have the opportunity for a public hearing before a Parliamentary committee.

(7) The nature of the local party system can be an important factor. If there is a party monopoly or dominance (see p. 111), it would be appropriate for the pressure group to concentrate its efforts on that majority party and perhaps withdraw from any other approaches.

It has been suggested that the more conspicuous their activities are, the less influence pressure groups are likely to exert.[31] This is largely because, as we have seen, local authority members feel there is a 'right' and a 'wrong' way for groups to approach them. The evidence from the Birmingham study suggests that

the local pressure group system seems to operate in such a way that the best-established groups ... are able to work through their close ties with decision-makers ... and ... operate in a relatively quiet and unnoticed way ... Paradoxically, the noisier and more visible the group the greater the likelihood of its being powerless in the political system.[32]

However, where the group or the issue cannot be accommodated in this behind-the-scenes fashion, the only alternative is for it to go beyond the council and make the matter more public and more obviously political.

The effectiveness of pressure groups

It is clearly difficult to judge the effectiveness of pressure groups at local level since their success will vary with the local authority, the issue or cause and the standing, resources and style of the groups themselves.[33] Slightly more specifically, we can say that a group will succeed or fail according to such variable factors as:

(a) the size of the membership, income and full-time staffing of the group;

(b) the extent of cross-membership and other contacts with the local authority, and its degree of acceptance or establishment;

(c) the 'direction' of its cause, that is whether it runs with, against or across established council policy. This will help to shape the authority's perception of the pressure group as 'helpful' or 'unhelpful';[34]

(d) the methods used by the group and the quality of their arguments;

(e) the extent of public and media sympathy with their cause;

(f) the organization, methods and arguments of counter-groups (such as developers *v.* conservationists);

(g) the general attitude of the local authority to pressure group politics.

The Birmingham survey suggests that pressure groups are well satisfied with the local authority response. But this may have been due to the fact that their aims were limited to single issues or issues that were congruent to council policy. Nevertheless, Newton suggests that in Britain pressure groups are accepted much more willingly than they are in the USA[35]; 80 per cent of his sample of councillors were described as 'facilitators' rather than 'resistors' of pressure groups. And throughout Britain the extent of support for such groups (especially welfare groups) is indicated by the substantial financial and material assistance which is provided by local authorities.

Pressure groups – threat or promise?

Like political parties, pressure groups are a fact of life. If they did not exist, perhaps they would have to be invented, since they bring with them a number of distinct advantages to the administration of local affairs: they provide expertise[36]; they help to smooth administration by securing co-operation and acceptability of policy; they act as a funnel or filter between the local authority and the various individuals, families, firms etc. who might otherwise separately convey their views and thus deluge the authority; they can scrutinize local government expenditure to detect value for money.

These groups also provide an additional method or source of involvement for the community: anyone can engage in pressure politics; it does not necessarily involve heavy expense, especially since the media seem so ready to provide free publicity for the sake of a story. Armed with the support of others in a group, the individual need no longer feel powerless against the juggernaut local authority. And membership of such a group does not bring with it a continuing commitment which public office or party membership normally requires. Where people feel alienated or estranged from their elected representatives, they can find an alternative voice in the form of a pressure group.

A large proportion of the general public belong to voluntary organizations. A survey published in 1967[37] showed that some 60 per cent of adults belong to one, and a significant proportion of these seem to be active members (though mainly in the non-political aspects of their group). In so far as these organizations do become politically active and establish contacts with the local authority, bridges are being built between the authority and the wider community: the authority has an additional means of gauging public reaction to their proposals and can explain their actions more fully than they could hope to do through the columns of the local press.[38] This mutual exchange of views and information may help to weaken the attitude of 'them and us' which unfortunately bedevils so much of local government's relationship with the public (see p. 264).

Casting a vote is a very generalized expression of opinion about policy: the most conscientious citizen can turn out to vote at every election and yet still have his particular interests overlooked in the manifestos and official policies. Besides, in many areas there are no elections, or the result is a foregone conclusion, and so there is little opportunity for influence. Pressure politics can articulate minority views and injustices which might otherwise go unheard and unacknowledged; in this respect they act as an educative force in society. Professor Richards suggests that pressure groups 'are a particularly valuable element in maintaining a spirit of local democracy as they frequently promote causes that cut across the lines of political party policies'.[39]

Finally, in favour of pressure groups it can be argued that they help to strengthen the democratic process by augmenting the resources of elected members. For those who take a somewhat conspiratorial view of the role of the official in local government, it may be reassuring to see pressure groups helping to restore the balance in favour of the elected member by supplying him with information which can augment that provided by the officers of the authority and may, wittingly or not, be biased.

We all have interests and attachments – personal, religious, racial, local, national. We reflect these, or an amalgam of them, when we cast our vote.

Voting is thus an individualized registration of our interests. Pressure groups are simply a group or collective form of the same process. As such, they are hardly anti-democratic, and most of them do not deserve the bad name which has derived from the lurid exposures of the influence which some of them have exercised on political decisions during this century (mainly at national level and especially in America).

However, there are certain aspects of pressure groups which do give rise to serious and widespread concern. Principally, they are criticized for distorting or undermining the democratic process of government in its traditional form, in which policy reflects the wishes of the public as expressed through their elected representatives. Through pressure groups, certain interests – especially powerful economic interests – are able to get an unreasonable amount of attention and so distort the balance of local provision, to the detriment of genuine needs. Thus we have a situation 'in which a minority of determined people are able to organize themselves into groups, apply pressure to the right quarter, and so influence decisions which affect us all. Parliamentary democracy has given way to politics by pressure.'[40] Essentially the criticism here is that the interests covered by pressure groups are too limited in scope, and that the already powerful groups accrue extra power through group pressure tactics.[41]

The uneven coverage of interest groups is partly due to the unequal distribution of wealth and other resources in society. It is also due to the fact that overwhelmingly pressure groups are created and run by people from a middle-class background, whose education and ambitions are said to make them 'born organizers'. Thus it could be argued, notwithstanding the prevalence of trade unions, that the working class are under-represented in the pressure group area of politics.[42]

Furthermore, although it has been said that pressure groups provide an opening for greater community involvement in public decision-making, in fact, while many people belong to organizations, most do so for their social, economic or spiritual functions rather than their political activities. A relatively small percentage – 14 per cent[43] – are involved in the organizational or bargaining aspect of their association or society. As Gyford says, '. . . the various groups and individuals which engage in local politics outside the ranks of the national political parties . . . represent a modest widening . . . of the area of debate'.[44]

The other main criticism of pressure groups is their mode of operation: their secrecy. In discussing 'the lobby' at parliamentary level, Professor Finer expressed the concern thus:

When we realize . . . that the debates upstairs [at private meetings of the parties] are conflicts between the claims of the rival lobbies in the parties concerned, surely it is clear that we, the general public, the people who have a right to know, are being denied the opportunity to judge between the true contestants – between the prime movers – between the real issues? Instead we are treated to the premasticated speech, tossed back and forth across the floor of the House, of blocs who have already formed their opinions in secrecy. This secrecy, this twilight of parliamentary debate envelops the lobby in its own obscurity. Through this, above all, the lobbies become – as far as the general public is concerned – faceless, voiceless, unidentifiable; in brief, anonymous.[45]

Room for Reform?

Thus may pressure groups exercise power without responsibility, and many councillors feel that if such people wish to press their 'rights' they should also accept duties and responsibilities, and become more open and accountable, perhaps by helping to shoulder the burden of office as elected members of a public authority. In practice, of course, many pressure groups do shoulder responsibility – for example in providing voluntary services to the community. Nevertheless, one simple reform could help to meet this criticism: the introduction of a register in each local authority area for all pressure groups which are in contact with the local authority. This could be available for inspection by the public and perhaps contain details of the organizations' aims, membership and funding.

Local authorities might also encourage the formation of groups and provide them with information and resources. This would enable a wider cross-section of the community to be represented and act as a counterweight to the big battalions already well placed. Some authorities already do this, for example by appointing community development officers and associations. And while in their own way, parish and community councils act as community 'watchdogs', some areas are establishing even more local 'neighbourhood' councils (see p. 276). As regards planning, local authorities are required to publicize their plans, to make people who might be affected aware of their rights, and to give them an adequate opportunity of making representations. In 1969, largely in response to the Skeffington Report of the same year,[46] the government recommended to local authorities that 'the formation of residents' associations should also be encouraged'.[47] In the wake of the Taylor Committee[48] many local education authorities have been encouraging community participation by appointing parents to school governing bodies (now mandatory under the Education Act 1980).

However, the opportunities for group formation and participation must be real: they need encouragement as well as resources. Participation 'involves doing as well as talking and there will be full participation only where the public are able to take an active part throughout the plan-making process'.[49] Or, in the words of the Seebohm Committee:

Community development in this country is seen as a process whereby local groups are assisted to clarify and express their needs and objectives and to take collective action to attempt to meet them. It emphasizes the involvement of the people themselves in determining and meeting their own needs. The role of the community worker is that of a source of information and expertise, a stimulator, a catalyst and an encourager . . . Community identity may also be developed through organizations such as community centres, clubs, play centres and tenants' associations, where the social service department could provide technical and professional help, information, stimulation and grant-aid.[50]

The Seebohm Committee was aware that 'there is certainly a difficult link to be forged between the concepts of popular participation and traditional representative democracy'.[51] But it also implied that the growth of the Welfare State has altered the relationship between state and people and requires something of a review or revision. The promotion of local groups is one such development. Furthermore, if sufficient such groups are created, then rather than adversely distorting local provision, they may instead provide an invaluable source of information about 'real' needs in the community. In the last resort of course it is the responsibility of the local decision-makers to strike the right balance between the various claims, and there is always the sanction (real or imagined) of the next election if they are seen to be failing in this respect.

The citizen with a grievance

Politics at local or national level is about the resolution of conflicting claims. Inevitably, where interests clash, someone wins and someone else loses, or more likely (in the event of compromise) both win something and lose something.

Local authorities mediate the conflicting claims and interests of the community. Theoretically, they attempt to promote its collective interests as expressed through the ballot box. In practice, owing to a host of imperfections both in the mechanism and the very concept of representation,[52] the pursuit of the public interest leaves a lot to be desired.

But even with a perfect system of representation (plenty of candidates, perfect communications, high voting turnout etc.) and with the best will in the world, local authorities are bound to upset some people: the 'general will' takes precedence over the individual in such matters as the compulsory purchase of property, the levying of taxes or the allocation of children to schools. But in a liberal-democratic society, while the majority may rule, they must not ride roughshod over minority interests. The individual must be given a chance to have his grievance investigated and redressed.

How should an aggrieved individual seek redress from his local authority?

Much will depend on the nature of his grievance: he may have been refused a licence or a council house; he may find that the council has given approval to an objectionable development near his house; he may object to the excessive amount of money being spent on local sports facilities or the inadequate amounts going to the home help service; he may protest generally about the level of the rates.

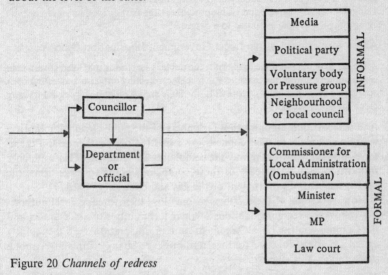

Figure 20 *Channels of redress*

We have already indicated some specific means of remedy – addressing questions to the district auditor (p. 217); presenting objections to the Minister (p. 226); taking legal action (p. 221); or contacting the local MP (p. 232). But the most obvious and sensible starting point is to contact the appropriate councillor, especially through his 'surgery'. In practice, it seems that councillors have one such contact per day, on average.[53] However, for various reasons (see p. 271) there may be problems in doing this. The alternative is to approach the local authority itself, though for many people this is a daunting prospect, overlaid with the problem of finding the right department or officer: in the last resort he can simply write to the chief executive officer or the chairman of the council.

Failing satisfaction here, or if he is uncertain of his case or the correct procedure, the complainant may turn to less formal channels: contacting his local or neighbourhood council (if there is one), approaching a local political party, getting in touch with a relevant pressure group or voluntary organization, informing (or just threatening to inform) the local media.

Although local authorities are not normally deliberately perverse or more self-defensive than other organizations, they do appear to be considerably defective in their machinery for dealing with complaints. The authors of one recent study have said:

> From our experience of representing members of the lower socio-economic groups, we have found local authority departments particularly difficult to deal with, not because of any unusual obstinacy on the part of officials or members, but because of a singular lack of adequate and visible procedures, the existing mechanisms frequently being convoluted and Byzantine to a degree.[54]

And a former head of the Local Government Information Office states:

> Unless something is done to alleviate the public's suspicions that local government is just another part of the bureaucratic machine, resenting criticism and setting itself apart from the community it represents, then it is unlikely that it will survive for very much longer in present form [sic].[55]

And it seems that amongst those members of the public (a small minority) who do complain to their councils, over half (54 per cent) proclaim themselves dissatisfied with the way the complaints are handled. (This is a higher proportion than is the case of those complaints going to large firms, the NHS, the central government or the gas and electricity boards.)[56]

However, some of these criticisms may lose their force as local authorities follow the recommendations of their local authority associations and the Commission for Local Administration in England. In 1978 they jointly issued a 'Code of Practice' for local authorities receiving complaints. Among other things, this suggests:

> Authorities should ensure that effective and continuing information is available to the public about channels through which queries can be raised or complaints made ... There should be easy access by the public to those responsible for dealing with queries and complaints whether officers or Members ... Contact points should be widely publicized, including the names and addresses of Members and appropriate officers. The procedure(s) should ensure that those raising queries are not unnecessarily passed from one place or person to another and that they are dealt with as locally and conveniently as possible ... Responsibility for dealing with queries and complaints must be firmly established ... There should be a willingness to see enquirers and complainants particularly when the issues are complicated or the facts need to be clarified ...[57]

In the meantime, local authorities have been improving their general administrative procedures[58] as a result of the reports issued by the Commission for Local Administration (CLA) – the citizen's 'ombudsman'.

The Ombudsman

Sometimes referred to as the 'citizen's defender', the ombudsman or 'referee' was introduced to deal with local government matters in 1974[59] (1976 in

Scotland). Technically known as 'Commissioners for Local Administration' (CLA), there is one for Scotland, one for Wales and three for England. Their function is to investigate and report on any claim by a member of the public that he has suffered injustice through maladministration by a local authority.[60]

'Maladministration' is not defined in the legislation, but refers generally to faulty administration in the *way* in which an authority's decision has been taken, rather than the actual merit of the decision. Thus maladministration is taken to cover administrative action (or inaction) based on or influenced by improper considerations (such as bias or unfair discrimination) or improper conduct (such as undue delay, failure to observe established procedures or failure to take account of relevant considerations). Much is therefore left to the interpretation or discretion of the Commissioners themselves.

However, there are a number of areas from which they are explicitly excluded. These include complaints about commercial transactions; job grievances and other personnel matters; certain education matters (including the giving of instruction and the internal organization of schools and colleges); and the investigation or prevention of crime (there is a separate machinery for dealing with complaints against the police). Local Commissioners cannot investigate any matter about which the aggrieved person has appealed to a tribunal or to a government Minister or has taken proceedings in a court of law. Nor do they normally pursue the matter if the person has the right of appeal to a Minister, tribunal or court (though this rule may be waived if the Commissioners are satisfied that it is not reasonable to expect the person to use those other rights or remedies). Furthermore, the Commissioners may not look into cases where most or all of the local inhabitants are concerned – a complaint against the general level of rates would not be accepted for investigation. Finally, there is normally a time limit of twelve months within which the complaint must be made (unless there are special circumstances).

The Commissioners will not normally investigate any complaint until it has been brought to the attention of the local authority and that authority has had a reasonable time in which to reply. If no satisfactory response occurs, the aggrieved person should put his complaint in writing and address it to a member (normally a councillor) of the relevant authority with a request that it be sent on to the ombudsman: only where the member fails to comply with the request is it permissible for members of the public to address their complaints directly to the Commissioners for Local Administration.

Unless the complaint is withdrawn or settled 'out of court', that is directly between the local authority and the complainant, and provided that it is within the legitimate scope of the CLA, an investigation takes place in which a CLA investigator interviews the complainant and will normally visit the local authority concerned, where he has the power (within limits) [61] to examine internal papers and take written and oral evidence from anyone who, in his view, can provide relevant information. However, all investigations are conducted in private.

When the investigation is completed, a report giving the CLA's findings will be sent to the complainant, the member and the authority (and any person complained against). The report is made publicly available, but does not normally give names of individuals. Where the report finds that injustice (anxiety, financial loss, inconvenience etc.) has been caused to the complainant by maladministration, the authority must consider the report and inform the CLA what action it proposes to take. (Where nothing happens, the CLA may make a further report and the process of publication is repeated.)

Each year the CLA have to prepare a general report on the discharge of their functions. This is received by a body representing the local authority Associations, which normally has the report published together with its own comments.

It is too early to be able to assess fully the contribution which the ombudsman system makes to local government, though one study has concluded that 'it has made a sound and useful start to its life', and its impact on local authority procedures has been 'considerable'.[62] Between 1974 and 1978, the English Commissioners received nearly 7,500 complaints – about 2,000 a year (roughly the same, for example, as the South West Regional Gas Consumer Council receives). However, the vast majority are rejected as outside their competence: about 50 per cent are received direct and not via a member as stipulated. In that same period a total of 573 investigations [63] took place and found the following (figures for 1983–84 in italics):

331 (58 per cent) injustice through maladministration (*202 = 63%*)
 24 (4 per cent) maladministration but no injustice (*33 = 10%*)
218 (38 per cent) no maladministration (*87 = 27%*)

(The figures to date for Scotland and Wales show similar amounts of maladministration.) Examples of injustice caused through maladministration include the following: a piggery being used without relevant planning permission and the council taking little action in response to complaints about noise and smell; incompetence in granting planning permission for two houses adjoining the complainant's bungalow; failure to act to prevent the demolition of a listed building; unsatisfactory handling of complainant's rate rebate; and undue delay in undertaking housing repairs. The majority of cases (some 70 per cent) involve housing or planning matters.

The CLA reports tend to be treated with respect by the local authorities. In nearly every case where injustice had been found, the CLA was satisfied with the subsequent action taken by the authority (an apology, provision of accommodation or financial compensation, alteration of procedures etc.); in only 6 per cent of cases do local authorities fail to take satisfactory action (the CLA's only sanction here is a second report and reliance on the force of public opinion, though some councils argue that central government constraints on local expenditure and manpower are restricting their ability to provide adequate services). The CLA was also largely instrumental in the creation of the Code of Practice for receiving and investigating complaints (see p. 260). And in 1978 legislation removed a considerable doubt and impediment on local authorities by allowing them to incur expenditure in order to recompense those who suffer injustice as a result of maladministration. And the 1980 Local Government, Planning and Land Act secured the CLA's right of access to relevant information and documents.

However, reviews of the work of the CLA, published in 1980 and 1983,[63] showed a considerable level of dissatisfaction with the service and also with council responses to CLA reports. Indeed over the years a number of criticisms have been levelled at the CLA. These can perhaps best be expressed as a series of questions: should the scope be extended into some of those areas at present beyond the legal competence of the CLA? Should the public be able to complain directly rather than go through the 'filter' of the member? Should the powers of the CLA be increased (either to insist on adequate redress or greater access to documents etc.)? Are there too many ombudsmen (they exist separately for the civil service, for the NHS, for local government), thus causing public confusion? Are the CLA themselves guilty of 'maladministration' in taking so long to complete their investigations (the average time in 1981 being 40 weeks)? Is the system sufficiently well publicized and should other Commissioners appear on television to explain their work as the Scottish ombudsman has done? Is the system (and is it held to be) sufficiently impartial? This last question arises from the fact that, though appointed by the Secretary of State, a number of the Commissioners have a local government background (as member or officer) and the whole system is financed by the local authority Associations. (The estimated cost of the CLA for England in 1983–4 was £1,094,846.)

Criticisms like these were levelled at the Parliamentary Commissioner for Administration (the ombudsman who investigates the civil service) when he was first established in 1967. Since then his role has been gradually amended so that he is evolving into a more effective and respected institution. It is hoped that the Commissioners for Local Administration will develop in the same fashion.[64]

However, there are some who would doubt the wisdom of any further extension. There is the fear that administrators will become over-cautious [64a] and that they will lose some of their valuable flexibility and informality (for example, by refusing to give 'off the record' advice to members of the public). Others have pointed to the costs which fall to local authorities

264 Local Government in Britain

as a consequence of CLA inquiries (the cost of officers' time, extra record-keeping etc. quite apart from any compensation costs or the re-structuring of procedures – for which reason even innocent local authorities are known to 'plead guilty' and settle with complainants, just to avoid the upheaval of an inquiry). And, understandably, there is also resistance from councillors. They, like MPs, claim that they are themselves 'ombudsmen' and that outside Commissioners are an intrusion.

There is some truth in this claim, as indeed the system recognizes by requiring complaints to be channelled initially through the elected representative. However, the evidence points to these representatives being inadequate to the task. This is partly because many have been poor at the constituency role (perhaps preferring to play the 'statesman' – see p. 132); partly because of lack of time (many MPs as well as most councillors are part-time); and partly because of a lack of expertise and power: councillors as individuals have little statutory authority and have limited access to internal documents.[65] The CLA should therefore be seen as an adjunct or 'back-stop' to the councillor.

Participation

Using conventional measures, British local government does not enjoy a high degree of public participation (i.e. enlarging involvement in the decision-making process). As we saw in Chapter 8 less than 1 per cent of the electorate ever serve or stand for election as councillor, a high proportion of seats go uncontested and the average turnout at local elections is only 40 per cent or less. A survey for the Maud Report[66] found that: between one fifth and one half of the informants were unable to name any service provided by their local authority; over two thirds said they had not heard of anything which their council had done during the previous month; less than one fifth had ever been in touch with a councillor for help or advice; only 7 per cent (1 per cent in counties) had ever been to a council meeting; and nearly one quarter felt alienated from the local authority. A different survey[67] found that amongst those who were aware of any participation exercise conducted by their local authority only 12 per cent had in fact participated by returning questionnaires, visiting an exhibition or attending a public meeting, and 42 per cent had declared themselves little or not at all interested in who wins local council elections. A social survey for Mathew Parris MP (April 1981) showed 57 per cent could not name any councillor for their area; 56 per cent could not name their own local authority; two out of three did not know which layer of local government is responsible for different services. And a survey for New Society (4 March 1982) shows that many people still believe hospitals and job-centres are run by local government. British local government is often held to compare unfavourably with other countries in these respects.

These are important findings, but their importance must not be exaggerated. Comparisons with general election results can be misleading, for at national level there is more publicity, the issues are clear, there is perhaps more at stake, electors who are mobile (moving house) have a sustained involvement and the MP will (unlike many local councillors) live in the constituency. Similarly, comparisons with local government elections in other countries must take account of their laws on compulsory voting, polling on Sundays or holidays or the fact that voters may be electing candidates to national as well as local office. Besides, having a high level of turnout does not necessarily imply a high level of interest, concern or understanding of what the councils are doing. Furthermore, as the Maud Committee itself pointed out,

It is of no particular significance that the public do not throng the public galleries of the councils; at any rate this does not seem to be peculiar to this country ... Local authorities provide a wide range of services to the community and relatively few people need to make contact with their authorities unless things go wrong. The lack of public interest in the work of local authorities may well suggest that the public are satisfied with the services which the local authorities provide. The Social Survey's findings in fact do not show that there is any high degree of dissatisfaction with the services or with the way in which local authorities are run.[68]

Other measures suggest a reasonable level of interest and commitment to local affairs. Thus an American survey found that in Britain 70 per cent of those interviewed felt that they ought to play an active part in local affairs and 78 per cent felt that they could if necessary alter 'an unjust local regulation'.[69] In another survey, some 65 per cent claimed to be 'quite interested' or 'very interested' in the work of their local council.[70] And in the survey for the Maud Report, 52 per cent said that they wanted to know more about their local council.[71] Furthermore, as we have seen (p. 255), some studies suggest that as many as two thirds of electors claim to belong to at least one voluntary organization, and some 80 per cent of local electors are readers of the local press.[72] As a consequence, it may well be that many people are interested in particular aspects of a council's work, rather than have an enduring interest in local government as a whole.[73]

Notwithstanding what is said above, the apparently low level of active interest in local government is regrettable. But it is not tragic. Nor is it reasonable to cry 'apathy', since some of the explanations lie in the machinery of local government itself rather than its citizens. The situation is therefore capable of improvement.

Improving participation

The Maud Report made a number of recommendations to raise the level of public interest and participation in local government affairs. These included:

(1) removal of some of the confusing features of local government, such as the aldermanic system and the varying systems of electing councillors;

(2) more education of schoolchildren (and their teachers) in the role and responsibilities of local government in the community;

(3) the development of closer relationships between local authorities and voluntary organizations;

(4) more in the way of advance information to the public on major issues or proposals coming before the council (that is something analogous to government White Papers);

(5) better arrangements at council offices for the public to gain access to responsible officers to raise matters which affect them personally or be put in touch with members if they are dissatisfied with the official response;

(6) easier access for the press to committee meetings; the press should be regarded as partners in the process of informing the public and should be given adequate facilities.

Some of these proposals have been implemented. For example, aldermen have been abolished except in 'honorary' form or in the City of London (see p. 136). Others have been rejected. For example, although local government elections are now held on the same day throughout the country, there are still two different systems operating (see p. 100), which leads to confusion. A number of the recommendations have been left to the discretion of local authorities themselves (public access to officers, for instance) and consequently it is difficult to generalize. Certainly a number have attempted to build up their relationships with voluntary organizations by, for example, establishing volunteer liaison officers or funding volunteer bureaux, but it is by no means systematic. In terms of education in schools, there has been no obvious move towards local government or political studies, despite the efforts of the Politics Association and a recommendation in 1978 by Her Majesty's Inspectors (HMIs), and current official thinking appears to be firmly in the direction of the 'core curriculum' (back to basic subjects) and/or a vocational (work-related) approach.

The other suggestions are dealt with below. But before turning to them it is appropriate to mention that there was some evidence in the survey for the Maud Report[74] that public understanding of local government was greater in the single-tier authorities than the multi-tier. If this is so then the reorganization to a universally multi-tier system of generally larger local authorities will not have aided public understanding of local government.

Communications

Communication is a prerequisite of participation. It has been described as the 'lifeblood of democracy', as it is a vital element in accountability and control. In its broadest sense, communication between the local authority and the community occurs by way of elections, co-option, political parties, pressure groups, area committees and neighbourhood groups, lobbying, open committee meetings, official notices, the media, letters and direct action. In this section, we are concerned with the latter aspects of communications.

Public relations. Communication is a two-way process: from the local authority to the community and vice-versa. It is commonly referred to as 'public relations', which has been defined as 'the deliberate, planned and sustained effort to establish and maintain mutual understanding between an organization and its public' (Institute of Public Relations). The Maud Committee stated that

Public relations are not just a matter of the mechanics of giving information to the public either through the press or over the radio, but also of individual behaviour and attitudes on the part of all who serve the local authority.[75]

This was endorsed by the Bains Report, which said,

... the public have a right to information about the affairs of their local council ... local authorities should themselves adopt an outgoing and positive attitude to the members of the community which they serve and should provide adequate resources, both finance and staff, to finance this.[76]

Legally, local authorities have long been obliged to make available to the public the minutes of their meetings, an abstract of their accounts, information about their expenditures, certain public notices (road alterations, school closures etc.) and a substantial amount of information about their planning proposals. In practice, local authorities provide more information than this (though there is considerable variation among them). In the 1970s, there was a significant increase in the number of civic newspapers, progress reports, open days, exhibitions and councillors' open forums. And the number of local authorities appointing a specialist officer – the public relations officer (PRO) – has increased from fifty to 200, while over 50 per cent of local authorities now have full-time specialist public relations units. Briefly stated, the task of the PRO is to supply information to the press and public, to instruct those staff responsible for dealing with the public and to organize open days, tours, exhibitions and displays of local services. He might also be involved in the investigation of complaints and the mounting of local campaigns (such as road safety or 'use your vote'). Some, however, are no more than advertising devices for encouraging industrial development or attracting tourists.

Such developments are advocated as a means of bridging the gap and creating a sense of partnership between the citizen, the elected member and the official. Others have seen it as a means of improving the image of local government, of preventing or remedying misunderstandings, of bringing before the public how much they owe to local government (by way of services) and of encouraging greater interest and participation.

However, many of these initiatives in communication have not been sustained. Some have been abandoned as an economy measure – in 1974 the Local Government Information Office, working on behalf of local government generally, was closed down – and others have become piecemeal exercises instead of being systematic and comprehensive. In many authorities there is a long-standing scepticism about public relations: a feeling that it is a waste of officers' time and the council's money; on the other hand there are officers and members (and perhaps journalists) who dislike the centralizing role of the PRO, whom they feel may 'steal their thunder'; some are also fearful of having more 'open' government.[77] Equally, there are members of the public who suspect that it is only a propaganda exercise (or 'whitewash machine') and that PROs (often ex-journalists) have developed a cosy relationship with the local media, with the latter publicizing the councils' conveniently prepared and predigested statements and other releases.

Meanwhile, under the Local Government, Planning and Land Act, 1980, local authorities are obliged to publish more information about rate demands and related financial matters and an annual general (or 'stewardship') report. The aim is to help ratepayers, electors and councillors make comparisons and judgements on their authority's performance. (Some authorities and services have been doing something like this for many years.)

The media

The development of local broadcasting has increased the importance of radio and television in the reporting and reflecting of local affairs (including phone-in discussion programmes and the broadcasting of live or recorded extracts from council debates: see A. Wright, *Local Radio and Local Democracy*, IBA 1982). However, the local press remains the most important communication link between the local authority and the community,[78] four out of five electors being regular readers of local newspapers.

Important as they clearly are, local newspapers have been subject to a number of criticisms. In the first place, they tend to present local government affairs in somewhat raw terms: committee meetings are summarized or extracts are culled from official minutes with little or no attempt to interpret them or place them into a wider context of council policy or community development. Consequently, so many of these items tend to become discrete snippets, devoid both of background or sustained interest.[79] Secondly, it has been argued that the local press (especially the weeklies) tend to create an artificial or distorted image of the locality as being essentially united and at harmony with itself, unaffected by social or political division.[80] On the other hand, the press may go to the other extreme and exaggerate the antagonisms which exist in the council and so understate the consensus which may exist on many issues (in the same way as the national press virtually ignore the work of the all-party committees of Parliament).

In general, the local press appears to give local government affairs a low priority, devoting few staff or only more junior staff to its reporting. And there is the temptation to seek reader-appeal by sensationalizing news items: after all, they are profit-seeking enterprises (mainly owned by large national companies), not philanthropic bodies working to promote democracy. However, as some editors recognize, the press does and should have a broadly educational and democratizing role, encouraging and leading an interest in civic affairs, rather than simply following or reflecting it.

However, the press is not altogether to blame, since to a large extent it is dependent on the local council for much of its information on local government matters[81] and it may not wish to jeopardize this relationship by being too critical or incisive in its reporting. The press has to walk something of a narrow path between too cosy, bland and passive a relationship with the local authority and a more critical stance which may result in upset, hostility and a closing up of the channels of communication. Furthermore, in contrast to national politics there are fewer obvious leaders for the media to focus on in local government. Conversely, there are too many local authorities, so that coverage becomes more diffuse and more superficial.

In many ways, councils are too secretive[82]: as Barbara Castle explained it, 'The tendency is always for the public to be told too little, not too much, because by their very nature, executives tend to be secretive.'[83]

In her maiden speech to Parliament, Margaret Thatcher introduced a Private Member's Bill which subsequently became the Public Bodies (Admission to Meetings) Act 1960. This clarified and secured the right of admittance of the press and the public to meetings of local authorities. This right was apparently extended by the Local Government Act 1972 (for England and Wales) and 1973 (Scotland) to allow access to committees of local authorities. However, much of the work of local government occurs in sub-committees and there is considerable doubt and variation of practice concerning the public's right of access to these.[84] Furthermore, the public and press can be excluded from full council and committee meetings if those bodies go into 'camera' or closed session by passing a resolution that 'publicity would be prejudicial to the public interest by reason of the confidential nature of the business to be transacted or for other special reasons'.[85] As a consequence of taking decisions in private session or at sub-committee level, it may be that the press and public become aware of an issue at a stage too late for them to exercise any influence.

The central government has shown its concern by issuing a circular to local authorities[86] which emphasizes that ready access to full information about a local authority's activities is essential if democracy is to flourish. It points out that the legislation of 1960 and 1972/3 sets out minimum requirement only, and it expresses disappointment at the limited moves by authorities to increase their freedom of information in dealing with the press and public. In particular the circular points out that meetings of sub-committees should be open in the same way as full meetings, and that when matters have to be dealt with at private meetings there should be a full explanation of the reasons for the secrecy. In addition, the government is now insisting that local authorities provide much more information about specific aspects of their work, including their finances, schools, housing and direct labour organizations (see p. 238).

Local authorities have raised strong objections to these impositions as yet another example of central interference (and suggesting that central government should put its own house in order[87]). And yet this greater publicity could be to their advantage: it can provide local authorities with an opportunity to blow their own trumpets, to display their achievements, to show they are giving value for money and to rally public support. In addition, by providing more information, they can give the public greater opportunities for comment and for airing views, and thus perhaps avoid frustration and resentment, and forestall outbursts of protest and various forms of direct action. It may also prevent the media providing only one side of a story and the public being given the wrong impression. This often happens in cases where confidentiality is important (as, for example, when children are taken into care), though in such cases the scope for greater explanation will clearly be limited.

Community politics

Communication is, or should be, a two-way process. Local government should be open to the receipt as well as the delivery of information. In the broadest sense this occurs through elections, pressure groups etc.

How, and how successfully, do local authorities receive the community's messages in the narrower, ordinary sense of the term? Ideally, the councillor is the main channel. But in practice there are severe limitations: there is substantial ignorance, lack of esteem, dissociation and even hostility towards councillors[88] due, in part, to the complexity of the local government system and its greater remoteness since reorganization in 1974/5; not all councillors are open to, or adept at, the constituency or 'tribune' role (see p. 132); and difficulties can arise where the councillor lives outside the area or belongs to the 'wrong' party.

Evidently, people prefer to deal with officers.[89] But there are problems here too: crossing the threshold of the town or county hall, locating the appropriate officer, dealing with receptionists etc. But in general, the main problem is the citizens' (the amateurs) lack of time, knowledge and resources: the local authority (the professionals) has all three. According to the Parris survey, (p. 264 above) 50 per cent of people feel too ignorant about the system to know who to complain to. And a further survey (Sobol[78]) showed that a majority thought it not worthwhile complaining. The consequence may be a sullen acceptance or resignation to council policies. But sometimes frustration breaks out into confrontation and direct action – demonstrations, rent strikes, occupation of nurseries or schools or squatting in houses, disturbing council meetings and inquiries or even rioting.[90]

Such events are no doubt partly a reaction to the current economic situation, with cuts in expenditure following years of growth in services and rising aspirations. In part, too, they may be a result of the quickening in the pace of social change, of urban redevelopment and loss of established communities. But it also reflects a reaction to the growth of government and an apparent lack of receptiveness on the part of the authorities. As the Skeffington Report put it:

In the past, local authorities have been more successful in informing the public than involving them. Publicity is comparatively easy, but effective participation is much more difficult . . . We understand participation to be the act of sharing in the formulation of policies and proposals. Clearly the giving of information by the local authority and of an opportunity to comment on that information is a major part in the process of participation but it is not the whole story. Participation involves doing as well as talking and there will be full participation only where the public are able to take an active part throughout the plan making process.

The report recommended the creation of greater opportunities for public participation in the planning processes of local government (they were largely enacted in the Town and Country Planning Act 1972). But the results have been disappointing in terms of public response. This may be partly due to the language (or jargon) used by the planners; it may be that the public are unprepared for consultation ('Participation does not come naturally, it has to be learned');[91] there is the suspicion too that the consultation is a sham, that the policy is crystallized and more than half decided, or at least the options (or parameters) have been pre-determined.[92] Consequently public meetings which aim to sound out public feeling often leave the public more confused or frustrated.

It is sometimes suggested that information and consultation is not enough: that real participation calls for real partnership, for the delegation of power to neighbourhoods and groups, for citizen control. The argument thus becomes more obviously about the distribution of power and resources in the community. And if the gulf between the governors and the governed becomes too wide, the latter may turn to direct action.

Consequently a number of other participative devices have been developed or suggested, for example in the Seebohm Report. Apart from the establishment of a variety of advice and aid centres (for such services as housing, planning, education, welfare and litigation) there is the encouragement of active involvement of clients in the provision or management of various services. These include mothers helping in nursery classes or playgroups, residents or members helping to run old people's clubs and homes, and volunteers helping in youth clubs or adventure playgrounds. In the field of education, it is intended that there should be more information and choice of schools, and there has been a significant growth in number of parent–teacher bodies (PTAs) and of parent representation on school governing bodies.[93] As advocated by the Plowden Report[94] there has been some movement towards the development of 'community education' in which schools and colleges are more open to the general public and become a resource for the wider community rather than exclusively for children between the hours of 9 am and 4 pm. In some areas there have been developments in tenant management of estates or tower blocks (and in some cases the establishment of tenant co-operatives). Recent housing legislation – the 'tenants' charter' – should provide more such opportunities.[95]

Some of these developments have been quite unofficial and due entirely to local initiative, such as the setting-up of action groups to monitor redevelopment or rehabilitation programmes, luncheon clubs, 'good neighbour' schemes or community bus services. They may be purely local or indigenous, or they may be an offshoot from a national organization (such as Shelter or Age Concern). The Seebohm Report drew particular attention to the importance of voluntary organizations in community development work (instancing the community projects taking place in North Kensington in London, Sparkbrook in Birmingham and Toxteth in Liverpool).

Similar developments have been started or encouraged (through cash or equipment) by local authorities, especially in response to the creation of educational priority areas (EPAs) and the urban aid programme.[96] Of particular interest has been the appointment of 'community development officers' (sometimes known as social development or social relations officers). Some are appointed by local authorities or other statutory bodies,[97] and others by voluntary organizations including neighbourhood councils. (Many are self-appointed in that youth workers, adult education organizers, librarians or social workers may develop a strong commitment to the community and adapt their role accordingly – in some cases adopting a radical stance and thus placing themselves and the authority in an awkward position.) Apart from giving information and advice to local residents, their function is to identify the needs and problems of the community and to help to deal with these either by calling on official resources or particularly by encouraging local self-help and initiatives. In this latter sense the community worker is acting as a catalyst.

A more radical approach to community work is being developed in Walsall and Kirklees through multi-purpose and greatly decentralized 'neighbourhood' – virtually walk-in – housing departments.[98] And a number of social service departments are developing the 'patch' system approach to social work services.[99]

Most of these initiatives in participation have occurred in urban areas. This is partly because urban community problems are more obvious or overt (though not necessarily greater)[100] than rural ones, and also because communication links are easier. But another reason is that urban areas lack local bodies (local councils) to represent them.

Local councils

In this book the emphasis throughout has been on the so-called 'principal' authorities, the regions, counties and districts. In this section attention is drawn to the more local, grassroots councils. These consist of parishes (in England) or community councils (in Wales and Scotland). In urban areas (formerly boroughs and UDCs) they are usually called 'town' councils (entitling them to a 'town mayor'). Collectively, they are all known as 'local councils' and their interests are promoted by the National Association of Local Councils (NALC), which is a federation of county associations (in England and Wales).

Under the Local Government Act 1972, parish (or town) councils were formed in England from existing parishes. Elsewhere in England (except London) parish councils would be formed (i) where the population contained 200 or more electors; (ii) where there were 150–200 electors and a parish meeting passed a resolution to have a council; or (iii) in a parish of under 150 electors if the district council agrees. Where there is a parish (or town) council, there must be an annual meeting open to all electors. Where there is no council, there must be such a meeting at least twice a year (though quite often in practice this does not happen). The parish meeting may appoint a committee. Altogether there are about 10,000 parishes in England, of which 7,200 have a council (containing over 70,000 councillors), about 150 of which comprise group or joint councils, each administering two or more parishes. Parishes are to be found predominantly in rural areas and range widely in area (from a few acres to nearly 100 square miles), in population (from 0 to 40,000) and in resources (from a few pounds to £70,000 in the product of a 1p. rate).[101]

In 1974, Wales was divided up into communities – about 900 in all – based on previous parishes or (where they were requested) urban districts and boroughs. Under conditions similar to those in England they have formed councils in about 750 of them. In certain areas (the larger urban areas)[102] community councils were not permitted; just as in England, it was felt appropriate that no community (parish) should have normally a population in excess of 20,000 (or 20 per cent of the population of the parent district). As a result only about 300 such councils in England and 90 in Wales were created in urban areas. (No parishes were allowed in London.)

The boundaries, status and electoral arrangements of these local councils are likely to change (marginally) as they are subject to review. This is the responsibility of the district councils, who must channel their recommendations through the Local Government Boundary Commission (see p. 56) to the Secretary of State, who makes the final decisions. (In Wales the initial community review is being undertaken by the Commission itself.) In addition, in England it is the district council which determines the number of councillors on a parish council (though the minimum must be five) and (both in England and Wales) the district council has the power to co-opt members on to the parish or community council where they are seriously deficient.

Parish and community council elections take place every four years, the next being in (May) 1987. Councillors are bound by the same conditions (in terms of qualifications, disclosure of interests etc.) as those in principal authorities and they may claim attendance allowances.

The functions of local councils are broadly four-fold: Firstly, they provide certain services (playing fields, community halls, bus shelters etc. – see Appendix 8, p. 302), many of which are run concurrently with the district council. Secondly, they have the power to spend the 'free 2p.' (see p. 235). Thirdly, they must be consulted about certain matters (such as footpath surveys by the county council and the appointment of managers to local primary schools) and they must be notified by the district council about certain other matters (including local planning applications, particular by-laws etc.). Fourthly, and perhaps above all, their function is to act as a forum for the discussion of local affairs and represent the interests of the local community to the district council and other local and national bodies generally. In 1980, this latter function has been graphically illustrated in a number of parishes in East Anglia, such as Brandon and Thetford, when under Schedule 12 of the Local Government Act 1972 they conducted local referendums on the siting of American 'Cruise' missiles in their area. For all of these purposes, local councils have the power to precept upon the district council (the rating authority).

The Local Government (Scotland) Act 1973 set up a totally different kind of community council system in Scotland. Although the community councils here have a statutory existence, they do not really form local authorities, since they have no statutory powers or any access, as of right, to public funds.

Initially the Scottish district and island councils were required to consult the public in their areas, then draft schemes for the creation of community councils (which were then submitted to the Secretary of State for Scotland for approval). Fifty-six such schemes have been approved, covering all fifty-three districts and three islands. As in England and Wales, there is considerable variation in the population coverage of the councils: most (75 per cent) have populations of under 5,000 (and 30 per cent have under 1,000), but twenty councils (in the cities) have populations of over 20,000. The schemes also vary in other respects – frequency of meetings and of elections, qualifications of candidates and of electors, methods of balloting etc.

The schemes also laid down certain conditions for the creation of the councils: at least twenty electors must sign a requisition for elections to be held, and usually a minimum number of candidates must stand. Since the schemes provide for (potentially) 1,343 community councils some 15,300 councillors are required (in effect, 1 for every 340 people in Scotland). This is in contrast to the 1,600 councillors in the principal councils. It presents a tall order and provides a sure test of community commitment. In practice, the response has been sufficient for 85 to 90 per cent of the proposed councils to have been successfully formed, though in most cases there have not been enough candidates to hold elections and only about one quarter of the council seats have been contested.[103]

According to the legislation, the general purpose of the community councils is:

to ascertain, co-ordinate and express to the local authorities for its area, and to the public authorities, the views of the community which it represents, in relation to matters for which those authorities are responsible, and to take such action in the interests of that community as appears to it to be expedient and practicable.[104]

For these purposes, the regional, island and district councils are empowered to provide the community councils with finance and other assistance such as may be agreed between them.

The community councils in Scotland, like the local councils in England and Wales, are intended to be broadly based organizations of official standing with which local communities as a whole can identify and through which they can speak and act. Unlike those in England and Wales, they are not a third tier of local government: 'their purpose being to complement local government, not compete with it'.[105] They have the important job of assessing and expressing local opinion, thus bringing to the attention of local authorities and other public bodies any matters of concern to their particular locality. In addition they can collaborate with local authorities in the organization and management of local facilities and services, and initiate community projects. It is a novel scheme in terms of public participation, and one which would, at least in the short term, appeal to many people in (urban) England who feel relatively deprived of a 'voice' at local level. The alternative which is being developed there is the 'neighbourhood council'.

Neighbourhood councils

The Royal Commissions on local government in England and Scotland each emphasized the necessity of local councils both to provide certain services and to represent the wishes of the inhabitants on matters that affect the local community. These roles were seen as crucial in view of the substantial reduction in the number of councils and councillors which would result from their proposals.

As we have seen, local councils have been established (or re-established) throughout much of Britain. However, in England the local councils predominate in the rural areas and the smaller towns. Very few exist in the large urban areas (and they are not legally permissible in Greater London: see p. 273), with the result that 75 per cent of the population of England live in 'unparished' areas. A further anomaly is that within the same district council some areas are entitled to have a local council while others are not. Consequently, there is strong pressure from many groups in the community for an extension of local councils to the urban, especially metropolitan, areas. This may occur naturally, as districts undertake their parish review (see p. 274). However, such an extension may meet resistance from many existing councillors, partly on the grounds that it would involve a further upheaval in local government so soon after the reorganization of 1974. There may also be opposition (as indeed there has been) arising from the fear of party political rivalry.

In the meantime an alternative is being pursued in the form of 'neighbourhood councils', otherwise known as 'urban parish councils'. These are non-statutory bodies which 'belong to the underworld of local government'.[106] They are based, as the name implies, on a neighbourhood of about 10,000 people (though ranging from under 3,000 to over 20,000). Their existence pre-dates reorganization and they are often the product of local community issues and local action groups which sprang up in response to those issues (see below). However, they have received added impetus from the reorganization of local government, with its creation of larger and what many feel to be remoter forms of local authority.

The government in the mid-1970s considered giving them statutory status, and has sought mildly to encourage their formation.[107] The Association for Neighbourhood Councils (ANC), a pressure group founded in 1970, has as its principal object the general introduction of neighbourhood councils on a statutory basis [108] in order to give them stability and status (credibility), and also to avoid the possible unrepresentative nature of voluntary groupings. The A N C (in contrast to the Scottish community councils) also wishes to see neighbourhood councils with financial independence (that is, with the right to precept on the rating authorities) and the power to provide certain services and amenities.

At present (1983) there are about 240 neighbourhood councils in England (compared to 150 in 1975). Because they are non-statutory, their size, finance, form and purposes vary considerably. [109] But typically a neighbourhood council has the following objectives: (1) to represent to other organizations (such as government departments, local authorities, public corporations and local industry) the needs and wishes of the local community. In this respect it will act as the 'ears, eyes and mouth' of the community on all aspects of community development. It may campaign for local amenities such as sports facilities, a shopping area, a play space or a community hall; or it may try to protect the local environment by scrutinizing local development plans or raising questions about derelict land or empty properties in the area; (2) to organize or stimulate self-help within the local community in order to improve the quality of life for the residents as a whole. This may include the clearing of dumped material from derelict sites, helping to set up holiday play schemes or 'good neighbour' arrangements; (3) to help those in the community in need of special facilities by providing services and amenities (such as voluntary playgroups, school crossings or youth clubs) and providing advisory services (such as 'problem shops'); (4) to foster or preserve community spirit or identity, and help to create a sense of community responsibility among residents. In other words, the neighbourhood councils may perform roles which are part social and part political. As regards the latter, this does not seem either in practice [109] or in theory [110] to imply party politics.

Neighbourhood councils are an important development in local government. Like the statutory parish and community councils they provide a 'voice for the neighbourhood'. Research has shown that most people identify with, or are conscious of belonging to, a definable area known as the 'home area'. [111] Local councils and neighbourhood councils cover such areas. And, being so local, these councils should be more accessible to the community and their members less anonymous than most councils, boards and commissions. Some people even envisage the development of sub-units based on groups of streets.

The Chairman of the National Consumer Council has recently spoken [112] of the 'smouldering discontent' among consumers over public services, and how for many people 'life involved banging their heads against the brick wall of bureaucracy'. In this context there is 'a very high level of unhappiness' with the attitudes of council staff. Such public feelings are dangerous at a time of mounting unemployment and simmering unease. He advised making public services more accountable to the public they serve by establishing and publicizing adequate complaints and redress systems. A similar warning that 'the monster machine of local government' needs to be geared to the real day-to-day needs of individual people has been expressed by the president of the Association of Directors of Social Services.[113] Neighbourhood councils can play a vital part in this.

We must, however, beware of over-stating their value, actual or potential. There is the danger that yet another council will confuse people or dilute their loyalties to existing local authorities. If they are to be a genuine and effective vehicle for the expression of community or grassroots feeling, they must not become or *appear* to become too formal, bureaucratic or cliquish. Some people may be put off if they see the council becoming too much a part of 'the establishment' and the machinery of consensus politics. Democratic structures do not necessarily pass power over to the people, but too often the power falls into the hands of small groups adroit at committee work (which is essentially a minority skill and interest).

Apart from elections therefore, there must be regular open meetings, newsletters, questionnaires and other means of allowing individuals to express opinions and raise questions – questions which might otherwise go by default because the individual feels overawed, powerless or bemused, or because he feels that the matter may be regarded as too petty. Like a speck of dust in the eye, seemingly small matters – litter, dogs, traffic, trees, transport – can loom large in the life of an individual or a small community. Over the past 20 years, local Liberal parties have built up strong support through their policy of taking a deliberate interest in such matters, including broken pavements – hence the term 'pavement (or community) politics'.[114] (During their brief period of political control in Islington in 1982, it was the S D P who initiated an opinion survey of public attitudes to that council and its services.)

Maintaining open channels of communication with the whole community, the neighbourhood and local councils can encourage the 'non-joiners' to participate, and this may be especially important in the inner-city areas. In this way, these councils can put community politics on a more regular basis by enabling ordinary people to band together to exert some influence on the decisions being made every day in town halls, government departments and company offices – decisions which may vitally affect their (our) lives. This is increasingly important as the scale and penetration of these decisions increase. The neighbourhood and other local councils, in acting both as 'watchdogs' and 'caretakers', can be a means of fusing or combining the old concept of representative democracy with the newer and particularly urban concept of participatory democracy.

14. Into the Eighties

Local government is part of the 'body politic' and as such it is in a state of continuous change and development. It has its critics – what social institution has not? In an educated, thinking and democratic society criticism is to be expected and welcomed, especially where it is constructive. Consequently, there are many opinions about the shape and direction that local government should take as we approach the twenty-first century.

First, there is the question of structure. The reorganization in 1972 (England and Wales) and 1973 (Scotland) created much dissent and left many elements disgruntled, though a new revision was out of the question in the 1970s. However, there was some (actual or proposed) change by stealth, involving the reallocation or readjustment of functions among local authorities. There was the Labour government's plan for 'Organic Change' in 1979 (see p. 59 above) which sought to restore to a number of district councils the responsibilities they had previously enjoyed as county boroughs. Under the Local Government, Planning and Land Act 1980, certain planning functions have been removed from the counties and consolidated into the districts. There has been a similar rationalization of concurrent functions under the Local Government and Planning (Scotland) Act 1982 (which followed the Stodart Report – see p. 63 above); further modest adjustments may occur as a result of the Montgomery Report (see p. 64). And, more generally, both the Labour and the Liberal parties advocate the abolition of the *ultra vires* rule, and propose that local authorities have 'general competence' powers (see p. 66).

The political parties have now detailed their policies for a more substantial restructuring of local government. The Opposition parties all propose a regional tier of government (with the Labour party also reviving plans for devolution to Scotland), and a single tier system of local government below it which would be based either on districts or counties (SDP) or on new unitary authorities (Labour). But if any of these parties win power at Westminster, any such changes are unlikely to be pursued in their first term of office: they would have more pressing claims to their attention. On the other hand, the Conservatives, now in their second term of office (since May 1983) are implementing a major reorganization [1] through the abolition of the metropolitan counties and the GLC, with their functions being transferred to appropriate district and borough councils or to *ad hoc* joint boards. It is argued by the Government that changed circumstances and practical experience have revealed these top tier authorities to be unnecessary and wasteful (see pp. 64, 84, 94 above). These authorities have also been Labour-controlled since 1980/81.

Clearly there is a lack of party consensus among the parties on this issue, and local government must live with the uncertainty which this situation engenders.

Secondly, local authorities are still trying to settle their own internal structures of committees and departments, and the appointment and role of their officers. Several more councils have decided (in the name of economy) to dispense with the post of chief executive officer (though in practice another senior officer is expected to assume the responsibilities of the former chief officer) and the corporate management system is being diluted (at least in England and Wales).[2] Furthermore, with the introduction of payment for councillors (for attendance at meetings and – currently in about a third of councils – the payment of special responsibility allowances) the full-time local politician (currently about 100) may become more widespread. Some would argue that such a development is long overdue since British local authorities are of a generally higher average size than in most European and North American countries, and their budgets exceed those of a number of independent sovereign states.

Thirdly, whilst party politics are providing a motive force for some of these re-assessments, the local party system is itself experiencing important changes. In the last ten years party politics have obtruded into more council chambers (see Table 9), and more recently (since 1981) we have seen the emergence of the Social Democratic Party which seeks, in alliance with the Liberals, to 'break the mould' of British politics. They have scored some notable election successes (described as 'political earthquakes'), and their achievements at local level have been impressive (in 1981 they had nine council members: in 1983 they had 815).

Of greater significance, however, are the changing trends within the major parties. They are more polarized and assertive today than they have been for over thirty years. This is partly because the Conservatives have espoused the ideology (otherwise known as 'conviction politics' and the 'resolute approach') of monetarism, i.e. deflation through sustained reductions in public sector expenditure. Partly as a reaction to this, Labour has moved to the Left and is proposing to institute a much more planned economy. It has been suggested that Labour changed as a result of having lost the 1979 election on a weak socialist programme and performance in office (1974–9). But it might equally well be contended that the composition of the parties is changing, with the replacement of the traditional upper-class dominance of the Conservatives by the new forces of a radical, thrusting, individualist middle class; whilst in the Labour party, the traditional trade union, working-class dominance is being displaced by the more radical, egalitarian and intellectual middle-class activists.[3] Voters have witnessed the results of these latter changes in the 'de-selection' by local Labour parties of some long-standing and moderate councillors. And officers are facing greater challenges to their advice and, perhaps, tenure.[3a]

Fourthly, voters in the 1980s may find a change in the electoral system – to a system of proportional representation (as in Northern Ireland's local government). This is promised by the SDP and the Liberals should they win power or gain a bargaining position at Westminster. There is also considerable public support for the new system.[4]

It is widely known that the national political scene dominates local election results (e.g. the GLC has never been won by the party holding national office; see also p. 122 above). However, recent evidence does suggest that local issues are now playing a more significant role in local voting decisions (see p. 122). This may be increasingly the case as government grants fall and the local rate begins to 'bite' (though central rate limitations – see p. 284 – will diminish the impact of this). Businessmen are also being urged (e.g. by the CBI) to get more involved in local politics, particularly with a view to moderating rate increases which bear so substantially upon them (see p. 205). Since the votes of business ratepayers form so small a proportion of the total vote (unless employers can mobilize their employees) there have been calls for a restoration of the business vote (an extra voting power which was abolished in 1969); or alternatively to have non-domestic properties partially or (as with agriculture) wholly de-rated. The Government's response in the Rates Act 1984, has been to de-rate empty industrial properties, to extend the right to payment by instalments (see p. 204), to promise a revaluation (of non-domestic properties) and to require rating authorities to consult local business interests before fixing the rate (or precept).

The fifth and most crucial area of change or contention in local government is finance. Until recently, local government expenditure increased as a result of new responsibilities (such as community care), of improved service standards (e.g. homes for the disabled) and in dealing with problems whose scale is growing (such as urban de-industrialization and environmental decay). The problems continue (a growing elderly population, mounting unemployment and increasing obsolescence of capital, buildings, sewerage etc.) and local authorities are finding it difficult to cope: they are experiencing 'resource squeeze' and 'fiscal stress'[5] because rates lack buoyancy (owing to irregular revaluations, see p. 203).

One strategy which is being explored is 'privatization'. This may take the form of total withdrawal of council provision and transfer of a service (e.g. sports facilities) to the private sector; or it may involve joint provision of a service with a voluntary or private agency (e.g. homes for the elderly). But most commonly it consists of 'contracting out' council services to private firms. These services may be for the public (e.g. refuse collection, as in Southend) or for the local authority itself (such as legal services, auditing, management consultancy etc.). Such practices are by no means new: local authorities have long engaged private firms for such things as architecture, building, engineering, industrial waste disposal, school transport etc. The main advantage of the arrangement is a possible lowering of costs, easier budgeting (with fixed-price contracts) and flexibility for work involving irregular work flows. But critics are fearful of a lowering of standards, of redundancies, of loss of service (through bankruptcies), or being held to ransom over subsequent charges, and above all of the adequacy of control and accountability; there are also doubts about the possible savings to be gained.[9a]

It has become an issue today because it is being pressed on local authorities by the Conservative central government. Under the Local Government, Planning and Land Act 1980 local authorities must go out to 'tender' (i.e. private offers) for certain levels of service expenditure, and councils' direct labour organizations (DLOs) must both achieve targets of profitability (return on capital) and publish details of their work and costings. In some authorities it has led to trade union strike action (e.g. Wandsworth in 1982). And some local authorities (e.g. GLC with contracts worth some £200 million) are countering privatization by insisting that private firms fulfil stringent conditions regarding health and safety, trade union recognition, fair wages, and the employment of women, immigrants and the handicapped. Indeed there is also the policy in some authorities (e.g. West Midlands, GLC) of setting up 'enterprise boards' which invest in local companies for the purpose of control, to secure local employment and economic growth, as well as providing a source of income.

Nevertheless, the overall savings from privatization will not be sufficient to free local authorities from dependence on central grants. And such grants provide a means if not a motive for central control.

Central–local government relations should be seen as *the* constitutional issue of the 1980s. It raises fundamental questions about the place of local government in Britain, accountability and the clash of mandates, and the future of Britain as a liberal–democratic state.

The problem has always existed because there is no clear statement of what the relationship is or should be. Britain has no written or codified constitution, and like so much else in our governmental system, the relationship of local government to central government is left to general understandings or conventions, usually characterized as partnership, co-operation or power-sharing. It is often held that in the course of this century, local government has been increasingly subject to central control. This is difficult to evaluate – like the alleged fall in standards of education or morality, measures are difficult to agree or calibrate. But there is now widespread agreement that the longstanding consensus or concordat between central and local government has been broken in recent years – essentially since the advent of the Conservatives in 1979.

It may be suggested that in the period of economic growth (up to the 1970s) local and central government enjoyed an easy-going relationship of incremental growth based on a perception of common interests. When this faltered, the strains began to show as both the Conservative and Labour governments sought to reduce the growth of State (including local government) expenditure, but the underlying consensus remained. This has now been shattered.

The Conservative government of Margaret Thatcher (elected 1979 and re-elected 1983) has adopted an unusually forthright and rigid framework for its policies – to the extent that members of the Conservative party (the so-called 'wets') have expressed concern at this uncharacteristic adoption of an ideology. The basis of this doctrinaire approach ('Thatcherism') is *monetarism*, which implies both anti-Statism – or getting the State 'off people's backs' (especially businesses) and curbing the money supply to control inflation. This involves reducing State expenditure – including that of local government.

The latter policy has been conducted largely through the local government grant system: partly by placing tight cash limits on grants (see p. 214); partly by reducing the proportion of grant support (in England from 61 per cent in 1979/80 to 52 per cent in 1984/5 and 48·8 per cent in 1985/6); and partly by changing the nature of the Rate Support Grant to include a block grant element (see p. 201). The block grant provides a diminishing percentage of grant aid (the 'taper') for expenditure which exceeds a given 'threshold' level (based on GREAs: see p. 201). Where there is a wholesale crossing of thresholds, then local authorities' grant entitlements are 'clawed back' to allow total grant entitlements to match the total grant available.

Soon after this system was inaugurated (1981) the Secretary of State (Michael Heseltine) announced (volume) 'target' expenditures for local authorities. Where a local authority's expenditure exceeds this guideline figure, it pays the penalty of withholding of grant (known as 'holdback'). These targets have altered so much that councils have protested at the difficulty of 'hitting a moving target' (others have called it Block Grant Bingo). But the real cause for concern is that rather than monitoring the overall grant figure, the government is telling each council what it should spend. Indeed there are fears that the government may actually begin to influence what councils spend on particular services; hence the considerable hostile reaction to the proposal for a separate block grant for education (see p. 220), and to the legislation which gives the government power to limit councils' subsidies for transport (under the Transport Act 1983) and (in Scotland) for council house rents.[6]

Many councils have 'overspent' the government's target figures and have lost all or some grant (nearly £800 m during 1982–4). However, they have been able to make good the loss by raising a supplementary rate (or precept). This avenue is now closed, for the Local Government Finance Act 1982 abolished the right of councils in England and Wales to raise supplementary rates/precepts, as was already the case in Scotland. The Act also clarified grant 'holdback' powers[7] and dropped plans for rate referenda.[8]

In Scotland, the Local Government (Miscellaneous Provisions) (Scotland) Act 1981 allows the Minister to reduce the grant to any Scottish council which is planning levels of expenditure (i.e. in the budget estimates) which he regards as 'excessive and unreasonable'. Thus facing a loss of grant, councils were expected to cut expenditure and so reduce the rates. In practice a number of (Labour) councils (e.g. Lothian) opted for losing grant. So under the Local Government and Planning (Scotland) Act 1982 the screw was tightened and the Minister can now actually limit the rate of any particular council – thus providing another example of 'fiscal centralism'.[9]

These powers are now being augmented and extended. Not only is the Scottish system of selective individual council rate limitation being applied to England and Wales (under the Rates Act 1984) but the Secretaries of State (for England, for Wales and for Scotland)[10] will now have the power, subject to Parliamentary approval, to institute a general rates limitation scheme covering all local authorities.

In the White Paper 'Rates' (Cmnd 9003, 1983) the Government argues that the estimated £770 million overspending of local authorities 1983/4 is largely caused by excessive spending by 20 per cent of local authorities (with the GLC and the ILEA alone responsible for £400 million). Thus if these so-called big spenders – the Secretary of State called them 'loony authorities' – have their rate levels limited or 'capped', then they will perforce restrict their expenditures since excessive expenditure plans will trigger grant penalties (holdback) and rate increases will no longer be able to compensate for such losses of grant. Councils are exempt if their spending does not significantly exceed their target or grant related expenditure (GREA) or £10 million p.a., and in addition they may seek 'derogation' whereby they negotiate a modification of the limits with the Secretary of

State. The general rate-capping mechanism may be called into play if 'local government as a whole continues to spend more than the Government believe the country can afford'. Meanwhile 'more economies are required from all authorities' through greater efficiency and the greater use of the private sector. In July 1984, 18 councils were nominated for capping.

Altogether these are massive central powers – the result of what Professors Jones and Stewart call 'panic ad-hocery'.[11] The balance of the constitution is being changed such that, in relation to local government, central government has come to resemble the Big Brother of George Orwell's *Nineteen Eighty-Four*: indeed rate-capping has been called 'knee-capping'. But before considering the significance of these powers, we should consider why the Government thought them necessary.

The White Paper gives the following reasons. Firstly to protect ratepayers in general against 'excessive levels of expenditure and therefore of rates'. Secondly, the cost of local government is felt to be 'too great a burden on the private sector' and is jeopardizing the economic regeneration of Britain: a reduction in rates will help to reduce the tax burden, increase incentives, increase competitiveness and reduce inflationary pressures. Thirdly, 'the Government necessarily have a major interest in local authority services which are national in character, such as education, or of national importance, such as the police ... [and in] the balance between these and other services'. Fourthly, and above all, the government is responsible 'for the broad conduct of the economy' and is 'determined, through firm control, to reduce public expenditure as a proportion of the Gross Domestic Product' so as to permit a reduction in public sector borrowing (PSBR) and thus a lowering of interest rates (to encourage investment).

Much can, and should, be said about these recent developments in central–local relations and their bases. On points of detail, critics have made the following observations: (a) rates form a small part (2–3 per cent) of business costs, and business taxation in Britain (including rates) is comparatively light by international standards; and while current legislation could significantly moderate non-domestic rate increases by requiring close consultation with business interests (see p. 281) the effect of selective rate-capping in reducing the tax burden is estimated at only about 0·5 per cent; (b) rates have risen no faster than the retail price index, and have reflected the inflation rate rather than contributed to it (compared to the impact of fuel prices and subsidies for housing and transport which the Government itself determines); (c) rate increases have largely been a reflection (as indeed intended) of the Government's own policy of withdrawing grants – both the penalty withholdings for 'overspenders' (amounting to £260 million during

1983–4) and the general reduction in Rate Support Grant (e.g. in England from 61 per cent in 1979 to 48·8 per cent in 1985), as well as central decisions on such matters as the development and pay of police, local government implementation of community care and the statutory sick-pay scheme, keeping redundant schools open and the introduction of the youth training scheme; (d) the current (1983–4) 'overspend' of £770 million is equivalent to little more than 0·5 per cent of total public sector expenditure, and local authorities as a whole have not strayed far from the Government's targets (despite the latter's arbitrary nature and frequent inadequate allowance for inflation); [12] indeed as a proportion of the GDP local spending has fallen from 15·9 per cent in 1974–5 to under 13 per cent in 1982–3, while central government's spending has risen from 33·3 per cent to over 35 per cent (excluding social security spending) over the same period; (e) some of the biggest overspending (and therefore penalized) councils face some of the greatest problems of unemployment and deprivation, and rate-capping could further hit many communities in terms of such vital services as schools, libraries, home helps, residential care and housing improvements; (f) the rate-capping mechanisms are unnecessary – indeed they amount to overkill, since the GLC and ILEA (together responsible for over half of the current overspend) and the metropolitan counties are to be abolished; and the doubling of the abatement penalties [13] in 1984 is already having a noticeably cautionary impact on local authorities; (g) there are considerable costs attached to the control process itself, with costs arising from the numerous meetings and mass of communications involved, the production and submission of information, the calculations and assessments, the appeals mechanism, the delays, the altered timetables and the overall uncertainty and demoralization which the whole procedure engenders: rate-capping introduces the ninth grant system experienced by local government since 1979.[14] Indeed, a recent report by the Audit Commission constitutes a devastating attack on the whole block grant system and thus undermines the basis of the government's attempts to control local spending.[15]

More generally it is acknowledged (though there are dissenters [16]) that the Government has a legitimate concern with total expenditure and with local expenditure as a component. But it can be argued that the Government need only control local government expenditure financed by borrowing and central grants; that rate-borne expenditure does not impinge on money supply and interest rates [17] and has a nil or only marginal impact on aggregate demand in the economy.[18] Certainly – and contrary to recent developments – the central government should avoid getting itself involved in the detailed budgets of individual authorities: such central interference only confuses accountability. As Jones and Stewart put it,

'Accountability to the Secretary of State is substituted for accountability to the local electorate',[19] i.e. if the Government 'allocates' a particular council an expenditure and a rate level to cover it, what accountability is there left between the local council and its citizens? Whitehall has displaced Town Hall.

Local rates should therefore be left as a matter for councils and their electors.[20] Admittedly there is a problem of adequate accountability here since only 35 per cent of local voters actually pay full rates. But this problem could be approached in a variety of ways[21] including the introduction of a local income tax (LIT): this would add substantially to those local voters (the ratepayers) who contribute to the financing of local expenditures. The Government has rejected LIT on the grounds that it would add to the burden of income tax, it would be costly to administer and it would not sufficiently identify itself as a *local* authority imposition. The Government also said that there was no consensus on the introduction of LIT. But there is no evidence of consensus on rate-capping or on the abolition of the metropolitan authorities.[22]

Furthermore, there is considerable doubt about the validity and wisdom of the whole policy of deflation through public sector expenditure reductions. Some (neo-Keynesian) economists argue that it will cripple Britain's industrial base and have intolerable social consequences – in terms of crime, family stress, health and social unrest (of which the urban riots of 1981 – in Brixton, Moss Side and Toxteth, for example – were only a foretaste).[23] Basically they argue for more State expenditure, and conclude that even if the monetarist policy is right in the long run, the price is too high. Some would go further and argue that the policy represents not just the political opportunism of the Conservative central government sequestering Labour councils, but that it manifests blatant class war: that the attack on local spending is an attack on the welfare services of the working class to provide tax cuts for the rich.

The price of the attack on local government may be too high in another sense. Local government is a system which diffuses power; it provides local opportunities for choice; and it provides alternative solutions (right or wrong) to local problems. It is the existence of local government which provides part of the 'checks and balances' of our unwritten constitution. Its existence helps to render inaccurate Lord Hailsham's description of our political system as an 'elective dictatorship'. Local government is part of the pluralism which characterizes the liberal-democratic state. It is this which is at risk as local decision-making is circumscribed and centralized. As Professors Jones and Stewart have said, with reference to the rate-capping legislation, 'The proposed Bill makes a constitutional change of the greatest significance. It removes from the local authorities that Parliament has set up as elected authorities the right of control over their own tax. It concentrates power to an extent unparalleled in this country since local authorities were created.'[24] Dr J. Cunningham (Labour's Shadow Minister) has declared it 'the biggest step yet ... down the dangerous road to a centralized authoritarian economy'. This was reiterated by the Chairman of the Association of County Councils who declared, 'The excessive power which central government is proposing will remove from the local voter and ratepayer the right to control their local budgets and determine their local priorities. This is the very essence of local democracy.' And indeed the (Conservative) Minister for Local Government (Tom King) said in 1980, 'If we started to determine [local authorities'] rate levies for them, then I'd accept that that would be a major threat to local democracy.'[25] In Parliament, the centralizing implications of the rate-capping legislation caused ex-Prime Minister Edward Heath to vote against his Conservative party and defy a 3-line whip: he was the first Prime Minister this century to do this.

Current governmental policies are moving Britain towards a 'mass society' – where intermediate bodies, between the Government and the people, are weak and vulnerable (as they were in Germany prior to Hitler's rise to power).[26] Thus apart from government policy towards local government, many semi-government agencies (quangos) have been disbanded;[27] trade union powers are being undermined by recent legislation; voluntary organizations are being starved of public funds; families are being hit by the stress of unemployment; and even H.M. Opposition is being threatened by the loss of its principal source of income (the trade union 'political levy').

Thus we return to the opening theme of this book: the proper role of local government in Britain. It is this which is currently under threat:[28] indeed it has been suggested that democracy is being sacrificed on the altar of economic dogma. Not only are local authorities being threatened with the loss of their centuries-old right to tax and budget as local circumstances suggest and the local community selects, but within the past five years local authorities have lost the power to make their own decisions about the sale of council houses, the level of transport fares, the level of council house rents and even the 'free 2p.' is under threat.[29]

There is fresh evidence of councillors being deterred from seeking to hold office:[30] in some areas, the political parties are placing advertisements in the press for suitable candidates.[31] A further consequence of the central pressures on local government is the greater risk of politicizing local officials, as they may find themselves in the middle of disputes between their local authority and the central government or the law.[32]

On the other hand, the normally non-political public may become politicized as it faces public sector expenditure cuts and the loss of services: after all, ultimately, rate-capping will only be successful in its objective if local services are held or cut back. At one time it was assumed that local government would be 'safe' from excessive central interference because, ultimately, the central government depends upon the goodwill and expertise of local government for the delivery of national environmental, economic and social services. This safeguard is now much less certain as the central government's commitment to such service provision diminishes. Central government does not need the co-operation and goodwill of local authorities to the same extent as before, since it is no longer so concerned about the delivery of State services and those programmes which the government does seek to protect or fashion may well be passed into the hands of the more pliant quangos, such as the MSC.

Local authorities can take advantage of a growth in local consciousness and activity: they can harness local and neighbourhood movements both as voluntary providers of community services and as 'power to their elbow' in their relations with the central government. Despite what is often said, there is a considerable reserve of faith or goodwill towards local government.[33] And since they are so dependent on central finance, local authorities need not appear as the villains of the piece (as they often did in the depression of the 1930s). Indeed local councils have an opportunity, which some are using, to stem the alleged increasing alienation of the public from established political institutions by being more open, showing understanding and demonstrating their relevance.

Appendix: 1

The Changing Pattern of Local Government

ENGLAND AND WALES					
SHIRE COUNTIES			**BOROUGHS**		**PARISHES**

1800	SHIRE COUNTIES			BOROUGHS			PARISHES
1830							
1860							
1890	County councils	County borough councils	Non-county borough councils	Urban district councils	Rural district councils	Parish	London County Council
1920							
1950							
1980	Metropolitan county councils	Metropolitan district councils	Non-metropolitan county councils	Non-metropolitan district councils	Parish/community		Greater London Council

		SCOTLAND		
	COUNTIES	BURGHS	KIRK/ PARISH	1800
Ad hoc bodies associated with local government — considerably absorbed by local authorities during this period though some reappear on a national or regional basis in the period since the Second World War				
				1830
				1860
	County councils			1890
London borough councils		Burgh councils	Parishes	
				1920
	County councils	Burgh councils	District councils	Counties of cities councils
				1950
Greater London borough councils	Regional councils	District councils	(Community councils)	
				1980

Appendix 2

The Functions of Principal Local Authorities (see page 296 for notes)

FUNCTION	ENGLAND AND WALES Metropolitan County	ENGLAND AND WALES Metropolitan District	ENGLAND AND WALES Non-Metro-politan County	ENGLAND AND WALES Non-Metro-politan District	LONDON GLC	LONDON Borough	SCOTLAND Region and/or Island	SCOTLAND District
Aerodromes	X	X	X	X		X	X	X
Allotments (a)		X		X		X	X(q)	X
Arts and recreation:								
– Art and crafts support, entertainment, art galleries, museums	X	X	X	X	X	X	X	X
– Libraries		X	X	(t)	(d)	X	X(s)	X
– Recreation (e.g. parks, playing fields, swimming baths etc.)	X	X	X	X	X	X	X	X
– Tourism encouragement	X	X	X	X	X	X	X	X
Caravans:								
– Site provision	X	X	X	X		X	X	X
– Site control, licensing	X	X		X		X	X(s)	X
– Gipsy sites, provision	X		X			X	X	X
– Gipsy sites, management		X		X		X	X	X
Cemeteries and crematoria		X		X		X	X(q)	X

	1	2	3	4	5	6	7
Consumer protection							
– Food and drugs (composition), trade description, weights and measures	X	X	(t)		X	X	X
Diseased animals	X	X			X	X	
Education (b) (c) and Careers guidance				(d)	X	X	
Emergency action, natural disaster	X	X	X	X	X	X	X
Environmental health:							
– Building regulations	X	X	X	X(x)	X(y)	X(q)	X(s)
– Communicable disease control	X	X	X		X	X(q)	X
– Food safety and hygiene	X	X	X	X	X	X	X
– Litter control	X	X (w)	X	X	X	X	X
– Public conveniences		(w)	X		X	X(q)	X
– Refuse collection, nuisance control, abatement, clean air	X	X	X		X	X(q)	X
– Refuse disposal	X	X	(u)	X		X(q)	X
– Rodent control		X	X		X	X(q)	X
– Street cleansing		X	X		X	X(q)	X
Fire service	X		X	X		X(r)	
Footpaths and bridleways:							
– Creation, diversion and extinguishment, protection	X	X	X		X	X	
– Maintenance, signposting, surveys	X		X		X	X	

FUNCTION	ENGLAND AND WALES				LONDON		SCOTLAND	
	Metropolitan County	Metropolitan District	Non-Metropolitan County	Non-Metropolitan District	GLC	Borough	Region and/or Island	District
Housing (e)		X		X	X	X	X(q)	X
Land drainage (h)	X	X	X	X	X	X	X	X
Licensing, inspection, registration (f)	X	X	X	X	X	X	X	X
Local licence duties collection (g) (e.g. dog and game licences)		X		X		X	X(q)	X
Markets and fairs		X		X		X		X
Planning:								
– Advertisement control, listed building control		X		X	X	X	X(q)	X(s)
– Building preservation notices, derelict land, conservation areas	X	X	X	X	X	X	X(r)	X(s)
– Country parks	X	X	X	X			X	X
– Development control, local plans, processing of planning applications (i)		X		X	X	X	X(s)	X(s)
– Development plan schemes, structure plans	X		X		X		X	
– National parks (b) (j)	X		X					

Police (b) (k)	X		X		X	X(r)
Rate collection (l)	X			X	X	X
Registration:						
– of births, marriages, deaths	X		X	X	X X	X X
– of electors	X		X	X		X
Sewerage (h)	X		X	X	X	X
Smallholdings			X		X	(v)
Social services, social work (b)	X			X	X	X
Traffic, transport and highways:						
– Highways (m)	X		X	X	X	X
– Lighting:						
Footway	X		X	X X	X X	X X
Highway	X		X(n)	X	X	X
– Parking: (o)						
Off-street	X		X	X	X	X X
On-street	X		X		X	X X
– Public transport, road safety, traffic regulation, transportation planning (p)	X		X(z)		X	X X

Notes on Appendix 2

(a) In England, where they exist, parish councils or meetings are the allotment authorities. In Wales, Allotments Acts powers are exercisable concurrently by district and community councils.

(b) Agency arrangements not permissible.

(c) The councils of non-metropolitan districts and inner London boroughs whose areas serve primary schools are minor authorities for the purpose of appointing managers of these schools except in areas where there is a parish or community council (or, in England, a parish meeting) which can act as a minor authority. Where the area serving the school comprises two or more of the authorities mentioned above they act jointly as a minor authority.

(d) Education is a borough function in outer London; in inner London education is provided by the Inner London Education Authority which is a special independent committee of the Greater London Council.

(e) County councils have certain reserve powers to provide housing subject to a request by a district council and/or the approval of the Secretary of State. The London boroughs are responsible for the provision of housing. The Greater London Council maintains a stock of housing which it inherited from the former London County Council and also has a strategic role (e.g. aiding the slum clearance programme of the inner London boroughs, provision of housing for Londoners outside London, re-housing GLC and London borough tenants whose accommodation needs change and providing accommodation through a nominations scheme for people on the borough waiting lists for housing). Much of the GLC stock is being transferred to the boroughs.

(f) Not all local authorities are equally responsible for this function; responsibility varies among authorities according to the nature of the activity being licensed/registered (e.g. counties register nursing homes and premises selling poisons; districts licence/register camp sites, race track betting promoters, premises storing explosives etc.). Much is undertaken with special reference to fire safety.

(g) Most local authorities collect local licence duties through the agency of the Post Office.

(h) Under the Water Act 1973 responsibility for water in England and Wales was passed to regional water authorities. They were also given responsibility for sewerage, but they are empowered to enter into agreements with district councils and London boroughs for the carrying out of this function locally. In Scotland, the regional councils are the responsible authorities.

(i) Some matters are reserved to the county and regional councils, i.e. applications straddling the boundaries of national parks and for minerals development.

(j)   Two joint planning boards have been set up to administer national park functions in the Lake District National Park and the Peak National Park. For other national parks these functions are administered by a special committee of the county council mainly concerned, which may include representatives of the other county councils and the district councils for the area of the national park.

(k)   Many county councils have combined their police forces (e.g. Avon & Somerset). Greater London and certain adjacent areas are policed by the Metropolitan Police Force (administered directly by the Home Office).

(l)   Rate demands issued by the district councils include precepts from county and parish councils; those issued by the London borough councils and the City of London include precepts from the Greater London Council. In Scotland the regional councils collect rates on behalf of the districts.

(m)   The Secretary of State for the Environment is highway authority for trunk roads. District councils may claim the right to maintain unclassified roads in urban areas (this power is distinct from the powers to act under agency agreements). The Greater London Council is highway authority for all principal roads in London other than trunk roads (i.e. the main strategic road network), while the London boroughs are highway authorities for non-principal roads.

(n)   Highway lighting responsibilities in Greater London are divided on the same basis as highway responsibilities.

(o)   In England and Wales off-street parking is provided as shown, subject to the consent of the county council or the appropriate London borough council. Subject to this consent Welsh district councils are also able to provide on-street parks. The G L C provides on-street parking on the application of the appropriate London borough council.

(p)   The metropolitan county councils and London Regional Transport are the passenger transport authorities and there are passenger transport executives responsible for day-to-day administration. Non-metropolitan county councils are responsible for the co-ordination of public transport in their areas but in some cases district councils run transport undertakings.

(q)   Islands, not regional councils.

(r)   Islands combine with the Highland region.

(s)   Regions only in Dumfries & Galloway, Highlands and Borders.

(t)   Some English districts have been granted limited agency powers for libraries. Welsh district councils may be designated exceptionally to exercise libraries, weights & measures and food & drugs authority functions.

(u)   Welsh district councils (unlike English) have refuse disposal functions (including the disposal of abandoned vehicles) as well as refuse collection. Similarly they are able to provide on-street as well as off-street car parks (subject to the consent of the county council).

(v)   In Scotland smallholdings are administered by the Secretary of State for Scotland and the Crofters' Commission.

(w)   Counties exercise a variety of environmental health functions which complement and impinge upon those of the districts. These include such things as control of toxic waste, the monitoring of noise and atmospheric pollution, the control of diseased animals (rabies, sheep scab etc.) and the analysis of samples (such as suspect food) sent by the district councils.

(x)   Inner London only.

(y)   Outer London only.

(z)   The GLC's transport responsibilities transferred to London Regional Transport (an offshoot of the Department of Transport) in June 1984, under the London Regional Transport Act 1984.

Appendix 3

Election Contests and Turnout 1945–70

Average % polls at local government elections (England and Wales)

Year	County councils	County boroughs	Non-county boroughs and UDCs	RDCs
1945	30·1	45·6	46·4	47·9
1949	42·5	52·2	47·0	51·6
1952	43·2	49·9	50·9	52·0
1955	36·5	43·8	45·0	48·2
1958	33·3	40·3	42·9	46·2
1961	35·7	40·6	42·3	45·0
1964	41·0	40·5	42·0	45·1
1967	38·7	40·3	42·8	42·8
1970	33·8	37·6	40·4	42·3

Uncontested seats (%) at local government elections (England and Wales)

Year	County councils	County boroughs	Non-county boroughs and UDCs	RDCs
1945	43·5	7·8	7·3	59·2
1949	52·1	7·7	19·2	66·5
1952	55·3	12·4	25·4	67·2
1955	60·7	18·5	31·5	72·7
1958	60·9	18·6	32·1	75·2
1961	61·2	12·8	28·5	73·9
1964	55·6	8·8	19·7	69·9
1970	55·0	6·0	23·0	70·0

Source: *Registrar General's Statistical Review of England and Wales 1970*, Part II; and the Maud Report, Vol. I, p. 93 (amended).

Scottish local authorities 1970

	Uncontested seats (%)	Voting turnout (%)
Scottish local authorities	50	44·1
Counties of cities	0	39·4
Large burghs	14	43·8
Small burghs	40	46·9
Landward areas	67	53·6
Districts	80	53·3

Source: Registrar General of Scotland: *Annual Report 1970*, Part II.

Appendix 4
An Example of Committee Structure (Somerset County Council 1980)

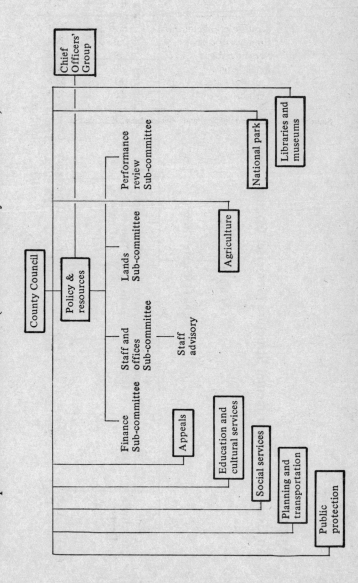

Appendix 5
An Example of Departmental Structure (Somerset County Council 1980)

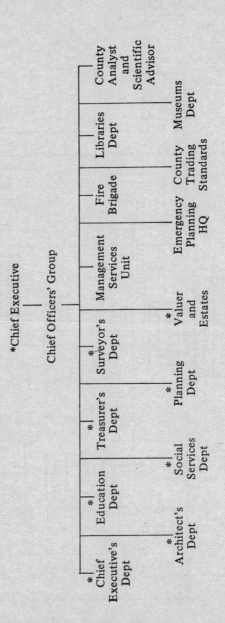

*Chief Executive

Chief Officers' Group

*Chief Executive's Dept	*Education Dept	*Treasurer's Dept	*Surveyor's Dept	Management Services Unit	Fire Brigade	Libraries Dept	County Analyst and Scientific Advisor
*Architect's Dept	*Social Services Dept	*Planning Dept	*Valuer and Estates	Emergency Planning HQ	County Trading Standards	Museums Dept	

*Indicates permanent membership of the Chief Officers' Group (COG)

Appendix 6

Somerset County Council's Education Department (1980)

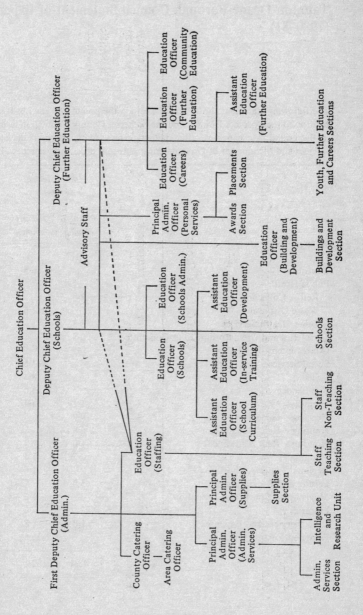

Appendix 7

Taunton Deane Borough Council Statement of Expenses (1980–81)

The following statement shows how the rate in the pound is made up. It sets out in relation to the Borough Council and the Somerset County Council, in terms of rates in the pound, the expenses, after deducting fees, rents, recoupments etc., of the services and the amount of Government grants and other monies receivable.

Services	Administering Authority		Total General Rate
	Borough council	County council	
	p	p	p
Education		86·5	86·5
Public Health –			
Refuse Collection	2·8		2·8
Waste Disposal		1·6	1·6
Other Health Services	3·3		3·3
Cemeteries and Crematorium Joint Committee	0·5		0·5
Concessionary Bus Fares	0·5		0·5
Social Services		13·6	13·6
Police		8·4	8·4
Fire Service		3·6	3·6
Highways	1·1	14·4	15·5
Housing – General	19·9		19·9
Housing – Rent Rebates	6·8		6·8
Housing – Rent Allowances	1·0		1·0
Planning	2·7	1·4	4·1
Regional Water Authorities		1·6	1·6
Leisure and Recreation	5·0		5·0
Magistrates' Courts and Probation		1·6	1·6
Libraries		2·0	2·0
Other Services and Expenses	1·8	·8	2·6
Provision for Inflation		26·6	26·6
	45·4	162·1	207·5

| Services | Administering Authority | | |
	Borough council	County council	Total General Rate
Deduct in respect of:			
Addition to Balances:		0·1CR	
Appropriations from Balances	1·4		1·3
Housing Subsidies	18·0		18·0
Government Grants Service Grants		9·7	9·7
Housing Rent Rebates Subsidy	5·0		5·0
Housing Rent Allowance Subsidy	·9		·9
	25·3	9·6	34·9
	20·1	152·5	172·6
Rate Support Grant – Needs Element	6·7	43·5	50·2
Rate required for Borough and County Council Services	13·4	109·0	122·4
Estimated product of 1p Rate	£146,651	£731,368	
Estimated Local Deficiency in Rateable Value	£5,007,318		

Appendix 8

Functions of Parish Councils in England and Community Councils in Wales

A. Powers to provide facilities and/or to contribute towards the provision of facilities by others

    1. Allotments

    2. *Arts and Recreation*
       Arts and Crafts, support and encouragement
       Community halls, provision
       Recreational facilities (e.g. parks and open spaces, playing fields, swimming baths etc.)
       Tourism, encouragement

    3. *Burials* etc.
       Cemeteries and crematoria †
       Closed churchyards, maintenance †
       Mortuaries, provision †

    4. *Environmental Health*
       Cleaning and drainage of ponds etc.
       Litter control
       Public conveniences
       Wash houses and launderettes

    5. *Footpaths, Roads and Traffic*
       Bus shelters *
       Footpaths – creation and maintenance; signposting *
       Footway lighting, provision *
       Parking facilities – cycle and motor cycle parks; off-street car parks *
       Rights of way, acquisition and maintenance
       Roadside verge, provision, maintenance and protection *

    6. Public Clocks

    7. War Memorials †

B. Specific powers to receive notifications and represent parish interests to other authorities

    1. District councils must notify parish councils in England and community councils in Wales of the following –
       a. planning applications received by them where the parish or community council ask to be so notified;

b. intention to make by-laws relating to hackney-carriages, music and dancing, promenades, sea shore, registry of servants and street naming;

c. intention to provide a cemetery in a parish or community;

d. proposals to carry out sewerage works.

2. County councils must consult parish councils in England and community councils in Wales about footpath surveys.†

3. Parish councils in England and community councils in Wales may in certain circumstances withhold consent to proposals for stopping up unclassified highways and footpaths.

4. Parish councils in England and community councils in Wales are 'minor authorities' for the purpose of appointing managers of primary schools serving their area.†

5. Parish councils in England and community councils in Wales may often act as trustees or make appointments to the trustees of local charities.

6. In England, the district councils may confer any power of a parish council on to a parish meeting.

* The exercise of these powers is subject to the consent of the county council.

† These powers or rights, as appropriate, are also available to parish meetings.

Appendix 9

An Extract from the Standing Orders of Somerset County Council

(reproduced by kind permission)

POLICY AND RESOURCES COMMITTEE

86(1)(a) The Policy and Resources Committee shall consist of 19 councillors, including the Chairman and Vice-Chairman of the Council and the Chairmen of [all the Council's committees]

(2) It shall be the duty of the Committee

(a) to consider and advise the Council regarding:

(i) their strategic policies, and for such purposes to consider the broad social and economic needs of the county (having regard also to any relevant national and regional considerations), to take into account (and to be consulted in the preparation of) any structure plans for the county, and to advise the Council on what their aims and priorities should be, and on methods and programmes for the achievement of those, either in whole or in part;

(ii) their overall level of expenditure both on capital and revenue account, their forward capital programme and the allocation and control of the financial, manpower and land resources of the Council;

(b) (i) to regulate and control the financial affairs of the Council and for such purpose from time to time to embody their directions relating to financial matters in a code of procedure which shall be observed by all committees of the Council;

(ii) to present to the February meeting of the Council each year estimates of income and expenditure of the Council for the next financial year together with a recommendation as to the amount which will be required to be raised by means of precepts in respect of that financial year;

(c) to keep under review the progress of any of the Council's work and services, the effectiveness of such work and services, and the standards and levels of, and the necessity for, existing services;

(d) to examine and make recommendations to either the Council or the committee concerned as the Policy and Resources Committee consider appropriate, on any proposal or decision of a service committee for new major policies or services or for any material changes in existing major policies or services, with due regard to any impact upon the Council's strategic policies or resources, for which purpose each service committee is hereby directed to refer any such proposal or decision to the Policy and Resources Committee before it is implemented;

(e)   to keep under review the main policies and aims of the Council and the arrangements for their implementation;

(f)   to ensure that the organization and the management processes of the Council are designed to make the most effective contribution to the achievement of the Council's aims; and to keep them under review, making recommendations as necessary for change in either committee or departmental structures, or the distribution of functions and responsibilities, or Standing Orders;

(g)   to advise the Council on the carrying out of any major building development schemes by the Council in association with any other local or public authority or private developer;

(h)   to ensure that the Council maintain effective liaison with other local authorities and appropriate bodies in respect of matters within the purview of the Committee;

(i)   to ensure the maintenance of an effective public relations service;

(j)   to determine polling districts for County Council elections;

(k)   to recommend to the Council the appointment of the Chief Executive, the Deputy Chief Executive and County Solicitor, the County Treasurer, the County Architect and the County Valuer and Estates Officer;

(l)   to make recommendations to the Council regarding the appointment of:–

(i) councillors to serve on the various committees (including the Staff Advisory Committee and the County Joint Committee);

(ii) persons to serve as additional members of committees;

(iii) councillors and other persons to serve on statutory and other outside bodies or committees thereof under whose constitutions the Council are entitled to representation except in those cases where this power is specifically reserved to another committee;

(m)   to act as the controlling committee in relation to the Departments of the Chief Executive, the County Solicitor and the County Architect.

FINANCE SUB-COMMITTEE

87(1)(a) The Policy and Resources Committee shall appoint a Finance Sub-Committee consisting of ten councillors including the Chairman of the Council, the Chairman and four other members of the Policy and Resources Committee;

(b) the Chairman shall be elected from members of the Sub-Committee who are also members of the Policy and Resources Committee.

(2) Subject to the overall control of the Policy and Resources Committee, it shall be the duty of the Sub-Committee

(a)   to advise the Committee as to

– the methods and procedures for controlling the financial affairs of the Council and to supervise their implementation and, where appropriate, give directions;

– the Council's annual capital and revenue budgets and forward capital and revenue estimates for successive years;

– members' allowances.

(b)   to make recommendations regarding the granting of supplementary estimates, provided that the Sub-Committee may in their discretion approve any supplementary estimate which the Council are obliged by law to incur or suffer or which is required to meet an unforeseen increase in the level of costs, prices or remuneration; [and in respect of certain other items].

(c)   to examine estimates of the cost of proposals by committees and to draw the attention of the Policy and Resources Committee to any points in connection with such estimates or proposals as they may think fit;

(d)   to act as the controlling sub-committee in relation to the County Treasurer's department.

Further Reading

The serious student cannot rely upon a single book for his knowledge of local government. Yet he faces the problem that the literature on local government is constantly growing in volume and diversity: new areas and themes are being explored and older ones are being revisited and researched and perhaps re-interpreted. This is both inevitable and desirable, for our understanding of local government cannot be fixed once and for all, and, in particular, it should not be based simply on an understanding of the statutory and other legal provisions (important though these are).

However, as a bibliography, a long list of books can be off-putting – and academics do get carried away (what enthusiast doesn't?). In what follows, therefore, I have aimed to provide a range of suitable reading from which the student can make his selections (bearing in mind that a number of the titles listed are alternatives). It is very difficult deciding what to leave out: even authors whose ideas are unacceptable can stimulate lines of thought and provide interesting insights and perspectives.

The list is essentially a list of books, though a few important articles are included. Other articles and books are mentioned in the chapter references. The keen student might also consult the bibliographies contained in *Local Government Studies* for July 1975; J. Gyford, *Local Politics in Britain*, Croom Helm, 1984; and H. V. Wiseman (ed.), *Local Government in England 1958–1969*, Routledge, 1969. There is also a select bibliography on local government published by the Royal Institute of Public Administration (RIPA). And in 1975 there was published an index of articles drawn from eleven journals entitled *The Essex Reference Index: British Journals on Politics and Sociology 1950–73*, edited by K. I. Macdonald, Macmillan, 1975.

Finally, anyone who wishes to keep himself up to date with developments in local government should regularly consult the journals mentioned in the last section of this list.

1. General reference

M. Minogue (ed.), *Documents on Contemporary British Government*, Vol. 2: *Local Government in Britain* (CUP, 1977). *Municipal Year Book* (published annually).

L. Golding, *Dictionary of Local Government in England and Wales*, EUP, 1962.

2. General and/or theoretical

J. Stanyer, *Understanding Local Government*, Fontana, 1976.

D. Hill, *Democratic Theory and Local Government*, Allen & Unwin, 1974.

W. J. M. Mackenzie, *Theories of Local Government*, LSE, 1961.

L. J. Sharpe, 'Theories and Values of Local Government', *Political Studies*, June 1970.

Lord Redcliffe-Maud and B. Wood, *English Local Government Reformed*, OUP, 1974.

P. G. Richards, *The Reformed Local Government System*, Allen & Unwin, 1980.

A. Alexander, *Local Government in Britain since Reorganization*, Allen & Unwin, 1982.

M. Boddy and C. Fudge, *The Local State: Theory and Practice*, SAUS, 1981.

P. Dunleavy, *Urban Political Analysis*, Macmillan, 1980.

J. Raine et al., *In Defence of Local Government*, INLOGOV, 1981.

E. Butler and M. Pirie (eds.), *Economy and Local Government*, ASI, 1981.

3. History

K. B. Smellie, *A History of Local Government*, Allen & Unwin, 1968.

J. Redlich and F. W. Hirst, *The History of Local Government in England*, ed. B. Keith-Lucas, Macmillan, 1970.

B. Keith-Lucas and P. G. Richards, *A History of Local Government in the Twentieth Century*, Allen & Unwin, 1976.

W. Thornhill (ed.), *The Growth and Reform of English Local Government*, Weidenfeld & Nicolson, 1971.

V. D. Lipman, *Local Government Areas 1834–1945*, Blackwell, 1949.

C. J. Pearce, *The Machinery of Change in Local Government*, Allen & Unwin, 1982.

4. The legal context

C. A. Cross, *Principles of Local Government Law*, Sweet & Maxwell, 1981.

W. O. Hart and J. F. Garner, *Local Government and Administration*, Butterworth, 1973.

R. J. Buxton, *Local Government*, Penguin Books, 1973.

S. A. de Smith, *Judicial Review of Administrative Action*, Stevens, 1973.

R. Jeffries, *Tackling the Town Hall*, Routledge & Kegan Paul, 1982.

5. Structure

Report of the Royal Commission on Local Government in England 1966–1969, (the Redcliffe-Maud Report) 3 vols., Cmd 4040, HMSO, 1969.

Report of the Royal Commission on Local Government in Scotland 1966–1969, (the Wheatley Report), 2 vols., Cmd 4150, HMSO, 1969.

Local Government in England: Government Proposals for Re-organisation, Cmd 4584, HMSO, 1971.

The Reform of Local Government in Scotland, Cmd 4583, HMSO, 1971.

C. Arnold-Baker, *The Local Government Act 1972*, Butterworth, 1973.

P. G. Richards, *The Local Government Act 1972: Problems of Implementation*, Allen & Unwin, 1975.

K. Newton, 'Is Small Really So Beautiful? Is Big Really So Ugly?', *Political Studies*, June 1982.

B. Wood, *The Process of Local Government Reform 1966–74*, Allen & Unwin, 1976.

J. A. Brand, *Local Government Reform in England 1888–1974*, Croom Helm, 1974.

J. Dearlove, *The Reorganisation of British Local Government*, CUP, 1979.

G. Jones, 'The Local Government Act 1972 and the Redcliffe-Maud Commission', *Political Quarterly*, April 1973.

S. L. Bristow, 'Criteria for Local Government Reorganisation and Local Authority Autonomy', *Politics and Problems*, December 1972.

R. A. W. Rhodes, 'Local Government Reorganisation: Three Questions', *Social and Economic Administration*, no. 8, 1974.

6. Functions

R. Bell and N. Grant, *Patterns of Education in the British Isles*, Allen & Unwin, 1978.

M. Kogan, *Educational Policy Making*, Allen & Unwin, 1975.

M. Kogan, *The Politics of Educational Change*, Fontana, 1978.

A. Byrne and C. Padfield, *Social Services Made Simple*, Heinemann, 3rd ed. 1984.

Report of the Committee on Local Authority and Allied Personal Social Services, Cmd 3703, HMSO, 1968.

J. Pratt *et al.*, *Your Local Education*, Penguin Books, 1973.

T. A. Critchley, *A History of the Police in England and Wales*, Constable, 1978.

S. Elkin, *Politics and Land Use Planning*, CUP, 1974.

J. Gyford, *Town Planning and the Practice of Politics*, University College London, 1978.

J. B. Cullingworth, *Town and Country Planning in Britain*, Allen & Unwin, 1976.

J. B. Cullingworth, *Essays on Housing Policy*, Allen & Unwin, 1979.

D. Regan, *Local Government and Education*, Allen & Unwin, 1977.

O. Hartley, 'The Functions of Local Government', *Local Government Studies*, February 1973.

D. Donnison and C. Ungerson, *Housing Policy*, Penguin, 1982.

7. Elections and councillors

Report of the Committee on Management of Local Government (the Maud Report), Vols. 2, 3 and 5, HMSO, 1967.

The Remuneration of Councillors, Vol. 2, HMSO, 1977.

J. Prophet, *The Councillor*, Shaw, 1979.

I. Budge *et al.*, *Political Stratification and Democracy*, Macmillan, 1972.

F. Bealey *et al.*, *Constituency Politics*, Faber, 1965.

G. Jones, 'The Functions and Organisation of Councillors', *Public Administration*, Winter 1973.

H. Heclo, 'The Councillor's Job', *Public Administration*, Summer 1969.

R. Gregory, 'Local Elections and the Rule of Anticipated Reactions', *Political Studies*, March 1969.

A. Samuels, 'On Ceasing to be a Councillor', *Local Government Review*, 4 July 1981.

P. Fletcher, 'An Explanation of Variations in Turnout in Local Elections', *Political Studies*, March 1969.

L. J. Sharpe, *Voting in Cities*, Macmillan, 1967.

8. Parties and politics

J. Gyford, *Local Politics in Britain*, Croom Helm, 1984.

J. G. Bulpitt, *Party Politics in English Local Government*, Longmans, 1967.

Report of the Committee on Management of Local Government (the Maud Report), Vol. 5, HMSO, 1967.

J. Dearlove, *The Politics of Policy in Local Government*, CUP, 1973.

A. H. Birch, *Small Town Politics*, OUP, 1959.

P. Saunders, *Urban Politics: A Sociological Interpretation*, Hutchinson, 1979.

W. Grant, *Independent Local Politics in England and Wales*, Saxon House, 1978.

A. Richards and A. Kuper, *Councils in Action*, CUP, 1971.

Local Government Handbook, Labour Party, 1977.

Conservative Political Centre, *Party Politics in Local Government*, Conservative Party, 1962.

G. Jones, 'Varieties of Local Politics', *Local Government Studies*, April 1975.

G. Green, 'Politics, Local Government and the Community', *Local Government Studies*, June 1974.

J. D. Lees and R. Kimber (eds.), *Political Parties in Modern Britain*, Routledge, 1972.

J. Richardson and G. Jordan, *Governing Under Pressure*, Martin Robertson, 1979.

9. Internal organization and procedures

J. Bourn, *Management in Central and Local Government*, Pitman, 1979.

R. Hambledon, *Policy Planning and Local Government*, Hutchinson, 1978.

T. Eddison, *Local Government Management and Corporate Planning*, Hill, 1975.

R. Greenwood *et al.*, *The Organisation of Local Authorities in England and Wales 1967–75*, INLOGOV, 1975.

R. Greenwood *et al.*, *In Pursuit of Corporate Rationality: Organisational Developments in the Post-Reorganisation Period*, INLOGOV, 1977.

A. Fowler, *Personnel Management in Local Government*, IPM, 1975.

J. Stewart, *The Responsive Local Authority*, INLOGOV, 1974.

Report of the Committee on Management of Local Government (the Maud Report), Vols. 1 and 5.

J. Skitt, *Practical Corporate Planning in Local Government*, Hill, 1975.

The New Local Authorities: Management and Structure (the Bains Report), HMSO, 1972.

R. S. Knowles, *Modern Management in Local Government*, Butterworth, 1977.

The New Scottish Local Authorities: Organisation and Management Structures (the Paterson Report), HMSO, 1973.

N. Boaden, *Urban Policy Making*, CUP, 1971.

A. Griffiths, *Local Government Administration*, Shaw, 1976.

R. Ashworth, 'Generalists and Specialists', *Local Government Review*, 27 June 1981.

G. L. Bayley, *Local Government: Is It Manageable?*, Pergamon, 1980.

D. Regan, *A Headless State*, University of Nottingham, 1980.

R. A. W. Rhodes and A. F. Midwinter, *Corporate Management: the New Conventional Wisdom in British Local Government*, University of Strathclyde, 1980.

J. K. Friend and W. N. Jessop, *Local Government and Strategic Choice*, Tavistock, 1969.

K. P. Poole, *The Local Government Service*, Allen & Unwin, 1978.

Report of the Committee on the Staffing of Local Government, HMSO, 1967.

D. Birley, *The Education Officer and His World*, Routledge, 1970.

Brunel Institute of Organisational and Social Studies, *Social Services Departments*, Heinemann, 1974.

B. Wilson, 'Who Would be a Chief Executive?', *Public Administration*, 1975.

R. J. Haynes, *Organization Theory and Local Government*, Allen & Unwin, 1980.

R. Greenwood *et al.*, *Patterns of Management in Local Government*, Martin Robertson, 1980.

C. Skelcher, 'From Programme Budgeting to Policy Analysis: Corporate Approaches in Local Government', *Public Administration*, Summer 1980.

C. Pinker and A. Dixson, *Solving Local Government Problems*, Allen & Unwin, 1981.

T. Bovaird, 'Recent Developments in Output Measurement in Local Government', *Local Government Studies*, September/October 1981.

10. Finance

A Handbook of Local Government Finance, CIPFA, 1982.

N. P. Hepworth, *The Finance of Local Government*, Allen & Unwin, 1980.

A. H. Marshall, *Financial Administration in Local Government*, Allen & Unwin, 1974.

Local Government Finance: Report of the Committee of Enquiry, Cmd 6453, HMSO, 1976.

Report of the Committee of Inquiry into the Impact of Rates on Households, Cmd 2582, HMSO, 1965.

The Future Shape of Local Government Finance, Cmd 4741, HMSO, 1971.

Sources of Local Revenue, RIPA, 1968.

A. R. Ilersic, *Rates and Local Government*, Michael Joseph, 1965.

D. S. Lees *et al.*, *Local Expenditure and Exchequer Grants*, IMTA, 1965.

W. L. Abernethy, *Internal Audit in Local Authorities and Hospitals*, Shaw, 1971.

L. Helmore, *The District Auditor*, Macdonald & Evans, 1961.

D. Ashford, 'The Effects of Central Finance on the British Local Government System', *British Journal of Political Science*, 4, 1974.

C. D. Foster *et al.*, *Local Government Finance in a Unitary State*, Allen & Unwin, 1980.

G. Jones *et al.*, *The Way Ahead for Local Government Finance*, INLOGOV, 1982.

T. Burgess and T. Travers, *Ten Billion Pounds*, Grant McIntyre, 1980.

R. J. Bennet, 'The Local Income Tax in Britain: A Critique of Recent Arguments Against Its Use', *Public Administration*, Autumn 1981.

R. J. Bennet, *Central Grants to Local Governments*, CUP, 1982.

Alternatives to Domestic Rates, Cmnd 8449, HMSO, 1981.

11. Central controls and other relationships

J. A. G. Griffith, *Central Departments and Local Authorities*, Allen & Unwin, 1966.

Report of the Committee on Management of Local Government (the Maud Report), Vols. 1 and 5, HMSO, 1967.

Local Government Finance: Report of the Committee of Enquiry, Cmd 6453, HMSO, 1976.

E. Sharpe, *The Ministry of Housing and Local Government*, Allen & Unwin, 1969.

D. N. Chester, *Central and Local Government: Financial and Administrative Relations*, Macmillan, 1951.

J. Swaffield, 'Local Government in the National Setting', *Public Administration*, Autumn 1970.

N. Boaden, 'Central Departments and Local Authorities: The Relationship Re-examined', *Political Studies*, 28, 1970.

Sir F. Hill, 'The Partnership in Practice', *Political Quarterly*, 2, 1966.

J. Boynton, 'Local Councils in Confrontation: the Current Conflict with the Centre', *Policy Studies*, April 1982.

N. Boaden, *Public Participation in Local Services*, Longman, 1982.

T. Gibson, *People Power: Community and Work Groups in Action*, Penguin, 1979.

O. Hartley, 'The Relationship between Central Government and Local Authorities', *Public Administration*, Winter 1971.

C. Hull and R. A. W. Rhodes, *Intergovernmental Relations in the European Community*, Saxon House, 1978.

K. Young, 'Inter-tier Political Relations in a Metropolitan System', *Local Government Chronicle*, 9 October 1971.

R. Rhodes, *Control and Power in Central–Local Government Relations*, Gower, 1981.

Local Government Studies, May/June 1982 (issue devoted entirely to central–local relations).

G. Jones, *Introduction to Central–Local Government Relations*, SSRC, 1980.

G. Jones (ed.), *New Approaches to the Study of Central-Local Government Relationships*, Gower, 1980.

12. Local councils

Report of the Royal Commission on Local Government in England 1966–1969 (the Redcliffe-Maud Report), Vol. III, Appendix 8, H M S O, 1969.

C. Arnold-Baker, *The Powers and Constitution of Local Councils*, National Association of Local Councils, 1974.

W. H. Ousby and B. G. Wright, *A Practical Guide to Local Council Administration*, Knight, 1976.

Department of the Environment, *Neighbourhood Councils in England*, HMSO, 1974.

Department of the Environment, *A Voice for Your Neighbourhood*, H M S O, 1977.

13. Participation

D. Hill, *Participating in Local Affairs*, Penguin Books, 1970.

G. Parry (ed.), *Participation in Politics*, Manchester University Press, 1972.

Royal Commission on Local Government in England, Research Study 9, *Community Attitudes Survey*, H M S O, 1969.

Royal Commission on Local Government in Scotland, Research Study 2, *Community Survey*, H M S O, 1969.

People and Planning: Report of the Committee on Participation, H M S O, 1969.

R. Benewick and T. Smith (eds.), *Direct Action and Democratic Politics*, Allen & Unwin, 1972.

D. Jones and M. Mayo, *Community Work*, Routledge, 1974.

A. Lapping, *Community Action*, Fabian, 1970.

W. Hampton and R. Walker, *The Individual Citizen and Public Participation*, Sheffield University Press, 1978.

C. Ward, *Tenants' Takeover*, Architectural Press, 1974.

S. Arnstein, *A Ladder of Citizen Participation*, Royal Town Planning Institute, 1971.

L. J. Sharpe, 'Instrumental Participation and Urban Government', in J. A. G. Griffith (ed.), *From Politics to Administration*, Allen & Unwin, 1976.

S. Baine, *Community Action and Local Government*, Bell, 1975.

W. Harvey Cox, *Cities: The Public Dimension*, Penguin, 1976.

A. Brier and T. Hill, 'Participation in Local Politics: 3 Cautionary Case Studies' in L. Robins, *Topics in British Politics*, Politics Association, 1982.

14. Public relations and the ombudsman

C. O. Bell, 'Local Government Ombudsmen: Progress Through Persuasion', *New Law Journal*, 11 June 1981.

D. Murphy, *The Silent Watchdog: The Press in Local Politics*, Constable, 1972.

A. Sherman, *Councils, Councillors and Public Relations*, Barry Rose, 1973.

A. J. Morris, 'Local Authority Relations with the Local Press', *Public Law*, Autumn 1969.

Justice Report, *The Citizen and His Council*, Stevens, 1969.

Justice Report, *The Local Ombudsman: A Review of the First Five Years*, Stevens, 1980.

N. Lewis and B. Gateshill, *The Commissioner for Local Administration: A Preliminary Appraisal*, RIPA, 1978.
Justice, The Local Ombudsmen. A Review of the First Five Years, 1980.

15. Case studies

(While some of the following works deal with a particular area, others deal with a particular policy or aspect of policy-making. Where this is not self-evident, it is indicated in brackets.)

A. Henney, 'The Cost of Camden', Camden Commercial Ratepayers Group, 1981.

G. Jones, *Borough Politics: A Study of the Wolverhampton Town Council 1888–1964*, Macmillan, 1969.

J. M. Lee, *Social Leaders and Public Persons*, OUP, 1963 (Cheshire).

J. M. Lee *et al.*, *The Scope of Local Initiative*, Martin Robertson, 1974 (Cheshire).

W. Hampton, *Democracy and Community*, OUP, 1970 (Sheffield).

K. Newton, *Second City Politics*, OUP, 1976 (Birmingham).

M. Stacey, *Tradition and Change*, OUP, 1960 (Banbury).

M. Stacey *et al.*, *Power, Persistence and Change: A Second Study of Banbury*, Routledge, 1975.

H. V. Wiseman, *Local Government at Work*, Routledge, 1967 (Leeds).

G. Jones and A. Norton, *Political Leadership in Local Authorities*, INLOGOV, 1978 (a selection of personal portraits).

N. Dennis, *People and Planning*, Faber, 1970.

N. Dennis, *Public Participation and the Planner's Blight*, Faber, 1972 (redevelopment).

J. Beishon, *A Local Government System*, Open University, 1973 (Brighton Marina project).

J. Gower-Davis, *The Evangelistic Bureaucrat*, Tavistock, 1972 (redevelopment).

R. Minns, 'The Significance of Clay Cross', *Policy and Politics*, 4, 1974.

R. Mitchell, 'Clay Cross', *Political Quarterly*, 2, 1974.

S. Ramson, 'Changing Relations between Centre and Locality in Education', *Local Government Studies*, November/December 1980.

D. Rowlands, 'The Impact of the Introduction of Corporate Management on the London Borough of Waltham Forest', Polytechnic of the South Bank, 1981.

D. Skinner and J. Langdon, *The Story of Clay Cross*, Spokesman Books, 1974.

M. Gillard and M. Tomkinson, *Nothing to Declare*, Calder, 1980 (the Poulson affair).

A. P Brier, 'The Decision Process in Local Government: A Case Study of Fluoridation in Hull', *Public Administration*, Winter 1970.

D. G. Green, *Power and Party in an English City*, Allen & Unwin, 1981 (Newcastle).

A. Blowers, *The Limit of Power: The Politics of Local Planning Policy*, Pergamon, 1980 (Bedfordshire).

A number of county councils have recently had their histories published, including Kent, Lancashire and the West Riding of Yorkshire.

16. London

G. Rhodes (ed.), *The New Government of London: The First Five Years*, Weidenfeld & Nicolson, 1972.

G. Rhodes, *The Government of London: The Struggle for Reform*, Weidenfeld & Nicolson, 1970.

D. Foley, *Governing the London Region*, University of California Press, 1972.

Report of the Royal Commission on Local Government in Greater London, Cmd 1164, HMSO, 1960.

Royal Commission on Local Government in England, Research Study 2, *The Lessons of the London Government Reform*, HMSO, 1968.

D. Donnison and D. Eversley (eds.), *London: Urban Patterns, Problems and Policies*, Heinemann, 1973.

E. Wistrich, *The First Years of Camden*, Borough of Camden, 1972.

W. E. Jackson, *Achievement: A Short History of the LCC*, Longmans, 1965.

P. Hall, *Radical Agenda for London*, Fabian, 1980.

H. Cutler, *The Cutler Files*, Weidenfeld, 1981.

17. Scotland

Report of the Royal Commission on Local Government in Scotland 1966–1969 (the Wheatley Report), 2 vols., Cmd 4150, HMSO, 1969.

J. P. Mackintosh, 'The Royal Commission on Local Government in Scotland 1966–1969', *Public Administration*, Spring 1970.

J. G. Kellas, *The Scottish Political System*, CUP, 1975.

G. S. Pryde, *Central and Local Government in Scotland*, Routledge, 1960.

J. B. Miller, *An Outline of Administrative and Local Government Law in Scotland*, Green, 1961.

V. D. Lipman, 'Some Contrasts between English and Scottish Local Government', *Public Administration*, 3, 1949.

H. M. Drucker and M. G. Clarke (eds.), *The Scottish Government Yearbook 1978*, Paul Harris, 1978.

H. M. and N. Drucker (eds.), *The Scottish Government Yearbook 1979*, Paul Harris, 1979, 1980, 1981, 1982, 1983.

E. Page and E. Midwinter, 'Remote Bureaucracy or Administrative Efficiency? Scotland's New Local Government System', *Studies in Public Policy* no. 38, Centre for the Study of Public Policy.

R. Young, *The Search for Democracy: A Guide to Scottish Local Government*, Heatherbank Press, Milngavie, 1977.

18. Wales

The Reform of Local Government in Wales: A Consultative Document, HMSO, 1971.

P. Madgwick *et al.*, *The Politics of Rural Wales*, Hutchinson, 1973.

T. Brennan *et al.*, 'Political Parties and Local Government in Western South Wales', *Political Quarterly*, 1, 1954.

I. B. Rees, *Government by Community*, Knight, 1971.

19. Journals

Local Government Chronicle (weekly).
Municipal Review (monthly).
Municipal & Public Services Journal (weekly).
Local Government Review (weekly).
Local Government Annotations Service: L O G A (bi-monthly).
Local Government Studies (bi-monthly, with an annual review).
Local Government Trends (annual statistical digest, CIPFA).
Local Government Comparative Statistics (annual, CIPFA).
Local Government Policy Making (3 times a year, INLOGOV).
Local Government Forum (2 or 3 times a year, LG Unit, Paisley College).
Public Money (quarterly, CIPFA).
Local Government News (monthly).
County Councils Gazette (monthly).
District Councils Review (bi-monthly).

20. Recent additions

J. Stewart, *Local Government: the Conditions for Local Choice*, Allen & Unwin, 1983.
K. Young (ed.), *National Interests and Local Government*, Heinemann, 1983.
J. Gyford and M. James, *National Parties and Local Politics*, Allen & Unwin, 1983.
G. Jones and J. Stewart, *The Case for Local Government*, Allen & Unwin, 1983.
S. Bristow *et al.*, *Redundant Counties?*, Hesketh, 1983.
M. Keating and A. Midwinter, *The Government of Scotland*, Mainstream, 1983.
D. Walker, *Municipal Empire*, Temple Smith, 1983.
A. Henney, *Inside Local Government*, Sinclair Browne, 1983.
T. Mobbs, *Local Government Policy Making Handbook*, INLOGOV, 1983.
Audit Commission, *Economy, Efficiency and Effectiveness*, HMSO, 1983.
Local Government: the Facts, SOLACE, 1983.
The Fight for Local Government, INLOGOV, 1983.
Future Changes in Local Government Structure, Functions and Finance, Association of
    District Councillors, 1983.
R. Bailey, *Access to Local Government Information*, LG & Health Rights Project,
    1983.
M. Cowan, *Politics and Management in Local Government*, RIPA, 1983.
D. Whitfield, *Making it Public: Evidence and Action Against Privatisation*, Pluto, 1983.
R. Rose and E. Page, *Fiscal Stress in Cities*, CUP, 1983.
R. Glasser, *Town Hall*, Century, 1984 (study of St. Albans council).
A. Midwinter, *The Politics of Local Spending*, Mainstream, 1984 (esp. Scotland).
K. Walsh, *Ethics in Local Government*, LGTB, 1984.
A. Doig, *Corruption and Misconduct in Contemporary British Politics*, Pelican, 1984.
J. Sharpe and K. Newton, *Does Politics Matter? The Determinants of Public Policy*,
    OUP, 1984.
Audit Commission, *The Impact on Local Economy, Efficiency and Effectiveness of the
    Block Grant Distribution System*, HMSO, 1984.
J. Seabrook, *The Idea of Neighbourhood – what local politics should be about*, Pluto,
    1984.

Notes and References

1. What Local Government Is

1. P. Holland and M. Fallon, *The Quango Explosion*, CPA, 1978. See also *What's Wrong with Quangos?*, Outer Circle Policy Unit, 1979, and D. N. Chester, 'Fringe Bodies, Quangos and All That', *Public Administration*, Spring 1979.
2. F. A. Hayek, *The Road to Serfdom*, Routledge, 1946, pp. 174–5.
3. See for example J. S. Mill, *Representative Government*, 1861, Chapter XV, and J. Toulmin Smith, *Centralisation or Representation?*, 1848, and *Local Government and Centralisation*, 1851.

2. An Evolving System

1. This reluctance was a consequence of the prevailing philosophy of *laissez faire*, which implied that the state should not interfere with private interests, especially in business. See D. Fraser, *The Evolution of the Welfare State*, Macmillan, 1973; A. J. Taylor, *Laissez Faire and State Intervention in Nineteenth Century Britain*, Macmillan, 1972; and E. J. Evans, *Social Policy 1830–1914*, Routledge, 1978.
2. For example, Liverpool promoted nine such Bills in Parliament in the period 1858–83.
3. The population of Britain, in the years 1801–51, increased from 10·5 million to 20·8 million. Over the same period, individual towns experienced the following population growths: Birmingham 71,000 to 233,000; Liverpool 82,000 to 376,000; Glasgow 77,000 to 345,000; Manchester 75,000 to 303,000; London 865,000 to 2·8 million.
4. Some counties, Yorkshire and Sussex for instance, were divided into separate administrative areas (North Riding, East Riding and West Riding; East Sussex and West Sussex) because of their size or shape. England's fifty-two geographic counties were thus divided into sixty-two administrative counties.
5. This figure included four towns – Canterbury, Worcester, Burton and Chester – which achieved county borough status despite having populations of less than 50,000.
6. A number of individual towns had acquired a variety of powers, for example to establish free libraries, museums, police forces, housing and tramways, largely through private Acts of Parliament.
7. See the *Report of the Committee on the Management of Local Government* (the Maud Report), HMSO, 1967, Vol. 1.
8. It has been suggested that some of the functions of the Countryside Commission, the Housing Corporation and the Scottish Development Agency could be taken

over by local authorities. See N. and H. M. Drucker, *The Scottish Government Yearbook 1979*, Paul Harris, 1978.

9. There were eight of these in England; Wales and Scotland had councils with similar functions. In 1979 the government announced the abolition of the Regional Councils.

10. *Report on Social Insurance and Allied Services*, Cmnd 6404, HMSO, 1942.

11. J. Wiseman, 'Local Government in the Twentieth Century', *Lloyds Bank Review*, January 1966.

12. The population of Scotland rose from 1·5 million in 1801 to 3 million in 1851. By 1861, nearly one third of Scotland's population was living in one-room dwellings, and Glasgow was described as 'possibly the filthiest and unhealthiest of all British towns in the period'. See M. W. Flinn, *Chadwick's 'Report on the Sanitary Condition of the Labouring Population of Great Britain'*, pp. 10, 99.

13. Following the Parliamentary Reform Act 1832, a number of non-burghal towns were designated 'parliamentary boroughs', entitling them to elect MPs and set up town councils.

3. The Structure of Local Government

1. See, for example: W. A. Robson, *Local Government in Crisis*, Allen & Unwin, 1968; *Report of the Royal Commission on Local Government in England* (the Redcliffe-Maud Report), Cmd 4040, HMSO, 1969; *Report of the Royal Commission on Local Government in Greater London*, Cmd 1164, HMSO, 1960.

2. *Report of the Royal Commission on Local Government in Scotland* (the Wheatley Report), Cmd 4150, HMSO, 1969, Vol. 1, paras. 1 and 2.

3. Parishes did not exist in Scotland, having been abolished in the Local Government (Scotland) Act 1929.

4. Some shared the provision of services through joint schemes, or they 'borrowed' from their neighbours.

5. *Ad hoc* provision includes such things as gas, electricity and National Assistance. Delegation occurred (usually) when an upper-tier authority arranged for services to be provided by lower-tier authorities (for example education or planning in 'excepted' districts with populations of over 60,000).

6. *Local Government: Areas and Status of Local Authorities in England and Wales*, Cmd 9831, HMSO, 1956, p. 4.

7. ibid., p. 6.

8. See H. V. Wiseman, *Local Government in England 1958–69*, Routledge, 1970, p. 30.

9. The Local Government Commission for England produced separate Reports and Proposals for: West Midlands Special Review Area (1961); West Midlands General Review Area (1961); East Midlands General Review Area (1961); South Western General Review Area (1963); Tyneside Special Review Area (1963); North Eastern General Review Area (1963); West Yorkshire Special Review Area (1964); York and North Midlands General Review Area (1964); Lincolnshire and East Anglia General Review Area (1964); and Lincolnshire and East Anglia General Review Area (1965). (All published by HMSO.)

10. Wiseman, op. cit., p. 1.
11. This did not apply only to seats on local councils: as Richard Crossman recorded in his diary when writing about his decisions on the reports of the Local Government Commissions and their possible impact on his parliamentary colleagues, '. . . each of them knows that as Minister of Housing [and Local Government] the decision I make may be life or death for them in terms of representation at Westminister'. See R. H. S. Crossman, *Diaries of a Cabinet Minister*, Cape, 1975, Vol. 1, pp. 87, 88. See also F. Mount, 'The History of a Mistake', *Spectator*, 6 October 1979.
12. Crossman (op. cit. above) explains how he took the initiative in setting up the Royal Commission in the fortuitous absence of his strong-willed and sceptical Permanent Secretary. The paradox is that this civil servant became a member of the Royal Commission!
13. Local Government Commission for Wales, *Report and Proposals for Wales*, HMSO, 1963, paras. 14, 16.
14. *Local Government in Wales*, Cmd 3340, HMSO, 1967.
15. Originally this was to be elected and executive – a response to the growing nationalist feelings in Wales at the time.
16. The Redcliffe-Maud Report, Vol. 1, para. 28.
17. *Local Government Reform in England*, Cmd 4276, HMSO, 1970.
18. *Report of the Royal Commission on the Constitution* (the Kilbrandon Report), Cmd 5460, HMSO, 1973. This report produced a number of schemes for devolving power to the regions of Britain, and led ultimately to legislation to set up elected assemblies in Scotland and Wales (subsequently repealed, see 37 below).
19. The Redcliffe-Maud Report, Vol 11, Memorandum of Dissent, Cmd 4040–41, HMSO, 1969.
20. It is estimated that the reorganized structure transferred twenty seats from Labour to Conservative. See F. Mount, 'The History of a Mistake', *Spectator*, 6 October 1979; B. Keith-Lucas and P. Richards, *A History of Local Government in the Twentieth Century*, Allen & Unwin, 1978, pp. 223–4; and P. Hall, 'The Country Fights Back – and Wins', *New Society*, 17 September 1970.
21. *Local Government in England*, Cmd 4585, HMSO, 1971.
22. *The Reform of Local Government in Wales*, HMSO, 1971.
23. Some district councils – former boroughs and UDCs – are entitled to call themselves 'boroughs' and some parishes are known as 'town councils'. In addition, some authorities have retained the title of 'city'.
24. *Local Government in England* (op. cit.), para. 13.
25. The adoption of certain business practices ('corporate management' – see Chapter 9) might be regarded as a further move in this direction. However, for the main thrust of the argument, see J. Dearlove, *The Reorganisation of Local Government: Old Orthodoxies and a Political Perspective*, CUP, 1979. See also the references in note 45, p. 331. While the Maud Report of 1967 (Vol. 2, p. 20) showed that 55 per cent of councillors were managers, farmers, professional workers or employers, and the Redcliffe-Maud Report of 1969 (Vol. 3, p. 132) quotes a similar figure of 51 per cent, the more recent Robinson Report (*Report of the Committee of Inquiry into the System of Remuneration of Members of Local Authorities,*

HMSO, 1977, Vol. 2, Tables 10 and 11) shows that at least 65 per cent of councillors are from non-manual occupational backgrounds, and that over 60 per cent of male councillors who are working are from just four groups of occupation (sales, clerical, administration/management and professional/technical). This change may please those who bemoaned the poor calibre of councillors, but it adds credence to those who, like Dearlove, interpret the reorganization of local government in class terms.

26. See G. Jones, 'The Local Government Act 1972 and the Redcliffe-Maud Commission', *Political Quarterly*, April 1973.

27. These services have been transferred into the hands of separate boards and authorities under the NHS Reorganization Act 1973 and the Water Act 1973.

28. Redcliffe-Maud Report, Vol. 1, para. 576 (iv).

29. *Organic Change in Local Government*, Cmd 7457, HMSO, 1979. The philosophy behind organic change is that the structure of local government should not be rigid but should vary between different parts of the country, taking into account local circumstances. However, it may be that the original proposals were a first step towards a general pattern of most-purpose district councils; see J. Stewart *et al.*, *Organic Change*, Institute of Local Government Studies, 1978, p. 4.

30. *Devolution and Regional Government in England*, Labour Party, 1975, p. 8. See also *Regional Authorities and Local Government Reform*, Labour Party, 1977.

31. J. Boynton, 'A Case for Leaving Local Government Alone for the Moment', *The Times*, 26 September 1978. In *Local Government in Britain Since Reorganization*, Alexander suggests that antagonism to the two-tier structure is muted through distaste for further reorganization.

32. There were some reservations by members about the allocation of planning functions and the structure of the island councils.

33. N. and H. M. Drucker, eds., *The Scottish Government Yearbook 1979*, Paul Harris, 1978. A. Dawson, *The Idea of the Region and the 1975 Reorganization of Scottish Local Government*, Public Administration, Autumn 1981.

34. 'The imbalance of size has been a natural target for criticism, but the boundaries of the Strathclyde region correspond broadly to a distinctive area with regional characteristics and large-scale problems. Any sub-division would have meant a weakening of administrative cohesion and an impairment of strategic opportunities' (*Brief on Local Government Reform*, Scottish Office, HMSO, 1974).

35. Elections were held in 1974 in readiness for the 1975 start.

36. It has been suggested that this was to give the districts a worthwhile role (see *Municipal Journal*, 16 May 1975).

37. Elected assemblies for Scotland and Wales were to be created under the Scotland Act 1978 and the Wales Act 1978. They were to exercise a number of legislative and/or administrative roles and thus off-load the central government as well as providing a focal point for the expression of local public opinion. However, all this came to a halt when the referendums (March 1979) failed to provide the necessary minimum support, and the Acts were repealed. An outline of the proposed schemes is to be found in the government's White Paper *Our Changing Democracy*, Cmd 6348, HMSO, 1975.

38. *Streamlining the Cities*, Cooper & Lybrand Ltd, December 1983 and February 1984.

4. The Functions of Local Government

1. Attorney-General *v.* Fulham Corporation (1921).
2. In practice even some mandatory responsibilities may not be fulfilled by local authorities, or they may be undertaken in purely token fashion, as the provision of county colleges after the 1944 Education Act and provision of health centres after the 1946 Health Service Act were. In other cases there may be uncertainty whether the responsibility is mandatory or not, as in the case of the provision of adult or nursery education.
2a. See C. Crawford and V. Moore, *The Free Two Pence*, CIPFA, 1983.
3. 'Local Government Today and Tomorrow', *Municipal Journal*, 1962, p. 27.
4. The Maud Report, Vol. 1, Chapter 4. See also the Redcliffe-Maud Report, Vol. 1, para. 323, and the Wheatley Report, Vol. 1, para. 640.
5. For example the York Corporation Act 1969 cost £6,000. However, under the Local Government Act 1972 (sec. 262) it was intended that certain powers conferred by local Acts should be made generally available to local authorities.
6. There are various types of order, and procedures differ for each. For further details, see C. A. Cross, *Principles of Local Government Law*, Sweet & Maxwell; W. O. Hart and J. F. Garner, *Hart's Local Government and Administration*, Butterworth; or J. A. Griffiths and H. Street, *Principles of Administrative Law*, Pitman.
7. The Redcliffe-Maud Report, Vol. 1, paras. 257–8.
8. The Wheatley Report, Vol. 1, paras. 361–9.
9. Joint committees are sometimes formed here too – e.g. Somerset County Council and Taunton Deane Borough Council had a joint planning committee until 1980 when under the Local Government Planning and Land Act 1980, counties lost most of their control responsibilities over 'county aspects' of planning.
10. In some areas, in order to avoid the messy administration which can sometimes occur when responsibilities are claimed, 'excepted districts' have been created whereby the district authorities may, for example, become responsible for the road maintenance of whole areas.
11. See, for example, the *Report of the Royal Commission on the Police*, HMSO, 1962. On the question of controls, see G. Marshall, 'Police Accountability Revisited', in D. Butler and A. Halsey, *Policy and Politics*, Macmillan, 1978.
12. In England the Department of Transport, in Wales the Welsh Office and in Scotland the Development Department of the Scottish Office.
13. Under the Transport Act 1968, certain areas of Britain were designated 'passenger transport areas' within which municipal transport was managed by 'passenger transport executives' (PTEs), full-time experts who worked under the control of 'passenger transport authorities' (PTAs), comprising part-time members, mainly representatives of the local authorities in the area. Since local government reorganization, the role of the PTAs has been taken over by metropolitan county councils and the Strathclyde Regional Council. However, the independence of the PTEs is sometimes felt to be excessive, and the Association

of Metropolitan Authorities has sought their absorption into the metropolitan county councils.

14. Largely a result of *People and Planning* (the Skeffington Report), HMSO, 1969.

15. This includes public as well as private developments, so that local authorities themselves have to make applications. However, certain government departments and government properties are excluded. In addition, certain aspects of 'permitted' development do not require specific applications for permission. These occur under a statutory instrument (the General Development Order) and include, for example, small house extensions.

16. Apart from private health provision, the health service provided under the Employment Medical Advisory Service, and health services in prisons and the armed forces, are technically outside the NHS.

17. See, for example, the Redcliffe-Maud Report, Vol. 1, paras. 259–367.

18. See, for example, the *Report of the Royal Commission on the National Health Service*, Cmd 7615, HMSO, 1979, para. 16.22.

5. London's Local Government

1. They were in fact called 'Progressives' and included many Liberals and some Conservatives. They were sometimes also known as 'Municipal Socialists', as they sought to emulate and surpass the achievements of Joseph Chamberlain, mayor of Birmingham in the 1870s.

2. This notion was examined by the Royal Commission on Greater London (Ullswater) in 1921–3. It lacked unanimity, producing three conflicting reports, and consequently no action was taken on its various recommendations.

3. From some 600,000 per day in the 1920s to nearly 1 million in the 1950s. See K. B. Smellie, *A History of Local Government*, Allen & Unwin, 1968.

4. Of these counties perhaps Middlesex was the most notable in this respect, having a number of boroughs which by the criterion of population size merited promotion to county borough status, except that this would have emasculated the administrative county.

5. The London boroughs were given some traffic management responsibilities.

6. See, for example, Professor Griffiths' evidence to the Royal Commission (para. 192). See also W. A. Robson, *Local Government in Crisis*, Allen & Unwin, 1967, Chapter XXXI.

7. G. Rhodes (ed.), *The New Government of London: The First Five Years*, Weidenfeld & Nicolson, 1972; see also the *Local Government Chronicle*, 4 March 1972.

8. *The Times*, 6 July 1978. See also R. Freeman, 'London through the Looking Glass', *New Society*, 27 March 1980.

9. See *Hansard*, 12 April 1982; *The Times*, 24 June 1982, 29 July 1982.

10. White Paper, *Public Transport in London*, Cmnd 9004, 1983.

6. Local Government Elections

1. Such as voting twice by impersonating someone else, etc. Anyone found guilty of

such offences is debarred from voting in the local area in which the offence was committed for five years from the date of conviction.

2. See A. Wigram and E. Lyon, *Local Government Elections – the Case for Proportional Representation*, CAER, 1979; B. Keith-Lucas, *Local Elections – Let's Get Them in Proportion*, Parliamentary Democracy Trust, 1978; and V. Bogdanor, 'Why the Local Elections System Makes Us Appear More Divided', *The Times*, 19 May 1980.

3. By-elections take place when vacancies occur on the council owing to resignation, death or disqualification of councillors. A councillor may be dismissed as a result of his unauthorized absence from council meetings over a continuous period of six months. However, a by-election would not take place in any of these situations if normal elections were due within six months, unless the council was deficient in membership by a third or more.

4. Up to 1979, members could be disqualified on the grounds of having been surcharged (in effect fined) the sum of £500 or more by the District Auditor. This power ceased as such under the Local Government Act 1972, but see pp. 217 and 340.

5. This principle implies that those who make the law should be different from those who operate it and from those who adjudicate when it is broken. For a rather fuller treatment, see C. Padfield, *British Constitution Made Simple*, Heinemann, 1983.

6. *Candidates' Expenses at Local Government Elections*, Home Office circular, RPA 263.

7. These electoral areas are reviewed from time to time by the Local Government Boundary Commissions (see p. 56), though the local authorities themselves may initiate alterations, counties seeking to change divisions and districts revising wards and parishes/communities. In the case of GLC elections, the boroughs assume the role of electoral areas.

8. The Maud Report, Vol. 3, pp. 72–80.

9. See, for example, A. H. Birch, *Small Town Politics*, OUP, 1959; W. Hampton, *Democracy and Politics*, OUP, 1970; F. Bealey *et al.*, *Constituency Politics*, Faber, 1965. Information has also been drawn from L. J. Sharpe, *Voting in Cities*, Macmillan, 1967, and *Power in Britain*, BBC, 1965.

10. See, for example, Hampton, op. cit., and P. Fletcher, in Sharpe, op. cit.

11. J. Stanyer, *Understanding Local Government*, Fontana, 1976, pp. 272, 284.

12. J. Stanyer, 'Why Does Turnout Vary?', *New Society*, 13 May 1971.

13. What these average figures do not show is the wide range of turnout among local authorities. For example, in the 1973 local elections the districts of Ceredigion and Dwyfor, in Wales, had turnouts of 93·9 per cent and 82·8 per cent respectively, while those in Middlesborough and Stoke-on-Trent were 18·1 per cent and 22 per cent. On the other hand, high voting turnouts can disguise the fact that a high proportion of seats have gone uncontested, and vice versa.

14. Such a view is at least implicit in the Government's White Papers *Local Government in England*, Cmd 4585, and *Reform of Local Government in Scotland*, Cmd 4583, both HMSO, 1971. See also the Redcliffe-Maud and Wheatley Reports. Some election figures for the old local government system are given in Appendix 4 (p. 295).

15. The Maud Report, Vol. 3, Table 113, p. 82.

16. G. W. Jones, 'Varieties of Local Politics', *Local Government Studies*, April 1975.

17. See, for example, W. H. Morris-Jones, 'In Defence of Apathy', *Political Studies*, Vol. 2, No. 1, 1954. See also L. J. Sharpe, 'Instrumental Participation in Urban Government', in J. A. Griffiths, *From Policy to Administration*, Allen & Unwin, 1976.

18. There is a tendency in rural areas towards a lack of contests because the incumbent councillor is often known personally by the electors, who may not wish to give offence by opposing him. Subsequently, many rural councillors become well entrenched and almost irremovable. This has been well illustrated in the study of the Scottish Communities – see R. Masterson and E. Masterman, 'The Scottish Community Elections, the Second Round', *Local Government Studies*, January 1980.

19. The Maud Report, Vol. 1, p. 134; see also p. 93.

20. The Maud Report, Vol. 5, pp. 48–9.

21. The last time there was an uncontested parliamentary seat in Britain was in 1951, when four constituencies went uncontested. See A. J. Allen, *The English Voter*, English Universities Press, 1964, p. 13.

22. See the Maud Report, Vol. 3.

23. J. G. Bulpitt, in *Participation in Politics*, ed. G. Parry, Manchester University Press, 1971, p. 290. There has been some change in composition since then (see Chapter 8) and some would argue that Bulpitt's warnings were justified: see J. Dearlove, *The Reorganisation of Local Government*, CUP, 1979.

7. The Political Parties

1. In order to cover these various situations, J. Stanyer has suggested a classification as follows: a 'developed' party system exists where parties contest elections and control the council; a 'semi-party' system is where they contest elections but hardly refer to their party labels while in office; a 'concealed' system is one where members are partisan behind the scenes of council work, but do not contest elections using party labels; a council is 'non-partisan' where parties are absent from elections and the council. J. Stanyer, *Understanding Local Government*, Fontana, 1976, p. 136.

2. See H. V. Wiseman, *Local Government at Work*, Routledge, 1967, and the Maud Report, Vol. 5, p. 100.

3. In 1956 a prominent (Labour) city council took it upon itself formally to condemn the British invasion of Suez. In June 1981 the GLC declared a boycott on South African goods as a protest against apartheid.

4. A five-fold classification is suggested by L. Corina, 'Elected Representatives in a Party System', *Policy and Politics*, Vol. 3, no. 1, 1974.

5. Political culture has been defined as 'orientations towards political objects' – A. Almond and S. Verba, *The Civic Culture*, Princeton, 1963. In the local government context, it implies the amalgam of people's judgements and attitudes about political institutions (the council, parties, the town hall etc.), personalities (the chairman, the officers, social workers) and processes (elections, rate collection etc.). It also

entails an element of how individuals see or feel about their own role in the local political system. e.g. Strathclyde provides an illustration with its tradition of left-wing distrust of voluntary organizations and a preference for working through the Labour party. For a concise account of the general concept, see D. Kavanagh, *Political Culture*, Macmillan, 1972.

6. Some of them could be said to have begun with the Birmingham Liberals under Joseph Chamberlain in the 1860s. See A. Briggs, *Victorian Cities*, Penguin, 1968.

7. J. Redlich and F. W. Hirst, *A History of Local Government in England*, ed. B. Keith-Lucas, Macmillan, 1958.

8. A nice illustration of the resistance to state provision was given by *The Times* in 1854 when it stated, 'We prefer to take our chance of cholera and the rest than be bullied into health.'

9. See W. Thornhill, *The Growth and Reform of English Local Government*, Weidenfeld & Nicolson, 1971, pp. 106–8, 112–13. See also Chapter 5 above.

10. Just as at national level more than half of the seats in Parliament went uncontested prior to the emergence of national parties. See T. Lloyd, 'Uncontested Seats in British General Elections 1852–1910', *Historical Journal*, Vol. viii, no. 2, 1965.

11. It is true that some councillors are deterred by the existence of political parties, but these appear to be few in number. See p. 124 above; also the Maud Report, Vol. 1, pp. 109, 145; Vol. 3, Table 207.

12. See for example J. G. Bulpitt, *Party Politics in English Local Government*, Longmans, 1967; H. V. Wiseman, *Local Government at Work*, Routledge, 1967; W. Hampton, *Democracy and Community*, OUP, 1970; K. Newton, *Second City Politics*, OUP, 1976; G. W. Jones, *Borough Politics*, Macmillan, 1969. This concentration of study may also be justified on the grounds that, while it may not cover a lot of local authorities, it does cover a lot of Britain's population.

13. See H. V. Wiseman, 'The Party Caucus in Local Government', *New Society*, 31 October 1963.

14. See the Maud Report, Vol. 5, p. 105.

15. There have been some bitter episodes with party groups disowning or de-selecting councillors; e.g. see 'Manchester Politics', *Economist*, 3 October 1981.

16. In addition they may also determine the choice of co-opted members. See p. 135. Indeed, well-established majority parties could change the number and structure of committees and to a large extent even the internal organization of the authority if they wished. See *Guardian*, 27 May 1981.

17. See the Maud Report, Vol. 5, p. 98.

18. ibid., p. 104.

19. See J. Gyford, *Local Politics in Britain*, Croom Helm, 1976, pp. 78, 84.

20. The Maud Report, Vol. 5, p. 193.

21. Gyford, op. cit., p. 82.

22. See the Maud Report, Vol. 5, p. 100.

23. See Gyford, pp. 86–7, G. W. Jones' article in *Local Government Studies*, April 1975, p. 31, and Table 7.5 in Bennett *Central Grants* (p. 316 above).

24. See Chapter 8. The October 1974 Parliament comprised only 4 per cent women and 7 per cent working-class members, while the middle-age groups (35–54), with 63 per cent, were well over-represented, and the younger (21–34) and older (55 plus) groups were under-represented with 8 per cent and 29 per cent respectively.

See C. Mellors, *The British M P*, Saxon House, 1978; also '*The Times*' *Guide to the House of Commons 1974*. On a wider perspective, the role of local politics as a stepping stone to national politics should be noted: Mellors shows that one M P in three has local government experience.

25. See L. J. Sharpe, *Why Local Democracy?*, Fabian, 1965.
26. See J. D. Stewart, 'The Politics of Local Government Reorganisation', in K. Jones, *The Yearbook of Social Policy 1973*, Routledge, 1974.
27. The Maud Report, Vols. 1 and 2.
28. Source: K. Newton, *Second City Politics*, O U P, 1976, fig. 2.2. In that book, the author declares that 'local elections are a sort of annual general election'. Another recent study concludes: 'On the whole ... municipal voting in big cities is a product of whatever factors happen at the time to be salient nationally.'
29. See Anthony Steen, 'New Life for Old Cities', Aims, 1981. Also G. Cameron, *The Future of British Conurbations*, Longman, 1981.
30. See C. Game, 'Local Elections', *Local Government Studies*, March/April 1981, and references therein; J. Ferry, 'Rates and Elections', *Centre for Environmental Studies Review*, January 1979; G. Jones and J. Stewart, 'The Local Factor in a Local Election', *Local Government Chronicle*, 18 June 1982, see also *Local Government Chronicle*, 17 June 1983 and *Municipal Journal*, 3 June 1983. In May 1979 the local elections happened to coincide with the General Election, and the authors of the second study mentioned in note 28 above show that electors (at least in Liverpool) made use of that unique opportunity to 'split' their vote and separate national issues from local by voting for one party in parliament and a different party in their local council: see W. Harvey Cox and M. Laver, 'Local and National Voting in Britain', *Parliamentary Affairs*, Autumn 1979.
31. The adversary or 'yah-boo' system as it occurs nationally is also heavily criticized: see S. E. Finer, *Adversary Politics and Electoral Reform*, Anthony Wigram, 1975.
32. See *Local Government Chronicle*, 5 March 1982, 18 September 1981.
33. The Maud Report, Vol. 1, p. 110.
34. ibid., Vol. 5, p. 109.
35. Gyford, op. cit., p. 68.
36. Source: *Municipal Year Books*.

8. The Councillors

1. By the Committee on Management of Local Government (Maud), 1967. See also C. Rallins and M. Thrasher, 'Disillusion, Age and Frustration – Why Councillors are Calling it a Day', *Local Government Chronicle*, 9 October 1981.
2. Councils are free to determine the timing of their meetings. Consequently, there are variations, but in very general terms county and regional councils and Scottish districts meet in the daytime (mornings or afternoons); other districts meet in the afternoon or evenings; and the London boroughs meet in the evenings.
3. R. V. Clements, *Local Notables and the City Council*, Macmillan, 1969.
4. The Maud Report, Vol. 2.
5. As with M Ps, this normally means that the union agrees to make a contribution towards the candidate's election expenses (in effect to the local party funds). However, in local government it is less systematic (e.g., agreements are not

signed) and the sums involved are small. Sponsorship normally occurs where the candidate is a member of the union and displays this fact on his election material.

6. The Maud Report, Vol. 1, p. 139.

7. This information is drawn from *The Remuneration of Councillors*, Vol. 2, HMSO, 1977, and the Maud Report, Vol. 2.

7a. See J. Gyford, 'Our Changing Local Councillors', *New Society*, 3 May 1984.

8. The Maud Report, p. 143.

9. Thus the chairmen of committees may take decisions on behalf of their committee, for example where the matter is urgent – see p. 152. Furthermore, it would appear that just one person may legitimately constitute a committee – see *Local Government Chronicle*, 30 March 1979, 13 April 1979, 4 May 1979.

10. This dilemma is made no easier when councillors are given such guidance as: 'Your over-riding duty as a councillor is to the whole local community. You have a special duty to your own constituents . . .' (Circular on the National Code of Local Government Conduct, 1975. See note 40 below.)

11. For various studies of this aspect, see K. Newton, *Second City Politics*, OUP, 1976; I. Budge *et al.*, *Political Stratification and Democracy*, Macmillan, 1972; J. Dearlove, *The Politics of Policy in Local Government*, CUP, 1973; J. M. Lee, *Social Leaders and Public Persons*, Oxford, 1963. In his study 'The Functions and Organisation of Councillors', *Public Administration*, Vol. 51, 1973, G. Jones suggests that, at that time, councillors broadly fell into three groups – 75 per cent mainly concerned with representing the ward and constituents' interests, about 5 per cent acting as general policy-makers and 20 per cent being policy-makers in particular service areas. See also Local Government Studies Sept/Oct 1982.

12. *Report of the Committee of Inquiry into the System of Remuneration of Local Authorities*, HMSO, 1977, Vol. 2.

13. The Maud Report, Vol. 1. Also MORI in *Sunday Times*, 19 June 1982. A recent survey of Scottish councillors give a figure of 120 hours per month: *Local Government Forum*, No. 4.

14. The chairman of the council in some English and Welsh authorities is known as the 'mayor'; in Scotland he is known as either the 'convenor' or the 'provost'.

15. See Addenda to the *Report of the Royal Commission on Standards of Conduct in Public Life* (the Salmon Report), Cmd 6524, HMSO, 1976; also see p. 142 above.

16. The Robinson Report, Vol. 1.

17. The Maud Report, Vol. 3.

18. In England and Wales, this system started under the Municipal Corporations Act 1835 and did not apply to many later types of local authority, including UDCs, RDCs and parishes.

19. However, it was not a clean break, as aldermen did not disappear from London until 1977 (GLC) and 1978 (London boroughs); and the City, being exempt from the 1972 Act, still has its aldermen. Furthermore, under that Act, principal local authorities in England and Wales are empowered to confer the title of 'honorary alderman' on anyone who has given eminent service as a past member of the council. He/she may then be invited to attend civic ceremonies, but that is all.

20. By law, police committees must comprise two thirds councillors and one third JPs. This could be regarded as compulsory co-option, but equally it may be seen

simply as a joint committee (see p. 151). The distinction is not always clear, especially where the co-option is of a representative nature (see p. 137), for example where a county planning committee provides for the built-in representation of additional members from district councils.

21. Equally co-opted members are disqualified like councillors, the one notable exception being teachers, who since 1902 have been regularly co-opted on to LEA Education committees.

22. E. L. Hasluck, *Local Government in England*, CUP, 1948. However, it should be noted that such complaints are not a new phenomenon, having been made at various times in the nineteenth century. See E. P. Hennock, *Fit and Proper Persons: Ideal and Reality in Nineteenth Century Urban Government*, Arnold, 1973; G. Jones, *Borough Politics*, Macmillan, 1969.

23. Dame E. Sharp in a speech quoted in the *Municipal Review*, November 1960. See also *Public Administration*, Winter 1962.

24. Professor B. Keith-Lucas, *The Mayor, Alderman and Councillors*, Liberal Publications, 1961.

25. The Maud Report, Vol. 5, p. 458; see also pp. 40–46 of the report.

26. ibid., p. 196.

27. The Salmon Report, p. 11.

28. The Maud Report, Vol. 1, p. 143.

29. *The New Local Authorities*, HMSO, 1972, para. 7.52. Concern at the calibre of members is still being expressed: see R. Garson, 'What Direction Should Local Government's Leaders Take Now?', *Local Government Chronicle*, 2 May 1980, p. 478.

30. T. Eddison *et al.*, *Strengthening the Role of Elected Member*, LGTB, 1979. *Support Services for Councillors* (Thomas Report), Association of Councillors, 1982. In recent years, the University of Bristol has run some courses for councillors, as indeed it did in 1979 for newly elected MPs.

31. The various relevant nineteenth-century laws were consolidated in the 1933 Local Government Act and are currently to be found in the Local Government Act 1972 (secs. 94–98) and the Local Government (Scotland) Act 1973 (secs. 38–42).

32. *Conduct in Local Government*, Cmd 5636, HMSO, 1974.

33. *Report of the Royal Commission on Standards of Conduct in Public Life* (the Salmon Report), Cmd 6524, HMSO, 1976.

34. *Conduct in Local Government*, p. 3.

35. *Report of the Royal Commission on Standards of Conduct in Public Life*, p. 11.

36. *Conduct in Local Government*, p. 11.

37. *Report of the Royal Commission on Standards of Conduct in Public Life*, Addendum by Mrs Ward-Jackson, p. 117.

38. An interesting illustration of this is provided by the former Chief Executive Officer of Wandsworth Borough Council who said that he was sacked for calling in the police to investigate suspected corruption. 'There is an immense amount of corruption going on and it is got away with because people know there is no thank you for reporting it' (*Local Government Chronicle*, 20 April 1979).

39. *Report of the Royal Commission on Standards of Conduct in Public Life*, p. 19.

40. Joint circular, *The National Code of Local Government Conduct*, HMSO, 1975.

9. Internal Organization: The Council and its Committees

1. Standing orders are the set of rules by which local authorities conduct themselves. They are rather like a written constitution, explaining the composition, powers and procedures of the local authority's component parts. For example, they would lay down the quorum required for meetings, the procedures for entering into contracts or those matters upon which committees or officers could make (delegated) decisions on behalf of the council. The central government issues 'model' standing orders for the benefit of individual local authorities. An example of a local authority's standing orders is given in Appendix 9.

2. See the Bains Report, *The New Authorities*, HMSO, 1972, para. 4.34.

3. The Maud Report, Vol. 1.

4. The Paterson Report, *The New Scottish Local Authorities: Organisation and Management Structures*, HMSO, 1973, para. 3.10, found some 20 per cent of their sample of local authorities reported having made significant changes in organization since the Maud Report.

5. For details of surveys of local authorities see Occasional Papers by the Institute of Local Government Studies (INLOGOV) 1969, 1970.

6. A. L. Norton and J. D. Stewart, 'The Bains Impact', *Local Government Chronicle*, 9 March 1973.

7. The Bains Report, p. xv and para. 2.3; the Paterson Report, para. 4.3.

8. See for example E. F. L. Brech, *Management: Its Nature and Significance*, Pitman, 1967.

9. For example whether monitoring should be undertaken by the P & R committee or should form a separate sub-committee function; or whether the chief executive should develop a small inner 'executive office'.

10. See the Bains Report, Appendix J.

11. With the possibility of joint meetings (ibid., para. 5.42).

12. The Paterson Report, para. 4.9.

13. ibid., para. 4.6.

14. J. D. Hender, *Municipal and Public Services Journal*, 15 September 1972.

15. This reflects the view of Sir Andrew Wheatley when he dissented from the Maud Committee Report on the grounds that this would keep council members generally better informed and would avoid the danger of the management board members becoming too remote or detached (see the Maud Report, Vol. 1, pp. 155–6). Bains did, however, follow Maud in pointing out that members have different interests, and implied that some of them could be satisfied in pursuing a purely constituency (rather than policy-making) role. (See the Bains Report, Chapter 3.)

16. See R. Greenwood *et al., The Organisation of Local Authorities in England and Wales 1967–75*, INLOGOV, 1975.

17. See R. Greenwood *et al., In Pursuit of Corporate Rationality: Organisational Developments in the Post-Reorganisation Period*, INLOGOV, 1977.

18. Greenwood, op. cit., p. 18.

19. Bob Hinings, 'Developments in Organisation and Management', *Local Government Studies: Annual Review*, April 1979. Birmingham City Council provides an illustration. When the Conservatives assumed control there in 1976, they pro-

ceeded to dismantle the corporate machinery and re-establish a more devolved, departmental structure.

20. Professor G. Jones has observed that, 'It is still doubtful if the corporate devices will invest the chief executive with the necessary authority to prevail against the tendency to departmentalism that is still inherent in the present system' (G. Jones and A. Norton (eds.), *Political Leadership in Local Authorities*, INLOGOV, 1978).

10. Internal Organization: The Officers

1. See J. H. Warren, *The Local Government Service*, Allen & Unwin, 1952.
2. This is augmented by general legislation such as the Contracts of Employment Act 1972, the Health and Safety at Work Act 1974, the Employment Protection Act 1975 and the Sex Disqualification Act 1975.
3. See the *Report of the Committee on the Staffing of Local Government* (the Mallaby Report), HMSO, 1967.
4. See the *Report of the Royal Commission on Standards of Conduct in Public Life 1974–76* (the Salmon Report), Cmd 6524, HMSO, 1976.
5. See A. Spoor, *White Collar Union*, Heinemann, 1967.
6. K. P. Poole, *The Local Government Service*, Allen & Unwin, 1978, p. 114; also *Public Finance and Accountancy*, February 1980, p. 26.
7. See the Salmon Report; also 'The Dangerous Ground in Public Life', *Local Government Chronicle*, 20 April 1979, pp. 425–7.
8. See Chapter 6. Teachers are an exception: they can be (and in Scotland must be) co-opted on to education committees.
9. *Report of the Committee of Enquiry on Industrial Democracy*, Cmd 6706, HMSO, 1977. In October 1979, the Secretary of State for Employment (James Prior) told a Confederation of British Industry conference that the government believed that greater employee involvement in decisions at work was the right road to good industrial relations and better productivity.
10. See R. Greenwood *et al.*, *In Pursuit of Corporate Rationality*, INLOGOV, 1977.
11. B. Wood, in *Party Politics in Local Government*, RIPA/PSI, 1979.
12. See R. Greenwood *et al.*, *The Organisation of Local Authorities 1967–75*, INLOGOV, 1975, and R. Greenwood and J. Stewart, *Local Government Studies*, October 1972.
13. Greenwood *et al.*, op. cit. (1975). Since then several local authorities have dropped their chief executive posts.
14. In the reports by Maud (1966), Mallaby (1967), Bains (1972) and Paterson (1973).
15. See R. Greenwood, 'The Recruitment of Chief Executive Officers', *Local Government Chronicle*, 19 October 1973. See also Alexander, op. cit.
16. See Greenwood *et al.*, op. cit. (1977) and op. cit. (1975).
17. Greenwood *et al.*, op. cit. (1975).
18. Further details may be found in the Treasury's *Glossary of Management Techniques*, HMSO, 1967.
19. See, for example, *Output Measurement – Discussion Papers*, published by CIPFA (and previously by the IMTA).
20. See, for example, the Local Government Operational Research Unit report, *Eval-*

uating Alternative Housing Management Strategies, HMSO, 1973; *Information Techniques in Local Authority Supplies Organisations*, HMSO, 1979; and *Planning Remedial Work on Local Authority Buildings*, HMSO, 1979.

21. See, for example, *Performance Management in Local Government*, published by Epping Forest District Council.

22. See the Layfield Report; also Walker and Henney (p. 320 above).

23. In 1974 the DES established the Assessment of Performance Unit to monitor national levels of pupil achievement. See *Output Budgeting for the Department of Education and Science*, Education Planning Paper 1, HMSO, 1970, and *Performance Indicators in the Education Service,* CIPFA, 1984.

24. Other notable legal cases such as Attorney-General *v.* De Winton (1906) and *Re* Hurle Hobbes *ex parte* Riley and another (1944) seem to imply that officers have a duty to the electors and may disobey council instructions. However, this would seem only to apply in cases where the legality of the council's instructions were in serious doubt.

25. The Maud Report, Vol. 5, p. 196. Elsewhere in that report officers are reported to say that 'only a minority of members on their committees make any real contribution' and 30 per cent to 40 per cent of the committee members 'were useless' (p. 42). The Royal Commission on London also noted that a good education officer 'is normally immensely influential in policy as well as in administrative questions' (*Report of the Royal Commission on Local Government in Greater London 1957–60*, Cmnd 1164, HMSO, 1960, para. 469). A recent example of LAMSAC's work concerned the computerization of refuse collection: in 1982.

26. The Maud Report, Vol. 1, para. 109.

27. ibid., Vol. 1, para. 145.

28. See *The Times*, 20 May 1982.

29. See *Community Care*, 4 March 1982.

30. See *Municipal Journal*, 21 May 1982. Also article by D. Peschek in *Local Government Chronicle*, 24 April 1981.

31. *Aspects of Administration in a Large Local Authority*, INLOGOV, 1967.

32. B. Keith-Lucas, 'Who Are the Policy Makers?', *Public Administration*, Vol. 43, 1965.

33. J. Gyford, *Local Politics in Britain*, Croom Helm, 1976, p. 43.

34. See, for example, M. Kogan and W. Van Der Eyken, *County Hall LEA*, Penguin Books, 1973. It is perhaps not without significance that this study of policy-making was based upon interviews with the *officers*, while the parallel study at national level (*The Politics of Education* by M. Kogan, Penguin Books, 1971) concentrated on elected *politicians*.

35. It is sometimes felt by some chief officers that education gets an unreasonably favourable share of the authority's resources because it has a powerful lobby behind it – parents. However, this can lead to those other officers reacting by 'ganging up' against the chief education officer.

36. See Kogan and Van Der Eyken, op. cit., and K. Wheare, *Government by Committee*, Oxford, 1955, Chapter 7.

37. See G. W. Jones, 'Varieties of Local Politics', *Local Government Studies*, April 1975. Another writer suggests that there may be differences between the political

parties when it comes to keeping a rein on officers: see J. Sharpe, 'American Democracy Reconsidered', *British Journal of Political Science*, Vol. 3, no. 1, 1973.

38. *Party Politics in Local Government*, RIPA/PSI, 1979.
39. See, for example, the clerk who wrote, 'In any cases where officials have tried to interfere with policy I have rapped them firmly over the knuckles' (Maud Report, Vol. 5, p. 268).
40. The Paterson Report recommended the provision of offices for committee chairmen (and perhaps party leaders), interviewing rooms at headquarters and local offices, libraries and information rooms, assistance with research, dictating, typing, copying and other secretarial services and adequate telephone facilities. See also T. Eddison, *Strengthening the Role of the Elected Member*, LGTB, 1979.
41. Under the reorganization of 1974/5, the number of members (excluding parishes and communities) fell from 42,000 to 26,000; the number of employed staff remained constant at over 2 millions (having risen from a figure of 1·4 million in 1952 and 1·8 million in 1962). A similar problem occurs at central government level with a virtually constant number of ministers having to control a greatly expanded civil service.

11. Finance

1. See A. T. Peacock and J. Wiseman, *The Growth of Public Expenditure in the United Kingdom*, OUP, 1961, and the *Report of the Committee on Local Government Finance* (the Layfield Report), Cmd 6453, HMSO, 1976.
2. In Scotland, teacher training and advanced further education (and mandatory grants) are not local authority functions and are financed directly by the central government.
3. The Layfield Report, Annexe 9.
4. See *National Income and Expenditure*, Central Statistical Office, HMSO, 1979; *Annual Abstract of Statistics*, Central Statistical Office, HMSO, 1980; *Social Trends*, Central Statistical Office, HMSO, 1980; and the *Local Government Trends*, CIPFA, 1980.
5. For example, the London Lotteries Club (comprising the GLC and twenty-one boroughs) raised £2½ million up to the beginning of 1980. See the *Local Government Chronicle*, 8 June 1979 and 1 January 1980.
6. The Community Land Act 1975 gave local authorities substantial powers to acquire land for development. This was being implemented slowly by councils, but under the Local Government, Planning and Land Act 1980 the 1975 Act was repealed and the scheme has ceased to operate.
7. A possible fourth group concerns the inter-local authority charges which occur under 'pooled' expenditure arrangements (see p. 77) and where the residents from one local authority benefit from the services provided by another; for example, students travelling to another LEA's college or children being placed in care outside the native local authority.
8. Individual councils may decide to adopt such a policy, but in some services (e.g. for free school meals) it may be laid down by the central government (as indeed

might the actual scale of charges; e.g., those for residents of old people's homes).

9. See *Housing Policy Technical Volume 3*, HMSO, 1977. Local authorities are obliged to keep a separate housing account.

9a. An Audit Commission report (8.84) was sceptical about the savings achieved by private refuse collection.

10. See *Local Charges as a Source of Local Government Finance*, IMTA, 1968; A. Seldon, *Charge*, IEA, 1979; A. Maynard and King, *Prices and Rates*, IEA, 1972; M. Beasley, 'How Rates Can Be Abolished', *Local Government Chronicle*, 4 January 1980; *Alternatives to Domestic Rates*, HMSO, 1981; *Service Provision and Pricing*, HMSO, 1981; Economic Affairs, July 1984. Another regular suggestion is that students be paid loans instead of grants. In February 1981, the High Court ruled that Hereford and Worcester LEA was breaking the law in charging for individual music lessons in school time: see *Where*, March 1981.

11. See K. B. Smellie, *A History of Local Government*, Allen & Unwin, 1946, pp. 112–14. Their expansion was mainly hindered by jealous Chancellors.

12. Some of these – police, education, roads – were paid on a percentage basis; others, such as housing, were paid on a unit basis, for instance £5 per house p.a.

13. See the White Paper on Local Government, 1929. In fact this is not easy to determine: it is very much a matter of judgement. For example the police services are closely overseen, but they probably would be even if there were no specific grant. On the other hand there is some evidence that the specific grants which go to housing and transport do bring with them a significant degree of central intervention. (See, for example, P. Richards, *The Reformed System of Local Government*, Allen & Unwin, 1978, p. 104.)

14. In England and Wales, they meet under the auspices of the Consultative Council on Local Government Finance. See Chapter 13. 'Relevant' expenditure covers most local authority expenditure but excludes housing subsidies and student mandatory grants, which are paid separately.

15. The percentage figure is higher in Scotland for historical reasons: the amalgam of general and specific grants in 1966 amounted to a higher proportionate figure in Scotland than it did for England and Wales. Also, in Scotland relevant expenditure is differently determined.

16. In effect, the local authorities transfer some rating responsibilities from domestic ratepayers to the central government to the extent of these figures. Until recently the figure for Scotland was 31p. but this was reduced in line with the 1978 revaluation.

17. See, for example, *Local Authority Needs and Resources*, Centre for Environmental Studies Research Paper no. 12, December 1974; also F. Cripps and W. Godley, *Local Government Finance and Its Reform*, CUP, 1976.

18. *Local Government Finance*, Cmd 6813, HMSO, 1977.

19. This implies a common, uniform precept across the county. In fact (essentially in London) there may be local additions to the basic precept where services are not evenly provided over the whole area.

20. A further consideration is whether neighbouring district authorities do so. Any such decision will automatically affect the yield of the county precept from which *all* county inhabitants benefit.

21. In Scotland the regions and islands appoint independent assessors (the Scottish Assessors Association). Their revaluations have been fairly regular (occurring in 1961, 1966, 1971 and 1978). This is in contrast to England and Wales, which since a partial revaluation in 1956 has only had a revaluation in 1963 and 1973.

22. Site values are said to have the merit of encouraging the development of empty sites. Capital values are said to be more realistic and easier to determine. The government accepted the advantages of the capital valuation method. See *Local Government Finance*, Cmd 6813, H M S O, 1977.

23. As an illustration, if the local authority's

estimated expenditure is		£40,000,000
and its estimated income is: grants	£20,000,000	
charges	5,000,000	25,000,000
then the rate-borne expenditure is		15,000,000
If the total rateable value is		20,000,000

then the rate poundage is $\dfrac{15,000,000}{20,000,000}$ = 75p. per £ R. V.

In actual practice, councils determine the rate on the basis of the 'product of a 1p. rate'. In the example, if 1p. rate raises £200,000, then to raise the required £15 million (which is 200,000 × 75) the local authority must charge 75 times the 1p. rate.

23a. Source: *Alternatives to Domestic Rates* Cmnd 8449, 1981; *Economic Progress Report*, January 1982; *Lloyds Bank Review*, July 1982.

24. There are some 28 million income earners compared to 20 million ratepayers. Under the Local Government Act 1980 elderly ratepayers in arrears can arrange to have their debts settled from their estate when they die.

25. Note: water and sewerage rates are not eligible for rebate (except for business).

26. In 1963 the *Report of the Committee on the Impact of Rates on Householders* (Allen), Cmd 2582, H M S O, suggested that while rates were regressive, they were broadly proportionate to incomes. It was this report which led to the rate rebate scheme in 1967. The Layfield Report (1976) said that rates were progressive up to £40 per week income, were proportional between £40 and £60 and were less than proportional over £60 per week. See also *Alternatives to Domestic Rates*, H M S O, 1981. In addition 2·45 million of those receiving Supplementary Benefit have their rates paid.

27. See the Allen Report and the Layfield Report, Annexe 19; also *The Times*, 19 April 1980 *Alternatives to Domestic Rates*, 1981.

28. S. Weir, 'The citizen and the Town Hall', *New Society*, 4 March 1982; T. Travers, 'Local Government is More Popular than Politicians Realise', *Local Government Chronicle*, 13 June 1980; C. Game, 'Budget Making by Opinion Poll', *Local Government Studies*, March/April 1982; 'Islington's Rates Survey', *Local Government Review*, 13 March 1982; Coventry's referendum, *The Times*, 26–28 August 1981; Layfield Report (Appendix) 1976.

29. Another case in point is the rate rebate scheme under which the central government reimburses local authorities 90 rather than 100 per cent.

30. See P. Self, in *From Policy to Administration*, by J. A. Griffiths, Unwin, 1978.

31. *New Sources of Local Revenue*, RIPA, 1956; S. Hindersley and R. Nottage, *Sources of Local Revenue*, RIPA, 1958; IMTA studies covering, individually, rates, sales tax, local income tax, charges and motor tax (1968–9); *The Future Shape of Local Government Finance*, HMSO, 1971.

32. *The Future Shape of Local Government Finance*, HMSO, 1971; *Local Government Finance*, HMSO, 1973.

33. *Local Government Finance*, HMSO, 1977, para. 6.12.

34. In 1934 and 1948 Public Assistance was transferred to the central government partly because of the burden on local authorities, but mainly for other reasons (uniformity, equity and to de-stigmatize the service).

35. The present (Conservative) government is wedded to a monetarist (or deflationary) economic policy: this implies a commitment to reduce the money supply which itself involves substantial reductions in borrowing by public authorities in particular (the 'Public Sector Borrowing Requirement'). However, apart from this there is a broad (party) difference of general philosophy regarding capital expenditure, with Labour largely seeking to spread the benefits and costs of capital projects over a number of years by borrowing, and Conservatives, broadly, believing in living within one's means and seeking to minimize borrowing. Furthermore, the move towards greater revenue financing may be seen as a further move towards the adoption of business methods, since much business finance is raised internally, including sale of assets.

36. Such legislation may for example set limits on local authorities' short-term borrowing as a percentage of its long-term, or it may govern their arrangements for the issue of bonds, mortgages etc. The Local Authority (Mortgages) Regulations 1974 are an example.

37. Partly because local authorities have been able to spend without approval from their own (revenue) resources and partly by leasing, but also because approved borrowing may run over a long period and become out of phase as capital projects get held up (or suffer what is called 'slippage').

38. Local Government Acts 1972 (Sec. 151) (England and Wales) and 1973 (Sec. 95) (Scotland). Under previous legislation some local authorities were required to appoint a finance committee.

39. Especially for capital expenditure. However, in practice this has become extremely difficult because of the uncertainties regarding government grants, economic policy, interest rates and inflation.

40. Local authorities will have some idea of RSG from their Consultative Council (see p. 232) meetings with the central government before the final November meeting. 'Cash limits' started in 1977 and represent the government's allowance for inflation, pay increases, fuel price rises etc. It is the maximum supplement which the government will make to the RSG. Thus where the actual inflation rate (say 20 per cent) exceeds the government's allowance in cash limit (say 15 per cent), local authorities have to find the extra resources themselves or cut their planned expenditure.

41. They could also choose (as did eight local authorities in England and Wales) to have partial audit by both district and approved auditors. In England and Wales 90 per cent had chosen district audit pre-1982.

42. Before 1972/3, the district auditor himself could actually disallow and 'surcharge' (fine). This was felt by many, for example the Maud Committee (1967), to be excessive, inhibiting local authority activities. Consequently, under the 1972 Act, leniency will be exercised where the persons concerned acted reasonably or in the belief that the expenditure was authorized by law. The Minister retains his discretionary power to approve expenditure of questionable legality. In the Camden wages case (Pickwell *v.* London Borough of Camden, April 1982) the auditor's claim of excessive and illegal expenditure was refused by the court.

43. R. Minns, 'The District Audit', *New Society*, 10 July 1975.

44. See E. C. Thomas, 'The District Audit Since Reorganisation', *Telescope*, November 1976; also L. Tovell, 'The District Auditor and His Place in Local Government', *Local Government Chronicle*, Supplement, 8 June 1979. W. Werry, 'What Does an Auditor Add Up To?', *Local Government Chronicle*, 29 January 1982.

45. See, for example, *The Local Government Audit Service*, the report of the Audit Inspectorate 1979, which makes critical remarks on bonus schemes, building contracts and pooling arrangements for polytechnics. In April 1982 the report criticized overtime payments.

46. Rating and Valuation (Amendment) (Scotland) Act 1984.

47. For example, *The Consumer and the State – Getting Value for Public Money*, National Consumer Council, 1979. See also 'Value for Money in the Public Sector', CIPFA 1980; C. Holtham and J. Stewart, *Value for Money*, INLOGOV, 1981.

48. With a view to keeping their committee structure within reasonable proportions, a number of authorities have had second thoughts about these.

12. Controls and Influences

1. *Ultra vires* may be procedural as well as substantive: thus if a council has not followed proper procedure in exercising its rightful powers (such as obtaining magistrates' approval before implementing a nuisance abatement order), the action is unlawful.

2. Attorney-General *v.* Fulham Corporation (1921), in which the council went beyond its powers to provide washing facilities by providing a laundering service.

3. R. *v.* Kent Police Authority (1971).

4. Metropolitan Properties Ltd *v.* Lannon (1969).

5. See H. W. Clarke, 'The Prerogative Order', *LG Chronicle*, 23 August 1974.

6. Recent cases include the GLC (December 1981) and the West Midlands MCC (January 1982), both of whose supplementary precepts (for subsidized transport) were quashed; similar protests by BL (*v.* Birmingham MCD, February 1982) and GUS (*v.* Merseyside MCC, December 1981) failed.

7. See W. A. Robson, 'The Central Domination of Local Government', *Political Quarterly*, January 1933; B. Keith-Lucas and P. Richards, *A History of Local Government in the Twentieth Century*, Allen & Unwin, 1978; the Maud Report, Chapter 4; and the Layfield Report.

8. For example *Standards for School Premises Regulations 1972*. Strictly speaking such regulations are a legislative form of control as much as administrative.

9. E.g. see *Local Government Chronicle*, 11 April 1980, p. 404. Another instance concerned Manchester's sixth forms: see *Guardian*, 12 January 1981.

10. In 1972 the Clay Cross Council refused to apply the new (Conservative) Housing Finance Act to its tenants: consequently eleven councillors were surcharged (£63,000) and disqualified from holding office. In 1974 the council went out of existence as a result of local government reorganization, but in the meantime the Minister established a Housing Commission to take responsibility for the housing functions of the local authority. The council refused to co-operate with the Commission and made its work rather difficult.

    An earlier case of a commission being sent in to replace a local authority occurred in 1927, when the Tredegar Board of Guardians was found to be too generous with poor relief. Outside local government, a more recent example concerned the Lambeth, Southwark and Lewisham Area Health Authority, which was replaced by Health Commissioners between 1979 and 1980. Most recently (November 1981–February 1982), the Minister was about to send his own agents in to administer the sale of council houses (and he had won a case in court to prove his right to do so) when the council, Norwich DC, acceded to the Minister's pressure to carry out the responsibility under the Housing Act 1980.

11. W. O. Hart and J. F. Garner, *Hart's Local Government and Administration*, Butterworth, 1973, p. 371.

12. See *Relations between Central Government and Local Authorities* by the Central Policy Review Staff, HMSO, 1977.

13. In 1970, for example, half of the lists of candidates for posts of director of social services were altered following submission to the Minister. See Lord Redcliffe-Maud and B. Wood, *English Local Government Reformed*, OUP, 1974, p. 127. In 1979, the government issued a White Paper, *Central Government Controls over Local Authorities* (Cmd 7634), which proposed to drop the ministerial vetting of candidates for such posts; this was not legislated for, however.

14. Local Government Act 1972 (Sec. 230) and Local Government (Scotland) Act 1973 (Sec. 199).

15. The 'Instruments' deal with the procedures of governing bodies – their size, membership, meetings etc. The 'Articles' are concerned with their powers and duties – appointing staff, the conduct of the school, its curriculum, lettings etc.

16. A White Paper is a government document declaring its policy; a Green Paper is a consultation document indicating the government's tentative ideas on policy, for discussion purposes.

17. Student grants, for example, within the education service. Such grants may take the form of 'percentage' grants (as in the case of the police, where the central government pays for half of the cost of local police forces). Alternatively, grants may be paid on a unit basis (such as the traditional form of housing subsidies, where a fixed amount of grant is given to local authorities for each house built).

18. If the government's allowance for inflation (the cash limits) is less than the actual rate of inflation, local authorities will find their resources stretched. Another constraint is the amount of planned expenditure which the government is prepared to recognize as 'relevant' for grant purposes, that is upon which it is prepared to make its proportionate contribution.

19. The building standards have been known as 'Parker Morris' standards after the committee which determined them in 1961. Cost yardsticks are in effect the maximum expenditure per house which the government recognizes as reasonable. In 1980, the government began to dismantle these controls.

20. See the White Paper *A Framework for Expansion*, Cmd 5174, HMSO, 1972.

21. B. Keith-Lucas, 'What Price Local Democracy?', *New Society*, 12 August 1976. See also W. A. Robson, *Local Government in Crisis*, Unwin, 1968; *Local Government Chronicle*, 9 October 1981, pp. 1041–2; the Maud, Wheatley, Redcliffe-Maud and Layfield Reports.

22. See the Central Policy Review Staff's *Relations between Central Government and Local Authorities*, HMSO, 1977; the Layfield Report; and J. A. Taylor, 'The Consultative Council in Local Government Finance', *Local Government Studies*, March/June 1979.

23. Secretary of State for Education and Science *v*. Tameside Metropolitan District Council (1976). See also A. Bradley, 'The Tameside Affair', *Listener*, 5 May 1977. In 1980, a similar event occurred in that the courts declared as unlawful the Minister's appointment of Health Commissioners in place of the Lambeth, Southwark and Lewisham Area Health Authority. In October 1981, the court held that the Minister had acted illegally (on a technicality) in withholding grant from six London Boroughs; in December Hackney successfully challenged his right to withhold part of their inner city 'partnership' grant.

24. For further details, see J. A. G. Griffiths, *Central Departments and Local Authorities*, Allen & Unwin, 1966.

25. See D. E. Ashford, 'The Effects of Central Finance on the British Local Government System', *British Journal of Political Science*, Vol. 4, no. 3, 1974; K. P. Poole, 'England and Wales', *Studies in Comparative Local Government*, Vol. 4, no. 1, 1970. cf. E. Page, 'Grant Dependence and Changes in Intergovernmental Finance', Strathclyde Studies in Public Policy, 1981; article by D. Wardman in *Local Government Chronicle*, 2 July 1982; A. Robinson, 'The Myth of Central Control', *The Listener*, 19 June 1982.

26. It is said that Richard Crossman resisted the proposals to place the NHS in the hands of local authorities (or any other separately elected bodies) because they were too successful in spending money, having the force of 'active' public opinion behind them. A similar point is made in L. J. Sharpe, *Why Local Democracy?*, Fabian, 1965.

27. M. Kogan, *The Politics of Education*, Penguin Books, 1971, p. 189.

28. Previous Ministers include Attlee, Morrison and Bevan. The current Secretary for the Environment, Patrick Jenkin, is an ex-councillor. The Minister for Consumer Affairs until 1981, Mrs Oppenheim, was also Vice President of the Association of District Councils. Lord Bellwin, the Minister for Local Government, was a prominent councillor and leader of Leeds City Council before the Conservative victory in the general election of May 1979.

29. For this information, I am grateful to Edward du Cann, MP, and also the House of Commons Public Information Office. See also F. Willey, *The Honourable Member*, Sheldon Press, 1974; P. Richards, *The Backbenchers*, Faber, 1972; A. Barker and M. Rush, *The Member of Parliament and His Information*, Allen & Unwin, 1971; *The Times' Guide to Parliament 1979*. However, it may be added

that M Ps are not always the allies of local government: by passing on complaints to the Minister rather than the local authority, the MP (perhaps unwittingly) draws the central government into local affairs. See G. Jones, 'M Ps – Eroding the Independence of Local Government?', *Municipal Review*, July 1972.

30. It is claimed that they may carry more influence with Ministers than do M Ps: this was suggested by the ex-leader of the Liverpool Council ('Brass Tacks', B BC, 17 July 1979).

31. See the Layfield Report, Annex 4.

32. *Local Government Finance* (1976).

33. *Local Government Finance* (1977), para. 2.9.

34. In 1854 *The Times* declared 'we prefer to take our chance of cholera and the rest than be bullied into health'.

35. In 1873, the town of Nottingham published an open letter to the president of the Local Government Board criticizing the degree of ministerial control: see Keith-Lucas, op. cit.

36. See Robson, op. cit.; L. T. Hobhouse, *Liberalism*, H.U.L., 1910, p. 233.

37. See Keith-Lucas, op. cit.; Robson, op. cit.; and see R. Darke and R. Walker (eds.), *Local Government and the Public*, Leonard Hill, 1977, Chapter 1.

38. In 1979 and 1980, the Minister was regularly expressing his concern at local government's failure to reduce its staffing levels, and suggesting that the bureaucrats were protecting themselves from the expenditure cuts. Local authorities replied that their numbers were sustained in part by government-imposed policies (selling council houses, charging for planning applications, allowing parental appeals against L EA school allocations etc.) which had substantial manpower implications. They also pointed out that 'bureaucrats' constituted only 2 per cent of the labour force. See A. Fowler, 'Who Are the Wicked Bureaucrats?', *Local Government Chronicle*, 11 January 1980.

39. Dennis Healey, Chancellor of the Exchequer, House of Commons debates (*Hansard*), cols. 296–7, 15 April 1975.

40. See Taylor, op. cit.

41. *The Times*, 19 February 1980.

42. *The Times*, 20 March 1980.

43. Though there are a number of theories: see W. J. Mackenzie, *Theories of Local Government*, L SE, 1961. See also L. J. Sharpe, 'Theories and Values of Local Government', *Political Studies*, no. 80, 1970; O. A. Hartley, 'The Relationship between Central and Local Authorities', *Public Administration*, Winter 1971; *The Times*, 8 July 1972.

44. Variations in the standards of local authority services are well documented. For example, see: the *Report of the Committee on Local Authority and Allied Social Services*, H MSO, 1968; S. Sainsbury, *Registered as Disabled*, Bell, 1970; B. Davies, *Variations in the Services for the Elderly*, Bell, 1971; B. Davies *et al.*, *Variations in Children's Services Among British Urban Authorities*, Bell, 1972; N. Boaden, *Urban Policy-Making*, C UP, 1971; Sharpe and Newton (p. 320 above). The Chartered Institute of Public Finance and Accountancy (C I P F A) regularly provide useful analyses of local authority expenditures through their Statistical Information Service, from which the following examples are taken:

Estimated expenditure per primary pupil (1981–2)

Dudley MD	£490	Powys CC	£733
Newcastle MD	£490	Kent	£517

Estimated expenditure per pupil in special education (1976–7)

Somerset	£930	Gwent	£2,154

Estimated expenditure per head for planning functions (1984–5)

Solihull MD	£2·63	Manchester MD	£12·75

Estimated expenditure per head for social services (1984–5)

Cleveland CC	£46·30	Shropshire CC	£27·81
Manchester MD	£99·62	Dudley MD	£32·44

Expenditure on consumer services (1975–6)

Powys CC over £1 m	Hertfordshire CC less than £200

Careers officers (1976–7)

Lincolnshire	23	Wiltshire	48

Meals delivered to pensioners (1976–7)

Doncaster MD provided four times those provided by Sheffield

Overall spending per head (1983–4)

Haringey LB	£697	West Sussex CC	£315
South Cambs. DC	£24·75	Blackburn BC	£122

It is unwise to draw too hasty conclusions from these figures: such 'league tables' can be misleading unless other factors are taken into account (such as need, costs, alternative provision etc.). A useful discussion of the reasons for variations is to be found in Boaden, op. cit., Note 40. A striking example emerged from a recent report of the Public Accounts Committee. This expressed concern at the substantial variations in expenditure among police forces – hardly the least centrally supervised local service. (See *Fifth Report from the Committee of Public Accounts: Procurement of Police Equipment*, House of Commons Paper 445, HMSO, 1980.)

45. See also P. Saunders, 'Local Government and the State', *New Society*, 13.3.80; and P. Saunders, *Urban Politics: A Sociological Interpretation*, Penguin, 1981.
46. See, for example, J. D. Godfrey and J. S. Stevens, *Training Gamekeepers to be Poachers*, RIPA Report no. 1, Spring 1980.
47. B. Davies, *Social Needs and Resources in Local Services*, Michael Joseph, 1968, and K. Judge, *Rationing Social Services*, Heinemann, 1978. But cf. Darke and Walker (eds.), op. cit., Chapter 14.
48. Darke and Walker (eds.), op. cit.
49. Saunders, op. cit. See also C. Cockburn, *The Local State*, Pluto, 1977; W. K. Tabb and L. Sawers, *Marxism and the Metropolis*, OUP, 1978; and M. Castells, *City, Class and Power*, Macmillan, 1978.
50. E.g. some of the work of British environmental health officers and meat inspectors is carried out in Europe by vets. This may have career implications.
51. A. Norton, 'Local Government and Europe', *Local Government Studies Annual Review*, 1979.
52. E.g. see 'European Pay Off', *Local Government Chronicle*, 14 March 1980.
53. R. A. W. Rhodes, *Local Government and the European Community*, INLOGOV, 1973, p. 7.

54. A. Norton, 'Relations between the European Commission and British Local Government', *Local Government Studies*, January/February 1980.

13. Local Government and the Local Community

1. See D. Peschek, 'Local Authority Technology Co-operation in Europe', *Local Government Chronicle*, 19 October 1979.
2. This post replaces that of the old Medical Officer of Health. Doctors are appointed by the health authorities, but since they work in and with the district councils, they have to be formally 'adopted' by those local authorities.
3. E.g. the GLC fares issue was started by Bromley council. On Manchester see: 'Greater Manchester 78', *Guardian*, 27 November 1978; 'Metropolitan Review', *Local Government Chronicle*, 14 March 1980; H. Elcock, 'English Local Government Reformed', *Public Administration*, Summer 1975; and M. Fitzgerald, 'Politics', *Local Government Chronicle*, 28 September 1979. The inquiry into the Toxteth riots in 1981 referred to the strained relations between the two tiers of local government on Merseyside.
4. C. A. Collins, 'Councillors' Attitudes', *Local Government Studies*, April 1980, p. 36.
5. For example, Manchester City Council *v.* Greater Manchester Council (1979) and Kensington and Chelsea LB *v.* GLC (1982).
6. One area of potential conflict in the field of planning is being somewhat diminished by the removal of many of the counties' planning control functions (known as 'county matters') to the district councils, under the Local Government, Planning and Land Act 1980.
7. J. D. Stewart, 'The Politics of Local Government Reorganisation', in K. Jones (ed.), *The Year Book of Social Policy in Britain 1973*, Routledge, 1974.
8. The Bains Report, Chapter 8.
9. Some are executive in nature: see, for example, T. J. Phillips, 'Area Planning Committees in Walsall', *Local Government Studies*, January 1979. See also Barbara Webster, 'Area Management', *Local Government Studies Annual Review*, April 1979; L. Corina, 'Area Councillors Committees', *Public Administration*, Autumn 1977; and R. Greenwood *et al.*, *The Organisation of Local Authorities in England and Wales 1967–75*, INLOGOV, 1975, section III.
10. Divisional executives were a form of decentralization within counties for the purpose of educational administration. They comprised members of the (county) local education authority and members of the district councils within the divisional area, together with some co-opted members. Their functions varied from county to county, but they normally exercised some powers delegated by the LEA.
11. Apart from the local authority associations, there are some separate associations representing members (the Association of Councillors, for example) and officers (the Society of Education Officers and the Association of Directors of Social Services, for example). These are primarily professional bodies: they do not negotiate pay or conditions of service, for which they may have separate bodies, such as the Association of Local Authority Chief Executives. There are also party groupings, e.g. Association of Liberal Councillors.

12. See D. Peschek, 'Can the Associations Become One Body?', *Local Government Chronicle*, 14 September 1979. However, one of the objectives of the ACC is the setting-up of a single body to speak for local government in England and Wales.

13. J. Kellas, *The Scottish Political System*, CUP, 1975, p. 143; the Layfield Report, p. 87. Though this contrast has diminished with the Local Government Acts of 1980 and 1982. See D. Heald, 'The Scottish Rate Support Grant', *Public Administration*, Spring 1980.

14. For example, the Local Government Training Board (LGTB); the Local Authorities Management Services and Computer Committee (LAMSAC); the Local Authorities Conditions of Service Advisory Board (LACSAB); the Local Authorities Mutual Investment Trust (LAMIT).

15. Such as the Bill drawn up by the AMA in 1979 seeking extensive powers for local authorities to help small firms in inner cities.

16. Mr Duncan Sandys in a speech reported in the *County Councils Gazette*, September 1956, pp. 195–6. See also A. C. Hetherington, *Local Government Studies*, April 1980, who notes the increasing readiness to hold talks with local authority association representatives at ministerial level.

17. As such they are 'partial' or semi-pressure groups. In practice many people belong indirectly to 'overt' pressure groups in so far as local (or first-order) groups may become members of a regional or a national network (second-order groups). For example, a local sports club may become affiliated to a regional/national body or standing conference which in itself provides no sporting facilities but seeks solely to further sporting interests.

18. D. Hill, *Participation in Local Affairs*, Penguin Books, 1970, p. 200; *Westminster Bank Review*, August 1979.

19. K. Newton, *Second City Politics*, OUP, 1976. He adds (p. 36) that there might well be another 5,000 which he had not included. There are about 400 such organizations in the area of Taunton, Somerset.

20. See J. Stanyer, *Understanding Local Government*, Fontana, 1976. But see also W. Hampton, *Democracy and Community*, OUP, 1970, p. 244.

21. The Maud Report, Vol. 2, pp. 184–5.

22. For example, the groups resisting the local introduction of nuclear power production may seek the aid of the energy-saving or alternative energy producers.

23. See Hampton, op. cit., Chapter 10.

24. Councillors in Britain, however, have been traditionally and notoriously involved in administrative details. See the Maud Report, Vol. 1.

25. Newton, op. cit. He also points to the very large amount of informal contacts, lunchtime chats etc. It must be quite obvious to councillors or local government officers why they are invited to social occasions or to act as speakers at meetings of local organizations. Nevertheless, even if their goodwill is not thereby engendered, such occasions do provide opportunities for them to be buttonholed or 'lobbied'.

26. J. Dearlove, 'Councillors and Interest Groups in Kensington and Chelsea', *British Journal of Political Science*, Vol. 1, no. 2, 1971, and *The Politics of Policy in Local Government*, CUP, 1973.

27. An example at national level is the RSPCA, which Professor Birch suggests has maintained its parliamentary reputation as a responsible body by successfully restraining the extremists within its ranks who would like to oppose blood sports. A. H. Birch, *The British System of Government*, Allen & Unwin, 1967.

28. Newton, op. cit., pp. 132–3.

29. See Dearlove, Hampton and Newton, studies cited above.

30. Newton, op. cit., Chapters 4 and 9. But cf. Hampton, op. cit., pp. 215 and 244.

31. Birch, op. cit., p. 99.

32. Newton, op. cit., p. 88.

33. Some interesting case studies are provided in Hampton, op. cit., Chapters 9 and 10, and in R. Darke and R. Walker (eds.), *Local Government and the Public*, Leonard Hill, 1977.

34. Dearlove's terms.

35. Newton, op. cit., p. 132. Cf. Hill, op. cit., p. 199.

36. In mobilizing the skills and energies of their members in the design and execution of local projects, pressure groups are acting rather like co-opted members at one remove.

37. The Maud Report, Vol. 3, pp. 114–17.

38. The need for this is well illustrated in Hampton, op. cit., p. 206–13, where he shows significant differences between what councillors perceive to be issues and what the ordinary electorate think.

39. P. G. Richards, *The Reformed Local Government System*, Allen & Unwin, p. 157.

40. P. Rivers, *Politics by Pressure*, Harrap, 1974, p. 7.

41. See Rivers, op. cit., pp. 16–20, and Hampton, op. cit., p. 216.

42. See, for example, Newton, op. cit., pp. 83–4; the Maud Report, Vol. 3, Table 159; Hill, op. cit., pp. 53, 89; G. M. Aves, *The Voluntary Worker in the Social Services*, Allen & Unwin, 1969, para. 38.

43. The Maud Report, Vol. 3, p. 167, Table 167.

44. J. Gyford, *Local Politics in Britain*, Croom Helm, 1976, p. 109.

45. S. E. Finer, *Anonymous Empire*, Pall Mall Press, 1969, p. 145.

46. *People and Planning: Report of the Committee on Public Participation in Planning*, HMSO, 1969.

47. Ministry of Housing and Local Government, Circular 65/69.

48. *A New Partnership for Our Schools*, HMSO, 1977.

49. The Skeffington Report, para. 5.

50. *Report of the Committee on Local Authority and Allied Personal Social Services*, HMSO, 1968, para. 480.

51. ibid., para. 494.

52. A. H. Birch, *Representation*, Macmillan, 1972.

53. Darke and Walker (eds.), op. cit., p. 73.

54. N. Lewis and P. J. Birkinshaw, 'Local Authorities and the Resolution of Grievances', *Local Government Studies*, January 1979.

55. Laurence Evans, 'Review of Public Relations', *Municipal Year Book*, 1975.

56. *Report of the Royal Commission on the Constitution* 1969–73 (the Kilbrandon Report), Study no. 7, Table 25.

57. *Complaints Procedures: A Code of Practice for Local Government and Water*

Authorities for Dealing with Queries and Complaints, Commission for Local Administration in England, 1978.

58. N. Lewis and B. Gateshill, *The Commission for Local Administration, a Preliminary Appraisal*, RIPA, 1978.

59. Local Government Act 1974 and Local Government (Scotland) Act 1975.

60. Except parish and community councils. The addresses of the CLA are: 21 Queen Anne's Gate, London; Portland House, 22 Newport Rd, Cardiff; 125 Princes St, Edinburgh. Contact normally takes place in the first instance through a member of the local authority.

61. Local authorities have some discretion to withhold records or information and can refuse to allow their officers to be interviewed by the ombudsman on grounds of confidentiality.

62. Lewis and Gateshill, op. cit.

63. *Your Local Ombudsman. Report for the Commission for Local Administration in England*, 1978. Published annually, the Report for 1981–2 responded to the 'Justice' appraisal (p. 313 above), endorsing its recommendations that CLA should be able to: receive complaints direct; secure legally enforceable remedies; deal with New Towns, school matters and contractual/commercial matters. The CLA also seeks the power to initiate investigations, while 'Justice' wanted independent (central) funding for the CLA. The 1983 Report was highly critical of council responses to findings of maladministration.

64. Lewis and Gateshill, op. cit., p. 59.

64a. E.g. see Audit Commission Report, August 1984 (p. 320 above).

65. For example R. *v.* Hampstead BC *ex parte* Woodward (1917); R. *v.* Barnes BC *ex parte* Conlan (1938); R. *v.* Lancashire CC Police Committee *ex parte* Hook (1980). Also C. Webster, 'What Right to Know Has the Member?' *Local Government Chronicle*, 9 November 1979; C. Cross, 'March with the Lawyers', *Local Government Chronicle*, 25 April 1980; H. W. Clarke, 'The Legal Right to Look at Local Authority Documents', *Local Government Chronicle*, 9, 16 July 1982; *Local Government Review*, 1983, pp. 226 and 451. See above, pp. 186–7.

66. The Maud Report, Vol. 3. A recent figure is 25 per cent: *New Society*, 4.3.82.

67. National Opinion Polls, 'Public Participation in Local Government', *Political Economic Social Review*, no. 1, 1975. For 42 per cent figure see *Local Government Chronicle*, 13 June 1980.

68. See the Maud Report, para. 323 and Table 91.

69. G. A. Almond and S. Verba, *The Civic Culture*, Princeton, USA, 1963.

70. The Kilbrandon Report, 1973, Research Paper no. 7, Table 4.

71. See the Maud Report, Vol. 3, Table 38.

72. The Maud Report, Vol. 3.

73. J. Bonner, 'Public Interest in Local Government', *Public Administration*, Winter 1954.

74. The Maud Report, Vol. 3, Chapter 1.

75. The Maud Report, Vol. 1, para. 448.

76. The Bains Report, paras. 7.35, 7.39.

77. H. Benham, *Two Cheers for the Town Hall*, Hutchinson, 1964, suggests that local authorities do not aim to maximize their communications with the public because they can administer services more smoothly without publicity. In particular it

appears that some Labour councils are suspicious, rightly or wrongly, of press publicity because they feel that newspapers are Conservative in general outlook: see D. Hill, *Participating in Local Affairs*, Penguin Books, 1970; D. Murphy, *The Silent Watchdog: The Press in Local Politics*, Constable, 1976.

78. *Publicity for Work of Local Authorities*, Department of the Environment Circular 47/75. Also see the Maud Report, Chapter 1, and the Royal Commission on Local Government in Scotland (Wheatley) Research Study 2, HMSO, 1969, p. 22, and S. C. Sobol, in *Local Government Studies*, September/October 1981.

79. H. Cox and D. Morgan, *City Politics and the Press*, CUP 1974; Hill, op. cit., Chapter 6.

80. I. Jackson, *The Provincial Press and the Community*, Manchester University Press, 1971.

81. For example, while the Public Bodies (Admission to Meetings) Act requires local authorities to supply agenda and other papers to the press it does not lay down how far in advance. And the Local Government Act 1972 was silent on the issue of papers for committee meetings, so that local authorities vary in their practices here.

82. 'Participation', *Studies in Comparative Local Government*, Vol. 5, no. 2, International Union of Local Authorities, The Hague, 1971.

83. R. Burke, *The Murky Cloak: Local Authority–Press Relations*, Charles Knight, 1970, p. vii.

84. A. Harding Boulton, 'Councils, Public and the Press', *Local Government Chronicle*, 31 March 1978.

85. Public Bodies (Admission to Meetings) Act 1960, Sect. 1.

86. *Publicity for the Work of Local Authorities*, Department of the Environment Circular 47/75.

87. Referring not just generally to more open government and freedom of information etc. but also specifically to the government's sharing information with local authorities in particular. Local authorities frequently show their frustration at being given too little information too late: they should therefore well understand the public outbursts of those who feel local government is playing the cards too close to its chest. Thus in fairness to the central government, it must be said that some local authorities do lack initiative and do need prodding.

88. See, for example, the Maud Report, Vol. 3, Tables 98, 99; L. Corina, 'Area Councillors Committee', *Public Administration*, Autumn 1977, p. 335; Lewis, op. cit., p. 13.

89. The Redcliffe-Maud Report, Research Study 9; the Wheatley Report, Research Study 2; Hampton, op. cit., pp. 87–8.

90. The riot in the St Pauls district of Bristol in April 1980 and in Brixton in April 1981 led some to suggest that 'no go areas' were beginning to develop in certain (especially immigrant) areas of mainland Britain.

91. Hill, op. cit., p. 150. See also Darke and Walker (eds.), op. cit., Chapter 10.

92. While planning is *not* easy and its results are distant in time, it has nevertheless been suggested that the participation element has been jeopardized by its being left in the hands of the professional planners to arrange: see Darke and Walker (eds.), op. cit., p. 83.

93. Under the Education Act 1980, it is now to be a legal requirement that parents be

appointed to school governing/managing bodies. This follows the recommendations of the Taylor Report, *A New Partnership for our Schools*, HMSO, 1977.

94. *Children and Their Primary Schools*, HMSO, 1967. Current legislation is seeking to extend parental choice of schools and also to give greater publicity to their activities – see the Education Act 1980.

95. The Housing Act 1980. In 1975, forty-six local authorities had introduced schemes for tenant participation and a further forty were considering doing so. See Darke and Walker (eds.), op. cit., Chapter 12.

96. Following the recommendations of the Plowden Report certain inner urban areas were given priority (or 'positive discrimination') in obtaining resources to improve their schools and educational opportunities: these were known as 'educational priority areas'. The 'urban programme' started in 1969 when special financial assistance was directed from the central government to certain local authorities containing areas of special social need. While early attention was focused on facilities for children, part of the funds have been used for 'Community Development Projects' which involved more intensive approaches by specially appointed staff who sought to gain the co-operation of all the local central and local social service agencies.

97. For example in rural areas many community development officers are funded by the Development Commission.

98. See *Guardian*, 16 March 1982; *New Statesman*, 19 March 1982.

99. See R. Hadley and S. Hatch, 'Social Welfare and the Failure of the State: Centralized Social Services and Participatory Alternatives', Unwin, 1981; Barclay Report, 'Social Workers: Their Role and Tasks', Bedford, 1982.

100. See A. Walker, *Rural Poverty*, CPAG, 1978.

101. C. Arnold Baker, *Local Council Administration*, Longcross, 1975.

102. Cardiff, Swansea, Newport, Port Talbot, Merthyr Tydfil and Rhondda. There could be changes here as a result of the current special review.

103. *Community Councils in Scotland*, Central Research Unit Paper, Scottish Office, September 1978. Early analysis of some of the second round of elections suggests an even smaller proportion of contested seats: see M. Masterson and E. Masterman, 'Elections of the Second Generation of Community Councils', *Local Government Studies*, Jan./Feb. 1980; *Local Government Chronicle*, 22.3.84.

104. Local Government (Scotland) Act, Sec. 51.

105. *Local Government in Scotland* (Scottish Office Brief), p. 7.

106. M. Minogue, *The Consumer's Guide to Local Government*, Macmillan, 1977, p. 111.

107. *Neighbourhood Councils in England*, Consultation Paper LG4/743/4, Department of the Environment, HMSO, 1974.

108. B. Dixey, *A Guide to Neighbourhood Councils*, The Association for Neighbourhood Councils, 1975.

109. J. Talbot and S. Humble, 'Neighbourhood Councils Defined', *Local Government Studies*, July 1977. Also *An Investigation into Neighbourhood Councils*, INLOGOV, 1977.

110. *A Voice for Your Neighbourhood*, Department of the Environment, 1977.

111. The Redcliffe-Maud Report, Vol. 1, p. 99 and Research Study 9; and the Wheatley Report, Research Study 2.

112. At an ICSA–CIPFA conference in November 1981. See also NCC publications, 'Bureaucracies', 1981, and 'The Neighbourhood', 1982.
113. See 'Community Care', 19 November 1981, p. 3.
114. See A. Godfrey, 'More Pavement Politics', *Local Government Review*, 28 November 1981.

14. Into the Eighties

1. It is intended that the new bodies and services will operate from April 1986. Although the 1985 GLC elections are cancelled (under the Local Government (Interim Provisions) Act 1984), the present members of the GLC have been given an extended period of office (to 1986). Discontent at the cancellation of the election in 1985 has led four members (including the leader, Ken Livingstone) to resign and re-fight their seats in the consequent by-elections. Further strife is foreseeable, with (Labour) councillors threatening to boycott the new joint boards.

2. See A. Midwinter, *Management Reform in Scottish Local Government*, Strathclyde University, 1982; D. Clapham, 'Corporate Planning and the Cuts', *Local Government Policy Making*, July 1983..

3. R. Dahrendorf, *On Britain*, BBC, 1982. See also J. Gyford, *New Society*, 3.5.84.

3a. See B. McAndrew, 'Complications of Overtly Political Officers', *Local Government Chronicle*, 22.6.84, and M. Clarke, 'What Has Happened to the Ground Rules?' *Local Government Chronicle*, 3.8.84.

4. A Marplan poll in February 1982 showed 62 per cent in favour of PR.

5. See K. Newton in L. J. Sharpe (ed.), *The Local Fiscal Crisis in Western Europe*, Sage, 1981; also P. Jackson *et al.*, 'Urban Fiscal Decay in UK Cities', *Local Government Studies*, September 1982.

6. Under the Rating and Valuation (Amendment) Scotland Act 1984.

7. There had been some uncertainty about the Minister's legal power to withhold grant from overspending councils; this was unsuccessfully contested (January 1983), e.g. by Camden council. It might be added, too, that at one stage the Bill included powers allowing the Minister to penalize councils on conditions drawn up retrospectively, i.e. after the financial year had begun: this was dubbed 'superholdback'.

8. The original Local Government Finance Bill 1981 would have allowed the Minister to require a local authority to hold a local referendum before it could impose a supplementary rate/precept (as some 30 councils had done that year, including the GLC for its 'Fares Fair' transport subsidies). The Bill was withdrawn in November 1981 after vehement opposition from the local authority associations and a number of MPs: they argued that (i) a referendum was difficult to validate if there was a low poll (it was only 26 per cent in Coventry's experimental rate referendum of August 1981) and if the wording was oversimplified; (ii) that if adopted, referenda should become applicable to central government extra-budgetary tax changes; and, above all, (iii) that referenda would emasculate local responsibility by undermining the value of

the ordinary electoral process and reducing councillors to mere delegates and cyphers.

9. See R. Jackman, 'Does Central Government Need to Control the Total of Local Government Spending?', *Local Government Studies*, May 1982; also D. Walker in C. Jones and J. Stevenson (eds.), *Yearbook of Social Policy 1980–81*, Routledge, 1982.

10. The latter under the Rating Act: see 6 above.

11. *The Times*, 7 November 1981.

12. P. Smith, 'How Targets Went Wrong', *Public Finance and Accountancy*, December 1983.

13. For 1984–5 the penalties involve a 2p. rate poundage holdback (or abatement) for the first 1 per cent of overspend, 4p. for the second 1 per cent, 8p. for the third 1 per cent and 9p. for each subsequent 1 per cent. In 1983–4, the figures were 1p., 2p., 3p., 5p. For 1985–6 they are 7p., 8p., 9p., etc.

14. G. Jones, J. Stewart and T. Travers, 'Rate Control: the Threat to Local Government', *Local Government Chronicle*, December 1983. A senior civil servant, Sir Antony Part (Permanent Secretary to the Department of Trade and Industry, retired) has commented in relation to the various grant formulae, 'They've got themselves so snarled up they hardly know what they're doing at the moment' ('Who Rules Britain?', BBC, 19 October 1982).

15. Referring to the uncertainties engendered by fluctuations of the block grant, in targets, in penalty systems and in the GRE assessments, the Report of the Audit Commission says that 'The conflicting signals which the grant system contains and the variations in these signals from year to year cause authorities to protect themselves by building up substantial reserves.' This exaggerates apparent overspending, so that in fact 'real overall local government spending last year was probably in line with target'.

The Report also comments critically on (i) the reliabilty of the information on which GREAs are based, so that some councils receive substantially more or less than their circumstances might warrant; (ii) the divergence of targets from GREAs, so that local authorities lose grant though their spending does not exceed GREA; (iii) the targets which, being related to past expenditure, provide a perverse inducement to spend more (i.e. at least up to target) since spending below target in one year may be 'rewarded' by a lower target (but the same penalties) next year: consequently, (iv) the grant system provides few incentives for local authorities to increase efficiency; (v) the fact that changes in local rates are not a reliable guide to individual councils' changes in expenditure; (vi) the continued central involvement in local affairs which has not been reduced as intended by the new system; (vii) the number of people (over 800) in local government alone who are occupied in grappling with the complex grant system, and (viii) the intricacies of the grant arrangements that (inevitably?) distract too many of the recipients into 'playing the system'. See also *Public Money*, September 1983.

16. E.g. see *Westminster Bank Review*, August 1981 and May 1982.

17. Indeed the main impact of public sector borrowing seems to be on the exchange rate rather than on interest rates, and the latter are largely influenced by external factors anyway, especially US interest rates.

18. G. Jones, 'How to Save Local Government', in *Town Hall Power or Whitehall Pawn?*, IEA, 1980; and J. Barlow, in *Local Government Studies*, May 1981.

19. *Municipal Journal*, 29 July 1983.

20. Since there are 42 million voters and only about 20 million ratepayers (see *Alternatives to Domestic Rates*, Cmnd 8449, HMSO, 1981) it is often suggested that many voters pay little heed to rates. This presupposes, at least, an indifference on the part of ratepayers' spouses. Nevertheless, a local income tax covering some 25½ million income tax payers might stimulate a wider interest as well as boost councils' income.

21. It has been suggested that elections be held on a proportional representation basis, that they should be held more often than every four years, that they be held earlier in the year to precede the councils' budget and rate-fixing decisions. Other suggestions include that of local referenda, the right of recall (of discredited councillors), popular petitions (to get items on to the councils' agenda), an elective mayor and the power of dissolution of the council.

22. E.g. A Harris poll in December 1983 showed that 59 per cent of those questioned disapproved of the plans to abolish the GLC.

23. See SOLACE report in the *Observer*, 18 July 1982; T. Blackstone in *The Times Educational Supplement*, 24 September 1982; and a MORI poll (*Sunday Times*, 6 September 1981) which found that nearly half of young unemployed respondents believed that violence to bring about political change is justified. See also B. Stevenson, 'Cleveland's Crazy Cuts', *Local Government Chronicle*, 14 January 1983, and B. Simon, *Marxism Today*, September 1984 (compare with the survey in the *Economist*, 4.12.82).

24. *Municipal Journal*, 29 July 1983.

25. W. Kornhauser, *The Politics of Mass Society*, Routledge, 1960.

26. Local government representation of others is being reduced, e.g. on MSC Area Boards, and under the Water Act 1983, on Water Authorities as these assume a management–consumer representation pattern similar to that of the NHS authorities: see p. 244.

27. It has been suggested that a Bill of Rights for local government may provide protection: see J. Stewart, 'Now is the time for our Bill of Rights', *Municipal Journal*, 5 June 1981. Also J. Raine (ed.), *In Defence of Local Government*, INLOGOV, 1981. And P. Self, 'Rescuing Local Government', *Political Quarterly*, July 1982.

28. This is because of the unpopular or dubious uses of grant-aid by some councils, particularly the GLC, where in using some of the 2p. 'locally determined spending' (see p. 235) for the benefit of certain minority and fringe political groups, it sometimes became known by the epithet of 'the political fund'. See also *Sunday Times*, 24 July 1983.

29. See R. Greenwood *et al.*, 'Making Government More Local', *New Society*, 25 February 1982. However, a Gallup poll in 1981 showed only 27 per cent were in favour of more decentralization from London to regional and local authorities.

Index

See also Glossary

MORE ABOUT PENGUINS, PELICANS AND PUFFINS

For further information about books available from Penguins please write to Dept EP, Penguin Books Ltd, Harmondsworth, Middlesex UB7 0DA.

In the U.S.A.: For a complete list of books available from Penguins in the United States write to Dept DG, Penguin Books, 299 Murray Hill Parkway, East Rutherford, New Jersey 07073.

In Canada: For a complete list of books available from Penguins in Canada write to Penguin Books Canada Ltd, 2801 John Street, Markham, Ontario L3R 1B4.

In Australia. For a complete list of books available from Penguins in Australia write to the Marketing Department, Penguin Books Australia Ltd, P.O. Box 257, Ringwood, Victoria 3134.

In New Zealand: For a complete list of books available from Penguins in New Zealand write to the Marketing Department, Penguin Books (N.Z.) Ltd, P.O. Box 4019, Auckland 10.

In India: For a complete list of books available from Penguins in India write to Penguin Overseas Ltd, 706 Eros Apartments, 56 Nehru Place, New Delhi 110019.

WE HATE HUMANS
David Robins

Every year the renewed wave of 'soccer hooliganism' revives the Great Debate: make parents responsible? Fence them in? Ban the professional game itself? Needless to say, the fans remain as impervious as ever. Theirs is a world which has its own history, enjoys its own rights and obligations and obeys its own logic, a logic of violence – which is also highly exportable.

The author spent seven years researching his subject, and his book tells the story of the youth 'ends' through the vivid descriptive speech of the fans themselves. Black and white, they are united against the law, and their voice is the unique voice of the Other England – a land where thousands of young people join the dole queue each year, dispossessed of expectations and often desperate. We ignore them at our peril.

FAMILY AND KINSHIP IN EAST LONDON
Peter Willmott and Michael Young

The two authors of this most human of surveys are sociologists. They spent three years on 'field work' in Bethnal Green and on a new housing estate in Essex. The result is a fascinating study, made during the period of extensive rehousing, of family and community ties and the pull of the 'wider family' on working-class people.

'Probably not only the fullest, but virtually the only account of working-class family relationships in any country. The general reader will find it full of meat and free of jargon' – *New Statesman*

'This shrewd – and in places extremely amusing – book combines warmth of feeling with careful sociological method' – *Financial Times*

'Observant, tactful, sympathetic, humorous ... I really feel that nobody who wants to know how our society is changing can afford not to read Young and Willmott' – Kingsley Amis in the *Spectator*

NURSERIES NOW
A Fair Deal for Parents and Children
Hughes, Mayall, Perry, Petrie and Pinkerton

The need for nurseries is greater in Britain now than ever before. *Nurseries Now* combines a consumer's guide to what nurseries are available with a sensible critique of the gaps and anomalies in the present system. The authors emphasize the importance of equal opportunities, of more choice for parents in child-care, and of a greater involvement by men in their children's upbringing. Nurseries alone cannot achieve these aims, and the book also looks at some of the other measures needed, including radical changes in the employment patterns of both sexes.

CLEVER CHILDREN
IN COMPREHENSIVE SCHOOLS
Auriol Stevens

Do you wilfully sacrifice children for political principles if you send them to a comprehensive school? In this sane and well-balanced assessment of comprehensive and selective school methods, the education correspondent of the *Observer* gives the facts – about mixed ability teaching, about the minimum size for a comprehensive with a good sixth form, about the challenge of research versus the slog of disciplined work, about provision for science and language teaching. She is sensitive both to the dilemma that faces parents as well as to the problems met by teachers who strive to fulfil the varied needs of their pupils.

INEQUALITIES IN HEALTH
Edited by Peter Townsend and Nick Davidson

The most important critique of the health service and general health standards written in this country since the war.

The government recently published a report called *Inequalities in Health* which has been acclaimed as one of the most significant pieces of research into the nation's health since the Beveridge Report in 1942. The report, however, did not find favour with the government and was not widely distributed.

In this Pelican Peter Townsend (author of *Poverty in the United Kingdom*) and Nick Davidson introduce and summarize the report and assess the enormous amount of material on such topics as regional, class and sex inequalities in health care. In addition they draw comparisons between the changing trends in health care throughout the world and point out the report's implications for the future.

THE NHS:
Your Money or Your Life
Lesley Garner

We all recognize the symptoms – growing waiting lists, inadequate facilities particularly for the elderly and the handicapped, dissatisfied doctors, strained industrial relations – but precisely what is the NHS disease?

Whilst few would agree with Illich's view that all health care is counterproductive, it is obvious from the increasing frequency with which the NHS hits the headlines that a fundamental reassessment is needed. In her calm and comprehensive study, Lesley Garner shows that everywhere – both at home and abroad, and regardless of economic or political bias – there is an increasingly impossible struggle between supply and demand.

But she also looks beneath the general problem arising from the very acceptance of the ideal of free health for all, to the specific problems of X, Y and Z. We may – we do, she argues – need a radical change in social attitudes and a redefinition of the terms of the 1946 NHS Act, but at other levels there are other solutions, and a national political debate must not be allowed to mask the need – and possibility – of worthwhile piecemeal improvement.